# On Cyber

Towards an Operational Art for Cyber Conflict

Gregory Conti

David Raymond

This book is dedicated to A4, O4, C3, C3, H3, N3, D2, F2, F2, S1, R1 & B1

0x0 *If the bit is set to 0, the packet has no evil intent. Hosts, network elements, etc., SHOULD assume that the packet is harmless, and SHOULD NOT take any defensive measures. (We note that this part of the spec is already implemented by many common desktop operating systems.)*

0x1 *If the bit is set to 1, the packet has evil intent. Secure systems SHOULD try to defend themselves against such packets. Insecure systems MAY chose to crash, be penetrated, etc.*

*- RFC 3514[1]*

# ABOUT THE AUTHORS

Gregory Conti ran West Point's cybersecurity research and education programs for almost a decade and is currently Director of Research at IronNet Cybersecurity. He holds a Ph.D. in Computer Science from Georgia Tech and is the author of *Security Data Visualization* (No Starch Press) and *Googling Security* (Addison-Wesley) as well as over 70 articles and papers covering cyber warfare, online privacy, usable security, and security data visualization. Greg has served as Officer in Charge of a forward deployed expeditionary cyber team, acted as a Senior Advisor in the US Cyber Command Commander's Action Group, and co-created US Cyber Command's flagship Joint Advanced Cyber Warfare Course (JACWC). He has spoken at numerous security conferences, including Black Hat, DEFCON, HOPE, ShmooCon, RSA, the NATO Conference on Cyber Conflict, and numerous academic conferences. His work can be found at www.gregconti.com and @cyberbgone on Twitter.

David Raymond is a retired Army officer, currently on faculty at Virginia Tech where he is Director of the Virginia Cyber Range. He also serves as deputy to the Virginia Tech CISO, teaches computer networking and cybersecurity courses, and runs a cybersecurity research lab for students studying computer science and computer engineering. David holds a Ph.D. in computer engineering and taught West Point's capstone course in cybersecurity for four years. He created West Point's cyber-competition team and is now the faculty advisor to Virginia Tech's student Cybersecurity club. David has published over 25 papers and articles on topics including computer architecture, wireless security, online privacy, and cyber warfare, and has spoken at several academic and industry conferences, including Black Hat, RSA, ShmooCon, and the NATO Conference on Cyber Conflict.

# CONTENTS

Preface     i

1   Introduction     1

2   Actors and Adversaries     12

3   Laws of Physics     29

4   Operational Environment     54

5   Terrain     68

6   Maneuver     88

7   Capabilities     121

8   Intelligence     140

9   Fires and Effects     179

10   Command and Control     213

11   Deception     242

12   A Look to the Future     259

References     275

# PREFACE

The history of the world is driven by technological advances and warfare. Armed conflict has been occurring since the dawn of recorded history. Individuals, tribes, city-states, and nations organized themselves and developed strategies and tactics to better protect their interests or acquire scarce resources to ensure survival. Combatants have always sought the upper hand through technology. Each advance—the development of bronze, the battering ram, the long-bow, machine gun, tank, or telegraph—required evolution in warfare. The groups that evolved faster and more effectively gained an advantage, sometimes a marked advantage, over their adversaries. Those groups that failed to evolve risked painful defeat and possible annihilation.

Over time, best practices were identified, and battlefield insights were codified into military doctrine and analyzed by military thinkers seeking to exploit weaknesses, illuminate strengths, and discover new innovations. In the twentieth century, we saw world wars of unprecedented scale and an amazing array of technology enabling the conduct of war. Airplanes, satellites, and submarines brought warfare to the sky, space, and under the sea. Nuclear weapons became an existential threat to humanity.[2] Policy makers and militaries grappled with each new technology, simultaneously trying to use it to their advantage while preventing their adversaries from doing the same. New military force structures were created to organize, train, and equip forces postured to exploit these new domains and the world saw an exponential increase in defense spending during these arms races of the twentieth century.

The twenty-first century brings the new challenge of cyber conflict. Depending on your definitions, computers have existed since the Victorian era, and networked communications since the telegraph, but with the development of the integrated circuit—making computers small and reliable—and the rise of the Internet—allowing distant and wide-spread digital communication—the stage was set for communication, entertainment, trade, and, of course, conflict in this new domain. The first link of the nascent Internet was established on 29 October 1969 between Stanford Research Institute and the University of California - Los Angeles. The World Wide Web (WWW) arose as an overlay on the Internet, alongside email, chat, and myriad other applications, and has since enjoyed exponential growth. At first, the Internet was the domain of scientists, who could not have envisioned what it would one day become, and the network possessed little in the way of security. Baked into the design of the Internet, however, were values held dear by its creators, principles that promoted trust, openness, and the free sharing of information.[3] The Internet proved remarkably resistant, but not impervious to damage and censorship.

As the Internet grew, companies raced to create a public presence on the WWW and interconnected their systems, striving to lower costs and increase efficiencies. The experiment worked. Users across this interconnected world gained access to information at a breadth, depth, and speed that seemed unimaginable only years earlier. Online commerce, digital banking, national governance, all became commonplace networked activities. The world quickly became invested and dependent. The complexity of information systems soared beyond human comprehension, and this complexity begat a corresponding increase in vulnerabilities.

It was, perhaps, inevitable that the Internet quickly attracted the attention of those who would take advantage of the trust and openness with which it was designed. Online crime arose, and entrepreneurial and disenfranchised technologists developed ways to first misuse the basic protocols that made the Internet function and later to subvert added security mechanisms to make a profit, first in isolated instances and later at scale. Viruses and worms began to spread widely and maliciously. People conducted day-to-day activities, important business, and even lifesaving activities on a fragile and largely unsecure network of systems where trust was misplaced or ephemeral.

Nations, at first caught off guard by the democratizing nature of the Internet, sought to regain control of their populations and tame slippery and inconvenient flows of information. Regimes toppled as activists, dissidents, and anarchists harnessed the power of social media while governments were powerless to stop them. Vulnerabilities that once were a nuisance threatened to undermine prosperity and way of life. Intelligence agencies quickly realized the unprecedented potential of digital communication, processing, and storage, and set up massive surveillance networks limited only by their imagination and resources. Entrepreneurial technologists and business people created companies that provided compelling offerings for search, social media, dating, and many other services, quickly rising to international prominence and daily use. A prevailing business model was that of no-cost services. The consumer became the product as companies acquired, correlated, and cataloged astronomical amounts of data and used it for targeted advertising, then sold that data to brokers for further use, and misuse. Some private companies amassed data stockpiles that rivaled intelligence agencies.

At first, it was difficult to convince most senior government and industry leaders that cyber security was a problem. Data began to spill, slowly at first, then in torrents. Some CEOs were fired as these disclosures damaged or destroyed their companies. Identity theft became rampant, while banks assumed the cost of consumer fraud at ever increasing rates. Government officials, military organizations, intelligence agencies, research facilities, and multi-national corporations all were subject to compromise by increasingly sophisticated actors. Some technology vendors began to take cyber security seriously and started building increased security into their products, but market forces overall did little to encourage widespread security. To many, the potential profit from releasing a product or service more quickly than the competition was worth the risk incurred by not taking the time to ensure it was secure. A dedicated cyber security industry emerged with products that placated business executives and government officials that something was being done, but a panacea remained far out of reach. Cyber security became a game of constant one-upmanship; each defensive advance was readily countered by an adversary.

Cyber attacks occurred across international borders with impunity, where similar kinetic attacks would have been addressed with the harshest of consequences. Attribution proved difficult, and deterrence faltered. Traditional actors who lacked the physical might developed effective cyber operations organizations. The United States, the sole superpower, soon found uncomfortably that it had near-peer adversaries in cyberspace.

Senior leaders no longer had to be convinced that cybersecurity was a problem. In an attempt to stem the hemorrhaging, policy makers, law enforcement, and military organizations worked to respond, but bureaucratic processes turn slowly. Law perpetually lagged technology and adversary tactics. Some of the proposed policy and legal solutions were interpreted by many to threaten the underpinnings of democracy. Countries vied for influence over key Internet protocols and infrastructure and tried to require backdoors in encryption systems that gave government officials easy access to the original unencrypted data.[4] Some countries emplaced firewalls around their networks as much to prevent destabilizing information from flowing in as to keep malicious actors out. Government, law enforcement, and military solutions were confounded by pre-Internet law, aging bureaucratic distinctions, confusing and limited legal authority, and a critical shortage of personnel with computer and network security expertise. Businesses were conflicted by misplaced incentives to rush products to market, maximizing return on investment, multinational global workforces, and a requirement to abide by the laws of the nations in which they operated. Companies with the resources and the vision to see that the cavalry wasn't coming to save the day invested in extensive cybersecurity organizations of their own, some with more than 1,000 people. Other less-resourced companies, as well as individuals, were left to fend for themselves. The defense industrial base mobilized and began to provide solutions due to significant increases in cyber security contract funding, but industrial age acquisition procedures slowed progress and increased cost.

In 2009, the United States created U.S. Cyber Command, a dedicated military organization authorized over 6,000 uniformed and civilian personnel under the charge of a four star commander and focused on the defense of military networks, providing support to other military commanders, and strengthening the United States' ability to withstand and respond to cyber attack.[5] During this period, other major powers either created or revealed the existence of cyber warfare units. In conjunction with the creation of U.S. Cyber Command, the United States went further and created service specific cyber commands for the Army, Navy, Air Force, Marine Corps, and Coast Guard.[6] Cyberspace itself was formally declared an operational domain, alongside air, land, sea, and space.[7] These developments started efforts toward cultural change. For example, the U.S. Army created a specialized Cyber Operations branch of equal stature with traditional maneuver branches including Infantry, Armor, and Field Artillery, creating a home for the once marginalized technologist community, who previously took cyber assignments at significant professional risk.[8] Charges, not entirely unfounded, of militarization of the Internet arose as a response.

While traditional kinetic warfare has had centuries of lessons-learned to build upon, much of what these new cyberspace organizations did was new and required the development of strategy and tactics from the foundation up.

This brings us to the present. The nature of war changes constantly. Kinetic war will still be bloody, but cyberspace operations provide nations with the ability to inflict serious damage to an adversary's economy, government, critical infrastructure, and populace in unprecedented ways. Attacks could bring down an economy, disrupt governments, destroy power plants, ruin the reputations and careers of senior officials, render vulnerable military weapon systems inert, shutdown hospitals, cause self-driving cars to run off the road, and cause strategic corruption of data backups.[9]    The most recent, and perhaps best, example is the cyber attack and subsequent information disclosure which heavily influenced the 2016 U.S. presidential election. Virtually every computing system we employ to live our twenty first century lives is at risk, both now and into the future. Where this will end is uncertain. At present, it is unclear whether militaries will be agile enough, and technically savvy enough, to keep pace with adversary cyberspace operations conducted by militaries and threat actors around the globe.   The time is now to figure out how wars will be fought in cyberspace.

## Why this Book?

The stakes have never been higher.   One ignores cybersecurity and its disruptive effects at their peril.   Nations are struggling to secure their boundaries and protect their rightful assets.  The emerging Internet of Things (IoT) promises much, from medical implants in our bodies, smartphones in every pocket, smart thermostats and toasters in our homes, autonomous cars in our streets, and smart cities that manage the lives of millions of people.  In short, we aren't slowing in our adoption of fragile technological infrastructure.   Technology and cyber security will increasingly touch all aspects of our way of life.  Nations, militaries, and law enforcement need the means to secure their people and their resources.  Of course, ignoring the problem of cyber conflict won't make it go away; instead ignoring the problem will only make matters worse and our way of life increasingly vulnerable.

The lack of an operational art for cyberspace operations is the inspiration for this book.[10]  Books have been written about traditional kinetic strategy and tactics from, at least, the era of Sun Tzu, about 500 BC.  Cyberwarfare books exist that study major historical events and provide high-level policy analysis. Technical books on information security have covered basic and advanced means of securing and attacking computing systems, usually individual systems, individual parts of larger systems, or small scale penetration testing and red teaming strategies. Discussion on how militaries actually defend, fight, and win in cyberspace, however, is absent.

We aim to fill the current gap by laying a foundation for the art of cyber warfare at the tactical, operational, and strategic levels, an admittedly ambitious undertaking, by focusing on underlying principles that are long lasting and not tied to the most quickly evolving of technologies.  We are thinking at scale. That is, how do nations, not just small teams, fight in cyberspace. Some aspects of cyberspace operations are quite similar to traditional military operations while others are fundamentally different. While the Laws of Physics cannot be changed, the quasi-"laws of physics" built into the Internet are based on human decisions and malleable code. The differences are subtle at times, but must be understood to succeed in cyber operations. Our book seeks to illuminate these areas.

## Who Should Read This Book?

We've designed this book to bridge the military and the technical, with the objective being a work that is useful and accessible to a wide range of audiences. Cyber operators will find insight into how they conduct their business. Military professionals and enablers of cyber operations will gain knowledge of the technical aspects of cyberspace operations and how to best integrate cyber into traditional military activities. Information technology, and especially information security, practitioners will see how military operations impact them and draw insights to help fend off nation-state adversaries that target their networks and data. Scholars and students will be able to make better sense of this little-discussed domain in order to incorporate it in the classroom, provide critical analysis, and identify promising areas of future research. Policy makers, business leaders, and their staffs will gain critical insight into the decisions they make involving technology investment and security policy. Our desire is to provide a high-impact work that can inform the many people working, regulating, living, and defending in cyberspace. We must note that we certainly aren't advocating militarization of the Internet. We do suggest, however, that by learning how advanced threat actors operate, we are all better prepared to defend ourselves, our networks, those who depend on us for protection, and thus our very way of life.

## A Map of the Book

This book takes a holistic approach to cyber conflict. Chapter 1, "Introduction," describes our theoretical framework and outlines the book's approach in greater detail. Chapter 2, "Actors and Adversaries," provides a look at the various entities that operate in cyberspace. Chapter 3, "Laws of Physics," examines intuitive and counterintuitive aspects of the domain. Chapter 4, "Operational Environment," and Chapter 5, "Terrain," study the operational domain of cyberspace and are complemented by Chapter 6, "Maneuver," which covers how units move and fight both in the physical domain and in cyberspace. Chapter 7, "Capabilities," examines the various cyber weapons that might be used, to what end, and with what realistic expectations. Chapter 8, "Intelligence," adapts time-tested principles from the intelligence discipline and applies them to cyberspace. Chapter 9, "Fires and Effects," considers how cyber weapons may be employed at scale to cause deliberate and well-considered effects, while avoiding unintentional and collateral effects. Chapter 10, "Command and Control," studies how large dispersed cyber/kinetic organizations will fight in synchronization across multiple domains. Chapter 11, "Deception," studies information flows and how these may be manipulated to one's advantage. We close with Chapter 12, "Conclusions and a Look to the Future," examining major themes that have arisen from the book and new challenges and opportunities that lay on the horizon as well as direction for future analysis and research.

## Acknowledgements

A book isn't the work of a lone individual, but the product of many hands. We would like to thank first the many Civilians, Soldiers, Sailors, Airmen, Marines—Active, Guard, and Reserve, Enlisted, Warrant Officer, and Officer—who conduct cyberspace operations and who live daily defending our way of life against aggressive threats to national security. We would also like to thank the members of the following communities: the United States Military Academy at West Point, the Viola Foundation, Virginia Tech, Georgia Tech, the Army Cyber Institute, DEF CON, Black Hat, ShmooCon, the Military Cyber Professionals Association, the Cyber Center of Excellence at Fort Gordon, Army Cyber Command, the National Security Agency, and U.S. Cyber Command.

Black Hat and ShmooCon were particularly helpful by allowing us to present at their conferences and refine the ideas this book contains. Our co-presenter and collaborator, Tom Cross, CTO of OPAQ Networks, made game-changing improvements to this work. We would like to thank our students from Black Hat Training who, through multiple two-day iterations of our *Military Strategy and Tactics for Cyber Security* course, gave freely of their expertise to help improve our thinking and subsequently this book. Ninjas such as you are a rare and elusive breed; we are in your debt.

Adam Tyra and Wesley Miaw made a fundamental difference by reading the entire draft manuscript and providing insightful and detailed advice. We particularly appreciated having one of cyber security's leading thinkers, Richard Bejtlich, participate in the first Black Hat class we offered and review portions of this book. Peiter "Mudge" Zatko, who in 1998 along with other members of the hacker collective L0pht Heavy Industries, famously testified before the U.S. Senate on the insecurities of the Internet, freely provided paradigm shifting insights in support of this work. We are also indebted to Dr. Michael Sulmeyer, leader of Harvard's Cyber Security Project, for organizing a workshop around this book at Harvard's Belfer Center bringing in some of the finest minds in the community to help refine the book's focus and content.

We'd like to thank Dan Conti for his work designing the book's cover. He did an excellent job of capturing the enigmatic nature of cyber conflict.

We would also like to thank Dr. John Nelson for his fine work editing significant portions of the manuscript. John has the rare combination of a background in technology, operational military experience, and mastery of the written word for this project. John, we are in your debt.

Finally, we would like to thank our DoD reviewers who conducted and approved our pre-publication review request. Note that all views expressed in this book are those of the authors and are not the official policy or position of our current or past employers.

Any errors or shortcomings in this book are entirely our own. We welcome any feedback to improve *On Cyber*. Please send suggestions, typos, and comments to oncyberbook@gmail.com.

Finally, as this book is about *war*, please don't interpret the ideas it contains or suggests as being legal or appropriate in any given context. Check with an appropriate legal advisor if you have any questions or concerns.

# 1 INTRODUCTION

*"Cyber is Conflict in Code for Control"*
*- Captain Roy Ragsdale[11]*

Cyber conflict is ongoing now.[12] Actors of all stripes—from empowered individuals to nation-states—fight to achieve their goals in cyberspace. They do so by conducting cyberspace operations, either alone or in conjunction with physical operations. All future military engagements of any magnitude will likely include some aspect of cyber operations, which seek to achieve objectives in or through cyberspace.[13] Cyber conflict certainly isn't isolated to military organizations. Enterprises are facing nation state aggressors on a regular basis in this domain. This type of war isn't as physically destructive as kinetic conflict, at present, but it is certainly undermining the national security of the United States and other countries.

Cyber conflict is harder to perceive since many effects occur in cyberspace alone, but there is no doubt that nations are active in cyberspace, stealing intellectual property on a massive scale, reading the U.S. president's email, placing backdoors at strategically important locations, subverting the supply chain of critical infrastructure, and attacking major corporations, including Sony, Sands Casino, HBO, and Saudi Aramco.[14] Much more is possible, but for now there are limited actors with both the will and the capability to do more damaging attacks, like take down power grids, disrupt stock markets, or shut down hospitals.[15] As we look to the future, cyber operations will certainly cause significant real world disruption, destruction, and even death. Over the past months we've seen attacks against the U.S. presidential election campaigns, allegedly by a foreign power, that directly influenced the U.S. election. Medical devices, automobiles, military weapon systems, satellites,

1

voting machines, and smart cities, all have proven vulnerable to cyber attacks. These attacks, both on the battlefield and at the national-level, are growing increasingly serious.

Technology's allure and potential efficiencies have drawn governments, businesses, militaries, and individuals *en masse* to adopt technical solutions that enable governance, commerce, and national security. You cannot live in modern times and avoid cyberspace. These digital systems are insecure, converging into risky monocultures, yet we depend on them. Nations that have a love affair with expensive weapon systems rely on them doubly so. Military systems that have a long procurement pipeline measured in years, or even decades, have vulnerabilities based on their use of dated software and hardware that must be addressed before they are exploited by their adversaries. Additionally, no nation has unlimited resources to dedicate to its military. The driving force behind new technologies is efficiency. It is unlikely that there are sufficient service members allocated to operate and maintain new, cyber-enhanced systems, and still maintain traditional "stubby pencil" back-up techniques for when those systems fail. Despite this constraint, training under degraded network conditions is absolutely necessary; all systems should have manual modes, and all units should occasionally train under constrained conditions in which they lack their technical tools. Every minute spent on technical training increases the unit's dependency on its digital systems.[16]

Actors who do not want to engage the United States and other powerful nations on a conventional battlefield will likely turn to cyberspace operations to wield power. The United States seeks unqualified dominance on the battlefield, but this isn't easy in cyberspace. The normal rules of military power do not apply. One cannot just count tanks on each side to determine the likely victor. The proliferation of technology, combined with a low cost of entry, allows non-traditional powers to arise and potentially impact everyone. Asymmetries abound, and we are seeing the rise of hybrid warfare that uses affordable and sophisticated technology and enables a threat actor to inflict disproportionate harm on its opponents.[17] Figure 1-1 depicts a military model of the spectrum of conflict and our assessment of the current state of cyberspace.

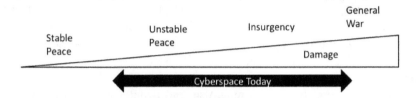

*Figure 1-1: In military doctrine the spectrum of conflict ranges from a stable peace to all-out war. As depicted by the arrow, cyberspace today is unsettled at best, with spikes of destructive activity by nation-state actors against companies as well as in the hybrid warfare strategy employed during the Russian invasion of Ukraine.[18]*

## A Hacker's Apology

This book is written for an audience of military and civilian information security professionals. For our information security readers, we offer a short disclaimer. This book is about "cyber." We acknowledge that this phrase chafes at some, especially the hacker and information security communities. We were in the room when "cyber" won a DEF CON Recognize award for worst cyber security buzzword.[19] We get it. But we've lost the battle. The term "cyber" isn't going away anytime soon, not when there are entire armies organized around it and most of the world is following suit. Information security has its place, the defense of systems and information, penetration testing, reverse engineering, vulnerability scanning, social engineering, and other concepts, but cyber transcends InfoSec. Where InfoSec could be a component of the tactics employed in cyber operations, cyber is about thinking at scale. Cyber considers how to defend nations in cyberspace, how armies fight in the cyber domain, how a nation-state might conduct a cyber siege of a city, and how a combat division might integrate cyber effects with kinetic battlefield operations.[20]

Additionally, the use of military jargon in computer security is starting to gain the same disdain that "cyber" has gained. People in the InfoSec community, particularly those in marketing, often misappropriate and oversimplify military terminology. Nonetheless military terminology and concepts are extremely powerful if employed correctly, an assertion this book seeks to prove.

With our disclaimer in place let's define *cyber* as we use it in this book.[21] We use *cyber* to mean attacking, defending, or collecting information from other computers, where *computers* is used broadly to mean electronic systems that collect, process, store, and communicate information.[22]    We consider *cyberspace* as the sum of the computing systems, networks, and data which permeate our global environment. These systems and networks are usually interdependent and include the Internet and isolated computing networks all the way down to the sensors, chips, and code that run individual devices.[23] *Electronic warfare* intersects with cyber operations, but focuses on military actions that use electromagnetic and directed energy to control the electromagnetic spectrum or to attack an adversary.[24] *Information Technology* (IT) operations are the provisioning, use, and maintenance of information technology infrastructure that we use day-to-day.[25]

In this book we use the language of warfighting because at its heart our book is about how nations fight wars in cyberspace. The inception of this book was based on a conversation we had with an information security friend who frequently encountered nation-state teams attacking his networks. He described a situation when he was forced to decide whether to cut off an intruder in his network or allow the intruder to continue to operate so he could collect additional information about the attacker's tactics and techniques. He lamented that there ought to be a term to describe this condition. We told him there is, it is called *intel gain/loss*, which led to a discussion about the military and intelligence community having concepts that are very applicable to the information security practitioner in industry. This random encounter at the ShmooCon hacker conference started our chain of thinking that took us through multiple conference talks and ultimately led to this book's creation. The military does indeed have terms and concepts useful for cyber security. The book will sound aggressive and warlike, which unfortunately is the nature of war. We will use appropriate military language throughout the book, but strive to make it accessible to a non-military audience. The military lexicon will help information security practitioners think differently, and at the right level of scale, when facing nation-state enabled threat actors.

This book isn't solely about how the military approaches cyber operations, although we think the military should use some of our ideas more often. Rather, it also describes how military thinking can be used to improve the way other organizations approach their own cybersecurity. Meticulous planning, detailed training, and deliberate decision-making are hallmarks of military operations, and many outside the military can learn valuable lessons from these standard practices. This book takes many of these military processes and planning techniques and applies them to cyber in a way that hasn't been done before—not even by the military.

*"A serious problem in planning against American doctrine is that the Americans do not read their manuals, nor do they feel any obligation to follow their doctrine."*
*- Attributed to Unknown Cold War-era Soviet Author* [26]

## A Soldier's Apology

For our military readers, this book is about military and nation-state cyber operations. By necessity, it isn't a doctrinal manual. For those unfamiliar with the military, doctrine is codified in the manuals and frameworks upon which military units operate. For some military personnel, doctrine is holy writ, and for others, something to be ignored. Most are somewhere in between. At present, military doctrine for cyberspace operations is unsettled and ranges from muddled[27] to a "great start."[28] There is not, and may never be, a canonical "right" answer. That means we are free to choose, extend, or ignore models and frameworks from the military doctrines of any nation. Most importantly, we are free to challenge doctrine before our adversaries do and, ideally, to get ahead of doctrine in order to improve future iterations.

At present, militaries are largely moving blindly into the era of cyber. Traditional doctrine doesn't always fit, and many aspects of cyber operations are counterintuitive to those with limited technical expertise. Our goal is to help provide a glimpse into future possibilities by providing an overarching framework with which to analyze and understand cyber operations and their impact on warfighting, as well as enterprise defense and national security. With that goal in mind, this book uses the language of technology and information security. At times, this language will be unfamiliar, but it is necessary to describe cyber operations with precision. We will attempt to define new terms as we go; however, we do ask that you meet us halfway and look-up terms you are unfamiliar with, lest the book become a primer on InfoSec and not a book on how nations fight wars in cyberspace today and in the future. For someone, who hasn't interacted with the information security community and studied its rich body of work, you may be surprised to find that much about cyber conflict is in the public domain.

Inside the military there are many naysayers[29] who tend to believe that cyber is the domain of "REMFs," soldiers in the rear echelon, people you can ignore. Believe this if you will, but you would be naively wrong. We are always in real or imminent contact with adversaries in cyberspace. We argue that militaries should focus on strategic threats in cyberspace and not be drawn to their comfort zone of focusing heavily on the tactical battlefield. Battlefield innovation is important, but it pales in comparison to the existential threats we face at the national level. When was the last time we faced an armored division in head-to-head combat? There might not be a next time because we might cease to exist as a nation if we fail to secure our critical infrastructure. If you are uncomfortable with technology and you won't believe in cyber unless an adversary's hands reach out from your monitor to choke you, then we ask that you reconsider. We must not ignore this slow bleed happening in the United States.

## Combat Power

Militaries fight by bringing combat power—including leadership, information, and the forces at their disposal—to bear against an adversary with the objective of eliminating the enemy's will to fight. These tools include intelligence, fires and effects, logistics, protective measures, and maneuver, all under a unifying command and control architecture.[30] At any given time, combat power is the sum of all of the combined destructive, constructive, and information capabilities a military unit can muster.[31] These powerful concepts apply equally well to cyberspace and cyber/kinetic operations. In this book, we'll examine each element of combat power in depth in the context of the cyber and cyber/kinetic domains.

Cyberspace is a battlespace impacted by a number of factors, including policy, economics, diplomacy, and military operations. For those of us familiar with the inception of the Internet and its accompanying nobly egalitarian goals, we wish that cyberspace wasn't a battleground, but the strategic value of the Internet has grown to such an extent that it can no longer simply be a garden for intellectual discourse and a playground for hackers. Cyberspace is too important to be ignored by those in power, and there they vie for dominance. Militaries seek to maintain freedom of action for themselves and deny the same to their enemies.[32] Freedom of action means the ability to operate as you wish without impediment, with the ultimate objective being to achieve cyberspace superiority and, by extension, superiority in the air, land, sea, and space so that your side has a decisive advantage in military operations. The extent that "freedom of action" and "cyberspace superiority" can actually be achieved in practice is yet to be determined.

## Levels of War

Militaries organize their actions into three primary levels: Strategic, Operational, and Tactical.[33]

- Strategic: The strategic level employs the elements of national power to accomplish national and multi-national objectives.
- Operational: The operational level is the art and science of employing tactical operations, allocating resources, and assigning tasks and missions to achieve objectives. It is at this level we think

of "campaigns," which are a planned series of operations, over time, designed to accomplish these objectives.

- Tactical: The tactical level is compromised of the planning and executing of battles, engagements, and other activities to achieve low-level objectives.

These three levels are useful in the context of cyber operations as well (see Figure 1-2). Information security operates primarily at the tactical level and is of short duration. Nation states take a longer-term perspective, implementing their strategies as a series of campaigns. InfoSec defenders who think in terms of campaigns are more effective than those who constrain themselves to tactics and isolated incidents.[34]

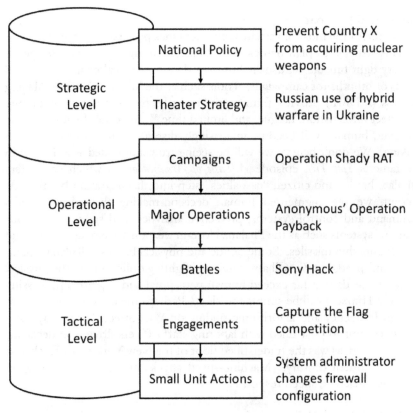

*Figure 1-2: The levels of war: strategic, operational, and tactical mapped to major aspects ranging from national policy down to small unit actions, and annotated with representative cyber operations examples.[35]*

## Readiness[36]

To fight and win, militaries must be ready. Readiness means that units are well trained, fully staffed, and equipped with the best available tools. They must constantly listen and learn to be more lethal, professional, and technically competent than their adversaries. To accomplish these goals, leaders must take care of their troops. These kinetic-centric dictums align closely with the needs of military cyber units, although the challenges are greater. Leaders must fight through a critical shortage of cyber talent,[37] overcome slow acquisition systems, adapt to constantly evolving technology, track agile adversaries, and ignore alluring private sector opportunities, to create an environment where the best people want to stay and build the most skilled and powerful cyber force.

## Automated Combat

War is one of the most physically taxing activities possible. During conflicts, humans struggle to plan battles and campaigns using imperfect intelligence on very tight timetables, usually hours or days for tactical engagements and weeks or months for campaigns. Tools such as the Military Decision Making Process (MDMP) provide frameworks to make the best decisions despite imperfect information, fatigue, and limited time.[38] As technologies advance, however, humans will become increasingly distant from real-time decision making. We don't believe we will be seeing truly automated war as seen in the famous *Star Trek* episode *A Taste of Armageddon*, in which computers simulate battles and citizen "casualties" step into disintegration booths. At present, we see augmented human decision-making through battlefield command and control systems, predictive analytics, and semi-autonomous weapons systems such as the Phalanx close-in weapon system, used to defend against anti-ship missiles. Some online and physical battles will always occur at human speed, but we will absolutely see fighting online and in the physical world at speeds that far exceed human perceptual and cognitive processing abilities. Humans will be simply too slow. Perhaps the closest analog is that of high frequency and algorithmic trading on Wall Street.[39] The days of a sweaty command post filled with laboring staff officers driving all decisions are numbered, as was the trader-filled floor of the New York Stock Exchange of the twentieth century. Machine-speed attacks at a grand scale require integrated machine speed responses.

## Multidisciplinary Cyber

Many mistakenly think that cyber is purely an InfoSec problem and squarely in the domain of expert technologists, particularly computer scientists. They don't understand that cyber is inherently multidisciplinary. To be honest, we did not buy into this idea at first, but we are now believers. Every discipline has some intersection with cyber (see Figure 1-3). Natural starting points are the disciplines of computer science, computer engineering, and electrical engineering. These people write the code and design and build computing systems, the ones with hands-on immediacy. But political scientists apply the rich toolset of international diplomacy and policy to tackle cyber-related challenges. And legal scholars and attorneys apply the law to enable legal cyber operations and punish transgressors. Political scientists and lawyers make up much of the nation's senior leadership who create law and policy to complement technical cyber security solutions. Much of information security revolves around economics. Economists study such things as malware economies to identify and help correct perverse incentives, analyze the impact of crypto currencies like Bitcoin, and trace back through complicated funding streams to identify online threat actors. Psychologists strive to create usable security and understand what causes people to perform unsafe online actions. Military science practitioners study strategy and tactics and act as cyber mission planners. Linguists study threat actor languages, including slang and jargon, to enable improved information collection. Historians bring us wisdom about the past, applying rich knowledge of warfare and technology so that we aren't doomed to repeat mistakes.

We have not fully plumbed the depths of the intersection between each discipline and how its tools and domain knowledge can be applied to both securing cyberspace and the conduct of cyberspace operations. Specialists are necessary to push the state of the art, but we also envision cyber leaders who have a solid technical foundation as well as advanced skills in policy, law, psychology, and a mix of other disciplines in the right amounts. We are still too early in the experimentation phase to get this ideal balance right.

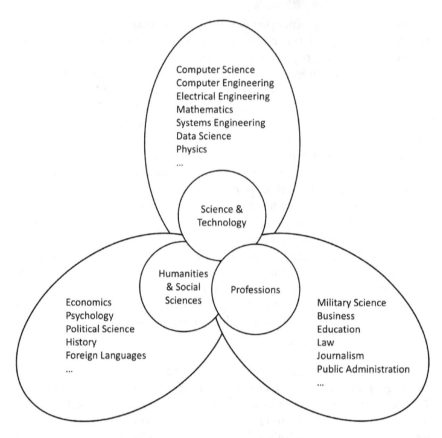

*Figure 1-3: Cyber is inherently multidisciplinary. Every discipline has important tools and domain knowledge that can be brought to bear against cyber security challenges and enable the conduct of cyber operations.*

Cyber operations can be covert and hard to detect, or noisy and deliberately disruptive. Much of the historical cyber operations occurring online have been quiet, with the exception of a few high profile attacks on Sony Pictures Entertainment, Saudi Aramco, and the Sands Casino, among others. Recently, we've seen the cyber operations employed by Russia in its incursions into Ukraine and their take down of the power grid.[40] Fueled by technological advancement, the rate of change in cyber warfare is much faster than advances in kinetic warfare. As a result, militaries are continually moving into unknown territory. Agile and innovative actors have the distinct advantage here. It is in the best interest of militaries to establish forward-looking organizations that are staffed by multidisciplinary cyber experts to continually explore over the horizon and prevent strategic surprise. The U.S.

Army did this by founding the Army Cyber Institute.[41]  In a time of resource constrains, dedicating resources to explore the future may feel painful, but is doubly necessary for cyberspace operations.

## Conclusions

Make no mistake: Cyber conflict is raging now. Much goes on unseen, but we see glimpses of the larger picture in the headlines every day. The military has many useful tools and frameworks for coping at scale with a spectrum of conflict, but militaries have a long way to go and may never catch up given the relentless press of Moore's Law and technical advancement. Most of these military tools need tailoring to be useful in the cyber domain, but we've presented several adapted examples and will add more throughout the book, as well as numerous new additions that we've designed ourselves based on our understanding of existing military doctrine. Militaries are designed to fight other militaries and are used to fighting at scale. Unfortunately, enterprises today are regularly attacked by nation-state enabled threat actors, and they need military grade strategies and tactics to survive. As we mentioned, military doctrine for cyber operations is immature, as evidenced by the litany of embarrassing military and government compromises and data spills that populate today's news headlines. However, traditional kinetic military thinking about fighting wars is mature and time-tested. In this book, we've worked hard to map and extend these robust kinetic principles to cybersecurity and cyber operations in novel and useful ways for both the enterprise and the nascent military cyber operations community.

The strength of the military's way is wrapped up in the process: deliberate planning, deliberate training, and highly structured decision-making. Most organizations don't plan their security operations. Instead, they rely on "heroes" (those highly knowledgeable and productive individual masterminds who save the day for everyone), best practices, and vendors. Just as the military cannot rely on its officers to all be Napoleons, organizations need a way to squeeze performance from insufficient cybersecurity resources. Flexible organizational structures and adaptive teams make this possible, not just talented individuals with exceptional intellectual capacity.

# 2 ACTORS AND ADVERSARIES

*"All history teaches that no enemy is so insignificant as to be despised and neglected by any power, however formidable."*
*- Jomini*[42]

When considering cyber operations, it is essential to identify and analyze potential actors. This chapter explores the types of actors active in cyberspace and examines specific aspects of each category. Seven billion people populate this planet, most of whom have some presence in cyberspace, and about 10 billion Internet connected devices proliferate cyberspace. Billions more devices aren't yet directly active on the Internet, but the trend is toward far greater interconnectivity. As an example, growth is expected to reach 24 billion Internet-connected devices in the next few years.[43] In order to consider the full range of possibilities, we consider each person and each electronic device to have a potential role in cyber conflict either as an aggressor, a defender, a victim, or simply a witness, whether they are directly on the Internet or indirectly influenced by it.

The distinction between aggressor, defender, victim, and witness is subjective. One person's patriot is another person's terrorist. Humans act based on their motivations, but devices follow code-based instructions derived from human guidance. Both humans and machines can switch sides based on changes in their logic. For example, a human might become an insider threat if he is enticed, convinced, or coerced in some way. Machines are susceptible to reprogramming in a way that can make them a quiet accomplice or an active aggressor.

Military organizations draw more precise distinctions. In traditional armed conflict, adversaries are organized into a limited number of categories: friendly, enemy, and neutral,[44] along with the less convenient partisan and terrorist groups. Friendlies can be further subdivided into a given nation's forces and allied forces. Under most circumstances, service members wear uniforms that allow quick identification, and their gear, vehicles, and weapon systems are similarly readily identifiable. To wear the uniform of an enemy risks charges of violating the Law of Armed Conflict, as does masquerading as a medic, chaplain, or other non-combatant. In cyberspace conflict, such clean lines and ready identification do not yet exist.

**Types of Actors**
There are many different types of actors with varying degrees of capability. This section groups them into a number of major classes. Actors may be considered friendly, enemy, or neutral depending on a given context and an observer's perspective.

*Individuals* – The least resourced category, individuals are just that, lone actors with varying degrees of expertise in cyber, ranging from little to moderate. Sometimes, however, individuals may be organized by a nation-state into a whole of a country's quasi-fighting force by employing their devices as a cohesive network of attack, defend, or analysis machines via software that provides external command and control.

*Insider Threat* – A trusted member of a group, particularly a governmental organization or business, who has privileged access to the group's data and operations. Because of the amplification effect of trusted status, a skilled insider has the ability to have a significant impact. An insider threat may be malicious and deliberately work against the goals of their employer, or may be non-malicious and create vulnerabilities through ignorance, apathy, or a desire to get their work done efficiently.[45] Thus, an insider threat is not always based solely on the actor's intentions.

*Lone Hackers* – Advanced- to expert-level operators who operate independently. Potentially capable of significant impact, exponentially so if the lone hacker is also a trusted insider.

**Hacker Collectives** – Groups of skilled operators who operate with some common agenda. The agenda could be the common good, political change, personal amusement, or some other reason. As a collective's size grows, infighting may degrade their once common mission. In addition to the general model, we see at least four sub-categories:

*Hactivist Groups* – Loosely organized groups of operators who share a common set of ideals and use electronic means to achieve them. These groups often strive to expose or punish what they see as abuses of power by politicians, religious groups, or large corporations.

*Patriotic Hackers* – Groups of operators who purport to operate out of patriotism. They may operate with the tacit support of their government, which often overlooks their behavior as long as government sponsors aren't embarrassed and national interests aren't damaged. Such support may include nation-state sponsors providing resources.

*Mercenaries* – Groups of operators who are transnational and accept payment from clients in return for services. These may be legitimate companies or looser knit collectives. Their compliance with the law is dubious, although some have suggested bringing back the concept of "letter of marque" and providing a degree of government legitimacy.[46]

*Extremist Groups* – Groups of operators whose activities are motivated by violent extremism. They may provide support for fund raising, operations security, recruiting, propagation of magazines and videos, command and control, and potentially offensive cyber operations. Violent extremist group cyber personnel are often hunted by adversary nation-states.

**Criminal Groups** – Criminal groups perform illegal activities, perhaps with tacit government support, that generate profit. In addition to tacit support, a criminal group may act as a proxy for a given government, which, in response, turns a blind eye to the group's activities. Such arrangements give criminal groups the ability to conduct illegal operations with impunity from punishment, while providing governments with plausible deniability of the actions taken on their behalf. More powerful criminal groups may have physical reach across national boundaries and financial resources easily in the millions of dollars.[47]

***Corporations***[48] – Corporations are business entities in any sector and are focused on providing a product or service to make a profit. They may be privately held and possess greater independence or publicly held and be accountable to investors and government regulators. Some may have altruistic motives, but others are aggressive, even exhibiting sociopathic-like behaviors.[49] Unless specializing in information security or technology, smaller companies are likely to dedicate limited resources toward information security, but larger companies may have robust defensive cyber capabilities and aggressively hunt for adversaries on their networks. Offensive cyber activities may be conducted or sponsored by corporations, depending on the legal and regulatory environment, but details rarely become public. In the United States, such behavior is highly discouraged and often deemed illegal.[50] Companies possess proprietary information, business secrets, and intellectual property that they desire to protect. Disclosure of such information can be devastating to their businesses and sometimes to national security.[51] Companies may have access to, or own, strategically key cyber terrain, such as source code for major operating systems, databases of search queries, global networks of managed security sensors, billions of user emails, key network hubs, or social networking data for hundreds of millions of users, among myriad other examples. Larger technology companies, and particular information security firms, may have robust intelligence collection capabilities through a global network of sensors or hire services that provide similar information. While only a rough approximation, the largest transnational companies have financial assets and other resources that are comparable to small- to mid-sized nation-states. However, corporations lack the law and policy-making powers, as well as military and law enforcement authorities entitled only to nation-states and thus must abide by the law and policy in the countries where they operate.

***Nation-States*** – Nations possess significant advantages as actors in cyberspace. They are able to set law within their borders, maintain intelligence agencies,[52] and train and equip military and law enforcement organizations. They also have an inherent right to defend themselves against invading adversaries and existential threats. Law enforcement routinely exists at the national, regional, and local level. Military organizations possess active duty and reserve forces, and service may be voluntary or compelled. The capability of nation-states in cyberspace operations is a function of their investment in cyberspace capacity and capability. Smaller nations are typically less resourced, but the asymmetric nature of cyberspace operations allows such actors to provide a credible threat.

***Machine Actors*** – It may feel ahead of its time, but machine actors are an emergent category that will surely grow in both scope and power in the future.[53] Machines operate at the behest of humans based on their programming. At present, machines typically act as tools for human operators either directly or indirectly, but there are ongoing efforts to increase machine autonomy using artificial intelligence (AI). The decision-making of AI is opaque and is likely to eventually far exceed that of humans. What was once well understood and under human control may operate in ways beyond the intent of their human creators, sometimes called the Rogue AI Problem.[54] This scenario is partially in the realm of science fiction, but not beyond the realm of the possible.[55]

To help better illustrate the various types of actors and their potential impact we've summarized them in Figure 2-1. Our list in this section, while including many, isn't necessarily comprehensive depending on your specific context and threat model. For example, we didn't include non-profit organizations or international standards organizations as actors, but you could if their inclusion made sense for your particular situation.[56]

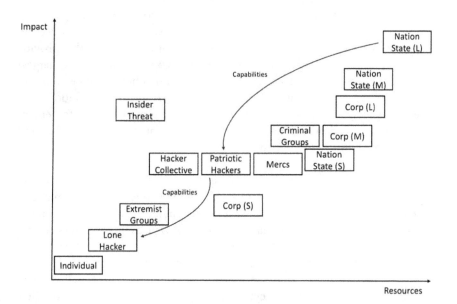

*Figure 2-1: Actors in cyberspace have varying degrees of resources that they can apply in cyberspace conflict. In some cases actors will share capabilities with allies or other parties, either purposely or inadvertently, resulting in a trickle-down effect. Note that insider threats, consider Edward Snowden, may have more than enough capability to create global persistent effects.*

## Characteristics

Each actor has widely varying characteristics based on his capabilities, resources, and incentives. Through careful analysis, actors may be modeled and used for further analysis.

*Sophistication* – Actors vary widely in their degree of sophistication. Some operate with mature techniques, tactics, and procedures under strong command and control utilizing vetted doctrine. Others are ad-hoc collectives that may suffer from infighting and unsanctioned operations. Some groups may employ tight operational security measures (OPSEC) to prevent attribution and thus mislead their adversaries. Evolutionary theory's *survival of the fittest*[57] insights apply to actors as well; less sophisticated actors may be attacked by more mature threats. Importantly, sophistication measures for adversaries' abilities to conduct cyberspace operations extend beyond technological know-how and into all other areas required to realize capability. For an example of how the U.S. Army scales its operations to the level of army vs. army combat, consider its DOTMLPF[i] construct - Doctrine, Organization, Training, Materiel, Leadership & Education, Personnel, and

---

[i] DOTMLPF. This initialization used widely in Army doctrine describes the range of courses of action that senior leaders can take to address emerging threats, new situations, evolving technology, and other occurrences that require strategic changes to the way the military operates. These changes can be addressed by one or more of these approaches, usually in synchronized combination. The initials stand for: *Doctrine* – Some changes require updates or additions to the doctrinal library, which contains manuals that provide a high-level description of how to approach operations. For example, new challenges imposed by the cyberspace domain have led to several new doctrinal manuals for the various services. *Organization* – Challenges in cyberspace have also led to new military organizations such as United States Cyber Command and its service-level counterparts. *Training* – New military organizations and responsibilities require re-tooled or completely new training courses and programs. The Army recently created the Cyber School at Fort Gordon, Georgia and has begun to train Cyber branch soldiers, non-commissioned officers, and officers there. *Materiel* – Changes to the strategic situation often require the research and development of new equipment such as tanks, aircraft, and ships. *Leadership and Education* – Strategic leaders need to understand new developments in order to lead units tasked to execute new types of missions. Each service has a "war college," or similar facilities to further educate senior military leaders. *Personnel* – Sometimes wholesale changes to the personnel system is warranted. An example is the Army's recently created Cyber branch, an entirely new career field for soldiers and officers. *Facilities* – Changes in the strategic situation often cause military bases to expand, contract, or cease to exist. For example, the fall of the Soviet Union resulted in dozens of U.S. military bases in Western Europe closing.

Facilities.[58] This mature and time-tested process provides a methodology for senior U.S. Department of Defense personnel to consider the range of potential solutions to operational and strategic challenges.

*Motivation* – Whether formally or informally organized, threat actors' actions stem from their own particular motivations and incentives. These may be uniform throughout a given organization or an actor may have a number of various cooperating factions, each with its own motives. For example, a loose-knit hacker collective will likely fall into the latter category while a patriotic hacker organization operating with tacit government support may be of a unified mind. The motivation of an organization will usually show in its behaviors, but only sometimes in its words. An intelligence organization might choose to be stealthy in its cyber operations, whereas a military organization might not care about attribution and operate in a very obvious and destructive fashion. A violent extremist group may adopt a Machiavellian "the end justifies the means" method of operation. Criminal groups and corporations will be motivated by business success, whether legal or illegal, which will in turn influence their decision making.[59] Motivations can sometimes seem to defy logic. A military unit serving a nation-state actor may simply strive to compromise and establish persistence on as many networks as possible, without regard to their value, in order to appear more skilled or efficient than rival organizations.

Dignity and pride also powerful motivations. In terms of cyber-threat analysis, the Hewlett-Packard Company's security research group did a remarkable job analyzing North Korea's anger over the pending release of the Sony movie *The Interview*, a controversial U.S. comedy in which two talk show hosts are asked to assassinate North Korean leader Kim Jong Un. In the report, analysts noted North Korea felt the United States "had gone beyond the tolerance limit in their despicable moves," lodging a complaint with the United Nations and stating, "If the U.S. administration connives at and patronizes the screening of the film, it will invite a strong and merciless countermeasure." North Korea's cyber attack on Sony Pictures Entertainment happened only a few months later.[60]

*Respect for the Law* – Legal factors weigh heavily on the capability of some actors, adding friction to cyber operations. In cases where attribution is likely, most nation-states are motivated to operate within the confines of international law to avoid sanctions from the United Nations and other international bodies. If an actor complies with the law, its options can be severely limited. Extralegal actors function with far fewer constraints and theoretically operate in the entire space of technically feasible options that they possess, boosting their effectiveness. However, each actor has a given tolerance for the limits of its illegal activity and may self-moderate. There is a hybrid option category, actors that operate unofficially but with government support; this is sometimes seen with criminal groups and patriotic hacker groups.[61] As long as these actors operate within explicitly or implicitly imposed parameters, the government will often turn a blind eye.[62] Of course no actor is entirely above the law, and there is often a risk of retribution. Governments themselves are still accountable under international law and norms, so they are unlikely to operate with impunity. Additionally, laws vary widely between nations. For example, the United States attempts to draw a distinction between intelligence collection by government agencies without passing intellectual property acquired to companies, whereas China's culture and law allows the theft and sharing with state-run companies as a means to gain an economic advantage.[63] Both are quite reasonable in their respective cultural context. Given the difficulty of attributing the source of attacks and pursuing legal action, most threat actors face little risk from not complying with the law. Threat actors have little to fear from law enforcement authorities in countries that aren't their own.

*Capability and Capacity* – Each actor has resources at its disposal, some trivial and some massive. A core aspect of an actor's capabilities is the skill level and amount of available human talent. A number of questions come to mind when considering threat capabilities. Does the actor possess cyber experts, and if so, in what areas of expertise? An expert who can discover or create vulnerabilities, write tools, and execute sophisticated cyber operations could be more valuable than a thousand novices. This is in contrast to physical operations where differences in training and talent are rarely so lopsided. Hardware and software are also critical components. What does a given actor possess in terms of processing power, bandwidth, and storage? What toolsets and 0-day assets do they have available?[64] Are they capable of creating their own tools, discovering vulnerabilities, or even creating vulnerabilities via supply chains, or is the actor heavily dependent on tools and exploits provided by others? Financial resources provide operational flexibility and allows the actor to hire talent, purchase hardware and software, and gain access to sensitive networks. Threat actors may also have rare or unique access to important information, networks, or facilities. Finally, given the sum of these resources and capabilities, what is the actor's overall capacity to conduct cyberspace operations, be they offensive or defensive in nature?

*Without strong law enforcement institutions, individuals in insecure areas will at times take matters into their own hands. This sort of environment is ripe for the emergence of an Anonymous group. Anonymous is "a classic 'do-ocracy'". The term "means rule by sheer doing: Individuals propose actions, others join in (or not), and the Anonymous flag is flown over the result. There's no one to grant permission, no promise of praise or credit, so every action must be its own reward."*

*— Paul Rexton Kan [65]*

**Agility** – An adversary that is well resourced with people and money isn't necessarily efficient and effective. Sometimes the opposite is true. Large organizations may be burdened with significant friction due to bureaucratic, ethical, or legal processes. Approvals for activities could take days, weeks, or even months. Command and control becomes more difficult as organizations grow in size and become globally dispersed.[66] Rigid hierarchies frustrate communication and empowerment of subordinates. Defense acquisition processes may take a decade or more, with project timelines clearly unsuitable for the rapid pace of cyber operations. Stakeholders in large bureaucracies, such as competing agencies, may maneuver politically to protect their resources and power rather than the superordinate mission of their higher authority, such as national security. Competing law enforcement agencies may vie for control of a given case or mission set. Military organizations may fight with intelligence agencies over decisions to collect information or cause physical damage to a given entity. Due to these and other inefficiencies, well-resourced actors may allocate increasingly greater resources to problems in an attempt to gain an edge over other actors. This model, while sometimes successful, does not scale well, and no actor has unlimited resources.[67] Smaller groups have a distinct advantage here, reminiscent of Gulliver being tied to the ground by the Lilliputians in Jonathan Swift's *Gulliver's Travels*. Despite possessing fewer people and less money, small actors have the potential for far greater speed in decision making, command and control, and rapid development of low cost solutions, particularly when unfettered by legal or procedural restraints. It's often not about numbers or size, but about flexibility, decisiveness, and know-how. A favorite example, from personal experience, is that of a training exercise conducted by the 24th Infantry Division in 1992. It was a command post exercise where commanders and their staffs fought a simulated wargame between the 20,000+ person division and a notional adversary. In this case, a single junior officer roleplayed the adversary. Because of the friction of layers upon layers of headquarters, the division responded very slowly. The lieutenant could make decisions rapidly and decisively. As a result, the single lieutenant ran circles around the division and the exercise had to be halted while the game masters inserted new rules to slow down the junior officer. This imbalance in agility is a key driving factor behind the vast asymmetries between actors in cyberspace.

Table 2-1 provides a summary that compares and contrasts each of the threat actor classes against the characteristics we just discussed, and assesses each actor's potential overall impact. Our analysis is generalized, and you may wish to expand the analysis for specific actors. In particular, we recommend creating an Order of Battle (OB) database that describes the organization, command structure, equipment, leadership, and other aspects of each threat actor you envision encountering.[68] We'll discuss these and other intelligence strategies in Chapter 8 – Intelligence.

**Trust**

Trust inside groups and among actors is a necessary component of survival, but misplaced trust can be deadly.[69] Most people trust their technology, assuming it will do what they intend it to do, or at least what it purports to do, and act in their own best interest. Such trust is misplaced and can be dangerous. As a given technology becomes increasingly popular, it becomes an increasingly greater target for subversion. Similarly humans who have important roles or important access will increasingly become a target for witting or unwitting compromise. Subversion of technology may occur anywhere in the supply chain, from design to chip fabrication, to assembly of components from dozens of factories, to storage in warehouses and long rides in trucks, until the device is in the hands of the user; and even then, it can be subverted remotely. Consider the dozens of global suppliers that provide components for our laptops and phones. The potential for subversion doesn't stop at this point. Those with physical access to the device, such as a cleaning crew in an office, may physically modify the hardware or software, for example, by installing an inline hardware keystroke logger on a critical system between the keyboard cable and the chassis. A bad software or firmware update could also do it, as can clicking a link to a malicious website in a phishing email, the installation of a malicious app from an app store, or a remote network-level attack that compromises one of your networked services. Even a compromised compiler, which translates human readable code into an executable program, would appear to the programmer to be doing its job, but could be including malicious instructions in the resulting program.[70] Shrink-wrapped commercial products are no panacea. Newspaper headlines frequently carry stories of pre-pwned, that is, already compromised, products being sold in stores.

21

*Table 2-1: Generalized analysis of cyberspace actors against key characteristics. Note that the overall impact isn't tied directly to size or resources; the actor's agility weighs heavily on their overall impact.*

| Actor | Size (IT & Cyber Operators) | Incentives | Law Abiding | Organic Capabilities | Capacity | Potential Impact |
|---|---|---|---|---|---|---|
| Individual | 1 | Variable | Variable | Uses existing tools | Low | Low |
| Lone Hacker | 1 | Variable | Variable | Discover vulnerabilities | Low | Variable |
| Malicious Insider Threat | Few | Variable | No | Discover vulnerabilities | Low | Variable |
| Hacktivists | 10s-1000s | Cause-based | Variable | Discover vulnerabilities | Moderate | Moderate |
| Patriotic Hackers | 10s-1000s | Patriotism | Variable | Discover vulnerabilities | Moderate | Moderate |
| Mercenaries | 10s-100s | Profit | No | Discover vulnerabilities | Moderate | Moderate |
| Extremist Groups | 10s-100s | Ideology | No | Discover vulnerabilities | Low | Moderate |
| Criminal Groups | 10s-100s | Profit | No | Discover vulnerabilities | Moderate-High | Moderate - High |
| Corporation (S) | 10s-100s | Profit | Yes | Use existing tools | Low | Low - Moderate |
| Corporation (M) | 10s-100s | Profit | Yes | Use existing tools | Moderate | Moderate - High |
| Corporation (L) | 100s-1000s | Profit | Yes | Create vulnerabilities | High | Moderate - High |
| Nation-state (S) | 100s – 1K | National security | Yes | Use existing tools | Moderate | Moderate |
| Nation-state (M) | 1000s | National security | Yes | Create vulnerabilities | High | Moderate - High |
| Nation-state (L) | 10K – 100K+ | National security | Yes | Create vulnerabilities | Very High | Very High |
| Machine | Variable | N/A | Variable | Discover vulnerabilities | Potentially High | Potentially High |

Companies may aid and abet subversive activities either purposely, exploiting their positions of trust, or inadvertently by exposing fabrication facilities or development tool chains to malicious tampering. Even non-networked development machines could be compromised through techniques such as dropping a thumb drive in a parking lot and having it carried inside a secure facility by unwitting users. There are techniques for reducing risk; examples include trusted chip foundries and isolated networks. However, no matter how pristine the environment, unless you are creating your computer from sand up, anywhere in this tenuous chain of design, manufacture, transport, storage, and use, a bad thing can occur. Additionally, aspects of the device have at one time or the other directly or indirectly touched the Internet, whether it is the chip designer's machine or an old utility included in the operating system. The end result is that both hardware and software can be compromised locally or remotely, individually and at scale, and it is very difficult to tell whether these devices are friend or foe at any given point in time.

Humans may also be compromised. Every human has weaknesses that might be exploited by an attacker—such as money, alcohol, or sex—that can be exploited to turn them into a coerced accomplice. Or a human may appear to be a loyal service member or employee, but have an alternate agenda. Of course, governments and businesses attempt to vet their workforce using such techniques as polygraph exams, background checks, and continuous monitoring of financial status and behavior, but, as history has shown, such means certainly aren't foolproof. However, contrary to hardware and software, it may prove difficult to compromise humans at scale, as each individual is different, and compromised people tend to reveal the secret sooner or later. The end result is that while many humans may be trustworthy, a number are not, so an actor may seem to be of one type, but actually be of another, and similar to hardware and software, it is difficult to tell whose side they are on and thus what type of actor they are. It would be convenient for us to just ignore this human element, but the many tiers of trust required in both people and technology and the potential for shifting of allegiance must be taken into account when making decisions and assessing risk.

*"The United States became the most formidable military in world history through a mutually beneficial alliance with corporations."*
*- Shane Harris[72]*

**Multi-Actor Collaborations** – Alliances are very likely between actors in order to pool capabilities and resources towards a mutually agreeable objective or under terms that provide desired benefits to each party.[73] The history of warfare is replete with examples: the Axis and the Allies in World War II, NATO, or industry's and academia's support for the Manhattan Project,[74] among numerous others. The end result is a summation of power, sometimes galvanizing the populations of entire nations, which collectively raises the impact of the team members, potentially up to or beyond the level of the strongest single superpower.[75]

Collaboration may also occur between sub-groups within a larger actor, such as law enforcement working with the military and intelligence agencies of a given nation-state. Such relationships may be tightly coupled and frequently refreshed, or loosely knit and infrequent. Collaborations may also occur between actors such as an intelligence agency partnering with companies or a national government providing tacit, state-sponsored support to a violent extremist group. Collaborations may be public and largely transparent, or surreptitious and attempt to hide in the shadows when public disclosure of the relationship may be damaging. In the latter cases, parties may try to limit evidence of the partnership to provide plausible deniability if knowledge of the relationship starts to become known. Collaborations will also vary in the degree of integrity and the depth of sharing. Rarely will all parties be truly transparent and share 100% of their resources and intelligence; in fact, each party will likely hold back some of their most valuable assets and stratagems.

Command and control across diverse organizations, especially from differing cultures, may be very difficult, slowing down or frustrating joint activities. Interoperability will also be complex. In the cyber domain, some militaries have enough difficulty networking systems between their own army, navy, and air force, let alone with international or non-governmental partners.

Alliances aren't all or nothing affairs. Threat actors may shift from one motivation to another, while still maintaining partnerships. For example, some Advanced Persistent Threat (APT) groups commit crimes when

24

government money isn't available, or criminal groups may sometimes do things the Government wants. People are complicated, so pigeonholing them in order to neatly predict behavior can fail.

Partnerships may falter and break apart. Trust in partnerships will vary widely based on current, anticipated, and historical behaviors of participants, but also based on the incentives for continuing the relationship. If one party is coerced, it is unlikely that they will remain submissive once the leverage employed is no longer sufficient. Partnerships based on business or financial incentives could shift rapidly when a better offer comes along. Alliances built upon shared ideology or national security could dissolve if one party is embarrassed through public disclosure regarding some aspect of the relationship. Other alliances may falter if it looks like one's present team is losing and it is prudent to switch allegiances or otherwise disband the relationship.

The arena of cyberspace operations has many examples of partnerships, some successful, some less so. The principle of collective defense is at the very heart of NATO's founding treaty and the NATO Secretary-General has made it clear that cyber attacks can potentially trigger a collective response.[76] The U.S. Department of Defense created the Defense Innovation Unit - Experimental in California's Silicon Valley to generate "cross-pollination and cross-collaboration" between the military and Silicon Valley companies.[77] A more mature public-private model than the DoD and Silicon Valley is found in Israel where Unit 8200 alumni have founded multiple cyber security start-ups.[78] One of the most famous international collaborations is that of Australia, Canada, New Zealand, the United Kingdom, and the United States, nicknamed the "Five Eyes," which share virtually all intelligence.[79]

Fighting via proxies, both human and machine, is another widely employed strategy. Large nation states have allegedly used online criminal groups, patriotic hackers, and hactivist groups to do their bidding when conducting cyberspace operations.[80] Importantly, devices, once compromised by an attacker, are often used to create a complex chain of machine proxies that obfuscate the source of an attack and weave through a number of diverse nations that may or may not assist in tracking down the source of an attack.[81] Command and control of botnets that exhibit very creative proxies are also regularly seen.[82]

Alliances are risky, creating additional vulnerabilities and an increased attack surface. Partnerships also add complexity, both in terms of humans interacting and networks/information systems interacting. For example, while a military's network infrastructure may be hardened, a successful attack may come in via a partner contractor.[83] Alliances bring rise to increased insider threat risk through violations of trust and enabled by some degree of privileged access by one of their personnel or a compromised machine. Among the first disclosures of Edward Snowden were relationships between the U.S. government and high-profile American companies.[84] Alliances themselves may evolve over time, and there is the possibility of a shift in allegiance, which could manifest itself in ill-timed and inconvenient, perhaps even devastating, ways. Compromising the code that drives military systems and other technology can create an equally devastating change in "allegiance" as well. For example, friendly and neutral networks and nodes have been used by online criminals to mine bitcoin, mass mail spam, and operate as pay-for-hire DDOS weapons. The same compromise of military systems would have staggering consequences.

Multi-nation alliances also generate legal implications. Problems may arise when a given activity is legal in one country but illegal in another. In these instances participants may decide to operate independently in these areas or tacitly use the other to perform actions that one actor may be unable to conduct at home, gaining operational agility by avoiding legal oversight. The latter example is particularly risky and severe consequences may occur if the activity becomes known. A variant is a nation-state using an extralegal actor to conduct illegal activities, with the same possibility of blowback. Even if an activity is technically legal there may be public relations damage if two unlikely actors collaborate, or even just allegedly collaborate; for example a well-regarded research university and a law enforcement agency attempting to de-anonymize users of a popular anonymity network.[85]

Neutrality is difficult to maintain; sometimes actors are forced to pick sides. For example, when neutral actors, like companies, are attacked by nation-states, they may decide to respond publicly.[86] Security companies are in a particularly tenuous position, as their malware and network-monitoring operations used to protect their customers encounter activities of nation-state, or nation-state enabled, threat actors.[87] Similarly, the companies themselves and others upon which great trust is based, such as certificate authorities, may be directly attacked.[88]

Tools used to perform various offensive or defensive measures, sometimes called capabilities, are also likely to be shared between partners, particularly from the stronger partner to a weaker partner, increasing the risk that these capabilities will be discovered or propagated further.[89]

Alliances may take many different forms in an attempt to aggregate power. Figure 2-2 illustrates representative models, but many other combinations are, of course, possible.

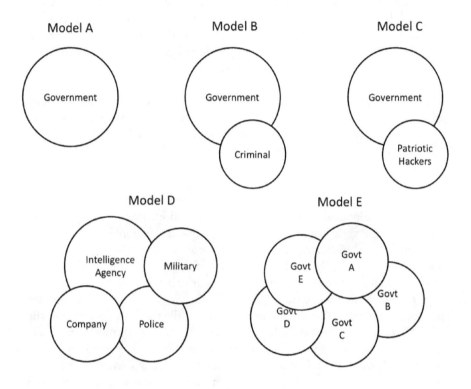

*Figure 2-2: Models of some potential collaborations. Model A represents a government operating without a partner. Models B and C, represent a government collaborating with extra-legal organizations to allow greater ranges of options. Model D depicts three government agencies collaborating with a commercial company. Model E is an alliance of five different governments.*

## Partnership Principles

While correctly aligned partnerships generate powerful results, forging true and lasting partnerships isn't easy nor necessarily desirable. A shared enemy, compatible motivations, or a like culture are starting points, but will only get you so far. At the most basic, partnerships are based on trust and relationships. This involves engaging with representatives that know and respect the community with which they wish to interact, ideally people who have a foot in both worlds, with the requisite credibility, communication skills, and credentials.[90] In each instance, the partner must bring something to the table, seeking to give more than it takes from a community. Proprietary or classified information is a potential hurdle frequently encountered.[91] Trust is paramount. When trusted with a confidence, whether formally restricted or not, it must be respected and protected carefully. The Snowden disclosures, which revealed corporate collaboration with the U.S. government is one example that caused severe embarrassment and significant financial loss in Silicon Valley.[92]

Alliances are often temporary; they may revolve around a particular activity and dissolve afterward. These principles may seem like common sense, but many military organizations in particular aren't wired to think in this empathetic way and often harm rather than help relationships.

## Conclusions

There are many more actors in cyberspace than we often consider, ranging from lone individuals to corporations to nation-states. We need to understand the varied types of actors, and expand our thinking beyond just the stereotypical malicious hacker in a hoodie or an online criminal group that steals credit card data. Most important of all are nation-state adversaries. They are well-resourced and can have missions that will likely not end until they achieve their objectives. Alliances must be made with care, but are powerful amplifiers of resources and can raise affiliating smaller actors to the level of cyber super-power, at least temporarily. Not all alliances are public. Smaller proxy actors, who have a nation-state partner at their back, may wield far greater power than one might assume. Publically owned and private corporations, particularly technology companies, should not be discounted in your analyses, as they possess great capabilities, sometimes comparable to nation states, but lack the legal authority to employ force.

Numbers of personnel don't matter as much in cyberspace. Actors who operate outside the law have a significant advantage, particularly if they take measures to frustrate attribution. Through careful analysis, we can better understand relevant actors including their offensive and defensive strength, their motivations, and their capabilities, in order to design appropriate stratagems. However, vulnerabilities resident in all forms of technology afford weaknesses such that smaller and less resourced actors can bloody the nose of major players. Asymmetries abound, and no one should be cocky.

# 3 LAWS OF PHYSICS

*"What is 'real?' How do you define 'real?'"*
*- Morpheus* [93]

Cyber operations represent conflict involving humans and the machines acting on their behalf. To better understand this conflict, we must understand the constraints faced by each. The Laws of Physics describe the fundamental constraints of the universe and ultimately explain what is and what is not possible in cyberspace. Scientists understand the Laws of Physics through observation and experimentation. In our daily lives, we observe the world through the lens of Newtonian physics, where objects behave according to Newton's Three Laws of Motion.[94] However, at the extremes of speed, time, size, and energy, classical physics and mechanics break down and counterintuitive relativistic and quantum theories emerge.[95] Cyberspace is unique in that it is a man-made construct, and while the underlying Laws of Physics still apply, many equally counterintuitive quasi-laws of physics are dictated by human designers. In this chapter, we explore the interplay between these man-made laws of physics and fundamental physical constraints to understand what is in the realm of the possible, and what is impossible, in cyber operations.

We as humans have evolved in this physical world and intuitively understand how it works. We throw a ball, and the catcher is able to track the ball and catch it with nary a thought. In cyberspace, the quasi-laws of physics are a blend of the formal Laws of Physics and the physical properties chosen by human designers.[96] Examples of these physical properties chosen by designers include fundamental decisions on how, when, and why to move data, what data is stored and for how long, and what processing occurs with the data. Designers make many other choices which define key properties of cyberspace, including how many hops a network packet may make on the network before it is discarded by a router, the frequencies used for wireless communication, how much memory a device possesses, and the clock speed of a particular server.

These quasi-laws of physics create interesting and often counterintuitive properties that can be difficult to grasp, especially for those who have less experience in technology. However, it is these effective laws of physics that constrain cyberspace operations. We must understand them or else cyberspace becomes a magic black box where we attempt the impossible. Attempting to violate the Laws of Physics, whether riding a bicycle, using a table saw, or in cyberspace will have unfortunate outcomes. Importantly, the Laws of Physics are absolute and applicable across the universe, but the man-made laws of physics are not absolute across the finite realm of cyberspace. Developers, network designers, system administrators, large Internet companies, standards bodies, and governments possess god-like superpowers to modify the quasi-laws of physics in the portion of cyberspace they control.[97] Over time, the quasi-laws of physics in cyberspace will bump up against theoretical limits, such as the speed of processors being limited by the speed of light. Heady stuff, but important to those who seek to fight and win in cyberspace. Leaders, cyber operators, and enablers need to know what laws are immutable and what can be changed. The side that understands these laws best and exploits them most ingeniously gains the high ground in cyberspace.

## Limits of Computation
While the Laws of Physics dictate physical constraints of cyberspace, there are also limits on the types of problems computation can solve. These limits are studied by scientists and mathematicians in the field of computability theory. Delving into this field will quickly take you into advanced mathematics, but doing so has practical implications. Central to the idea of computation is the Turing Machine, hypothesized by Alan Turing, which is an abstract model of a computer system. Computer theorists use this and other models to determine the limits of computation. A well-known problem from computability theory is the halting problem, which examines whether or not an arbitrary computer program and an input will ever finish running. Alan Turing proved that the halting problem is impossible to solve. Related is the work of Gödel, whose incompleteness theorems demonstrated that any logical model of reality is incomplete. Even if a given problem is solvable, another challenge is its complexity. Some algorithms may execute quickly, others are infeasible given today's hardware, and yet others are potentially solvable but would require more than the lifespan of the universe to run.[98]

There are optimizations, such as more efficient algorithms, but again the attempt may not achieve the desired goal within available time, processing, and storage constraints. The key takeaway for the cyber professional is that computers are not magical devices that can solve any problem. Many are feasible, but some problems are impossible to compute.

## Mechanics of Bits

The science of mechanics studies the behavior of physical bodies under the action of forces, such as gravity or magnetism, and is divided into three branches: statics (forces acting on a body at rest), kinematics (potential motions of a body), and kinetics (explains or predicts what will occur given a specific set of conditions).[99] Mechanics deals with *physical* bodies, but there are important analogs in cyberspace. Bits, the zeroes and ones in digital systems, are the fundamental unit of information in cyberspace.[100] They do not just reside there; each bit has a physical manifestation, such as a pulse of light on a fiber optic cable, as an electrical charge on a motherboard trace, as a magnetic state on a hard drive, or as a modulated wave of energy travelling through space. These examples represent both data at rest and data in motion. Depending on the context, bits may be considered data or code (instructions). Bits in the physical world must obey the Laws of Physics, as water flows downhill via the easiest path. Bits in cyberspace flow according to algorithms. How they are created, erased, acted upon, moved, or blocked is deterministic, that is, there is no randomness involved. Information systems follow strict logic and should always generate the same output given the same starting conditions.[101] Cyberspace's algorithms are under the control of humans and can alter the operations on bits. In other words, bits can flow uphill, but only if the algorithms and their human masters, friend or foe, dictate. While the humans can change the rules, the system is still deterministic. The same starting conditions and inputs always to the same code yield the same ending conditions and outputs. It is often possible to do such things as replay network traffic, step backward and forward through a running program, and employ predictive analytics to help forecast future states of a system.

## Limits of Sensing

Humans and machines sense and interact with the world around them, but ultimately have only a partial understanding of reality. Humans employ their senses of sight, hearing, taste, touch, and smell. Machines use sensors that detect and measure aspects of the environment, such as temperature, light, sound, and movement. Neither approach is perfect, of course, and it is worth noting that at least for the moment, machines' sensors are designed and programmed by humans and therefore have a human-centric bias in that by design they sense things that humans find relevant. In cyber conflict, humans, machines, and hybrid human/machine teams compete in cooperation with, and potentially against, one another. The fundamental sensing limits of each matter a great deal. Events that occur outside the limits of these senses, human or machine, will not be detected accurately, if at all. Ultimately, machines must act upon information. The design and layout of most cyber operations must facilitate some access to data or else the operation is pointless.

Human vision detects light in the visible portion of the electromagnetic spectrum, but quickly becomes blind to energy, such as infrared and ultraviolet, which falls outside this narrow band (see Figure 3-1). Hearing in most humans is constrained to frequencies from 20-20,000 Hz. There are minimum and maximum thresholds of hearing ranging from -0.5db to 85db or higher, which can cause hearing loss.[102]

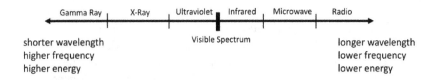

Figure 3-1: Human perception is limited to a small slice of the electromagnetic spectrum, while engineers and scientists have developed sensors that function across a much greater range.[103] Both human perception and machine sensing are subject to exploitation and deception techniques.

A machine's sensing depends on the characteristics of its sensors. Sensors may be passive and powered by external energy, or active and expend energy to sense the environment, like a flash on a camera. Sensors work by taking samples of the environment and are limited in their precision and frequency (see Figure 3-2). Sensors are subject to continual technological advance but are currently limited by the imagination and capabilities of the humans who design them, while human senses are effectively static. For example, improvements in human hearing will happen at the speed of evolution and occur over eons, while audio sensors like laser microphones, which can listen to conversations through a window, or parabolic microphones, which can eavesdrop on conversations from hundreds of meters, exist today, and we can expect additional advances that similarly exceed human capacity in the near future. However, there are fundamental limits. One such limit is illustrated by the Heisenberg uncertainty principle, which describes basic limitation in accurate measurement.[104]

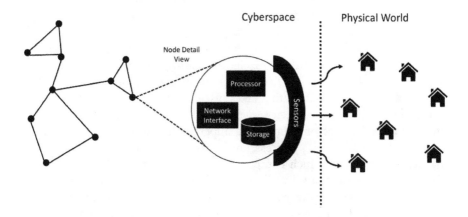

*Figure 3-2: Detail view of networked computer. It contains a processor, storage, and a representative network interface. Its suite of sensors allows it to sense the physical world.[105]*

Consider a smart phone that is equipped with a proximity sensor, ambient light sensor, motion sensor/accelerometer, magnetometer, moisture sensor, gyroscope, and multiple microphones, cameras, and radio transmitters.[106] Each sensor's manufacturer typically provides specifications about the official limits of a given sensor's capabilities. However, such specifications, while useful, only tell part of the story. Besides providing opportunities for deception, the manufacturing process results in differences between batches and even between individual sensor devices. In fact most probably exceed the advertised minimum sensing capability to ensure that the devices meet the requirements of application areas in which they are deployed. For example, if a company advertises that the motion sensors it sells are effective to 20 feet, they want to be sure that they are effective to at least that distance. In cyber security, we are only just now learning the vulnerabilities and unintended uses of modern sensors. For example, security researchers from the Georgia Institute of Technology used a mobile phone's accelerometer to covertly identify keystrokes when placed on a desk near a keyboard.[107] Others have used the accelerometer to create a distributed network of smartphones to detect earthquakes.[108]

Humans and machines do not always operate independently, but rather as a hybrid team where one enhances the senses and cognition of the other. This is the domain of human computer interaction (HCI), which seeks to help users accomplish goals quickly and effectively. An example of human/machine synergy is night vision goggles, which improve human vision in low light conditions. Augmented reality, in which a computer

33

overlays information onto the human's field of view, is another. These hybrid relationships extend human capacity and allow such things as observation from a great distance.

Both human and machine sensing are fallible. If events occur outside the bounds of a given human's or machine's sensing it may be undetected, for example, a motion sensor that only detects movement above a certain threshold or a conversation that takes place outside of earshot. Events can occur faster than the eye can see, a fact taken advantage of in the movie theater where frames of a movie are imperceptibly stitched together in the minds of an audience, a process known as the phi phenomenon.[109] The JPEG image format which compresses images by about 90% also exploits human perceptual limits by eliminating information such as subtle color differences that are imperceptible to the viewer. The opposite extreme is also possible since humans are optimized to more keenly perceive certain classes of inputs. Preattentive processing is particularly interesting in this regard. *Preattentive processing* is the human's processing of inputs, such as shape, pattern, motion, and color, without conscious thought. Advertisers exploit preattentive processing in their online advertisements though garish coloring and videos that autoplay, among numerous techniques.[110] At an even greater extreme is the concept of dazzling, when the human perceptual system or a machine sensor becomes overloaded.[111]

Sensing may also be deliberately deceived; just consider optical illusions created by psychologists and the misleading tricks they play on our senses. There have been and will continue to be more aggressive uses of deception in warfare. During World War II, deception units recorded the sounds made by of various types of vehicles and played them back from loudspeakers to trick enemy forces. Camouflage is another textbook example. Military scientists, informed by the limits of human perception, work to develop camouflage patterns that help people and objects blend into the background, or visibly shift apparent points of vulnerability so that enemy fire does not have the intended effect. With the advent of human/machine and machine-only weapons, scientists are developing tactics that deceive machine sensors, such as a heat source in an inflatable tank being used to trick a thermal targeting system. Even more advanced strategies are possible, such as tricking a driverless car's sensors to make it run off course.[112] As we look to the future, it is possible that deception may become increasingly difficult for actors as more and more of cyberspace and the physical world becomes instrumented with sensors, resulting in an increasing number of different observers that must be fooled.

## Limits of Cognition

Both humans and machines have the ability to acquire, remember, and process information. Of course the respective biological and algorithmic models for doing so are quite different. Understanding these differences, and the human and the machine's respective strengths and limitations, is a core aspect of cyber operations.

Human are great at abstract thought and have strong linguistic and pattern matching capabilities even in ambiguous situations, but are lazy, slow, tire easily, and are (compared to computers) bad at math. Humans understand context well, but have severe limits on short term and long term memory, including notoriously poor recall,[113] a fact that is evident when suspected criminals are exonerated through forensic evidence despite damning testimony by eye-witnesses. Human communication distance is very limited without the use of enabling technologies. Humans are creative and solve ill-defined problems well, fallible, resourceful and sometimes brilliant all at the same time. Due to the complexity of producing code, humans are far from perfect at precisely instructing computers.[114]

Machines are fast, at least against well-defined problems that can be algorithmically specified, but lack true intelligence. Computers do not tire and have precise recall of digital data. Mechanical errors are rare. Computing machines are essentially giant, rigid calculators with layers of code to help them solve problems of increasing complexity. The machine cognition required to solve these problems looks increasingly like human intelligence as we understand it, but at present machines are better at narrow tasks (Weak AI). Strong AI that can solve general problems remains on the technological horizon.

Machines and humans have amazing strengths as well as glaring weaknesses. As a general practice, human/machine systems are designed to complement the strengths and weaknesses of each other. Regardless of whether the entity is a human, machine, or hybrid, adversaries seek to exploit cognition to their advantage. A common approach is to increase their opponent's work factor, which is the amount of effort one must exert to accomplish a given objective, by designing tasks with significant cognitive or computational complexity to complete ( see Figure 3-3).[115] Deception acts as a force multiplier by causing one's adversary to squander or misuse their resources like available time and energy.[116]

A final aspect we'd like to discuss is *precognition*, knowledge of events before they happen. Assuming that Extra Sensory Perception (ESP) is not viable, humans lack precognition.[117] However, humans are able to predict future events from present and past data. Machines are able to do the same using techniques called predictive analytics, a branch of data mining that estimates probabilities of future events by identifying complex and often non-intuitive patterns that led to past events.[118]

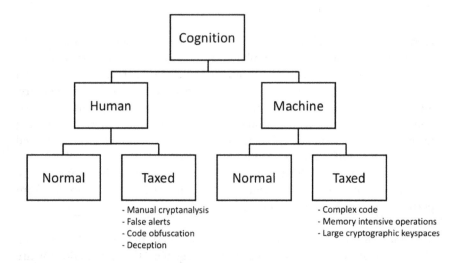

*Figure 3-3: Comparison of human and machine cognition, and representative examples. Note that adversaries will seek to create conditions that tax and exploit human and machine cognitive and perceptual capabilities.*

**Energy**

While efficient, intensive computation still takes significant amounts of energy. For example, the cryptocurrency Bitcoin required about the energy needed to power an average home for a day and a half, just to generate one coin in 2015.[119] At the nation-state level of computation, energy consumption is extreme. For example, in 2011 the National Security Agency was the largest consumer of electricity in the state of Maryland.[120] Even commercial grade data centers are extremely energy hungry. Microsoft is exploring the use of underwater data centers that use water as low cost coolant and to generate electricity from the ocean's motion.[121] Facebook created a data center at the edge of the Arctic Circle for similar reasons.[122] Battlefields are notoriously austere environments, and power consumption will likely be limited at command posts and severely limited for personnel travelling on foot who have to resort to batteries or solar power.

Beyond energy requirements for computation, another significant consideration is energy attenuation in communications, the loss of strength of a signal as it moves through a medium like the air or water. In long runs of fiber optic cable, repeaters regenerate the optical signal to keep it strong over long distances. Radio signals at frequencies and strengths popular for wireless communication, like 2.4 GHz, have ranges limited to several hundred meters, unless amplifiers, repeaters, or specialized antennas are used.[123] The advantage here is that when seeking to localize certain types of cyber or electronic warfare activity or their effects, radio transmissions naturally degrade and are less likely to cause collateral damage.

**Time, Rate, and Distance**
We envision three primary scales of time associated with cyber operations: human time (measured in seconds to days or more), network time (measured in milliseconds), and machine time (measured in microseconds or faster). From the machine perspective, human response time approaches infinity due to infinitesimally slow human speeds over even short distances. From the human perspective computer and network operations are effectively instantaneous for short distances with only a minor delay over terrestrial distances (see Figure 3-4 for a graphical depiction).

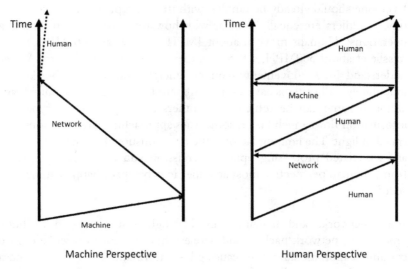

*Figure 3-4: Graphical depiction of time from the machine's and human's perspectives. Note that machines far outpace humans. From the machine perspective, humans move in slow motion. From the human perspective machines function instantaneously (not to scale).*

Operational reach—how far an army can successfully employ military capabilities—is also an important consideration in cyberspace operations.[124] In the physical domain, as armies move farther from their supporting bases, they extend their lines of supply, ultimately reaching a point where they can go no further for lack of fuel, ammunition, food, or other resources. In cyberspace, operational reach depends on the interconnectivity of systems. For devices directly connected to the Internet, operational reach may extend around the world. In other situations, such as isolated business networks, operational reach is more limited, reaching perhaps only as far as the home computers or mobile devices of employees. Operational reach may vary significantly with time. Virtual Private Networks (VPNs) may provide intermittent access, for instance when an employee works from home in the evenings and connects temporarily to work systems. Cyberspace operational reach may be enhanced by physical operations, such as a drone that can be flown into position over a targeted site to relay wireless communications.[125] The same as in the physical world, cyberspace obstacles may be used to limit operational reach, like a firewall that blocks external network connection attempts. Again, these can be bypassed via physical operations, such as covertly sneaking a device onto the internal network that tunnels back to the outside to pass information or enable remote access.[126]

Everyone should already be familiar with the concept that distance = rate * time. Soldiers are equally familiar with how this works in typical military operations: Humans move at about 4MPH, vehicles at 30-60MPH, a cruise missile at about 500MPH, a B-52 bomber at about 650MPH, etc. We also understand that movement requires energy and cannot be kept up indefinitely. All systems have a finite onboard fuel capacity and limited range, although some can be refueled and others are single use. In cyberspace, information flows much faster, sometimes approaching large fractions of the speed of light. The limiting factor is the time consumed by circuitry en route and associated processing upon transmission and reception. Regardless, from a human perspective most activities in cyberspace happen at incredible speeds.

While networks and machines are blazingly fast compared to human timeframes, network packets and wireless transmissions can collide on the communication medium, thus causing lost information. Having an accurate time-based understanding of events is important to both human and machine processing. As one example, race conditions happen when a desired outcome depends upon a set of events occurring in a certain sequence. In system security, race conditions like requesting permission to open a file and actually opening the file cause problems. For this case, a user might request a file that he has legitimate authority to access and be given permission by the operating system, but as an attack might swap the file for a symbolic link and be able to open a sensitive file instead.[127]   With proper governing protocols in place, such as Transmission Control Protocol (TCP), machines can handle out of sequence information, but without these safeguards the information can be discarded or confuse the processing system.  Humans have even greater difficulties. [128]  Network packets are particularly interesting, as they don't necessarily take the same path through a network, and time of flight between source and destination can vary greatly.[129]

Human scales of time and patterns of life play a useful role in cyber threat intelligence analysis.  Humans aren't nocturnal, and analysts can glean some insight into the time zone of actors based on digital evidence.  Some analysis centers even put clocks on the wall with common threat actor time zones.[130]

Certain cyberspace operations happen at human speed over the course of months, but as we look to the future, we should consider that while preparation for attacks might happen at human speed, some attacks will be automated and executed at machine and network speeds.[131]   Network defenders who attempt to defend against a network speed attack without automated defenses risk being overwhelmed.[132]

**Presence**
If you read Henri de Jomini's *The Art of War*, you'll note that he went to great lengths to describe the importance of roads and troop marches to move military forces into the right position at the right time on the battlefield.[133]  Troops needed rest, food, and footgear and had to brave the weather and terrain, sometimes marching 20 miles or more per day.  Commanders worked to provide for their troops' needs so that they arrived with essential fighting power intact.

Presence takes on a different character in cyberspace.  Locally, humans use interface devices such as keyboards and mice to interact with software, processors, and storage on their machines.  From the human point of view, this interaction on a local machine is instantaneous.  As the human, or alternatively code in a machine-to-machine communication, accesses remote services, their communications flow through a series of network nodes until they, or more accurately, their tools, interact with the destination server.  On an Internet Protocol (IP) network, these intermediate nodes perform some minimal processing, such as examining source and destination addresses to make routing decisions.  In the event of congestion or failure of a link, routers attempt to find an alternate path.  Sometimes multi-path routing is used, which employs multiple paths to help provide resilience and increase bandwidth. In effect, we have an ephemeral chain of nodes from the source providing presence at the destination.[134]     We are discounting the intermediate nodes, where presence is merely the pass-through of bits, and there is not a significant element of control.  However, a tactic sometimes used in cyberspace operations involves compromising and gaining control of intermediate nodes between attacker and target and using that control to create a chain of intermediaries to mask one's identity and location, or to gain closer access to a given target goal. This is often called *pivoting*.[135] Building this chain of compromised systems can be tricky, and once attackers gain access, they will often create persistent backdoors on the machines to allow easier access in the future.[136]

An attacker's virtual presence on a target system may be eliminated by logically diverting the network flow or physically breaking the connection. So, while presence may be possible around the world, presence can be disrupted by simply pulling out a network cable, setting a device to "airplane mode," or turning off the device, either locally or remotely.  Note, however, that attackers have developed innovative ways to communicate thorough non-traditional channels like ultrasonic sound and infrared, so attempts at network disconnection may fail against an adaptive adversary.[137]  However, if the attacker is able to install code on the target machine, the code could work on their behalf in the absence of human guidance even if the connection is dropped (see Figure 3-5).

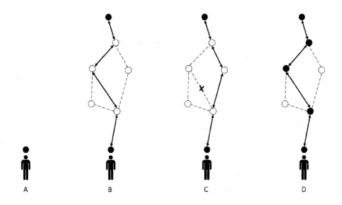

*Figure 3-5: Examining presence in cyberspace.  A human user may have physical presence at a given device and use it locally (A).  A user, or code acting on his behalf, may transit a network and have a remote presence on a destination device (B).  If a network link goes down or become congested, routers send the traffic to functioning links (C).  The attacker may iteratively compromise a chain of nodes and pivot through them creating a virtual presence on each (D).*

## Counterintuitive Implications[138]

Given these theoretical foundations, it is useful to study their implications. It is important to understand where cyberspace operations are similar, and importantly, where they challenge conventional wisdom, in order to be most effective.

*Code Respawns* – While physical hardware may be destroyed through physical or cyber attack,[139] data and code can be restored at the point of the latest uncorrupted backup. The hardware is just the generic substrate; the ghost in the machine is the data and the code (executable programs, firmware, and the operating system). If the data is not backed up, and operators reinstall the operating system and other applications, the machine is functional but might be severely degraded operationally. A corollary is that a device can be rendered temporarily, or perhaps even permanently, non-functional if its firmware is corrupted or destroyed. In some cases, just as damage can be inflicted remotely, remote healing is possible by carefully pushing software and firmware updates as well as rerouting processing through alternate systems. We see this in the high-stakes repair by NASA engineers of distant satellites, probes, and robots.[140]

A corollary of code respawning is that cloning is possible. Infinite copies of information may be made at near zero cost, a concept at the heart of the information economy. These copies may be of data, code, or complete system images. Importantly, nearly frictionless duplication means that producing identical copies of cyber weapons at scale is effectively free.

*Expect Mutations* – Data and code may be mutated in innumerable ways to frustrate malware analysts, to find vulnerabilities, to avoid detection, and to operate in ways unintended by designers. For example, *fuzzing* is a software testing technique in which vulnerability researchers provide massive amounts of random or carefully crafted input in order to find flaws in code. Other examples of code mutation are when malware developers obfuscate their code to hamper others trying to reverse engineer their work, or cyber criminals finding malicious software on the Internet and modifying it for their own ends.

*Long Distances Collapse, but Short Distances Expand* – Cyberspace allows almost instantaneous communication on a global scale, at least on the human timescale. However, "almost" instantaneous communications creates a human noticeable time lag, about a quarter of a second to bounce to a satellite and back on a terrestrial scale. At present, this latency is manageable in remote control of drones, but can make the difference between victory and defeat in online gaming where rapid human-computer interaction over a network is required. As humans expand into space, long distances still collapse but not to zero; it takes approximately 3 minutes to communicate between Earth and Mars, a distance of about 34 million miles.[141] At much shorter distances, such as inside computer CPUs, the impact of distance is also, and ironically, readily felt. Processing is limited by the speed of light and the processor's ability to dissipate heat. We see attempts to push up against this boundary with liquid cooling and smaller processor dies.[142] High-performance computing and high-frequency trading machines used in financial markets are two sources of related innovation, but still ultimately bounded by the speed of light. The limits of speed and distance will certainly be felt in global, machine- and network-speed combat.

### Cyber "Bullets" Don't Hurt, Except When They Do
Except in the most esoteric sense, information doesn't have mass.[143] Therefore the physical force information itself can exhibit is not a factor. However, information, when packaged as a set of instructions sent to a computer, can certainly have physical effects, such as crashing an aircraft's flight control systems in flight or instructing a pacemaker to behave erratically. Directed energy weapons and electromagnetic bombs may also have significant physical effects ranging from disabling electronic circuits to searing flesh.[144]

***It Rains in Cyberspace*** – More precisely, weather in the physical world impacts the physical devices and electromagnetic spectrum upon which cyberspace depends. Excessive rain may flood data centers taking them offline. The sunspot cycle may generate solar radiation, which disrupts Earth's power and communications, particularly impacting satellites. Thus the physical world can have effects in cyberspace and, as described previously, cyberspace can affect the physical world.

***You Can't Fire Cannons at the Internet*** [145] – The Internet, and hence much of cyberspace, effectively routes around damage. As a blanket statement, the networks do route around damage, but such routing is constrained by the number of available paths at each network node. Generally, the closer one gets to either endpoint, the fewer the paths. Therefore, the ability to route around damage is somewhat overrated. Additionally, it is quite possible for damage in the physical world to unintentionally impact cyberspace, such as foul weather or an errant backhoe.[146] An attacker might intentionally damage physical infrastructure to shape an adversary's use of cyberspace, perhaps by damaging undersea cables or jamming digital communications.[147]

42

***An Enemy Combatant Can Be Grandma's Toaster*** – On a traditional battlefield, it is usually straightforward to identify opposing combatants: They wear uniforms. In the event of insurgent groups who don't wear uniforms, you can usually still tell who they are because they are carrying weapons and shooting at your friends. However, in cyber conflict the identification of adversary actions, let alone reliable identification of adversaries, is much more difficult. You won't necessarily know if you are being shot at, or by whom, until the effects ultimately reach you. Even so, those effects might be delayed by seconds or years. Adding to the difficulty, computers, mobile devices, and commercial products come shipped to you and are initially "allies," but one unpatched vulnerability can result in an assertive adversary taking control of those devices, causing them to become an unknown accomplice—even your smart, Internet-connected television, refrigerator, or toaster.

***Adversaries Are Invisible*** – We argue that adversaries are always invisible in cyberspace. Or, more precisely, we can never actually see them directly. Defenders have nothing but the reflections and shadows of adversarial activity to use for attribution and analysis. Some of these echoes are translated by the computer into human-readable form, and this output is removed once again from its original context by each person's interpretation of what she sees on the screen. As a defender, this is one of the biggest challenges—activity that looks like teenagers to one person might look like a nation-state to someone else. In other words, information flow is invisible. Yes, we have automated systems that can detect signatures or suspect behaviors and limited visualization systems that allow humans to peek into cyberspace; however, much of what goes on in cyberspace is beyond human sensing. Not only are flows of information invisible, but data at rest is also invisible, and both are subject to modification in ways that may not be detectable. If you consider that computers store information merely as sequences of ones and zeros, history itself can be re-written by editing security logs and altering other information stored by the target system. What a system reports to have happened may or may not have actually taken place.

***Time Is Malleable*** – Like information in cyberspace, time is malleable. Computers do not magically understand the flow of time. Most computers do have a clock that tracks system (human) time as well as a microchip that, like a metronome, ticks away at constant intervals and keeps processing synchronized. Until recently system clocks required being set by the user. The U.S. Government broadcasts time signals from the time signal radio station WWVB to transmit the time to millions of clocks and wristwatches that contain a WWVB receiver. On the network, the Network Time Protocol

(NTP) keeps things synchronized closely with Coordinated Universal Time (UTC). Clocks drift, but a protocol keeps things very closely in synchronization. Time, however, can be attacked. Clocks can be manually reset and synchronization signals spoofed, providing an opportunity to manipulate systems where time is an important component.[148] A historical example is the practice of setting a computer's clock to an earlier date in order to continue to use software whose license has expired. In a sense, time can flow both forwards and backwards. Remember, since computers are deterministic machines, it is often possible to step backwards or forwards through the execution of a program, or even to freeze an application or a complete system (often a virtual machine) in time to restart it in the future with no degradation.[149]

***Access Is King*** – Despite the intense interconnectivity of much of cyberspace, not every device can reach every other device. *Air gapped*, that is, physically isolated networks create walled gardens that are impossible to reach using routine network traffic.[150] Some individual devices, while they fit in our broad definition of cyberspace, are not networked, although some might have the capability to do so. Some systems may be connected and the user unaware, an issue increasingly common with modern automobiles and mobile devices. Even on physical connected networks, firewalls, routers, switches, Virtual local area networks (VLANs) and more formal network segmentation strategies create virtual boundaries that are difficult to cross. *Access* is the ability to reach a device to receive or transmit information, control it, or generate some effect, despite these safeguards. Breaching an air gap may sound impossible, but the enterprising actor can create asynchronous communication software, place it on a thumb drive in a parking lot outside a secure facility in hopes it will be taken inside.[151] Penetration testers use devices like the Pwn Plug and attempt to physically sneak them past security personnel and other safeguards to place them on a target network where they will then connect back to the attacker.[152] Another strategy is to use lesser known communication paths like Near Field Communication (NFC), built into many phones, or to mail the target a malicious DVD purporting to be something else. The key concept is that defenders seek to deny physical or virtual access to their systems, while attackers seek to overcome safeguards and gain access to devices and systems.

***The Attacker Has the Advantage over the Defender*** – In conventional military thinking, an attacker needs a 3:1 advantage in force to overcome a defending unit which is otherwise equal.[153] At present, we believe the inverse is generally true in cyberspace operations, the attacker has the advantage. In order to compromise a system, the attacker probes the perimeter seeking a vulnerability, while the defender must plug every conceivable hole. The complexity of computing systems makes plugging every hole impossible, and even if the defender were partially or completely successful, the attackers can then shift their efforts by seeking to compromise human operators or gain physical access. This isn't to say that attackers have no challenges at all, for they often start with little information and need to learn much on the fly. An attentive system administrator could detect an attacker's activities and alert the enterprise.[154] Defenders also have a home field advantage (and theoretically complete information on their own networks and systems) and the ability to deploy deception techniques.[155] Even so, advanced network actors will work to gain better knowledge about the target network than the defenders, giving them an even greater advantage in an attack.[156]

However, when considering advantage in cyberspace operations, it is important to understand at which level of war this analysis might be true, under what conditions, and to what extent. In general, we believe attacker advantage is less true the higher up the strategic thinking ladder you climb. For example, at the tactical level an attacker can usually craft a tool to beat a specific defense. Operationally, it's more even. Strategically and at the level of national policy, advantage appears to be an open question. The reason is that as one moves from tactical to strategic levels, the less cyber is dominant and the more physical resources seem to matter.

Mankind's collective understanding of the dynamics of advantage in cyberspace operations is limited, but the importance of such knowledge is huge. This is an important open question and merits future research and experimentation. Our presumption that attacker advantage is a "law of physics" in cyberspace may be false; instead advantage may be a symptom of our failure to conduct defense well. There are key things that we do in physical defense, including hardened people, weapon systems and fighting positions; carefully placed obstacles; knowledge and exploitation of terrain; pre-planned artillery targets; and detailed intelligence collection. However, how well do we do these things in cyberspace? Do people know their own networks better than their attackers do? Do we exploit natural advantages that we have over attackers, such as physical access to systems and the ability to communicate and collect intelligence, without attacker knowledge? We don't think so, and that is why we are failing. Future thinking may well indicate attacker advantage isn't really a law of physics, but more a reality of the state of the art of our practices, immaturity of our doctrine to make us better defenders, and evidence that we have far to go.

*Soldiers Need to Understand How Their Weapons Work* – There are two basic types of cyber operators: tool[i] users, who use the tools given to them; and tool makers, capable of designing their own tools.[157] This distinction between users and makers is important. A tool user may have received some training on how to employ a tool, but a tool maker will understand the tool at a fundamental level, including its operation and the intended and unintended effects it might generate. In cyberspace operations, toolmakers are able to go off script and modify tools and techniques on the fly as the mission dictates, something far less likely and far more dangerous with tool users. The ability to improvise is critical for actors who seek the asymmetric advantage of agility.

*Soldiers Should Sometimes Make Their Own Weapons* – Each actor, from individual hackers to nation-state sponsored cyber operators, are capable of designing their own tools of the trade. If the actor lacks in-house expertise, he will likely hire or coerce required talent or even employ freely available tools from the Internet. Custom tools and capabilities may be offensive, defensive, or dual use. We envision tiers of capability development: agile code development and scripting at the tactical edge of cyberspace operations, more robust in-house capability available through reach-back support or teams of dedicated developers, and longer-term, contract-based development for complex efforts. The takeaway here is that cyber operators can't be disarmed if they or their organizations are capable of making their own weapons.

*Missed Shots Can Go Around the World* – If a soldier fires a rifle at a target and misses, the bullet may go a mile or so before it falls back to Earth and stops. In electronic warfare, electromagnetic signals attenuate, reducing the chance of unintended effects.[158] In cyberspace, incorrect targeting such as a mistyped IP address could inadvertently reach the other side of the planet. In automated malware, like worms or other tools, an error in the code could cause the software to propagate broadly and impact unintended

---

[i] In this discussion, a *tool* is a piece of software designed and developed by a cyber operator with either an offensive or defensive purpose. Tools are developed either to gain unauthorized access to an adversary's system, usually in a way that is hard to identify and attribute, or to defend systems or networks from an adversary's attacks. Offensive tools, or programs, are usually carefully crafted to exploit a vulnerability in a piece of software that is known (or suspected) to be running on a target system or device. Defensive tools are designed to identify or even sabotage an adversary's attempts to gain unauthorized access to friendly computer systems or networks.

targets.[159] We may think we are using a precise sniper rifle and instead end up spraying unintended effects around the planet, creating unforeseen collateral damage.[160] The physics we see play out in a game of pool has little relevance to the manner in which network packets transit the globe because a packet's movement is dictated by code. Proper training and tight control measures are essential to reduce mistakes. Importantly, what may be viewed as a legitimate mistake by the originator could be viewed by those impacted or even a disinterested third party as something deliberate and nefarious.

**Your Weapon Systems May Work Once, Twice, or Not at All** – If you've watched *Star Trek – The Next Generation*, you are familiar with the Borg, the arch-enemy of the Enterprise and humanity. In several episodes the Enterprise crew use their phasers on the Borg, but the Borg quickly adapt. Because they are an interconnected collective sharing a hive mind, the adaptation is spread throughout the Borg community instantly. Cyberspace operations face similar challenges. A vulnerability that exists today may be patched tomorrow. Antivirus venders might detect a type of malicious software and add a signature that they share with millions of users, and note that all anti-virus vendors aren't necessarily allies of the United States.. An astute system administrator may notice suspicious activity and reconfigure their systems to render future attacks impotent. The dynamic of vulnerabilities, capabilities, and target systems frustrates cyber planning and the degree of certainty that a given effect will take place at the right time, if at all. This uncertainty is quite foreign to those who expect the predictability and repeatability of kinetic attacks. Such timely and high-reliability effects are difficult, and sometimes impossible, in cyberspace operations.

> *You can't hide secrets from the future with math.*
> *You can try, but I bet that in the future they laugh*
> *at the half-assed schemes and algorithms amassed*
> *to enforce cryptographs in the past.*
> *Best of all, your secret: nothing extant could extract it.*
> *By 2025 a children's Speak & Spell could crack it.*
> *- MC Frontalot* [161]

**You Can't Hide Secrets from the Future** – The lifespan of secrets is finite. There is lots of sensitive information developed in government facilities and in closed corporate labs. These secrets may be kept for a while, but over time they trickle out through accidental disclosure, sharing with partners, transparency laws and declassification procedures, reverse engineering, cryptanalysis, and potentially many other ways (See Figure 3-6).[162] This seepage is combined with the possibility of independent discovery by academic or individual researchers, creating an inexorable trend toward public knowledge.[163] It's usually just a matter of time until even the most carefully hidden secrets are divulged.

*"Moore's law"[ii] is the observation that, over the history of computing hardware, the number of transistors in a dense integrated circuit has doubled approximately every two years.[164]*

In the digital world information is slippery, and history is replete with examples of data spills, but advances in technology also help unmask some of the best kept secrets. Increases in processing power over time, fueled by Moore's Law, are also particularly significant. Consider the Data Encryption Standard (DES) algorithm, developed in the 1970s and once an official U.S. Government Federal Information Processing Standard (FIPS), which fell prey to the relentless advance of technology. About twenty years after DES became an official standard, the Electronic Frontier Foundation (EFF) built a special purpose machine that could crack DES encryption in 56 hours. The EFF machine, Deep Crack, cost less than $250,000. Six months later, Deep Crack decrypted a message in less than 24 hours.[165] As MC Frontalot rhymed, in the future a child's Speak & Spell toy could crack it.[166] This rapid evolution of technology has important implications, most notably, that cryptographic algorithms will likely fail over time and retroactively open up to the analyst any historical communications ever used by that algorithm.[167]

---

[ii] In 1965, Gordon Moore, co-founder of Intel and Fairchild Semiconductor, famously predicted that the number of components per square inch on an integrated circuit would roughly double every year for the next 10 years. In 1975, that prediction was scaled slightly to predict a doubling every two years. Moore's predictions have since been referred to as Moore's Law. Moore's Law has been used to predict increases in computing power for the last half century. While other experts have predicted the demise of Moore's Law due to physical limitations related to the manufacturing process, it has proven to be surprisingly robust. With continuing advances in nanotechnology and quantum computing, Moore's Law could potentially hold true for many years to come.

A final, but key point is that some secrets don't need to be protected forever. On the battlefield, ciphers just need to resist attack for a short period because even if the underlying message is discovered, it is no longer of intelligence value. This weaker operational requirement has historically allowed tactical forces to employ simpler and easier-to-use ciphers since they were good enough.

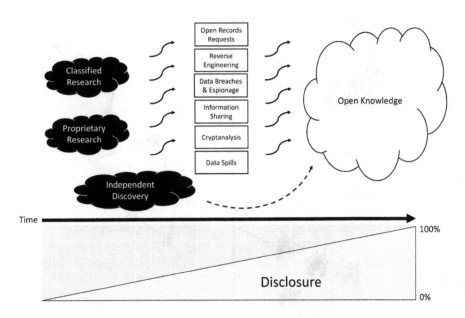

*Figure 3-6: Information wants to be free.[168] Sensitive information is developed in classified and proprietary arenas, where it is subject to a number of forces ranging from theft and espionage to deliberate sharing to reverse engineering. Over time, we argue, information disclosure will eventually approach 100%.*

**Cyberspace Is More Like a Parallel Dimension than Physical Space** – Despite the hardware and bits that comprise cyberspace having a physical presence, cyberspace has unique and special virtual properties. Chief among them is the compression of distance, the facility for remote presence, and communication speeds approaching the speed of light. These attributes combined with the lack of human visibility into the realm, make cyberspace more like a parallel dimension than a physical space. An attacker at one point on the globe can enter cyberspace, bypass traditional physical security measures, and potentially strike a target that is impregnable in the physical world (see Figure 3-7).[169] When the mission is complete, actors need only break the virtual connection, and their virtual presence dissipates. With the advent of additive manufacturing, it is even possible to virtually "teleport" objects by sending digital models to distant 3D printers, which create physical items to support remote requirements.

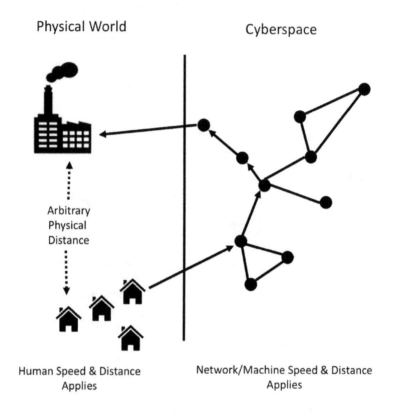

Figure 3-7: Comparison of speed and distance in cyberspace. In cyberspace information moves at percentages of the speed of light, and as a result distances collapse, but not to zero. Attackers can enter cyberspace, bypass physical security measures, remerge around the globe, and cause physical effects.

**Humans are Losing Ground to Machines** – We see this in the physical world where jobs are being eliminated by robots and artificial intelligence.[170] Even the world's champion humans fall in their respective domains, like Chess, Go, and Jeopardy.[171] If we take a step back and consider the situation, data is growing at an exponential rate, the average screen size available to view data is growing at a linear rate, and human cognition is constant (see Figure 3-8). The inevitable result is the increasing inability of humans alone to cope with data in general, and cyber conflict in particular. Processor Speed is much faster than Network Speed, which is much faster than Human Speed. Effectively, humans move in slow motion. Success lies in humans teaming with machines, exploiting the strengths of each. Further in the future, we see a time approaching, called the Singularity, when artificial intelligence reaches then rapidly surpasses human intelligence. Estimated dates vary. Futurist Ray Kurzweil estimates the date to be 2045 (see Figure 3-9).[172] While we don't know the specific date, we do believe the Singularity will take place, after which the future becomes increasingly uncertain. For now, cyberspace actors, particularly nations with very large populations, can devote increasingly more humans to challenging problems in an attempt to stay ahead of their adversaries. Ultimately, however, future success requires automation.

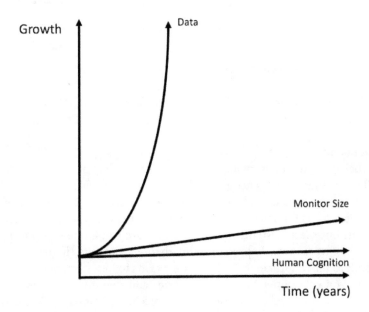

*Figure 3-8: The combination of exponential growth of data, modest growth of display size, and static human cognition implies that humans will be able to process an increasingly smaller sliver of available data. Automation in cyber operations is a necessity.*

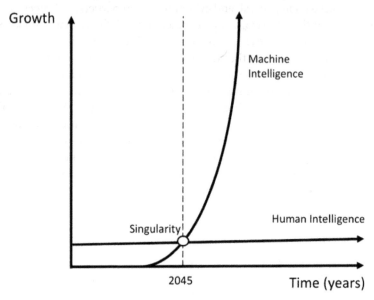

*Figure 3-9: Machine intelligence continues to grow rapidly while human intelligence remains constant. A point will eventually come when the machine bests the human, dubbed the Singularity, which is estimated by futurist Ray Kurzweil to be 2045.*

## Conclusions

In cyberspace, the man-made laws of physics overlay the true physical Laws of Physics. Practitioners need to understand both. While the Laws of Physics are immutable, much of how cyberspace functions in practice can be controlled by its human creators. Machines operate at a speed far faster than humans, but machines and communications are still limited by the speed of light. As we approach practical and theoretical limits, it may prove too difficult to make sufficient hardware-only gains to best opponents; therefore, we envision cyber operations organizations adjusting their strategies, tactics, and hardware and software solutions to provide advantage. While we can optimize code to get an edge up, we must understand that there are limits to the types of computation that computers can solve. Human and machine sensing both have limitations; to operate outside the range of either means one can operate without being properly identified or tracked, but again, human perception is constant and machine perception is continually improving. Human virtual presence in cyberspace is possible at great distances, but is ephemeral. Simply disconnecting a network cable can break a remote connection. Software, however, can be left behind to provide persistence and act on one's behalf without human intervention.

These limits and realities of cyberspace generate many important, but often counterintuitive implications. Information, including code-based cyber weapons, may be copied in a friction-free and low-cost manner. Machines may be physically destroyed, but sometimes they can be restored by reinstalling key system software, firmware, and data. Distances collapse in cyberspace, but the speed of light still rules. Events in the real world, such as weather or deliberate damage, may impact cyberspace, and cyberspace can cause effects in the physical world. The high speed and global nature of cyberspace demand that cyber operators understand how their tools work at a fundamental level, lest they cause unintended effects and lose agility. To best exploit these realities, cyber operators, planners, and leaders need to understand how cyberspace functions. It cannot be simply a magic black box.

# 4 OPERATIONAL ENVIRONMENT

*"Unlike the land, sea, air and space domains, cyberspace is continuously evolving and adapting along with each entrepreneur, inventor and actor that uses it." [173]*
*- Lieutenant General Edward Cardon*

Humans are very experienced with conflict in the physical world. Traditionally militaries have organized for conflict in four domains, and those domains are used to characterize the physical environments in which military forces operate. The Land domain was first, but with the addition of disruptive new technology, militaries now recognize other new domains. With the advent of ship building came the Sea domain; aircraft forced the acknowledgement of the Air domain; and rockets, satellites, and orbital vessels led to the acceptance of the Space domain. Organizations tailored to engaging in combat in each domain emerged as armies, navies, and air forces. The Laws of Physics held in these natural domains, and appropriate strategy and tactics emerged, fueled by advances in technology.

The birth of computers and networking and the eventual ubiquitous nature of the Internet as a deeply intertwined component of prosperity and national security led nations to declare cyberspace as a fifth domain. This changed some long-held beliefs about what a domain is. No longer just describing physical aspects of the environment, the cyberspace domain implies that the definition of domain is expanded to include abstractions beyond physical space when describing an operational environment. This represents a significant change, and change can be hard for some. Debates occurred between many traditional military leaders and some of the more adaptive, forward looking, and typically younger, service members, but the change held. The United States created U.S. Cyber Command, along with service-specific subordinate cyber commands for its Army, Navy, Air Force, Marine Corps, and Coast Guard. We haven't yet gone as far as creating a separate military service for Cyber, but some predict that it will come in time.

Cyberspace is novel in that it is man-made, and while the fundamental Laws of Physics still apply, many underlying attributes of the Cyberspace domain are very much under the control of human architects. Cyberspace crosscuts each of the physical planes, akin to a parallel plane. Most people and technology have a presence both in the physical world and in cyberspace.

Surrounding each of the five planes is the Electromagnetic (EM) spectrum, the field of electromagnetic radiation that surrounds everything (see Figure 4-1). Examples include visible light, radio waves, and X-rays. The EM spectrum is special in that it is present in each of the physical domains and provides the communications substrate upon which cyberspace operates. The spectrum is finite and can become crowded, so governments and militaries seek to perform spectrum management to prevent one organization's communications from inadvertently colliding with others'. Militaries use the EM spectrum to communicate information, which in turn leads to attempts by adversaries to jam signals, delay communications, or more subtly deceive users through misleading messages. Direction-finding tools are used to find the location of sources of electromagnetic radiation. In fact, the EM spectrum is so fundamental to military operations that there is an ongoing discussion about whether it should be designated as a sixth operational domain.[174]

Cyberspace represents flows of information to machines and humans. As we discussed earlier, these flows of information have a physical manifestation and can create physical effects by altering the logic of computing systems. Information also has a cognitive component, and the right flow of information at the right time will alter the decision making of humans, whether they be governments, militaries, insurgent groups, businesses, or individuals. We can expect militaries to operate in cyberspace not just to cause physical effects on the battlefield or to gather intelligence, but also to carefully target the decision making capabilities of allies, adversaries, neutral parties, and populations. The strong influence of social media on the recent U.S. presidential election by a foreign power is a good example.

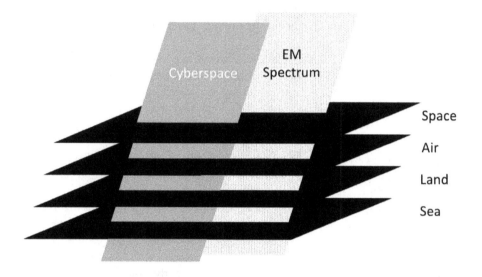

*Figure 4-1: Diagram of the natural operational domains of Sea, Land, Air and Space, the cross-cutting man-made domain of Cyberspace as well as the Electromagnetic spectrum, which permeates all other domains.*

The U.S. Military uses the concept of an Operational Environment (OE) to describe and analyze the conditions, circumstances, and influences that affect military operations.[175] This helps military members better understand the larger context in which they operate and how these aspects affect their employment of capabilities.[176] Actors work to shape the operational environment to their advantage to deter aggressors, seize the initiative, dominate in conflict, stabilize regions, and assist civil authority for themselves and allies. Most militaries would prefer to shape the operational environment to prevent conflict, but when it is necessary to seize the initiative, the goal is to dominate on the battlefield and return back to peace. See Figure 4-2 for a graphical depiction of such efforts from U.S. Military doctrine.[177]

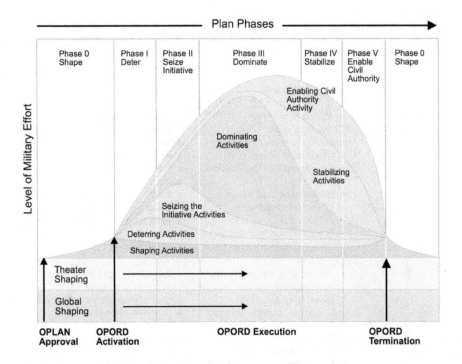

*Figure 4-2: Notional depiction of phases of conflict. The U.S. Military prefers to shape the operational environment to prevent conflict, but prepares Operations Plans (OPLANs) to be ready. If conflict cannot be prevented, the U.S. Military issues Operations Orders (OPORDERS) to guide increasingly more aggressive military activities, with the goal of stabilizing the environment and enabling civilian leaders to transition to peace. Shaping of the military environment occurs throughout. (Image: U.S. Department of Defense)*

Operational environments are complex and constantly changing. One useful framework for analyzing the operational environment uses the initialization PMESII-PT. Despite the unwieldy acronym, the concept is powerful and comprehensively includes key aspects that one should understand when considering operations in cyberspace: political, military, economic, social, information, infrastructure, physical environment, and time.[178] Table 4-1 provides key attributes for each of these areas. Note that the U.S. Army traditionally applies PMESII-PT to land domain activities, [179] so we've extended it to illustrate the framework's application in cyberspace operations.

*Table 4-1: Using PMESII-PT to analyze an operational environment. The left column illustrates the traditional application. The right column applies the framework to cyberspace.*

|  | Traditional Application | Cyberspace Application |
|---|---|---|
| Political | • Attitude toward your country/group<br>• Centers of political power and type of government<br>• Government effectiveness and legitimacy<br>• Influential political groups<br>• International/Inter-actor relationships<br>• Major historical events | • Online political activity<br>• Electronic voting<br>• Online governance activities<br>• Political messaging<br>• Political fundraising<br>• Recruiting<br>• Political influence on cyberspace policy and standards<br>• (Inter)national organizations governing use of the Internet and online access |
| Military | • Number, size, and capabilities of conventional military forces (Army, Navy, Air Force)<br>• Government paramilitary/cyber forces<br>• Non-state paramilitary forces<br>• Unarmed combatants<br>• Nonmilitary armed combatants<br>• Military functions (including command and control, maneuver, intelligence, target acquisition, protective measures, logistics capabilities, intelligence) | • Number, size, and capabilities of military cyber forces<br>• Unofficial/sanctioned cyber forces<br>• Non-state paramilitary cyber forces<br>• Noncombatant users and groups in cyberspace<br>• Nonmilitary combatants in cyberspace<br>• Maturity of SIGINT capabilities |
| Economic | • Per capita income<br>• Key industries, agriculture, and natural resources<br>• Employment status (poverty, percent unemployment)<br>• Economic activity (exports, imports, inflation rate, debt)<br>• Illegal economic activity<br>• Banking and finance | • Electronic commerce activities<br>• Permeation of ecommerce<br>• Currencies (including cryptocurrencies) used online<br>• Major payment card systems<br>• Cost of online access<br>• Online economic activity<br>• Illegal online economic activity and marketplaces<br>• Online banking and finance<br>• Regulatory requirements |
| Social | • Demographics (population growth, density, immigration/emigration)<br>• Volatility<br>• Education (literacy rate, education level)<br>• Major ethnic groups | • Degree of population with Internet access<br>• Social media penetration and popularity<br>• Technical literacy<br>• Cyber cafes<br>• Common online slang |

| | | |
|---|---|---|
| | • Major religions<br>• Major urban areas<br>• Language(s) used<br>• Criminal activity (effects on population, economy, and infrastructure)<br>• Centers of social power<br>• Cultural norms and values | • Online culture and social norms<br>• Online communities and activist groups<br>• Cyber criminal groups<br>• Online anonymity<br>• Identity spoofing |
| Information | • Media outlets (and their political slant)<br>• Intelligence capabilities<br>• Electronic warfare capabilities<br>• Computer network operations capabilities<br>• Deception capabilities<br>• Freedom of media<br>• Perception of media toward various relevant actor groups | • Government filtering of the Internet<br>• Online news sources<br>• Use of censors<br>• "Sock puppets" / paid trolls[180]<br>• "Fake" news stories<br>• Extremist group online activities<br>• Government-mandated cryptographic backdoors<br>• Online deception capabilities<br>• Freedom of online journalists/bloggers<br>• Online sentiment toward relevant actor groups |
| Infrastructure | • Developed/developing regions<br>• Building density<br>• Utilities present<br>• Transportation (routes into major cities, major choke points)<br>• Fragility to adverse events | • Major data centers<br>• Major ISPs<br>• Major cell providers<br>• Satellite ground stations (commercial / government)<br>• Undersea cables<br>• Cell/Microwave towers<br>• Reliability of power grid<br>• Back-up power sources<br>• Continuity of Operations (COOP) facilities<br>• Average home ISP bandwidth<br>• Key infrastructure interdependencies |
| Physical Environment | • Type of terrain<br>• Major landforms<br>• Natural hazards<br>• Climate<br>• Weather<br>• Historical natural disasters | • EM spectrum usage<br>• Natural or man-made sources of EM interference<br>• Broadband penetration levels |
| Time | • Cultural perception of time<br>• Key dates | • Time synchronization mechanisms and location (e.g. Network Time Protocol (NTP) servers, Atomic Clock) |

## Cyberspace Permeation

If we dig a little deeper into the idea of the operational environment, we see it is built upon increasingly ubiquitous technology.[181] Technology pervades our lives, from implants inside our bodies[182] to satellites in space, most designed to improve quality of life (see Figure 4-3). Each of these devices once had, currently has, or will eventually have a presence in cyberspace. Imagine a city, with its millions of people, projecting itself into the ether of cyberspace: billions of "trusted" devices that create an ever-changing environment, allegedly performing some function designed to enhance people's lives. Each also has processing capability and storage, and most have sensors to sample aspects of their environment, and wireless network capabilities to facilitate communications. The complexity of this digital ecosystem is beyond human comprehension, creating an astronomically vulnerable attack surface.[183] Cyberspace is congested, and dominance is contested. Large swaths of cyberspace are built and operated by private industry, but the permeation of cyberspace into our daily lives is the result of private citizens who adopt new technologies. The sum of these devices provide the substrate for cyber conflict.[184] These devices, and the flows of information among them, will be co-opted, manipulated, and sometimes destroyed by actors with the power and motivation to do so.

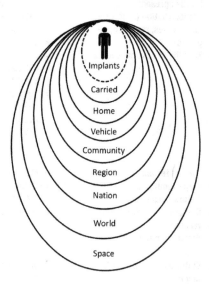

*Figure 4-3: Analyzing the instrumented world. Humans are vigorously integrating technology into their lives, workplaces, and environment. This integration and increased dependency that comes with it create a fertile landscape for cyber conflict.*

To understand our instrumented world, we think of concentric rings emanating from each individual. In each ring are devices, sensors, networks, and systems, with each sphere serving as a battlefield. Engagements can take place in any or all of these rings, even inside your body. This isn't the realm of fantasy. Former Vice President Dick Cheney had doctors disable the wireless functionality of his heart implant to prevent assassination attempts; cell phones have been turned into mobile tracking devices; hospitals' information systems are being held hostage for ransom money; and hackers, many think from Russia, have taken down portions of the Ukrainian power grid.[185] There are even allegations of state-sponsored cyber criminals attempting to influence U.S. presidential elections that have led to international sanctions.[186]

*Implants* – The most intimate of all technologies are those embedded in our bodies. Today these implants consist of medical devices, such as pacemakers and defibrillators and radio frequency identification (RFID) for tracking people and animals. We expect there will be a dramatic rise of future implant use as the technologies get smarter and scientists resolve issues between interfacing biology and technology. Right now the U.S. military is investing heavily on advanced implants to allow computers to communicate directly with the human brain.[187] Once a major breakthrough in neural interfacing takes place, the battlefield will shift from hacking commercial and military computing systems to literally hacking the brains of combatants. Imagine a situation where your very thoughts can be intercepted via vulnerable electronic systems designed by the lowest bidder. When that happens, we recommend buying stock in neural firewalls, intrusion/extrusion detection systems, and tamper-evident seals. These businesses will be booming.

*On Our Person* – One business area that is already booming is consumer technology. Consider all the technology you carry on your person when you travel: smartphones, tablets, book readers, fitness bracelets, electronic key fobs, and smart cards, for instance. And those are just the things we make the conscious decision to carry. Our clothing might still bear the electronic RFID tagging from the box store where we bought it.

*Home* – In our homes we have larger and more capable computing devices than the ones we carry on our persons, with increased network bandwidth and processing power. Take a look around your home and you'll see networked gaming consoles, smart televisions, alarm systems, set top cable boxes, printers, smart power meters, smart lightbulbs, and smart thermostats. The future lies in the Internet of Things, where increasing numbers of devices and appliances will be connected to, and a part of, the global information grid.  Business incentives push these devices not just to provide services, but also to possess myriad sensors that collect information on the environment and use it for easier purchasing and to allow data collection and user profiling for targeted advertising.[188]  One smart TV manufacturer warns customers not to discuss sensitive or personal information within earshot of the device as these conversations might be unintentionally intercepted.[189]  Importantly, these devices aren't static. Many have code that can be altered or updated remotely by the manufacturer.  Governments see the Internet of Things as a rich resource for tracking and surveillance, and for good reason.[190]

*"We don't have cars anymore;*
*we have computers we ride in.*
*We don't have airplanes anymore;*
*we have flying Solaris boxes connected to*
*bucketfuls of industrial control systems."*
*- Cory Doctorow [191]*

**Vehicle** – Automobiles and the freedom they provide are a core part of the American ethos.   Unfortunately, vehicles and transportation systems, whether personally owned or community-based, represent another zone of potential combat.  As Cory Doctorow points out, such systems are no longer just simple mechanical systems, but complex computer systems that we ride inside.  As with virtually all other types of computing systems, vehicles have proven to be vulnerable to attack and manipulation. For example, in 2008 a Polish teen modified a television remote control device and used it to control the local train system, causing a derailment.[192] Vehicles are also studded with sensors, radio transmitters, and a ubiquitous black box, providing such services as automatic toll payment, location tracking, concierge assistance, automatic accident alerting, vehicle performance tracking, and fleet monitoring services.  Many insurance companies allow you to save money if you agree to provide data to them from sensors in your car that track speed, acceleration and deceleration, turns (to include G-forces for each), and time-of-day.[193] These advantages inadvertently create an additional attack surface[i] for actors to engage during cyber conflict.  Law enforcement agencies have remotely activated in-car microphones to monitor conversations,[194] tire

---

[i] Attack Surface. This term is used to describe the myriad avenues through which an information system is vulnerable to cyber attack. As a system becomes more complex, the attack surface increases, making it more vulnerable. Countermeasures, such as network firewalls, can help decrease a system's attack surface; however, these systems are almost never completely effective in protecting against all existing vulnerabilities.

pressure monitoring systems broadcast unique serial numbers,[195] automated toll payment systems are being exploited to track user driving behavior,[196] and GPS systems allow continuous location tracking of taxis and riders.[197] Two independent security researchers discovered security flaws that provided the capability to remotely control many key aspects of certain models of automobiles. The vehicle manufacturer issued a recall for 1.4 million vehicles, perhaps the first automotive recall due to an active adversary rather than a design flaw.[198] Imagine what highly resourced threat actors would be capable of.

*Community* – At the community level, we transition from individual people and personal technologies to businesses and wide-area systems serving large groups. This category includes population centers ranging from small villages to megacities, so the population and technology densities will vary widely. There are, however, important common characteristics, particularly critical infrastructure which exist across the range of community sizes. The U.S. Department of Homeland Security lists 16 sectors at the strategic level, and we've highlighted the sectors most applicable to communities in Table 4-2.

While the DHS list is focused at the national level, we've extended their framework with examples from the local community. The DHS list is deficient because of its dismissal of "non-critical" infrastructure. Some of that infrastructure may not be critical from a strategic perspective, but can be considered so at local levels, particularly so because of its cumulative potential and capability of causing mass panic and break down of social order. Examples include public and private schools, bars, day care centers, law firms, churches, and the many aspects of the local community that are important to the population. Workplaces are of particular concern as they house innovation, processes, and proprietary information that make the economy run. We encourage you to think holistically about these and other facets of the community when conducting your analyses.

*Table 4-2: Common Critical Infrastructure Sectors and Representative Examples at the Community Level*

| Sector | Community Examples |
|---|---|
| Commercial Facilities | Casinos, hotels/motels, theme parks, shopping malls, sports stadiums, bars and nightclubs |
| Communications | Telephone and cable infrastructure and control systems |
| Manufacturing | Local manufacturing plants |
| Emergency Services | 911 systems, emergency notification systems |
| Energy | Power substation control systems, residential smart meters, dams |
| Financial Services | Local banks, ATMs, point of sale terminals |
| Food and Agriculture | Farms, grocery stores, automated irrigation systems |
| Government Facilities | Local government record keeping systems, electronic voting systems |
| Healthcare/Public Health | Hospital, medical clinic, and doctors' office medical technology and record keeping systems, pharmacy prescription systems, internal sensors and regulators |
| Information Technology | Internet service providers, cyber cafes, home networks |
| Transportation Systems | Toll payment systems, smart parking meters, air traffic control systems, gas stations, smart highways, GPS navigations systems |
| Water and Wastewater Systems | Water and sewage treatment plant industrial control systems |

Ironically, the least technically advanced communities are sometimes the most resistant to cyber attack and exploitation. One reason Ukraine was able to quickly recover from the recent hack on portions of its power grid is because manual controls were still in place in their recently upgraded control centers. This is less likely to be the case in more modern systems where such backup functionality may no longer exist.

Local governments often look for more efficient ways to govern by investing in new technologies. We see change driven by governments, law enforcement and other agencies as well as private industry.[199] Networked red light cameras require fewer cops on the beat, smart power meters reduce energy waste, and shopping malls track consumers as they shop. Perhaps the most pronounced change is seen in cities competing for leadership in "smart city" initiatives. Consider Barcelona, which was ranked the top smart city in the world by Juniper Research. A smart city seeks to improve the quality of life of its citizens, an admirable goal and one we would enjoy seeing realized. We see amazing innovation, apps portals for community-focused software, emergency response service for the elderly via telecare necklaces, community Wi-Fi, barcodes placed around the city for citizens to scan to learn more about a particular location, and even technological platforms to help city leaders make decisions in real time.[200] However, each initiative dramatically increases a community's attack surface.[201] If not properly secured, we may see smart cities turned into dystopic surveillance systems or simply razed to the ground by cyber siege.

Walk down any Main Street in America and try to count the surveillance cameras. Dozens of them peek out from banks, ATMs, shops, gas stations, parking areas, and police stations. Many commercial parking areas use surveillance cameras to both discourage and investigate vehicle break-ins and other crimes. Facial recognition systems designed to identify known terrorists and criminals have been used in football stadiums, Olympics venues.[202] Facial recognition technology was even used in downtown London in 2011 to identify suspects after widespread rioting following the August 4th police shooting of Mark Duggan during a vehicle stop.[203] It is not hard to imagine these surveillance systems being used along with other cellular and wireless technology to surreptitiously track individuals' movements from parking lot, to shop, to bank, to gas station.

An increasingly important trend in this area is the growth of megacities. Megacities are defined as cities with populations of 10 million or more people and are characterized by massive scale, intense population density, complexity, connectedness, and surface and sub-surface development.[204] Global drivers that are fueling this growth include war, increased numbers of disenfranchised youth, scarcity of resources, climate change, and unemployment.[205] Some of the largest megacities are merging into mega-regions like the East Coast of the United States. In China, the Hong Kong, Shenhzen, and Guanzhou region is home to approximately 120 million people.[206] Megacities and mega-regions present immense challenges to conventional military forces, and their footprint in cyberspace will eclipse many nations. Megacities and mega-regions must be part of future planning for both those seeking to defend those populations as well as cyber operators planning to exploit them.

**Region** – Sometimes it is useful to have a tier between the community and national level since regions often have unique attributes and are usually semi-autonomous. In some countries, regions might be states, provinces, or territories. Regions are characterized by having multiple population centers, regional military (National Guard) forces and law enforcement agencies, and large-scale facilities serving regional or global customers, such as hydroelectric dams, chemical plants, nuclear power plants, and large-scale agriculture. Regional presence in cyberspace is largely a linear extension based on the increased size of the population, regional governance, and specialized facilities.

**Nation** – Nation states are geographic regions that share common governance, language and cultural similarities and possess sovereignty. Entrance into and exit from nations in the physical world is often strictly controlled, and physical borders are well-understood. In cyberspace, these borders are blurred, but the concept of borders does still apply. Due to the intensely interconnected nature of cyberspace, it is very difficult to secure national borders in cyberspace, although some nations have tried. Examples include North Korea, which has severely limited Internet access to a few elites, government institutions, and academics, and China's Great Firewall, which attempts to regulate Internet access. Some nations are technologically advanced and possess a rich presence in cyberspace while other lesser-developed nations have very little presence and protection. Even in underdeveloped nations, citizens still seek Internet access and employ technologies such as mobile phones and Very Small Aperture Terminals (VSATs), which allow individuals and institutions to access it. The result is that Internet activities quickly leave the geographic confines of a given country. Lesser-developed nations sometimes leapfrog over older technologies, such as copper-based telephone service, to more advanced technologies, such as advanced cellular infrastructures. Many nations attempt to control disruptive information flows, but it is common for citizens to attempt to bypass government controls despite legal consequences and, in some cases, the very real possibility of physical harm. Nations employ surveillance technologies to monitor their populations to provide for their national security and stabilize the government. Despite even the best of intentions, such deeply embedded surveillance systems may be used for less altruistic purposes today and in the future.

**World** – Nations are interconnected through a series of surface and undersea fiber optic cables and satellites links, which have historically been subject to exploitation and attack. In cyberspace, network traffic is commonly routed through other nations, much of it through the United States in particular. Internet routing infrastructure has also been subject to misconfiguration and attack that can shift the flows of traffic significantly.[207] Not all of the Earth's surface is occupied by nation states. Commons, such as the oceans, are shared by all, although there are certainly disputed regions. There are numerous international and intergovernmental organizations, most notably the United Nations, that attempt to advance collective agendas, keep the peace, and protect the rights and equities of the organization's constituents. Similarly, many large companies are global, with presences in multiple nations. Companies with global workforces are at increased risk for insider attacks and compromise through remote offices and diverse, and sometimes adversarial, national allegiances.

*Space* – The USSR launched the first satellite, Sputnik, in 1957, and since then mankind has used space for communications, science, and remote sensing. There are more than 1,000 satellites active in space and many more that are apparently inoperable. In particular, the region about 22 thousand miles into space, where satellite orbits match the rotation speed of the earth, is the home for hundreds of geosynchronous satellites that provide critical and continuous communications support. Significant satellites require years of effort to construct and can remain in orbit for many decades. Satellites are controlled by terrestrial ground stations, which transmit command and control instructions. As a result, satellites are remotely controlled and use aging technology. It should be noted that remotely controlled, aging technology has historically proven to be particularly susceptible to cyberspace attack.[208] Militaries are dependent on space systems for communication, global positioning, and intelligence collection. Expect space-borne cyberspace operations to be part of future large scale conflict between superpowers. How could it not?

## Conclusions

Understanding the Operational Environment is essential to effective cyberspace operations and how they fit into a given actor's overall strategy of attack and defense. The PMESII-PT framework—political, military, economic, social, information, infrastructure, physical environment and time—is a powerful tool for analyzing the larger context. The Operational Environment is swathed with interconnected sensors, processors, and data storage, creating the terrain of cyberspace, which actors seek to defend and upon which they conduct operations. Cyber operators must understand that the rapid proliferation of technology is increasing the density and complexity of cyberspace. With this change comes both peril and opportunity.

# 5 TERRAIN

*"Of all the mountainous countries, the tactical defense of Switzerland would be the easiest, if all her inhabitants were united in spirit; with their assistance a disciplined force might hold its own against a triple number."*

*- Jomini* [209]

No deliberate military operation is planned without a detailed terrain analysis. Combat is inherently about using battlefield terrain to your advantage. Whether you are on the offensive or the defensive, choosing where you fight can make the difference between winning and losing. Cyberspace is no different; understanding the environment in which you are operating is critical. Cyberspace is, of course, much more than just physical network devices. In this chapter, we introduce and describe cyber terrain, show why it is crucial for successful cyber warfare, and discuss how to leverage it.

On the physical battlefield, terrain is the land and the features it contains. Militaries have mature techniques for analyzing physical terrain, and the traditional understanding of "terrain" has changed to incorporate other aspects of the operational environment, such as human terrain,[210] political terrain, man-made terrain, and urban terrain. However, while we can employ some of these concepts in cyberspace operations and adapt others, there are still gaps. In this chapter, we seek to provide a coherent framework for understanding and analyzing cyber terrain. Such a framework is necessary because physical terrain has effects on cyberspace operations; likewise, cyberspace operations can affect physical terrain that impacts kinetic operations. For our purposes, we define cyber terrain as the systems, devices, protocols, data, software, processes, cyber personas, and other network entities that comprise, supervise, and control cyberspace. [211]

An understanding of terrain is integrated with other mission planning factors including designated mission, enemy, troops available, time, and civilian considerations. The U.S. Army uses the mnemonic METT-TC to help commanders recall these key factors even while under the stress of combat.

Thus far we've considered two primary worlds: physical and cyberspace. We've broken down the physical world into the land, sea, air, and space warfighting domains. Now we are going to further refine the model to provide a higher resolution look into the operational domain of cyberspace (see Figure 5-1). Note that our evolved model links the cyberspace planes with the physical world at the Geographic Plane.

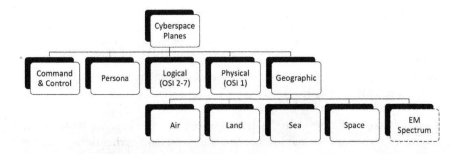

*Figure 5-1: We've extended our model to include a higher resolution look at the operational domain of cyberspace. Note the geographic plane of our cyberspace model intersects with the physical domains of air, land, sea, and space, where the physical components of cyberspace reside. We've also added the Electro-Magnetic spectrum.*

### Cyber Terrain and Levels of War

Cyber terrain features exist at all three levels of war: strategic, operational and tactical. At the strategic level, which is concerned with national policy and theater strategy, cyber terrain would include transatlantic cables and satellite constellations, among other examples. At the operational level, which focuses on campaigns and major operations, cyber terrain might include a telecommunications central office or a regional data center, and at the tactical level where battles, engagements, and small-unit actions take place, cyber terrain could include the wireless spectrum or even a particular Local Area Network (LAN) protocol. It is important to note that cyber terrain features are often virtual, and thus aren't necessarily tied to a given geographic location, or the geographic location might be irrelevant.

## Cyber Space Planes

Rather than one monolithic plane, our revised model breaks cyberspace down into five layers: Command and Control, Persona, Logical, Physical, and Geographic.[212] Important terrain resides at each of these layers, some vital to success in cyberspace operations. When we talk about achieving effects in or through cyberspace, these layers are where it happens. As you study these layers, it is important to note that each layer depends upon the one below it. For example, if one destroys the networking equipment at the Physical layer, the Logical, Persona, and Command and Control may collapse if redundant systems are not employed. And above it, destroying account credentials on the Persona plane would prevent usage of the lower planes.

*Command and Control Plane* – The command and control plane provides the oversight and authority to start, stop, modify, or redirect a cyber operation or activity. It is comprised of elements of cyberspace that either perform a supervisory function or provide a conduit for command and control. Examples include botnet herders,[i] military command and control nodes, system administrators, and administrative accounts. The command and control plane is a popular counter-attack vector for defense against large automated systems, such as botnets.[213]

*Cyber Persona Plane* – The cyber persona plane is where we have online identities and accounts that are used to authorize and authenticate all users and computers in a given online domain. Cyber personas can become rich online identities. Alternatively, sparse online identities can be used when one wants to limit his online exposure. Carefully cultivated real-world identities that are developed over years of use are common. Online personas may be deceptive by design, such as unknown actors posing as senior military leaders, and all types can be discarded when necessary.[214] Identities can be one human or machine per identity (1:1), one human or machine to many identities (1:N), many humans or machines using a single shared identity (N:1), or many humans and machines using multiple shared identities (M:N). As an example, an administrator account credential shared among many network administrators is an N:1 relationship of humans to cyber personas.

---

[i] Botnets and herders. A botnet is a term used to describe a large number of compromised systems under the control of a single individual or entity, often referred to as the bot herder. Systems are compromised through malicious email attachments or other methods, and once compromised, each system, called a bot, calls back to the bot herder's computer. This command channel is kept open so that the herder can direct the bot to take action, such as participate in a distributed denial-of-service attack. The user of the bot usually never knows that their system is sometimes being used surreptitiously by someone else for malicious purposes.

*Logical Plane* – The logical plane is what people usually envision when thinking about cyberspace. This is where applications run, word processing files exist, data is encrypted, errors are corrected, routing decisions are made, network nodes communicate end-to-end, and packets[215] traverse network links. It contains layers 2-7 of the Open Systems Interconnection (OSI) model:[ii] data link, network, network, transport, session, presentation and application. The logical plane also contains many other code-based components that make computers run.[216] Two major aspects are the operating system and software applications. Software applications are the computer programs you typically use on a computer. If these applications are network aware, they will likely contain layers 5-7 of the OSI model: Session (Layer 5), Presentation (Layer 6), and Application (Layer 7). Applications communicate through a series of interrupts and system calls with the operating system. The operating system handles memory management, allocates and deconflicts requests for resources, and uses device drivers to communicate with hardware devices. The operating system is what mediates communications with the motherboard, which connects computer hardware components such as the processor, memory, video output, and hard drives. Below the operating system on the motherboard and inside of CPU chips, there are other code-based components, including firmware and microcode, which blur the line between the Logical and Physical Planes. There are exceptions to these rules. For example, virtual machines replicate much of the hardware functionality in software. (see Figure 5-2 for a graphical depiction).

The Logical Plane, where operating system and application software resides along with network and other protocols, is where a lot of tactical cyber combat takes place. The network aspects of the Logical Plane conflict have been popular as an attack vector since the 1990s, but at the lowest levels of the Logical Plane, where it comes into contact with the hardware, the battle is heating up.[iii] For example, information security researchers have

---

[ii] OSI Model. The Open Systems Interconnect model is a conceptual model developed in the early days of the Internet to describe a hierarchy of protocols necessary for communication between nodes on the Internet, or any network for that matter. The idea is that different protocols can be interchanged at any of the seven layers; physical, data link, network, transport, session, presentation, and application; as long as the interfaces provided to adjacent layers are standardized. It is a concept that is widely understood by information security professionals.

[iii] The Memory Hierarchy. Computers contain different kinds of memory for different purposes. *Registers* are small memory components located on the computer's processor, which the processor uses during computations. Registers represent only a small portion of a computer's memory. A computer's *Random Access Memory*, or *RAM*, is volatile, in that the data is lost when the computer is turned off. Data in random access memory is stored in transistors and is swapped back

discovered techniques to hide malware logically below the operating system, which make the code undetectable to antivirus software.[217] Malware authors have found ways for their code to exist only in Random Access Memory (RAM) and never be saved to hard disk, greatly frustrating detection, analysis, and elimination.[218] The Basic Input Output System (BIOS), which provides bare bones communication with hardware components and is used to bootstrap the operating system, has had serious security flaws and been subject to attack.[219] Further complicating the situation is that inside a computer are many smaller, fully functional computers, each with its own processor, memory, firmware, and storage, often with direct and unprotected access to other components of the computer.[220] Understanding these low-level interactions between hardware and software is important to the security professional and worthy of further study beyond the short overview we've provided here.

---

and forth to the registers on the processor for computation. Finally, *secondary storage*, or *non-volatile memory*, includes hard drives and other media that continue to store data magnetically or optically even after the power is turned off. Data in secondary storage takes much longer to access than RAM, and it is swapped back and forth to RAM in order to be manipulated by the processor.

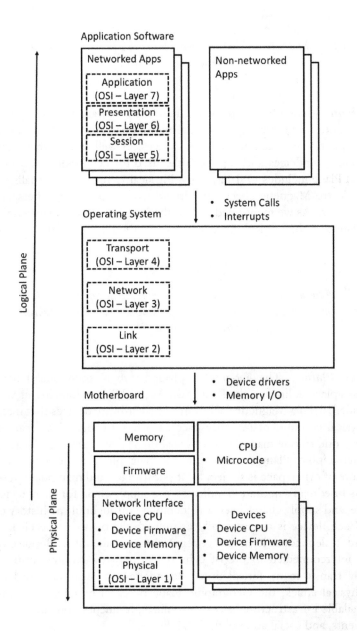

*Figure 5-2: Overview of the interaction of the Logical Plane and the Physical Plane. Note that even on the motherboard there is embedded code in the form of firmware, microcode on the CPU, and even the logical traces of chips, thus blurring the crisp lines between the Logical Plane and the Physical Plane.*

*"The Biggest Lie About Your Computer is that it's Just One Computer"*
*- Dan Kaminsky* [221]

**Physical Plane** – The physical plane is where the hardware components of cyberspace reside. These components are the physical boxes, chips, circuit boards, peripheral devices, and network devices, as well as the fiber optic cables, including undersea and copper cables used for networking, and thus the Physical Plane includes OSI Layer 1 – Physical Layer. Conceptually we place the Electro-Magnetic spectrum here when it is used for cyberspace communications. As we mentioned earlier, the lines are blurred between the Physical Plane and the Logical Plane, likewise for the Physical Plane and the Geographic Plane.

*"Basically all the world's computer parts come from the same supply chain that runs from Korea, down through coastal China, over to Taiwan, and down to Malaysia."*
*- Thomas Friedman* [222]

**Geographic Plane** – The geographic plane is where traditional kinetic warfare takes place; it links to the Land, Sea, Air, and Space domains, as well as the broader Electro-Magnetic spectrum. The hardware devices that make up the physical component of cyberspace each has a geographic location, resulting in a one-to-one mapping of Physical Plane devices to their location on the Geographic Plane. Because of their physical presence, the infrastructure of cyberspace is subject to physical attack and manipulation.[223] As Thomas Friedman's quotation indicates, the supply chain for each device is extensive, and supply chains been a vulnerability throughout the history of warfare. Each device is commercially or individually owned, so each falls under location-dependent legal and governmental jurisdictions. Because of the highly interconnected nature of cyberspace, network communications can quickly transit many jurisdictional boundaries and national borders. Beyond physical attack, the Geographic Plane raises many considerations, such as available infrastructure, access to utilities, frequency and severity of weather events, and social and political stability.

**Terrain Analysis**
Terrain analysis is central to preparing to defend or attack, and it is a critical component of Intelligence Preparation of the Battlefield (IPB), which we'll cover later in the book. The military has a systematic method for analyzing

the environment and uses it to inform commanders and staffs how the physical environment will affect operations. The core of terrain analysis is done using the OAKOC framework.[224] OAKOC stands for Observation and Fields of Fire, Avenues of Approach, Key Terrain, Obstacles and Movement, and Cover and Concealment, each of which sheds important light on the cyber environment when preparing for operations. To this we've added a sixth factor, Legal Authorities, because law-abiding nation-states cannot engage in cyber combat without having lawyers nearby, to make OAKCOLA.

***Observation and Fields of Fire*** – This category seeks to understand "who and what you can see" and "who and what you can engage"[225] from various positions on the terrain, for both you and your adversaries. Examples of what you might be able to observe from your current location include networks, subnets, individual network addresses and other metadata, servers, computers, network devices, wireless signals, operating systems and applications, among others. There are many things you might engage. Examples include open network ports, vulnerable applications, wireless access points, and critical services. As we discussed earlier, observation in cyberspace isn't easy, so considering observation and fields of fire will help you place network traffic sensors and configure visualization and SEIM[iv] systems appropriately. For devices at a network edge, observation is limited to a given network segment. Observation is greatly improved as one moves to a centralized location on the network such as a core router. Contrasted with the physical or geographic planes, observation may be both closer and better concealed.[226]

*Fields of fire* refers to what you can engage from a given location and is often dependent on line-of-sight. Line-of-sight in the analog realm is what you can see from a given location. Not all weapons, however, require line-of-sight to a target in order to engage it, and those that don't are referred to as indirect fire weapons. Artillery can lob rounds high over terrain features and other obstructions. On the network, you can usually hit what is network reachable, which might mean around the world or even in space. Because you are unlikely to have a sensor in place at the target, you will often fire off your packets and trust that the Internet's routing protocols will take them to their destination. We'll discuss the related concept of Battle Damage Assessment (determining the actual effects caused by an attack) later in the book.

---

[iv] A Security Event and Incident Management (SEIM) system is a computer system used in network operations centers to monitor ongoing network activity in order to identify security incidents. These devices often aggregate information from other network security devices, such as firewalls and intrusion detection systems.

Another example of an indirect fire cyber weapon is a phishing email; the destination isn't observed, but the email will likely hit its target inbox (for more examples, see Table 5-1). Cyber operators are used to operating partially in the dark. Consider the Blind SQL injection attack, which because the target server returns only a generic error message (or no error message at all) the attacker must send a large number of queries to gather the desired target data. A related concept is obstacles, which we will cover shortly. Obstacles can be used to filter or block observation and attacks.

*Table 5-1: Examples of observation and fields of fire by plane.*

| | Observation | Fields of Fire |
|---|---|---|
| **Command Control** | Botnet C2 traffic visible on chat applications such as IRC, observation of threat actor C2 on social media, wiretap, CALEA[227] enabled law enforcement access to leadership communication systems | Access to Command-and-Control server, social engineering via telephone |
| **Persona** | Threat actor online personas | Access to persona account credentials |
| **Logical** | Packet sniffing, access to DNS server | Network reachable devices, ability to probe network services |
| **Physical** | Wi-Fi traffic, ability to physically observe antenna size and orientation | Physical access to network cabling, routers, wiring closets |
| **Geographic** | Observation of ingress and egress of personnel to facilities, employee wearing access badge in public, access to CCTV system | Physical access to facilities |

**Avenues of Approach** – Avenues of approach are the paths that an adversary might take to reach you and how you might reach an adversary's positions. In traditional conflict, enumerating avenues of approach involves analysis of trafficability of roads and trails, and whether they support the expected mode of travel, such as tracked vehicles, wheeled vehicles, or foot march. Trafficability is often heavily dependent on weather. Physical avenues of approach are usually identified by the size of unit they can support (for example platoon, company, or battalion). In cyberspace there are different dynamics. Akin to threat vectors in information security, avenues of approach can include the logical plane for network based attacks, the electromagnetic spectrum for Wi-Fi and other wireless attacks, and even humans for geographic plane attacks. An insider accomplice is at a particular advantage as they are already inside perimeter defenses.[228] The purpose of avenues of approach is to reach the attack surface of the target (see Table 5-2 for examples).

*Table 5-2: Examples of avenues of approach by cyberspace plane*

| Command Control | Target's command and control systems, malicious software sent to senior leader, Whaling[229] |
|---|---|
| Persona | Email to targeted persona's inbox, social media sites of employees |
| Logical | Internet paths to Internet connected devices, VPN access from home users, subcontractor network access, HTTP access to a database server |
| Physical | Electromagnetic spectrum, access to fiber optic or copper cables |
| Geographic | Roads leading to data center, HVAC, tailgating through security check points, elevators and service entrances to a target facility |

When analyzing potential avenues of approach, analysts should consider how direct a particular route is to the objective, the degree of concealment the avenues provide (such as high volumes of legitimate traffic that can obfuscate attack traffic), whether friendly or enemy sensors are in place along the route, whether there are alternate routes, available bandwidth, and any obstacles that one might encounter. We've found that a useful conceptual model is to imagine a sphere around your person, home, or workplace and ask yourself what can cross that boundary. We've created Figure 5-3 to show this method and to illustrate various physical, wired, and wireless avenues of approach to a notional target device. We recommend conducting a similar analysis of potentials avenues to critical assets within your organization, employing a healthy degree of paranoia. It is very difficult to anticipate and counter the moves of an agile and adaptive adversary who will seek out unanticipated avenues of approach or attack vectors.

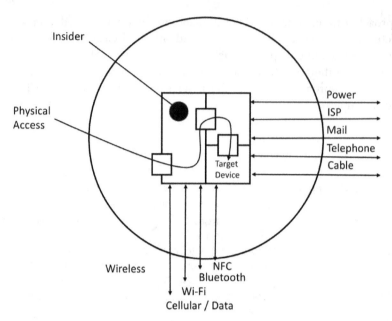

*Figure 5-3:* To help assess potential avenues of approach in your environment, it useful to think of it inside a sphere and determine what information or objects flow across that boundary. In the center of this diagram is the floorplan of a small three room office. We've labeled it with likely information, object and resource flows to consider when determining avenues of approach.

**Key Terrain** – Key terrain refers to areas that, if held, give the attacker or the defender a distinct advantage. On the traditional kinetic battlefield, key terrain might include a bridge that supports movement of your tanks to a tactical objective or a hilltop that allows observation and lines of fire down into enemy positions. In kinetic warfare, the concept of key terrain is most often applicable at the tactical level. In cyber operations, key terrain exists on every plane and may be the same or different for the attacker and defender. Key terrain has important temporal characteristics; what may be key terrain at one moment may not be the next. By analyzing key terrain, both attackers and defenders can better focus their efforts (see Table 5-3 for examples).

**Decisive Terrain** – Decisive terrain is key terrain that provides an overwhelming impact on the mission. It isn't present in every operation, but when decisive terrain is present, it must be seized or retained to avoid mission failure.[230]

*Table 5-3 – Example Key Terrain by Plane. Key Terrain provides a marked advantage if seized or held and exists on every plane in our model.*

| Command and Control | Nuclear launch C2 systems, Active Director controller, authentication servers |
|---|---|
| **Persona** | Admin/root accounts, back-up credentials, developer accounts, CIO/CEO's email account (or their spouse's) |
| **Logical** | Critical applications, configuration files, firmware, password file,[231] root name servers[232] |
| **Physical** | Wiring closet, core router (especially its RS-232 port[233]), option ROMs,[234] data center, border routers, routing protocols |
| **Geographic** | Security office |

### Cover and Concealment

Cover and concealment in the physical world are straightforward concepts and apply to both attackers and defenders. Cover provides protection from a given type of incoming fire, like a brick wall or bulletproof glass. Concealment masks your location from observers, but it doesn't protect against weapons fire if you are targeted. These concepts have ready analogues in cyberspace operations (table 5-4 breaks out examples by plane). In addition to cover and concealment, there are two more conditions to complete the picture. These states occur when you can see an adversary. If the target isn't protected by cover and you can reach it, then the target is unprotected. If the target is visible, but beyond the effective range of your weapons, then the target is out of range (table 5-5 makes these concepts clearer).

*Table 5-4: Examples of cover and concealment by cyberspace plane.*

|  | Cover | Concealment |
|---|---|---|
| **Command Control** | Heavily encrypted command and control channels. Air gapped command and control networks. | Using covert channels for command and control, such as IRC, DNS, and HTTP. |
| **Persona** | Limited social media presence. Invite-only social media accounts versus public access. | Deceptive online identities, super-user accounts with non-traditional names. |
| **Logical** | Virtual Private Networks, VLANs, virtualization, closed ports, removal of unnecessary services and utilities, polymorphic code, tunneling traffic over HTTPS. | Obfuscated code, network camouflage techniques, anonymity networks, attacks that occur only in memory, tunneling IPv4 network traffic over IPv6. |
| **Physical** | Faraday cage, TEMPEST shielding, wired only communications, tamper resistant sensors. | Fake wireless access point traffic, disguised network facilities and antennas, frequency hopping communications. |
| **Geographic** | Underground data centers. | Physical camouflage, dead drop transfer of electronic media. |

*Table 5-5: Comparing cover and concealment with adversary options.*

|  | Adversary can see | Adversary cannot see |
|---|---|---|
| **Adversary can engage** | Unprotected | Concealment |
| **Adversary cannot engage** | Out of Range | Cover |

***Obstacles and Movement*** – As forces prepare for combat, they often emplace obstacles to impede their adversary's mobility. Obstacles may be natural or man-made, and both can be used to shape adversary behavior. Traditionally these would include:

- Obstacles with disrupting effects that break up enemy formations, interrupt their tempo, or cause early commitment of anti-obstacle resources such as combat engineers
- Obstacles with fixing effects that cause the enemy to slow or stop,
- Obstacles with turning effects that cause the enemy to move in a desired direction
- Obstacles with blocking effects that prevent the enemy from maneuvering into a certain area.[235]

These concepts apply well to cyberspace operations (see Table 5-6). However, there are many more effects that we can generate, especially if we exploit the unique properties of cyberspace and employ deception. We'll cover those strategies more in depth in Chapter 9 - Fires and Effects and Chapter 11 – Deception.

*Table 5-6: Examples of fixing, turning, disrupting, and blocking obstacles in cyberspace*

| Fixing | Turning |
|---|---|
| • Tarpit[236]<br>• Sticky advertising<br>• Honeynets<br>• Network segmentation<br>• Code obfuscation<br>• CAPTCHAs | • DoD Warning Banner<br>• BGP attacks<br>• DNS redirection<br>• Sinkholes<br>• VPN<br>• Anti-virus quarantine server<br>• DMZ or perimeter network |
| **Disrupting** | **Blocking** |
| • IDS<br>• Degrading network reliability<br>• DDOS<br>• Wireless jamming<br>• Fake Personas<br>• TCP RST<br>• Fake access points<br>• Bandwidth limitations | • Firewall<br>• IPS<br>• ACL<br>• Air Gap<br>• Cutting cables<br>• Web content filtering<br>• Sandboxing<br>• Hardened servers<br>• NAT<br>• Anti-Virus<br>• White/black listing<br>• VLAN |

Obstacles you put in place to frustrate your adversary might inadvertently impact your own organization as well. For example, web content filtering deployed to prevent inadvertent downloading of malware from infected websites may block your users from accessing legitimate content.[237] As you emplace obstacles, consider how they may affect your own organization and its efforts. Despite your best intentions, practices such as disabling links in emails or stripping email attachments can limit your organization's ability to operate and can lead to personnel purposely working around those protections, for example by using personal email accounts for work activities.

Obstacles can occur on any plane and may be technical, physical, policy, or human. Although more common at the tactical level, obstacles may be placed at the operational and strategic level as well. Properly architecting your network infrastructure by employing network segmentation and air gapped networks is a good starting point (see Figure 5-4). Adaptive adversaries will attempt to bypass obstacles by maneuvering to another plane. For example, an attacker frustrated by network security may try a social engineering attack to trick a help desk into providing legitimate remote user credentials, or an adversary who encounters a strong wired network defense may shift to a wireless network attack.

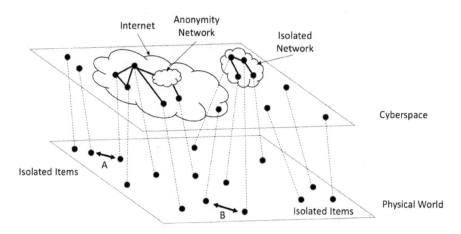

*Figure 5-4: Projection of physical world technology into cyberspace. Some devices are connected to the Internet, some are connected to isolated (or air gapped) networks, and still more are not networked at all. Isolation can be defeated if someone accidently or deliberately bridges the two, see A and B.*

*Legal Authorities* – With actors who respect the rule of law, legal authorities and administrative policies have important impacts on cyber terrain. Since cyber terrain is dynamic and malleable, changes or applications of law and policy can rapidly shape its character. In the United States, the distinction between authorities provided to Department of Defense agencies by Title 10 of the US Code and authorities offered intelligence agencies under Title 50 provide examples of how legal authorities shape cyber terrain. Title 10 and Title 50 clearly delineate the types of cyberspace activities that various U.S. government agencies may legally undertake. While penetration of another country's networks by military personnel operating under Title 10 authorities could be seen as an act of war, similar activities undertaken by intelligence personnel under Title 50 in order to collect intelligence-gathering might be completely acceptable from the perspective of international law (see Table 5-7 for examples of how legal authorities can shape cyber terrain).

Conducting OAKCOLA analysis will help you gain the best positional advantage. Assume your adversaries are doing the same.

*Table 5-7: Examples of how legal authorities and policies can shape cyber terrain.*

| Plane | Examples |
|---|---|
| Command and Control | Selection of senior cyber leaders, required approval authority for given activities, organizational mandates on network structure |
| Persona | Policies on usage of online personas and social media activities. |
| Logical | Self-censoring of online activities, processes for authorizing usage of operating systems and application software, support or prohibition of certain networking protocols |
| Physical | Peering agreements to voluntarily connect networks, process for authorizing usage of brands/models of networking hardware, BYOD policies |
| Geographic | Acknowledgment of borders between nations and regions. Geographic limitations of various forms of online activities. |

*"God made the other four [domains]. You made the last one. God did a better job."*
*- General Michael Hayden* [238]

## Other Related Concepts of Terrain Analysis

OAKCOLA provides a good starting point for cyber terrain analysis, but it isn't complete. Here are some other important aspects.

***Control of Terrain*** – Because cyber terrain is largely invisible, it isn't always obvious who controls various aspects of it. We see this in compromised industrial control systems. The owner and operator of, say, a dam may believe they have full control, but in reality a threat actor might have access in a way that allows them to control operation of the dam at their will. Taking the issue of presence and control even further, multiple threat actors may be present in a system in addition to the legitimate operator and have full control of the system, such as several security industry malware analysts with control of the same botnet command and control network. Fratricide in these circumstances is likely. You might imagine multiple "friendly" actors simultaneously working to take control of an enemy asset, each unaware of the others. These situations can be prevented by close collaboration among agencies, along with communication and de-confliction efforts.

***Terrain Classification*** – In classic terrain analysis, there is the concept of Unrestricted, Restricted, and Severely Restricted terrain, which helps commanders decide when and where they might maneuver their forces. These classifications are useful when considering cyber terrain. Unrestricted terrain is free from any restriction on movement. In cyberspace, unrestricted terrain might be high-bandwidth links without obstacles. Restricted terrain hinders movement and might contain some obstacles or possess limited bandwidth. Severely restricted terrain is all but impassible, although limited movement may be possible. It is possible, however, to improve mobility by disabling obstacles like firewalls or increasing bandwidth by limiting the access of others. Faced with severely restricted terrain, an actor is likely to simply seek out another route, perhaps on another cyberspace plane.[239] Terrain classifications are not absolute and depend on multiple variables. A determined adversary may find a unique solution that will allow passage through even Severely Restricted terrain, just as Allied Soldiers did during World War II, retrofitting tanks with "tusks" to cut through the hedgerows that served as natural obstacles in the Normandy countryside.[240]

***Shaping of Terrain*** – Geographic terrain changes slowly, even with the help of tools and bulldozers. Cyber terrain is both dynamic and malleable. It may be created, modified, or destroyed at scales of time ranging from human speed to machine speed. Avenues of approach may likewise appear, shift, or disappear at similarly high speeds. Such movement may be the deliberate decision of humans or by protocols and algorithms that operate routinely. Deliberate attacks or accidental misconfigurations can also shift the terrain dramatically, as in our previous example in which Internet routers belonging to China Telecom advertised incorrect traffic routes and directed 15% of net traffic to China for 18 minutes.[241] Thus cyber terrain itself can be a target and be shaped by an adversary in ways not possible in the physical world.

Technologies such as Software Defined Networking, which is based on the OpenFlow protocol, allow networks to be programmatically configured and centrally managed at network speeds to adapt to changing traffic patterns and networking requirements. Another example is fast flux DNS, where an actor updates DNS records rapidly to map a large number of constantly changing IP addresses under a single domain name. This means that the network could be constantly shifting under one's feet. Automation in cyber operations is a requirement to keep up with changing cyber terrain.

Capable defenders should have the advantage here, as they control the terrain in their own network. Wise defenders will shift the terrain under their control across all the planes to their advantage even while under attack. Much of the shaping should be done in advance, for example, by reducing the number of enterprise connection points to the Internet to facilitate centralized network monitoring. Network isolation and other strategies may be done on the fly. Some countries have even suggested the creation of an Internet disconnect "switch" or Internet kill switch to be used in emergencies.

***Terrain Mapping*** – When operating on cyber terrain, accurate maps are a clear advantage. One way to map networks is through passive traffic analysis. This technique is stealthy, but requires careful placement of network sensors, something that is not always feasible.[242] Active network mapping provides higher resolution information and is often faster, but requires active packet transmission into the probed network. Active mapping may not be an issue on your own network, but might be observed on an adversary's network. Network defenders can continually monitor their networks, systems, and services, as long as they don't generate so much traffic that they degrade network operation, which might be especially of concern on production networks. In theory, and sometimes in practice, network owners have complete knowledge of their own terrain. In addition to attackers and defenders, neutral third-parties may perform network mapping, sometimes

Internet-wide, and make the data publicly available.

Due to the size and rate of change of some networks, it is difficult even for their owners to possess accurate maps. Reconnaissance is the first phase of most operations but probing does not necessarily portend an attack. It is likely that attackers will attempt to build maps of target networks months or more in advance. Network attackers may employ slow and passive network mapping techniques to avoid detection, or only scan for certain systems and vulnerabilities. This means that attackers will almost always be working from old maps and incomplete coverage.

Obstacles and deception play an important role in network mapping. Firewalls, router access control lists (ACLs), and intrusion prevention systems typically frustrate, but don't necessarily prevent network mapping attempts. Attackers will often try to make their active mapping blend in with other legitimate traffic. Defenders might use honeypots to attract and detect mapping attempts.[243] A network map will look different in the face of these various defensive technologies and may very well appear different depending on the route taken into the network.

While to the cyber operator mapping may be most intuitive at the logical plane, it can occur on any plane (see Table 5-8). Social media sites are particularly interesting because they provide links from online personas to all of their friends and followers, allowing the creation of large social graphs. Cyberspace mapping is especially powerful when conducted across all the cyberspace planes and the results combined. The end product is not merely a flat physical map, but a multi-dimensional map that can allow inter- and multi-plane planning, maneuver, and operations.

*Table 5-8: Examples of mapping techniques and sources by plane. Cyberspace mapping is particularly powerful when analysts combine the results into multi-dimensional maps to facilitate inter- and multi-plane maneuver.*

| Plane | Examples |
| --- | --- |
| Command and Control | Traffic analysis of communication networks, organizational phone directories |
| Persona | Social media mapping, email address web mining, web page scraping |
| Logical | Network mapping for services, IP addresses, MAC addresses, document metadata, DNS records |
| Physical | Asset location inventories, war driving,[244] war dialing,[245] EM spectrum surveys |
| Geographic | Traditional mapping |

*"Our military networks are not defensible"*
*- General Keith Alexander*[246]

## Conclusions

Terrain is where actors maneuver and cause effects. A clear understanding of the terrain is essential in all aspects of cyber conflict. Virtually every challenge in cyberspace operations can be better understood and overcome when the terrain is decomposed into the five planes: Command and Control, Persona, Logical, Physical and Geographic, as we've done in this chapter. Each plane has its own unique terrain features, characteristics, and obstacles that must be understood in order to operate effectively. OAKCOLA (Observation and Fields of Fire, Avenues of Approach, Key Terrain, Cover and Concealment, Obstacles and Movement, and Legal Authorities) provides an overarching framework for analysis.

Presence on terrain may be difficult to detect, and multiple threat actors may be present and the physical owner unaware. Terrain may be shaped rapidly, one of the rare advantages the defender possesses. Consider the power that administrators of Twitter, Second Life, and Google have over their respective ecosystems. Currently many organizations have an exposed cyber flank, and even if your networks are generally not defensible at present, they can be re-architected so that they are.[247] Cyber terrain can and should be mapped. Passive mapping is quiet, but may not gather sufficient information. Active mapping provides much better resolution, at the expense of stealth. The most powerful mapping will occur across all five planes and generate a multidimensional picture of the cyber battlespace. We should expect constant reconnaissance by persistent, well-resourced threat actors.

There are many different types of cyber terrain, ranging from computer memory to online personas to virtual machines, industrial control systems, anonymity networks, the deep web, darknets, distributed data centers driving cloud-based computing solutions, even the billions of devices comprising the Internet of Things. Some are disconnected, some are in austere environments, others reside in highly dense megacities. Terrain is an essential aspect of cyber conflict that must be understood to be effective; we will continually discuss ways to leverage cyber terrain throughout this book.

# 6 MANEUVER

*"Without a solid grasp of what cyber maneuver can (and can't) do for the battlespace commander, cyber operations will be limited not by resources or technical limitations, but by the imagination of those who wield it."*

*— Dr. David Gioe* [248]

Maneuver in military operations uses movement and weapons fire to place combat forces in a position of advantage over an adversary.[249] Maneuver may occur in a single operational domain or take place across multiple planes in synchronization; it is far more powerful when commanders orchestrate and combine the diverse elements of power at their disposal,[250] such as air power, armor, infantry, artillery, and cyber, to apply strength against enemy weakness at the appropriate place and time. In conflict, adversaries seek to maneuver against each other and use terrain and obstacles to frustrate their enemy's ability to do the same. The concept of maneuver applies well to cyberspace operations; although unlike maneuver in the physical world, it will sometimes take place at machine and network speeds on terrain that constantly shifts. Wise commanders will use the malleability of cyberspace to continually shape terrain to their advantage and the enemy's disadvantage.

Technology has always changed the way we maneuver. Troops who once walked into battle would later move faster and strike deeper using horses, trains, trucks, tanks, airplanes and long range weapons. Cyberspace adds global reach, often at nearly instantaneous speeds. Militaries, especially air forces and multi-service joint teams, have experience in multi-domain warfare, but cyberspace adds a counterintuitive new dimension that adds complex problems and opportunities. The planes of cyberspace are each areas where the attacker and defender maneuver, whether it be in a computer's memory or across a global network of Internet of Things devices.

Classical forms of maneuver apply surprisingly well in cyberspace operations: frontal assault, turning movement, envelopment, penetration, and infiltration. But we will also introduce and analyze other forms of maneuver that are only possible in cyberspace. Multi-domain and multi-plane maneuver is particularly potent. Imagine a paralyzing attack in cyberspace timed to support invading armored units rolling into a neighboring country.[251] The possibilities are limited only by one's imagination, as Dr. Gioe aptly puts it in his epigraph above.

Effective cyber maneuver requires the technical skills and understanding of the operator, timely and accurate intelligence, and often a legal team. An adept operator will overcome or bypass an obstacle that might stymie the efforts of less skilled or poorly resourced actors. Without reconnaissance and intelligence, cyber operators' situational awareness is limited to what they can observe from their own particular vantage point. In law abiding countries, attorneys are necessary to help determine which terrain may be used for maneuver and which terrain is off limits, whether the terrain is in their homeland, an allied nation, a hospital, a commercial aircraft, or a thermostat.

Maneuver is more than just movement, which is simply moving forces from A to B. Maneuver is movement, often while firing at the enemy or receiving enemy fire, to place your forces in a position of advantage over an adversary. Flexibility and adaptability are key. Both the attacker and defender maneuver differently due to constraints placed upon them, a topic we will explore in this chapter. Maneuver keeps the enemy off balance and the situation uncertain, and this alone makes cyber maneuver worthy of study.

*"It's probably only a slight exaggeration to say we are fighting an attrition battle [in cyberspace] where we are the only ones being attrited."*
*— Carl Hunt* [252]

## Major Forms of Warfare

To understand maneuver, particularly maneuver in the context of cyber operations, we must understand various major philosophies of military strategy: attrition warfare, maneuver warfare, wide area security, hybrid warfare, and unrestricted warfare. Attrition warfare[i] is characterized by combatants who attempt to wear down an adversary, usually in head-to-head combat. In attrition warfare, the side with more resources usually wins.[253,254]

Maneuver warfare[ii] represented a major advance in military operations.[255] Maneuver warfare emphasizes movement and seeks to seize, occupy, and hold ground in order to gain positional advantage and bring the right amount of force to bear against an adversary weakness at the right point in time. Every conflict consumes resources, but maneuver warfare, for agile actors, is a powerful means of conserving resources and magnifying impact with fewer personnel. Maneuver warfare practitioners are able to seize the initiative, set the tempo, and decide when to fight. If done correctly, maneuver warfare disrupts the enemy's ability to plan and respond effectively. The foundations of maneuver warfare include initiative, decisive action, flexibility, adaptability, lethality, synchronization, attacking in depth, and empowered junior leaders who understand their superior's intent.[256]

---

[i] A classic example of attrition warfare was the Battle of Verdun, which occurred on World War I's Western Front in 1916. During this prolonged battle near the French city of Verdun, the German army hoped to deal a death blow to the French army and take France out of the war. Between February and December 2016 there were an estimated 700,000 casualties, split almost equally between France and Germany, during fighting for a portion of the Western Front with little strategic value.

[ii] In the opening days of World War II, the German army introduced their *blitzkrieg*, or "lightning war," tactics. In an effort to avoid the stalemate of trench warfare observed during World War I, the Germans took advantage of the rapid advances in armored vehicle technology during the interwar years and used a tactic in which they would concentrate forces at a single point to penetrate allied lines in what was referred to as *schwerpunkt*, or "focal point" After the initial penetration, German units would pour through the breach and attack rear areas, forcing the allies to fight in two directions at once. This tactic was extremely effective during the early years of the war, such as during the German invasion of France and Belgium in 1940.

The U.S. military considers Wide Area Security (WAS) as a complement to maneuver warfare. Wide Area Security is usually used in lower intensity conflicts and attempts to protect populations, forces, infrastructure, and activities by denying the enemy positions of advantage and retaining the initiative.[257] If done poorly, as we see often in cyberspace, Wide Area Security begins to look a lot like attrition warfare, as Colonel Hunt notes in the epigraph above.

Two other forms of warfare that are powerful counterstrategies to U.S. hegemony on the traditional battlefield are unrestricted warfare and hybrid warfare. Unrestricted warfare is described well in a book written by two Chinese People's Liberation Army colonels. The book highlights the U.S. dependence on technology on the kinetic battlefield and suggests alternate methods of attack over longer duration, including terrorism, legal and political action, targeting of critical infrastructure, and undermining economic systems.[258] We see these very activities playing out today against the United States to great effect. Hybrid warfare is an emerging, and not yet formally defined, concept that advocates combining irregular warfare, information operations, and cyber warfare with conventional warfare. This type of warfare frustrates attribution and makes it difficult to bring traditional military counter force to bear. The Russian invasion of Ukraine demonstrated the powerful effectiveness of hybrid warfare.[259]

Each form of warfare brings important insights to cyber conflict. Attrition warfare suggests strategies that overwhelm the human, network, and machine resources of one's adversaries. Maneuver warfare exploits the fluid nature of cyberspace to rapidly strike at points of vulnerability and disappear, as well as shifting the terrain of cyberspace to support offensive and defensive operations. Wide Area Security provides an aspirational goal of what strategic cybersecurity might look like if we overcome the vast vulnerabilities that exist today. Unrestricted warfare indicates that attacking a nation's critical infrastructure through cyberspace leverages an ill-protected flank essential to a nation's well-being. Unrestricted warfare also tells us that antiquated law and policy, combined with limited legal authorities to conduct cyber operations, puts the United States at a distinct disadvantage. Finally, hybrid warfare shows us that ambiguity in cyber operations will frustrate even the most powerful nations on a global stage. Future cyberspace operations strategies might blend all these attributes together into something that transcends any one philosophy.

*"Part of the art of being a commander [is] in the choice of terrain to allow flanking attacks or prevent them."* [260]

### Flanking Maneuvers and the Battle of Marathon

One of the most fundamental techniques in combat is the flanking maneuver. Traditionally, an army formation's front lines (or in the cyber context, the *attack surface*) are best able to withstand enemy attack because this is the portion of their force that they expect to directly encounter the enemy. Their flanks, that is their sides and rear and even the sky above, are usually much weaker. Forces choose fighting positions with clear fields of fire to their front that interlock with those of the units on their left and right to create devastating kill zones. If time allows, defending units will dig fighting positions that reduce exposure and provide additional protection. Orientation plays a key role. The enemy is to your front; your allied fighters are on your left and right; your supplies and possible escape routes are to your rear. An adversary that can maneuver effectively and attack the flanks or rear of a defending force can "roll the flank," causing the defense to break down and forcing defenders from their defensive fighting positions. If the attacking unit is able to attack the flank with the element of surprise, the results are often far worse for the defender. A successful attack into a defender's flank can even result in a *rout*, a disorganized flight from the battlefield by defending forces.

All capable commanders work to prevent enemy flanking maneuvers by anchoring defensive lines on terrain impassible to their enemies, or by deploying forces specifically to defend exposed flanks.[261]

The Battle of Marathon (490 BC) is a classic example of maneuver and the effective use of terrain, see Figure 6-1. In the battle, the Greeks chose their location carefully, placing their forces on high ground with their flanks guarded by wetlands and mountains. This positioning of forces prevented their Persian adversaries from using their highly effective and mobile horse cavalry. During the battle, Greek forces moved to the Persian center and engaged in fighting. By drawing Persian forces and attention to the center, the Greeks were able to attack with forces on both Persian flanks in a pincer movement that became to be known as a double envelopment.

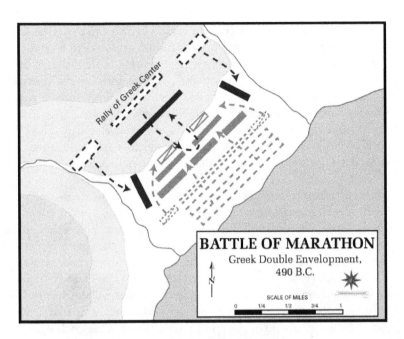

*Figure 6-1: The Battle of Marathon between the Greeks and the Persians in 490 BC is a classic example of attacking an enemy's flanks (Image: U.S. Army).*[262]

> *"War is not an exercise of the will directed at inanimate matter…*
> *In war, the will is directed at an animate object that reacts"*
> *- Clausewitz*[263]

While we have used an example from antiquity to illustrate a flanking maneuver, the concept is no less powerful in cyberspace operations. Consider a network. Network engineers and security architects generally devote a lot of attention to the portion of the network where their external-facing services are offered, such as web servers, email servers, and file servers. This portion of the network is considered the "front lines" of the network, and another term borrowed from military operations is often applied to it: the DMZ, or *demilitarized zone.*[iii] The DMZ, however, is usually not the only

---

[iii] A DMZ, or demilitarized zone, is a portion of a network in which network engineers must let down some defenses in order to allow network traffic from external entities to access services like web servers and email. The network gateway between the DMZ and the organization's internal network is carefully secured and monitored in case a threat actor gains unauthorized access to a system on the DMZ. Because DMZ systems aren't afforded the level of security

pathway into the network, especially in networks that offer wireless access. Network engineers work to shape organizational networks to limit exposed network flanks by reducing connectivity and routing traffic through limited and heavily protected entry/egress points. Inside this fortified perimeter, there may be additional protections, such as VLANs and network segmentation, which further subdivide the network into controlled sub-regions. On individual machines, defenders will likely eliminate unnecessary network services and employ host-based antivirus software, firewalls, and intrusion detection systems to help identify and block malicious activity.

However, cyberspace operations are more than just network operations. Consider any organization, military unit, or individual and project their cyberspace presence across all the cyberspace planes and physical domains. These myriad points of potential attack comprise the *attack surface* of a defender. Attackers will probe for and exploit unwatched avenues of approach (attack vectors) to reach this attack surface and identify vulnerable flanks *on any cyberspace plane or domain.* We argue that rolling the flank in a cyberspace attack is straightforward. Simply find an unanticipated or weakly protected flank, maneuver inside, and wreak havoc. One such example is when attackers created chaos by penetrating hospital security and installing ransomware that shut down operations.[264]

Flanking attacks can also be used to strike moving forces, such as the flanks of an armored cavalry regiment moving across a desert. In cyberspace, consider network-based attacks that occur on extended flanks created by network connections as they transit the network from point A to point B, such as a Man in the Middle Attack, which can edit, slow, or delete network flows, and even insert malware.

## Types of Maneuver
Later in this chapter, we will examine forms of maneuver that exist only in cyberspace and do not have analogs in classical maneuver, but first we will map classical forms of maneuver into cyberspace operations.[265] In this section, we have included aspects of maneuver that take into account the unique properties of cyberspace. In combat, no two attacks will be the same, and each will pose new challenges for the defender, but these approaches are the basic building blocks. Cyberspace operations can be quite obvious if network defenders are properly monitoring activity, but contrasted with kinetic maneuver, cyberspace maneuver is often more covert and will

---

offered to the rest of the network, they are much more closely monitored than other systems so that attempted and actual compromises are identified as soon as possible.

frequently employ deception. This is because many attacks can be easily negated by changes in computer or network configuration, architecture, or patch level. In many cases, cyberspace attackers need not attempt to conceal their activities. If the defender doesn't possess technical countermeasures, cannot readily identify the attacker, must keep systems network-connected at all costs, or if the attack comes through innocent third-party proxies, there is no need for the attacker to be stealthy.[266]

## *Nth Order Envelopment*

An envelopment is a form of maneuver designed to apply attacker strengths to enemy weakness. Attackers probe the attack surface of their adversary's organizational perimeter to find or create a point of vulnerability in their flanks or rear. At the same time, the attacker often launches another diversionary or supporting attack that draws, or "fixes," the defender's attention (see Figure 6-2). The attacker could attempt to fix both human and machine attention, but humans are a more likely target. As a real world example, consider the employment of a DDOS attack[iv] or an obvious phishing campaign that draws network defenders away from their hunt[v] and defensive overwatch duties, while the primary attack takes place on a flank or rear area. Single envelopment entails attacking a single flank, double envelopment targets two flanks, but because of the multidimensional aspects of cyberspace and the physical planes, we aren't limited to two. Nth order envelopments can strike the attack surface across any number of dimensions. The envelopment can turn into an encirclement if the attacker can compromise each of the communication paths possessed by the defender.[267]

---

[iv] A distributed denial of service, or *DDOS*, attack is one in which hundreds or thousands of systems send traffic to a victim host or network in an effort to overwhelm it and make it unavailable for legitimate network traffic. In some cases the malicious traffic comes from machines that belong to individuals who are cooperating to attack the target, a tactic known to be used by the hacker collective Anonymous. In other cases, the traffic comes from botnets, or networks of compromised systems that are controlled by a single attacker, sometimes referred to as a *bot herder*.

[v] *Hunt* refers to a network defense technique in which cyber operators hunt for potential malicious actors on their own network. While traditional defense is reactive, hunting is proactive. This mission does not necessarily assume compromise. Hunters search for indicators of compromise and then take actions to remove access to their systems by attackers.

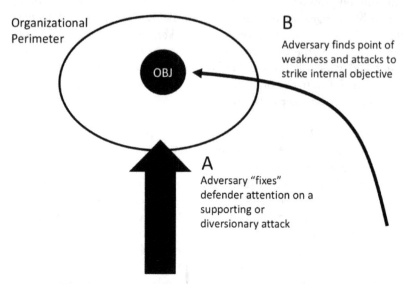

Figure 6-2: Envelopment. In an envelopment the attacker draws the attention of the defender with a diversionary or supporting attack (A), while the primary attack strikes at the flanks or the rear (B).

"A significant factor in maneuverability in cyberspace is access to the target node"
- U.S. Military Doctrine[268]

### Infiltration

Infiltration is a covert form of maneuver during which an attacker quietly identifies a point of vulnerability in the attack surface of the organization and moves inside (see Figure 6-3). Infiltration can occur both through physical access and remotely via a network. The purpose of the infiltration could be to collect information, maintain persistent access, or cause some effect such as damage or disruption. Once inside, the attacker can then disable internal security controls to allow follow-on attacks. Infiltration can occur quickly or very slowly, perhaps even over the course of several years. Examples might be an employee who takes time to carefully build trust and access in order to put themselves in a position to steal proprietary data from their employer's network, or an attacker who subverts an IT supply chain to insert malicious firmware. Because infiltrations seek to remain covert, attackers will often severely limit external communications to frustrate detection.

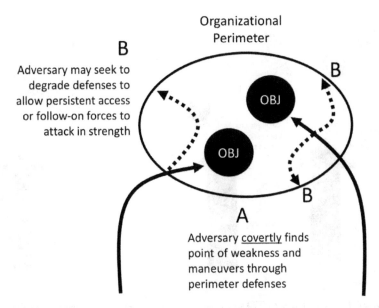

Organizational Perimeter

**B**
Adversary may seek to degrade defenses to allow persistent access or follow-on forces to attack in strength

OBJ

OBJ

**B**

**B**

**A**
Adversary <u>covertly</u> finds point of weakness and maneuvers through perimeter defenses

*Figure 6-3: Infiltration. Infiltration is a covert activity in which the attacker exploits a vulnerability and moves inside the organizational perimeter (A). Once inside, the attacker or their code can exfiltrate information, cause disruption, or lay dormant to maintain long-term access.*

### Frontal Assault

A frontal assault occurs on a broad front and brings force against force. The analog in cyberspace is more likely manpower, bandwidth, and processing power against manpower, bandwidth, and processing power (see Figure 6-4). The most obvious frontal assault in cyberspace is a DDOS attack, which seeks to overwhelm the processing resources of the defender, oftentimes their web servers or electronic commerce systems. Brute force attacks also fall in this category, such as an attacker who repeatedly attempts to guess SSH passwords with little or no attempt to hide his activities.

In jurisdictions where cyber counter attacks (often referred to as "hacking back") is illegal, or in cases where it is difficult to rapidly attribute attackers, a frontal assault can be very effective. In some cases a defender may employ mitigation strategies, such as coordinating with Internet Service Providers to filter malicious traffic before it reaches the target, or acquiring additional resources to help absorb the attack. A last resort is to simply disconnect from the network. Failing these strategies, defenders are left to employ human-speed law enforcement or political means to counter a network-speed attack.

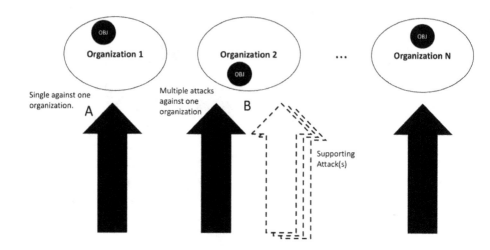

*Figure 6-4: Frontal Assault. The attacker attacks on a broad front, against one (A) or multiple organizations (B). In a well-defended network, a frontal assault often becomes a contest of human, network, processing, and storage resources.*

### Penetration

Rather than attacking on a broad front like a frontal assault, a penetration seeks to mass resources and penetrate defenses at one or a small number of spots (see Figure 6-5). The attacker doesn't necessarily go to great lengths to hide his activities or cover his tracks. Such a quasi-overt nature is seen with some Advanced Persistent Threat actors and often with government red teams and industry penetration testing teams. In the kinetic realm, it is impossible to miss a frontal assault and all but impossible to miss a penetration attempt. Ironically, in cyberspace operations, a frontal assault may even be missed by an inattentive defender ("Hey the network is running slow."). If the attack is covert, a penetration becomes an infiltration.

Network defenses may be hardened, but ultimately the goal of a network is to communicate. The two primary means for doing so are email and the World Wide Web, which also encompasses social media. Allowing communication requires that network administrators provide paths through their network perimeter, thereby leaving systems open to attack. While there are various systems designed to cover these avenues of approach and filter malicious email, attachments, and websites, such systems are imperfect.

Phishing[vi] is particularly powerful because it allows the targeting of specific individuals as well as large swaths of an organization. From the attacker's perspective phishing is a push technology in which the attacker takes direct action against a victim. The web is a pull technology, requiring users to visit compromised websites either by clicking links or through misplaced trust, as in a watering hole attack[vii] where an attacker subverts a legitimate website and causes it to inadvertently host malicious content. Most modern websites require that clients communicate with them through an encrypted HTTPS tunnel, which provides an advantage to the attacker because it often limits network defender's visibility on their users' online activities.[269]

Once the attacker gains an initial foothold on an internal system, the attacker will pivot through this initial node and maneuver toward his objective by attempting to compromise other systems within the network. As with other forms of maneuver, the attacker may not immediately create visible effects, but instead may simply maintain access until he can take advantage of it. For example, an attacker might gain control of many systems until he has amassed sufficient numbers to launch a DDOS attack.

You might consider a variant of the penetration as an asymmetric frontal assault. An attacker need not overwhelm all resources to be effective, but can target his force against a particular limitation and have, via interdependencies, an amplified effect. For example, an attacker may not seek to consume all available bandwidth or processing power of a server, but instead target memory allocation[270] or algorithmic weaknesses and force worst case scenarios.[271] Beyond just causing a server or device to crash, brute force attacks may cause systems to fail in ways that make the entire network more vulnerable, such as a logging server filling up and being unable to collect

---

[vi] Recall that a phishing attack is one in which an unsolicited email containing a malicious file or link to malicious website is sent to members of a target organization. If the recipient clicks on the file or link, their system may become compromised if host- or network-based defenses against the specific malware is not in place. A *spear phishing* attack targets specific individuals in an organization in order to not alert network defenders that an attack is underway. *Whaling* refers to specifically targeting senior executives or other high-ranking officials in an organization with phishing emails under the assumption that the potential reward for the attacker will be much greater.

[vii] Instead of directly targeting an organization, a watering hole attack targets web sites (and perhaps other services) that members of the target organization are likely to use, placing malware on those websites so that when members of the target organization visits those sites, they risk potential compromise. If the target organization has a very strong cyber defense, using this indirect approach is often much easier for the attacker.

forensic data, or a switch that turns into a simple hub when its CAM table[viii] is full.[272]

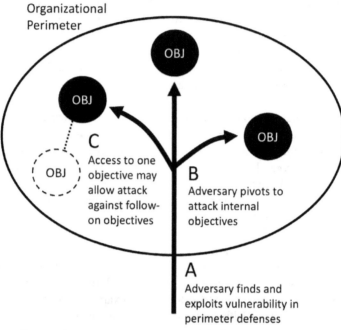

Organizational Perimeter

OBJ

OBJ

OBJ

C

OBJ

Access to one objective may allow attack against follow-on objectives

B

Adversary pivots to attack internal objectives

A

Adversary finds and exploits vulnerability in perimeter defenses

*Figure 6-5: Penetration. An attack on a narrow front (A) that is not of a covert nature and seeks to penetrate network defenses. Once inside the network perimeter, the attacker will pivot (B) and maneuver toward one or more objectives. Attackers may opportunistically exploit success by further pivoting toward other objectives (C).*

---

[viii] Switches, hubs, and CAM tables. Hubs and switches are network devices that connect computers on a local area network, or LAN. The difference between a hub and a switch is that when a computer communicates through a hub, the incoming traffic is transmitted to all other devices connected to the hub. A switch is a smarter device that uses a content addressable memory, or CAM, table to keep track of which device is connected to each individual switch port. The switch can then send incoming network traffic only to the specific destination device. This improves both efficiency and security, since other devices connected to the switch will not be able to eavesdrop on communications not intended for them. Some switches revert to hub functionality when they are overwhelmed with traffic and their CAM table fills up. Attackers can take advantage of this functionality to allow them to eavesdrop on traffic between network devices.

## Turning Movement

A turning movement[ix] avoids adversary defenses altogether and strikes in the rear area or along supply lines (see Figure 6-6). In the kinetic realm, such an attack would force defenders from the planned fighting positions, such as fox holes, and cause them to maneuver toward a foe in their rear area. In cyberspace operations, we see turning movements in the subversion of supply channels and attacks against systems the defender is dependent upon, especially critical infrastructure. These could include attacks against utilities like power generation, financial records, water supplies, and transportation. Note that physical proximity isn't required; objectives for the turning movement may even be thousands of miles away in their home garrison or even their home.

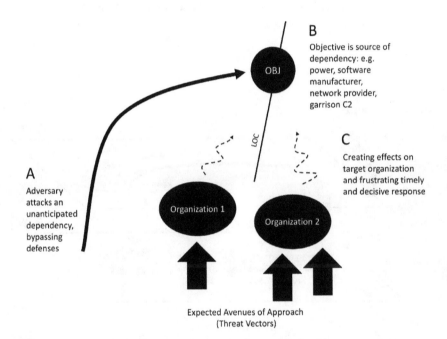

*Figure 6-6: Turning Movement. The attacker bypasses defender strength (A) and targets a source of dependency for the defender (B). Successfully depriving the target of needed resources will disrupt the defender and generate a disorganized response.*

---

[ix] Major General William Tecumseh Sherman's attack from Atlanta to Savannah during the American Civil War in late 1864 was a classic turning movement. The attack, deep in the Confederates' rear area, put pressure on Confederate General Robert E. Lee to defend Confederate territory and likely slowed reinforcements from joining Lee's forces in Virginia. Lee surrendered just a few months later in April 1865, after this and other devastating Confederate defeats.

## Multi-Domain Maneuver

One of the most important aspects of cyberspace operations is the interplay of the physical domains with cyberspace maneuver. Each of the major forms of maneuver that we just described can, and sometimes should, take place across multiple planes. See Figure 6-7 for an example of synchronized maneuver across cyberspace and the physical world. Attacks across multiple domains force the defender to defend in multiple dimensions. The defender's dilemma is further complicated by the limited visibility of cyberspace. A powerful aspect of multi-domain maneuver is that attackers can shift to the cyberspace domain to bypass physical obstacles and to the physical domain to bypass cyberspace obstacles (see Figure 6-8). An attacker might, for example, bypass the best network defenses by breaking into an adversary's data center and gaining physical access to target devices.

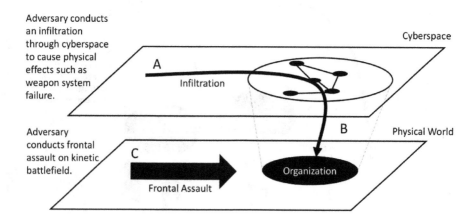

*Figure 6-7:* Each of the maneuvers we discussed may be executed alone or in synchronization across multiple operational domains. Here an attacker uses a cyberspace infiltration (A) to cause degrading effects in the physical world (B) while facilitating a land-based frontal assault (C).

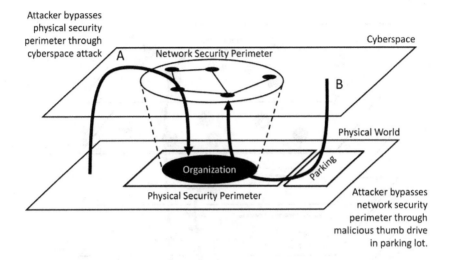

Attacker bypasses physical security perimeter through cyberspace attack

Cyberspace

A

Network Security Perimeter

B

Physical World

Organization

Parking

Physical Security Perimeter

Attacker bypasses network security perimeter through malicious thumb drive in parking lot.

*Figure 6-8: Adversaries may alternate between the physical and virtual domains to bypass strength. Here an attacker uses a cyberspace attack to bypass a strong physical security perimeter (A) or alternatively bypasses a strong network security perimeter through a physical domain attack (B).*

### Inter- and Intra-Plane Cyberspace Maneuver

Maneuver doesn't just take place across the domains of air, land, sea, space, and cyberspace; it also occurs across the planes of cyberspace itself. Figure 6-9 depicts examples of classical maneuver executed via cyberspace. However, there are many more nuanced approaches. Code itself, such as network worms, can maneuver and propagate to other network nodes based on their programming. Cloud hypervisors[x] can modify, move, delete, or restart virtual machines to frustrate attacks, or even create hardened attack platforms. Some malicious software can escape from a virtual machine and compromise the hypervisor below it. Malicious software can reach below the operating system and compromise the firmware or the Master Boot Record (MBR) of a hard drive. There are almost unlimited and quite technical examples, but the key idea is that maneuver takes place in cyberspace itself as the attacker and defender vie for a position of advantage.

---

[x] Advances in computing technology have created the ability to run computers and servers as virtual machines, where physical components such as processors and memory are replicated in software. Virtualization provides significant flexibility since computers can be created, copied, and destroyed almost instantaneously. A hypervisor is specialized operating system software on which virtual machines are run. Examples include VMWare's ESXi and the open source XenServer software.

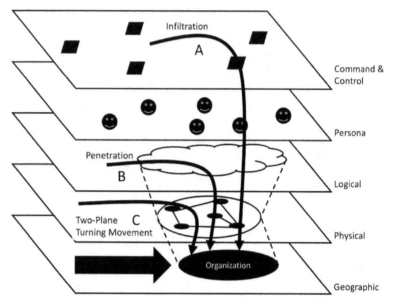

*Figure 6-9: Attackers and defenders—both human-driven and autonomous code-based—may maneuver up and down the cyberspace planes to bypass obstacles or create desired effects.*

*"Rapid and continuous [maneuver] multiplies the effect of an army, and at the same time neutralizes a great part of that of the enemy's, and is often sufficient to ensure success; but its effect will be quintupled if the marches be skillfully directed upon decisive strategic points of the zone of operations, where the severest blows to the enemy can be given."*
*- Jomini*[273]

### Characteristics of Cyber Maneuver[274]

Cyberspace isn't all just TCP/IP networks. We can maneuver through memory, inside weapon systems, through cloud-based architectures, through overlay networks, virtual worlds, SCADA systems, or in air gapped government enclaves. The previous examples hint at the some of the unique, as well as common properties of cyber maneuver. Here we will examine them further.

### *Virtual and Physical Maneuver*

We've discussed cyberspace maneuver at length, but let's take a closer look. Maneuver may take place virtually and physically, inside a system, in a datacenter, on a network, or pretty much anywhere else that cyberspace exists. Inside a system, code may move between various physical components, including physical storage, memory, and firmware and virtually through protection rings provided by the operating system and hardware. See Figure 6-10 for an example of protection rings found on many computing systems.

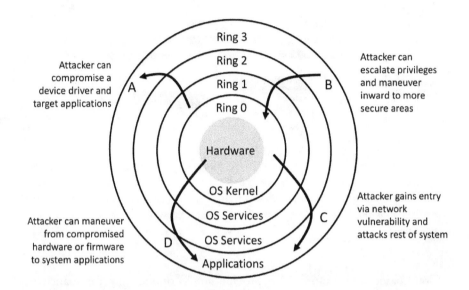

*Figure 6-10: Maneuver frequently occurs within systems. For example, the attacker might compromise a device driver in a wireless mouse and target applications (A), use privilege-escalation techniques to move to more secure areas of the system (B), exploit a network vulnerability and attack applications (C), or use a supply chain compromise to maneuver from hardware to system applications (D).*

On a network, maneuver can take place at any level. This is true for all seven layers of the OSI model, but also applies to networks in general. For clarity, here we'll use a simplified version of the OSI model (see Figure 6-11).[275] Note the virtual connections between the source and destination computers at the Application, Transport, and Network layers. Attackers and defenders may conduct maneuver through each of these virtual connections. For example, at the Transport layer, where network-aware services such as email and web servers reside at numbered locations called ports, the defender might dynamically shift the ports in use from the standard defaults. At the Network layer, an attacker may map and target specific IP address ranges, or at the Application layer, a defender might switch to a more secure browser. Attackers and defenders may also shift physical locations as well. For example, when the Republic of Georgia fell victim to cyber attack in 2008, they transferred critical services to servers hosted in the United States. On the electromagnetic spectrum, defenders may employ Frequency Hopping Spread Spectrum techniques to rapidly change frequencies to frustrate interception, one of many potential strategies.

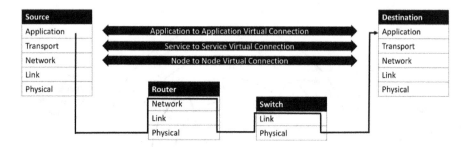

*Figure 6-11: Simplified version of a TCP/IP network. Communications descend through layers of the network stack on the source node, through intermediate routers and switches and back up through network stack layers at the destination, thus creating virtual application-to-application, service-to-service, and network node-to-network node connections.*

Cloud-based architectures also provide ample opportunity for maneuver. Many architectures are composed of multiple virtual machines orchestrated by a hypervisor. These machines may be started, stopped, rebooted, or recreated at will, and be connected in virtual and physical networks. One example of defensive maneuver is the temporary use of a virtual machine that is discarded after a desired period, at which point a duplicate system is started from a pristine master copy. So even if an attacker is successful in gaining a foothold on a given VM, his progress may be halted when the VM is discarded. Alternatively, attackers may try to escape from a virtual machine, or a sandboxing technology, and compromise the hypervisor or even the underlying hardware, see Figure 6-12.

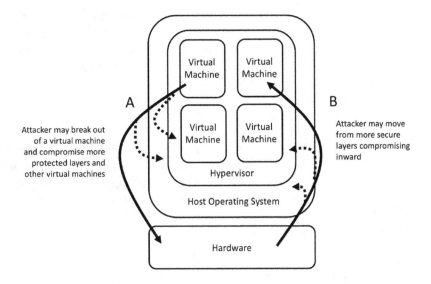

*Figure 6-12: Simplified virtual machine (VM) system, a core technology of cloud architectures. Attackers may break out of a virtual machine and move to attack more secure layers (A) or move from more secure layers compromising confidentiality, integrity, and availability of the host OS, hypervisor, or virtual machines.*

*In a blink, mayhem descended. Strange glitches emerged.*
*Stocks fell like rocks, only to shoot back up minutes later.*
*— Todd Frankel [276]*

### Agility

As we discussed in Chapter 3 - Laws of Physics, distance, speed, and time have unique characteristics in cyberspace. Here we consider the related concept of agility. We define *agility* as the ability to rapidly change one's direction and form of maneuver in response to changing conditions or enemy activity. When more than one human or machine entity are involved in a given operation, agility requires synchronization to weave a larger tapestry of operations. On the kinetic battlefield, agility may be constrained by human limits. An infantry soldier can only recall a limited number of maneuvers under the duress of combat, and can only move so fast on foot. But when humans and machines are combined into hybrid weapon systems—like a tank, drone, or fighter aircraft—humans are enhanced by the machine they employ. The interface between the human and the machine is of critical importance. The human pilot gives instructions to the machine, and the machine correspondingly reacts. The machine, the environment, and the adversary all provide feedback to the human, indicating the success or failure of these instructions. The human then responds with additional instructions. Better training for the human, increased capability of the machine, and improved interfacing between the two help hybrid man-machine systems increase their combined limits. With proper synchronization and cross-communication, this concept scales from individuals to teams to armies. These points are intimately linked to the OODA loop proposed by Colonel John Boyd, in which combatants must observe the situation, orient themselves, decide what to do, and then act. Each combatant seeks to cycle through this loop faster than her adversary. She who does this best gains the initiative and disrupts her enemy's mission accomplishment. The German use of speed and agility in their World War II *blitzkrieg* (lightning war) across Europe was devastating. German armored and motorized forces moved so far, so fast that they quickly outmaneuvered and disrupted their adversaries who were unable to respond to the attacks in time.

Another way to understand agility in cyber operations is found in the martial arts, where the concept of flow plays an important role. Through practice and experience, martial artists fight with decreasing levels of conscious thought, transitioning fluidly from technique to technique with economy and shattering impact. While the martial arts are limited by human frailties, cyber operations open up new vistas for flow and agility at network and machine speeds. As technology progresses and artificial intelligence evolves we expect machines to take more and more decision-making responsibility, freeing humans for other tasks. Humans will increasingly be removed from the decision-making loop and decision making in cyber combat will become increasingly automated.

We see glimpses of future combat with Wall Street's high frequency and algorithmic trading firms. The arena of combat for these firms is the complex system of financial markets. In this arena, contestants design bleeding-edge streamlined hardware, acquire the fastest and geographically closest data centers to trading computers, and create optimized algorithmic trading strategies.[277] Big money is at stake, and continuous innovation is the key to success. Cyber operations have equally high stakes, and innovation is similarly important.

### Anonymity and Invisibility
Maneuver is most effective when adversaries do not detect it. We should expect actors to take measures that hide their activities and mask their identity. A well-known anonymity tool is The Onion Router, or Tor, one of a number of anonymity networks that anonymizes users' online activities by passing communications through a network of volunteer-run intermediate nodes. Tor and other similar strategies are not perfect, but do provide

significant protection, especially from non-nation state resourced adversaries. Another class of tools is the anonymizing proxy that strips identifying information from communications and acts as a trusted man-in-the-middle.[xi,278] In addition to passing communications through an anonymity network, actors will likely seek to reduce the unique signatures of their tools, techniques, and tactics. Anonymity does not guarantee invisibility, but it lessens one's uniqueness and frustrates attribution and counterattack.[279] Encryption, especially encrypted tunnels like virtual private networks, or VPNs, reduce signatures of online activity and allow maneuver with a degree of cover and concealment. Similarly, the dark web, or more generally darknets,[xii] provides protection for those concerned about prying eyes, as do virtual worlds and online gaming environments, which allow communications inside closed ecosystems.

### Command and Control
Humans and code maneuver based on their own decision-making abilities, whether biological or algorithmic, and external guidance. Some forms of malicious software have their maneuver instructions embedded within them, such as network worms.[280] Others connect back to command and control servers for additional instructions. In most military organizations, humans make maneuver decisions based on their understanding of the current situation and their commander's intent. Depending on circumstances these maneuver decisions will be centralized, distributed among a team of cooperating actors, or autonomous. We'll cover these subjects in greater depth in Chapter 10 – Command and Control.

### Trafficability
Whether in the physical or virtual worlds, the trafficability of the terrain either enables or limits maneuver. Maneuvering across a network involves moving across a path of linked network nodes. The nodes may either be under your control and open to occupation or transit, defended by someone else and need to be compromised or bypassed to move further, or configured to automatically route traffic. The default behavior of these latter neutral nodes

---

[xi] A man-in-the-middle attack utilizes a system or operator who is placed logically between a network user and their communicating partners. Some offensive cyber operations seek to surreptitiously place a man-in-the-middle in network communications in order to eavesdrop on seemingly secure communications.
[xii] Darknets are networks that are hidden from most other Internet users by not participating in the global Domain Name Service architecture. They are used by organizations to communicate away from the prying eyes of other network users. The dark web is a collection of websites that are similarly not accessible on the open internet and are used widely by cyber criminals to sell illicit goods and services.

may support the movement you desire, or the nodes or the algorithms they employ may need to be subverted to allow the desired movement. Maneuver thus requires the ability to chain together a series of interconnected nodes that allow transit to your desired objective, overcoming any obstacles (typically by gaining access) along the way. This access (the cyber equivalent of gaining and holding ground) will be limited in time unless you have full control of the device. Ideally, a defender has physical access to systems she is defending. Physical access can always trump virtual activities. He who physically controls systems can reinstall system software, remove or replace hardware, or simply cut power or disconnect them from the network. Access isn't all or nothing; multiple parties, likely including the legitimate owner of the device, may share access. There are also degrees of access, such as limited user-level access or unconstrained root or administrative level access.[xiii] When attackers occupy new ground, they must make sure it is appropriately secure. To maintain access required for maneuver, attackers will seek to maintain persistence on each device, even patching the system to prevent subsequent takeover by other attackers. While the discussion thus far has considered nodes, the links themselves can also allow or limit desired maneuver. Constraints such as uncommon networking protocols or limited bandwidth are also possibilities that will slow or stop cyber maneuver.

### Maneuver and Effects
Maneuver is designed to place forces in a position of advantage over an adversary. Typically this means being in a position to collect information or create effects on a specific target, now or in the future. The ultimate goal in cyber conflict is to directly or indirectly create effects in the physical domains as well as the electromagnetic spectrum. Importantly, much maneuver on networks takes place between network nodes with routing of packets being handled by intermediary network devices like routers and switches. Each link between the nodes will effectively act as a portal from attacker to target with only a limited ability to affect the link itself. Additionally, traditional

---

[xiii] Administrator or root device accounts. Security best practices dictate that computer users only have system permissions that allow them to conduct activities consistent with their position or job. Standard users are normally able to run application software and create and access files in specific locations on a computer's file system, but are often not allowed to install software or change fundamental system configurations such as Internet addresses. This protects the system from malware that might try to make those changes on behalf of the user. System administrators have special accounts called "Administrator" accounts on Windows computers and "root" accounts on Unix and Linux computers, which allow full control of the computer. A cyber operator who gains unauthorized access to a user-level account will try to use that access to elevate their privileges on the system to that of an Administrator or root user in order to gain full access to the system.

maneuver allows weapon systems to mass their effects against a given target. Think of an armor battalion's tanks coming on line and firing at an enemy position. Massing of effects via maneuver takes on a different character and is likely to mean either blanket denial of service attacks or striking of multiple targets from a distributed group of attack machines.

## Mapping and Navigation

To maneuver most effectively, operators must have keen awareness of those around them, know where they are, and have a map to guide them. A key challenge is that cyberspace is constantly shifting and ripe for deceptive countermeasures, so while maneuver without a map is possible, an adequate map is almost essential for successful maneuver. Mapping, as we've discussed, can be passive or active. Passive mapping provides less resolution, but is much less likely to be detected. Active mapping provides greater visibility, but requires riskier active probing. Most attacks will begin with a reconnaissance phase to help collect this information. The purpose of network mapping is to develop high-quality intelligence products, including the construction of an Order of Battle (OB) database with location and system information for your area of operations. We'll discuss situational awareness (SA) and OB databases in much greater detail later in the book. Additionally, maneuver in the physical domains is highly dependent upon cyberspace-based technologies, such as the Global Positioning System (GPS) and friendly force (blue force) tracking systems, which will commonly be targets of attack in future conflict.[281] When considering mapping, we should remember that cyberspace isn't infinite, and that large portions could be mapped in advance of conflict (See Table 6-1).

*Table 6-1: Estimated size of cyberspace by plane.[282] The key idea is that while large, each of these layers can be enumerated, at least in part, by determined cyberspace actors.*

| Cyberspace Plane | Rough Order of Magnitude |
|---|---|
| **Command and Control** | Millions of human leaders, thousands of senior human leaders, billions of Internet users |
| **Persona** | Billions of accounts |
| **Virtual** | Billions of IPv4 addresses, millions of Internet routes, millions of domain names, more than a billion websites, trillions of Internet searches annually, exabytes of data, 2^128 IPv6 addresses (but most not in use) |
| **Physical** | Millions of routers, billions of cell phones, millions of servers |
| **Geographic** | Fixed at size of the Earth |

## Legal Authority

Cyberspace maneuver, especially between dispersed network nodes, will quickly cross regional and national borders, raising questions of legal authorities to operate in a given location. Care must be taken to ensure your maneuver and effects occur in areas where it is legal for you to operate. Consider a corporation that is victim to a cyber attack. The organization may engage in cyber maneuver, but only up to its legal limits, likely inside its own network only. When one moves beyond their organizational network borders, they will likely encounter commercial assets that won't be wholly owned or controlled by the government, military, or even the given nation's corporations.[283] Furthermore, third-party infrastructure may be damaged in the conduct of cyber maneuver and may cause legitimate claims of damage.[284]

## Channelization and Choke Points

On the kinetic battlefield, not all maneuver can occur on any type of terrain. Similarly, network communications are constrained to physical or logical paths that permit maneuver to varying degrees, either by design or happenstance. When the terrain forces maneuver or multiple information flows or activities into a given path or limited selection of paths, it is called channelization. We see channelization in transatlantic cables. When terrain forces maneuver through a single location, again either by design or nature, we call this a choke point. Choke points and channelization provide defenders key locations to intercept, modify, and block traffic. If this type of terrain doesn't exist already, defenders may create them. Attackers gain an advantage if they successfully bypass these heavily watched areas and attack via an unsuspected avenue of approach, including another cyberspace plane or operational domain. Attackers may also use encryption to mask their activities as they pass through or leverage the heavier traffic in these areas to blend-in, appearing as noise or legitimate traffic.

## Maneuver Control Measures

While maneuver may occur at the spur of the moment in exigent circumstances, coordinated maneuver is far more powerful. Militaries use maneuver control measures to increase efficiency and maximize the power of maneuver. One core concept is well-defined boundaries between units so that each unit knows where it has primary responsibility and autonomy. The boundaries are geographic and marked on maps. Firing weapons or moving into an adjacent unit's sector requires coordination or risks fratricide. Borders between sectors are best when tied to a visible terrain feature such as a road or river. So there won't be confusion, one unit or the other must be given clear responsibility for such features to be sure that it is included in one or the other unit's defensive plan.

Maneuver control measure concepts apply well to cyberspace operations, but should be extended beyond the geographic domains into the planes of cyberspace. As cyberspace operations evolve, we must be flexible in our thinking. Geographic boundaries still play a part, but other virtual boundaries are equally or more important. We see virtual maneuver control in the radio frequency spectrum as well, ranging from radio silence to Frequency Hopping Spread Spectrum (FHSS) where those communicating synchronize their maneuver across the electromagnetic spectrum in close coordination multiple times per second.

Laws, policies, and willingness to accept risk affect cyber maneuver control. In general, organizations should define clear boundaries across each of the planes to the extent possible, so personnel know where and when they can operate and whom they must coordinate with when crossing boundaries. These boundaries are cleaner and easier to define on networks one owns, but we cannot neglect offensive scenarios. Multiple organizations performing computer network operations on the same network node, for example, will cause significant problems. Maneuver control measures may, in the heat of battle, cause forces to lose momentum. Smart adversaries will exploit adversary maneuver control limits to their own advantage. We saw this during the Vietnam War, when enemy fighter pilots would escape across the border into the sanctuary of neighboring countries while U.S. policy forbade pursuit. We also see this today when actors strike U.S. corporations and the corporations are unable to strike back.

Maneuver control measures are only one part of the larger command and control of cyberspace operations and must be linked to fires coordination and proper threat identification. We'll cover these topics in greater depth in Chapter 9 – Fires and Effects, and Chapter 10 – Command and Control.

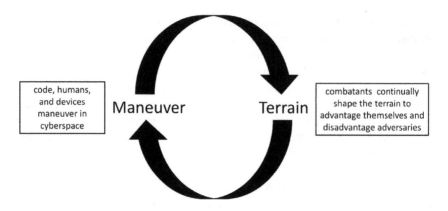

| code, humans, and devices maneuver in cyberspace | Maneuver | Terrain | combatants continually shape the terrain to advantage themselves and disadvantage adversaries |

*Figure 6-13: Combatants will use maneuver and shape cyber terrain in an attempt to gain advantage over the other in a continuous cycle at speeds that far outpace similar attempts in the physical world.*[285]

### Shaping Cyber Terrain

Cyberspace maneuver is deeply intertwined with shaping the terrain of cyberspace (see Figure 6-13). Even without offensive or defensive actors attempting to influence its behavior, the Internet, by design, is highly dynamic. The Internet and its constituent network paths constantly shift to alleviate traffic congestion, accommodate new routes, or to route around failure. It is possible to consider maneuver at a highly abstract level, such as autonomous code moving from machine to machine or an attacker sending commands to a remote machine via an interactive session, but these scenarios implicitly assume static terrain.[286] However, skilled attackers and defenders will seek to not just maneuver to a position of advantage, but shape the appropriate terrain, including emplacing obstacles, to their benefit.[287] In the physical world, soldiers quickly run out of time and energy to shape terrain, as anyone who has dug a fox hole or erected a pontoon bridge across a river knows. In cyberspace, the dynamics are different. We can instruct machines and code we control, or at least influence, to rapidly alter their structure. It is difficult to draw a crisp line between maneuver of code and shaping of terrain, as much of the substrate of cyberspace is code, but regardless, the interplay is important. In Table 6-2 we've provided examples of maneuver and shaping of terrain by cyberspace plane. As you examine the table, note that shaping cyberspace terrain doesn't only happen in cyberspace, a backhoe or a bomb can damage the physical devices that drive cyberspace too. We should also see that infrastructure need not be a fixed location. Network nodes can be on vehicles, planes, robots, or other devices that themselves move. Also consider the opposite: Cyberspace activities can also facilitate or degrade physical maneuver by compromising cyber-physical systems, like

114

the onboard computer of an aircraft, the locks on the doors of a building, or the traffic lights in a city. For those familiar with the U.S. Military's Continuum of Military Operations, we consider Phase 0 (Shape the Environment) as a different concept than shaping cyberspace. In kinetic military operations, Phase 0 focuses on activities that build and reinforce friendly relationships and alliances.[288] However, there are certainly strategic initiatives that an actor might take to shape cyber terrain, such as supporting a desired Internet standard.

*Table 6-2: Examples of Cyber Maneuver by Level of War and Cyberspace Plane*

|  | Tactical | Operational | Strategic[289] |
|---|---|---|---|
| **Command and Control** | Fast Flux DNS, activate weapon systems' autonomous modes | Call or send text messages to senior threat leaders | Switching to alternate governmental C2 network |
| **Persona** | Reset passwords for administrator accounts, establish honeypot social media accounts | Adopt new multi-factor authentication system for Enterprise | Impersonate a government leader on social or broadcast media |
| **Virtual** | ASLR, rapid patching of enterprise systems, direct malware into containment, adjusting firewall rules, rapidly adding new IDS signatures, TCP wrappers | Software Defined Networking, rapid patching of systems in theater of operations, enterprise wide network camouflage[290] | Rapid patching across government agencies, issue new governmental OS image, development of cloud-based war computers, moving servers to more robust infrastructure of another country.[291] |
| **Physical** | Movement of radio transmitters, FHSS | Employ new drone systems or system capabilities | Reissue of keying material |
| **Geographic** | Bridging an airgap network through physical means | Bomb theater communication centers to shape network usage | Establish a national cyber command center |

*"The portion of the theater of war from which an enemy can probably reach this front in two or three marches is called the front of operations."*
*-Jomini[292]*

### Operational Reach

Operational reach—how far an army can successfully employ military capabilities—is also an important consideration in cyberspace operations.[293] In the physical domain, as armies move farther from their supporting bases, they extend their lines of supply and ultimately reach a point where they can go no further for lack of fuel, ammunition, food, or other resources. In Jomini's time, he considered all forces that could reach the front lines in two to three days as being in the fight. On a network, we are looking at times as fast as two to three seconds. In cyberspace, operational reach depends on the interconnectivity of systems. For devices directly connected to the Internet, operational reach may extend around the world. In other situations, such as air-gapped networks, operational reach is more limited, reaching perhaps only as far as the home computers or mobile devices of users that have an air-gapped network at work. Operational reach may vary significantly with time. Virtual Private Networks may provide intermittent access, for example, when an employee works from home in the evenings. Cyberspace operational reach may be enhanced by physical operations, such as a drone that can be flown into position over a targeted site and relay wireless communications.[294] At the same time, operational reach may be limited by law, policy, or diplomatic constraints that limit the spectrum of tools, tactics, and procedures that one might employ. As in the physical world, obstacles may be used to limit operational reach, like a firewall which blocks external network connection attempts. Again, these obstacles may be bypassed via physical operations, such as covertly sneaking in a device onto the internal network that tunnels back to the outside to pass information or enable remote access.[295]

*"In traditional land combat, commanders typically think in terms of a flat battlefield.
Air force doctrine, as one might expect, defines both a horizontal and vertical
battlespace and views the air domain as an exposed flank of ground forces."*
- Jeff Becker and Todd Zwolensky [296]

## Offensive and Defensive Perspectives on Cyber Maneuver

Before we close the chapter we wanted to dive a little deeper into how
maneuver varies between offensive, defensive, and exploitive operations.

### Offensive Maneuver (CNA)

Offensive maneuver is designed to gain and hold terrain to enable making
contact with and destroying, degrading, disrupting, or otherwise defeating an
adversary. While surprise is beneficial, surprise isn't necessarily paramount.
Offensive cyber operations can often be conspicuous. Aggressors may not
care if they are identified, although ambiguity is usually preferred. Brute force
offensive maneuver may not require as extensive reconnaissance as
exploitative maneuver. Maneuver that requires fixing a defender's attention
could be done with weaker or less capable cyber forces as a small number of
operators, even a lone individual, can readily generate noisy attacks that
consume human time and attention.

### Exploitive Maneuver (CNE)[297]

Exploitive maneuver seeks to gain access to information and systems, hold
desired terrain for persistent access, identify weaknesses, perform
reconnaissance, and avoid detection and attribution. To be effective, such
activities are covert, and cyber operators on exploitation missions will seek
to leave no visible trace in system logs[xiv] and the minimum possible network
presence. Detection of activities and attribution of actors is highly
problematic for exploitive maneuver. While offensive maneuver is designed
to facilitate kinetic or cyberspace effects, exploitive maneuver seeks to avoid
observable effects.

There are commonalities between offensive and exploitive maneuver, such
as access. Access is the driving factor for exploitive and offensive maneuver.

---

[xiv] Most computing devices log various types of events for troubleshooting and
security incident response. Computers, servers, and network devices, such as
switches and routers, log many types of events, such as successful and failed login
attempts, privilege escalation, and hardware and software failure. These logs often
provide a trail of clues corresponding to system compromise, so skilled cyber
operators will take the time to edit these logs to hide their tracks.

Attackers will conserve their tools, weapons, accesses, and capabilities, using the least valuable first and seek to bypass or remove obstacles to enable their maneuver. Attackers will work to find an unwatched or overly trusted avenues of approach to serve as an attack vector.

### Defensive Maneuver (CND)

Defensive maneuver is designed to defend and hold desired terrain, while avoiding or limiting the success of offensive or exploitive activities, provide confidentiality, integrity, and availability of resources, and possibly position defenders to better initiate a counterstrike. Defenders may employ hunters who maneuver on their own networks to identify, observe, and root out adversaries. A network defender should have greater knowledge of their own networks and other cyberspace resources than their aggressor, although this may or may not be the case, depending on the maturity and professionalism of the organization. Defense in cyberspace without the ability to strike back, or even a credible deterrent, is more like siege warfare than maneuver warfare.

Defenders should shape terrain to reduce their attack surface and eliminate avenues of approach, channelizing adversaries and forcing them through observed choke points, and shunting them into containment areas or sand boxes if possible. They should leverage their dominant advantage of full physical and logical access to their own systems. Defenders will also emplace obstacles as necessary to constrain, divert, or prevent adversary maneuver. They will seek to observe attackers and shape the environment so that attackers disclosure their intent, objectives, and techniques, tactics and procedures—especially their advanced capabilities—while wasting attacker time and other resources.

We've provided examples of offensive and defensive cyber maneuver in Table 6-3.

*Table 6-3: Examples of Cyber Maneuver by Cyberspace Plane*

| Layers | Defense | Exploitation | Attack |
|---|---|---|---|
| **Command and Control** | Switch to use of human couriers | Employ (semi-) autonomous systems and code to limit need for remote C2 | Fast Flux DNS for Botnet C2 |
| **Persona** | Reissuing of passwords | Switching to false online personas | Switching to false online personas |
| **Virtual** | Address Space Layout Randomization (ASLR), Software Defined Networking, rapid patching, white listing, black listing, moving target defenses[298] | Maneuver through anonymity network, use of zero-day exploits | Maneuver through anonymity network, disable malware when inside a virtual machine, design malware to avoid AV detection |
| **Physical** | Movement of radio transmitters, FHSS, reissue of keying material | Wardriving, wardialing, shifting a satellite location in space | Wardriving, wardialing, shift a satellite location in space |
| **Geographic** | Institute tighter data center physical security, issue new identification cards to employees, move to Continuity of Operations (COOP) site | Activate trusted insider/spy | Bridging an airgap network through physical means |

*"Cyber maneuver dynamically modifies tactical network configuration, hosts and applications that is undetectable and unpredictable to potential enemies, but that is still manageable for network admins"*
*- John Keller [299]*

## Conclusions

Maneuver—the placing of forces into a position of advantage over an adversary—is a powerful strategy in both kinetic and cyberspace operations. Like placing chess pieces into key positions on a chessboard, maneuver in cyberspace allows a prepared attacker to execute a mission with speed and effectiveness that is difficult to counter. Defenders, too, can use maneuver to great effect, exploiting their intimate knowledge, full control, and physical access of the systems under their command to throw the attacker off balance.

The heart of maneuver is protecting and exploiting flanks. Cyberspace offers myriad flanks to consider, many known but some yet to be discovered. Defenses crumble when an attacker finds a new or weakly protected attack vector that approaches systems from unanticipated directions. Limited resources prevent defenders from covering each of these avenues of approach, while complexity ensures that no system's attack surface is entirely secure, even if patches are entirely up to date. When faced with a system that a given attacker is unable to bypass through technical means, the attacker can pivot and employ maneuver in the physical domains or the electromagnetic spectrum. Maneuver not only occurs in networks, but also across all the planes of cyberspace from command and control to personas, and even deep inside system memory, firmware, storage, and hardware.

Maneuver requires practice, training, and testing. Defenders must ensure continuity of operations as they put maneuver-based defenses in place. One mistake and the system could become inoperable to users or vulnerable to attackers. Attackers require intelligence to maximize the power of maneuver, and defenders employ intelligence to analyze most likely and most dangerous attack vectors to better allocate scarce defensive resources. Exploitive maneuver requires subtlety and guile; these attackers seek to avoid any visible effect while they collect information or seed malicious software into target systems. Offensive maneuver, while always benefiting from surprise, is at times noisy and destructive, creating a tension between offensive maneuver and exploitative maneuver objectives.

Cyberspace is far more dynamic than geographic terrain and is constantly shifting. Attackers and defenders will thus manipulate architectures, protocols, and configurations to their advantage. Thus, maneuver in cyberspace is very fluid and limited only by the imagination of the attacker or defender within the ultimate broad constraints of the laws of physics.

# 7 CAPABILITIES

*"Give a man an 0day and he'll have access for a day,*
*teach a man to phish and he'll have access for life."*
*- the grugq[300]*

Capabilities are the tools of cyber conflict. The term *capability* has a broad meaning. The U.S. Military defines a capability as "a device, computer program, or technique, including any combination of software, firmware, or hardware designed to have an effect in or through cyberspace."[301] Examples include the ability to compromise a specific type of computer system, encrypt a hard drive without the user's approval,[302] identify a specific type of malicious software, or overwhelm a web server with traffic through a Distributed Denial of Service Attack (DDOS) There are many other possibilities, even oddball things like inverting a user's display.[303] In some cases capabilities produce an obvious effect, either in cyberspace or the physical domain, however when the capability is designed for espionage or data exfiltration, visible effects are unwanted.

Capabilities are limited by one's imagination, technical feasibility, and the resources an actor has to invest in their creation. The employment of capabilities in practice is another matter. Whether a capability will be used in a given instance is impacted by legal constraints, ethical considerations, fear of attribution and retribution, bureaucratic infighting, and concern over leakage of the capability to others. Actors of all levels will stockpile vulnerabilities for the day they are needed. Capabilities may be stolen,[304] shared amongst collaborating actors, duplicated, or withheld by an actor to retain an advantage.

Some capabilities are weapons. Describing a capability as a weapon invites legal scrutiny, but may provide budgetary advantages in militaries that prioritize funding to weapon systems.[305] Capabilities often take the form of weaponized tools for offensive use, but may be dual use. A classic example is a penetration testing tool,[306] which can be used by defenders to test network security and by attackers to find weaknesses and break-in. Some capabilities aren't designed to be weapons, like full disk encryption applications, data backup software, secure messaging applications, remote surgery robots, weather satellites, and password hash cracking software. However, the distinction between a given capability being a weapon or a defensive tool can be subtle, often depending on the intent of the user and the context of the tool's use. There is an important distinction that what one does with access is separate from the method that one used to gain access, a distinction that penetration testers and cyber operators sometimes forget.

*my name's viktor, elite code scripter*
*from a soviet satellite that's cold in the winter*

*pack my own malware, write my own crypters*
*with more entropy than a mersenne twister*

*evade antivirus and ids filters*
*to leave the scene cleaner than mops and a swiffer*

*a few years ago our economy crashed*
*and the paper that we use is worth more than the cash*

*- Dual Core[307]*


**Capabilities as Commodity**

Capabilities are valuable commodities because of their scarcity, expertise required to create, and cost to develop. The value of a given capability isn't fixed however, and typically degrades over time. Capabilities are most valuable when they haven't yet been used and their existence is undisclosed. Once their existence is known, defenders can develop countermeasures that reduce or limit the capability's effectiveness and hence its value. Each use, even in a small scale way, increases the probability of discovery. The most prized capabilities are tightly controlled, lest their effectiveness become diluted.[308] Viable business models exist for those seeking to profit from the discovery and sale of capabilities, including the creation of markets that specialize in the selling of zero-day exploits.[309] Their value is a function of the security and market share of the target system, the exclusivity of the capability, and the potential benefit from controlling or employing the capability.[310] Some vulnerabilities may be discovered accidentally or deliberately through a concerted effort. Each passing day increases the likelihood that a vulnerability meant to be the target of a certain capability will be discovered and patched. Companies actively seek to remove vulnerabilities in their software, some running bug bounty programs to elicit support from a larger community, and issue patches that remove known weaknesses they are incentivized to fix. An existing patch does not render a capability useless; many individuals and organizations do a poor job of ensuring that their systems are patched within days or even weeks of patch release. An existing patch does, however, reduce the probability of a tool's effectiveness, and the longer the vulnerability is known, the less often a capability will be effective. Technology itself evolves, and even if a piece of targeted hardware or software isn't patched it could lose market share and become increasingly irrelevant, dramatically reducing the utility of a capability. Many capabilities' values approach zero due to age or disclosure. These capabilities might still be included in open source exploit toolsets and be used for educational purposes, regression testing, or against aging targets that still possess old weaknesses.[311]

## Vulnerability Discovery

Vulnerabilities are flaws or weaknesses in a system's design, implementation, operation, or management that could cause effects on a target.[312] Vulnerabilities provide the opening that allows the creation of offensive capabilities, or the requirement for defensive capabilities. Vulnerabilities aren't just resident in software. They are also in the firmware, network protocols, security procedures, human users, physical security, and just about any other aspect of the entire system.

There are many reasons for vulnerabilities, but there are several primary causes. Complexity is the bane of security. Many systems are so complex that they are far beyond the ability of a single human to comprehend and are certain to have flaws.[313] The Microsoft Windows operating system, for example, is estimated to contain approximately 50 million lines of code. In some cases the theoretical foundation may be sound, such as the mathematics underlying cryptographic systems, but the implementation may be flawed. Products are often rushed to market without adequate consideration of security, creating an apparently never-ending source of vulnerabilities. Lack of secure coding practices is another reason, leaving the door open for buffer overflow,[i] SQL injection,[ii] cross site scripting,[iii] and other exploitation tactics. Legacy systems are yet another source of unpatched vulnerabilities and legacy technologies, like dated cryptographic protocols, may still be resident in modern systems to allow interoperability.[314]

An important aspect of vulnerabilities is that some exist if a technology is to be used it all. Consider a web server. A web server exists to communicate with web browsers. If many web browsers visit the server at one time, sooner or later the webserver will become overwhelmed, slow down, and possibly crash. Normally, web servers have far more capacity than required for day-to-day use, but a malicious actor could deliberately send a great deal of traffic in an attempt to crash the server. This denial of service attack is difficult to mitigate, particularly if the attack comes from many different locations. Taking the web server offline isn't a solution, because the server exists to handle web page requests from many different locations. The situation largely degrades to one of bandwidth and processing power of the target versus that available to the attacker. While DDOS mitigation techniques and commercial services are available to help reduce illegitimate traffic to the server, attackers may respond with asymmetric techniques that more efficiently consume resources on the server with less network traffic.[315] Sometimes the server can be caused to crash with even a single malformed

---

[i] A *buffer overflow* is a vulnerability in which a program does not check user input to make sure that it will fit into the memory buffer that the program has reserved for it. For example, a tax preparation program may ask for your first and last name, and reserve memory space for 50 characters for each. If a user enters more than 50 characters and the inputs are not corrected (perhaps truncated), the buffer can overflow into portions of memory that is supposed to contain other data, or even program instructions. Sometimes the result is that the program crashes; sometimes the program behaves in unanticipated ways. Buffer overflows can often be leveraged by attackers to make a program behave in a way that is not intended, and can actually benefit the attacker, perhaps by giving control of a system or access to data that they would normally not be able to access.

[ii] *SQL Injection* is a vulnerability in web sites that interact with a database. The majority of modern websites display data from a database. Consider shopping websites, news websites, and social media, which are all backed by small or large databases. If a web page has a user input field, such as a search field, that interacts with the database and the user input is not properly filtered, a malicious individual might be able to enter SQL, or 'simple query language' statements into the input field and have them interpreted by the database to display content that the attacker is not supposed to be able to see, such as user account information or credit card numbers stored in the database.

[iii] *Cross Site Scripting* is another web-based attack. Most modern web pages rely on various types of scripting, such as JavaScript, to display their content. An attacker can sometimes cause a web server to cause the attacker's script to execute in other site-visitors' browsers for malicious purposes.

packet or request.

Those seeking to discover vulnerabilities will try to create a condition that system designers never envisioned. They will try to force an application to process input that will cause it to fail, either because of the input's contents, size, frequency, or burstiness. Attackers will explore edge cases and otherwise poke and prod systems in ways the designers didn't intend, and are frequently successful. Oftentimes, the failure of a system is not the fault of the creator, but is due to idiosyncrasies of the programming language that was used to develop the application, or the compiler that translated the programmer's commands into an executable program. The failure could also be caused by the operating system on which an application is running. Even if it were possible to create completely error-free application code, a system could still be vulnerable due to an insecure operating system or human intervention.

Depending on the discoverer, some vulnerabilities are made public immediately. Others go through a responsible disclosure process where the individual who discovers the vulnerability gives the manufacturer an opportunity to patch the system before news is made public. An unknown number are kept secret, bought and sold, and quietly stockpiled.[316]

How attackers prioritize their vulnerability research is driven by their objectives. An online criminal group will target systems being used to process money, such as popular end user operating systems, ATMs, and point of sale terminals (the modern equivalent of cash registers). The market-share of a given technology is often a driving factor. When studying the number of known vulnerabilities for a given operating system or web browser, it may appear that one is more *secure* than another, but a more likely case is that one is more *popular* than another, attracting additional attacker attention. A nation-state adversary may care about popular systems, but they may also prioritize their efforts against obscure systems used by their targets, with the canonical example being the Siemens systems used to control nuclear centrifuges.[317]

To discover vulnerabilities, the attacker probes the attack surface of the system. The attack surface is the exposure of reachable and exploitable vulnerabilities, and exists across the cyberspace planes and the physical domains.[318] With enough effort, the attacker can usually find a weakness. Such probing may occur in a one-to-many fashion with a threat actor scanning large portions of the Internet, be sector-specific like recent cyber-attacks that leveraged vulnerabilities in software used for international inter-bank money transfers,[319] or be highly specific and very quiet like Stuxnet.

Figure 7-1 illustrates this concept. Probing is also constrained by the attacker's resources and their fear of attribution and retribution. The time available to the attacker is a key aspect of their search for vulnerabilities. Some attackers, like a penetration testing team, have only a short period to discover vulnerabilities, while nation-state aggressors may have months or years of time to allow persistent, long-term probing, waiting for that one mistake.

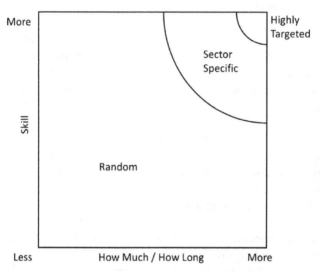

*Figure 7-1: Comparison of attacker skill and resources against targets.*

## Capability Development

Every actor in cyberspace has some intrinsic ability to perform cyberspace operations, but actors vary significantly in sophistication, capacity, and desired impact. Even end users and their computers might be used as part of a larger effort, such as a hacktivist group's recruiting of supporters to employ its DDOS tool, or a criminal group using compromised home machines to send spam.[320] However, there are three basic tiers of actors. At the lower tier are those that can employ capabilities developed by others, for example, leveraging tools found in an open source exploit toolkit or an easily acquired DDOS tool. More advanced are those that can discover new vulnerabilities and create capabilities around them, such as vulnerability researchers who find vulnerabilities in existing systems or software and can write the necessary code to exploit those vulnerabilities. At the top are actors who can create vulnerabilities by subverting the software or hardware design, development, and supply chain.[321] This latter category typically consists of actors at the nation-state level.

Capability development is both an art and science. There is no single surefire way to find vulnerabilities and then weaponize them. However, there are traditional techniques. In source code reviews experts look for vulnerabilities in the original human readable source code that are often due to insecure coding practices.[322] Fuzzing uses automation to send malformed input to software, operating systems, and networks seeking vulnerabilities.[323] Reverse engineering[iv] is another powerful approach and involves disassembling hardware, software, and firmware looking for weaknesses.[324] Some vulnerabilities are even advertised in the press or go viral on social media.[325] In many cases, identical hardware may be purchased on second hand markets, such as online auctions, to facilitate vulnerability discovery.[326]

Creating capabilities at the right time, at the right place, and at the right level of sophistication and usability is a function of an actor's agility and resources. Some capabilities are inexpensive, for example, the defensive measure of putting opaque tape over the web camera on a laptop. Other capabilities are very time consuming and expensive to develop. Costs can be lowered by reusing components of existing capabilities, possibly acquired from publicly available exploits, and just modifying them for a new use. Reusing components comes at the cost of increased likelihood of detection and attribution.[327]

Some vulnerabilities are fleeting windows of opportunity. Actors may be pressed with an operational requirement to develop a capability rapidly, such as a red team finding a vulnerability during the course of a penetration test. Whether an actor is able to develop a capability in time depends on their knowledge, skill, and importantly, their agility. An organization such as a

---

[iv] Programs are represented in a computer's memory in binary, or machine code, as a series of zeros and ones that are interpreted by the computer's processor when the program is executed. Machine code is the lowest level of programming languages. A step up from there is human-readable assembly code, a mapping of machine code to basic operations, such as adding two values or moving data from one place in memory to another. While assembly language is human-readable, it is extremely tedious and time-consuming to write code in. High-level languages, such as C, C++, Fortran, and others, are much easier to write and to later read and modify, but programs written in these languages must be processed by a program called a compiler, that converts the code into machine code. This conversion is not completely standardized across compilers, so the same program converted by different compilers is likely to result in different machine code. By understanding how compilers convert a particular high-level language to machine code, an attacker can take advantage of loopholes that the programmer doesn't even know exists to find vulnerabilities.

nation's intelligence agency might require such a tedious process to approve the use of a given tool they may often not be able to react in time. Their OODA loop just doesn't turn fast enough. However, an empowered, autonomous and perhaps extralegal actor might find and employ a workable solution in time for it to be effective. The requirement for agility suggests having capability developers resident on the operational team in question. Face-to-face coordination and a first-person awareness of the problem aids efficiency. Reachback[v] support to offsite resources is a slower, but potentially equally effective strategy, particularly if there is an appropriately skilled team member forward who understands the operational challenge and can clearly and accurately describe the problem to the reachback team.

Forward teams may be in austere conditions and possess limited resources, while reachback teams reside in established facilities and have greater resources at their disposal. Reachback team responsiveness is proportional to how many other forward-deployed elements they are supporting and their work ethic, despite being farther from the fight. A classic example of the reachback approach was the support received by the Apollo 13 crew during their ill-fated mission. The mission control team tapped exceptional resources and provided instructions to craft the necessary solution out of the severely limited parts available on the spacecraft, saving the day. In the context of cyber conflict, the passing of information from a reachback team could easily involve the passing of code-based solutions and designs for building items forward, sometimes described as *expeditionary making*.[328]

Other capabilities require long, tedious, and expensive efforts to develop. For nation-state actors, success or failure in the development of capabilities is often tied to the efficiency and effectiveness of their defense acquisition processes. There are also companies that focus on developing and supplying digital weaponry that are potentially very agile compared to traditional defense acquisition mechanisms.[329] See Figure 7-2 for an overview of capability development and employment.

---

[v] *Reachback* refers to a forward deployed element's ability to call on units in the rear area to develop intelligence or create tools for use during the deployed unit's mission. A reachback team is an organization, often a military intelligence unit, in a rear area that directly supports a unit deployed to a combat area, and reachback can also be leveraged in cyberspace operations. A cyber operations element that is conducting an on-site penetration test of an organization's network might rely on a team at the penetration tester's headquarters that is better staffed and equipped to develop particular types of capabilities.

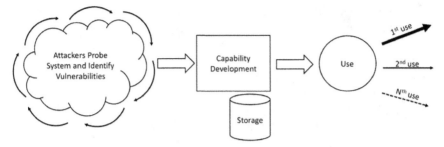

*Figure 7-2: Capability development process. Attackers probe a system and identify vulnerabilities which are then weaponized and turned into capabilities. Capabilities are then stored and employed, with their utility degrading over time and usage. Both vulnerability discovery and capability development may be performed in-house or outsourced to third-parties.*

## Characteristic of Capabilities

Each capability has different characteristics that inform when and how it should be used.[330] These characteristics fall into three major categories: operational, technical, and administrative as depicted in Table 7-1. As you examine each, consider that you could further subdivide each category and add details and metrics tailored to your operational context. You will see that cyber capabilities are far more complex and probabilistic than simply firing a bullet at a target. This can be particularly difficult to understand for some kinetic military leaders who would like to be able to leverage cyber capabilities, such as senior military officials who are accustomed to applying the straightforward effects of rifles and artillery.

*Table 7-1: Each capability has operational, technical, and administrative characteristics that inform how and when the capability should be employed. Advanced actors will likely maintain databases of these or similar characteristics to better manage their capabilities.*

| Operational | Technical | Administrative |
|---|---|---|
| - Effects | - Communications | - Cost |
| - Targeting | requirements | - Supplier |
| - Command and | - Access requirements | - Estimated lifespan |
| Control | - Environmental | - Usage history |
| - Risk assessment | requirements | - Legal authorities |
| - Intelligence | - Propagation | - Prevalence |
| requirements | - Speed and efficiency | - Training and |
| | | certification |

## Operational Characteristics

The Operational category includes attributes that explain employment of the capability in an operational context.

*Effects:* What does the capability actually do and what effects will it have? This category lays out the physical and virtual effects the capability is designed to cause as well as an analysis of potential unintended effects and collateral damage, including an assessment of severity. Effects include destruction, degradation, deception, access to sensitive information, corruption of data, and myriad others.[331] We'll discuss effects in greater detail later in Chapter 9: Fires and Effects.

*Targeting:* What targets does the capability work against? A capability may be effective against a wide range of targets, such as any computer running a Windows operating system, or it may be effective against only a very precise type of technology with a specific operating system software version, processor chip, and patch level.

*Command and Control:* Does the capability afford or require remote instructions once it has been put into use? Can it be given instructions to produce effects at some designated time in the future or under a certain set of conditions?[332] There is a tension between command and control and autonomy. The autonomy of a capability refers to the degree of required human oversight. The most autonomous capabilities have logical behavior embedded in them and allow no further updates or command and control instructions once initiated. Once launched, the internal logic determines the path the capability will take. One such completely autonomous program that exploited an operating system weakness was the Morris Worm,[vi] which wreaked havoc on the Internet in 1988. The program's vast spread was unanticipated by the creator, but once it started to propagate, there was no way for him to stop it. Greater autonomy lowers the risk of discovery via command and control communications, but increases the risk that a flaw in the logic will have unintended outcomes. Importantly, command and control can't be guaranteed. Unlike other weapons, cyber payloads sometimes can be intercepted and redirected back onto their original owners.

---

[vi] A *worm* is a malicious program that is self-propagating. Worms are designed to infect a system, create one or more copies of themselves, and go on to infect other systems, with a typical goal of infecting as many systems as possible. Many worm programs contain logic that seeks out passwords and other sensitive data on systems and sends the collected information back to the worm writer.

*Risk Assessment:* Use of a capability always incurs some degree of risk. There is detection risk. Is the capability likely to be discovered? Are there known signatures that defenders might exploit to detect the capability? Does the capability exhibit behavior that is likely to draw attention from humans or machine behavioral intrusion detection systems? There is disclosure risk. Many capabilities, if discovered, may be used with or without modification by the discoverer. The capability may be hardened with encryption to help prevent such secondary use. An example is that of the Gauss malware, whose payload is heavily encrypted and believed to be tied to the exact specifications of an as yet unknown target system.[333] An actor must understand the reliability of a capability. Capabilities do no always function 100% of the time. As we've discussed, most capabilities assume the existence of specific vulnerabilities on a target system that might have been discovered and patched before the capability is deployed. How likely is it that the capability to do what it purports to do? Has it been tested sufficiently? There is also the risk of countermeasures. How can the capability be defeated? What is the likelihood of countermeasures being employed? Failure to conduct a thorough risk assessment invites negative consequences, both for the actor who deployed the capability, and those who depend on the successful execution of the cyber operation.

*Intelligence Requirements:* Each capability requires a certain set of circumstances for its effective use. What questions must be answered, and to what depth, before an actor can employ a capability with confidence?

### Technical
Each capability has technical specifications and requirements that actors should understand to be most effective.

*Communications Requirements:* Some capabilities require communications to facilitate command and control, receive updates, probe systems, and pass information back and forth, such as passing code for advanced capabilities inward to the target system or exfiltration of desired data. The frequency and volume with which the capability communicates, and via what path, heavily influences the chance of discovery, particularly by watchful targets. Some communications are encrypted, decreasing the chance of others learning exactly what information was passed, but is likely still susceptible to traffic and metadata analysis.[vii,334] The integrity of the communications channel is

---

[vii] *Metadata analysis:* metadata is data that can be used to describe other data. An example is network traffic analysis, in which Internet connections between computers and other connected devices can provide information about whom a certain individual is communicating with, even if the content of the communication is encrypted or otherwise unreadable.

also of critical importance. If the adversary can subvert the information flows they can hijack a system or transmit deceptive materials.[335]

*Access Requirements:* Some capabilities can be executed remotely over a network, while others may require local or physical access. Some may require a degree of privileged access to the target or an intermediate system, such as a local user account, a superuser account, or a trusted inside accomplice.

*Environmental Requirements:* Many capabilities require a specific minimum bandwidth, processor, memory capacity, operating system, or electric power sources in order to be deployed. The size of the capability, whether it is the dimensions of a physical device or the number of bytes in a block of code, impacts whether the capability will be discovered. Smaller capabilities are easier and faster to transmit and reduce the likelihood of detection. If the capability involves a physical object, what are its dimensions and will it function using battery power (and if so for how long). If code-based, how large are the components in bytes and lines of code?[336] Are there hardware and software interdependencies required to make the capability work? What language(s) were used to create the capability?

*Propagation:* How does the capability propagate from one system to another? What is the expected growth and decay of its propagation? If responsive to command and control, is it possible to stop, slow, or increase the spread of the capability? Can its target lists be updated?

*Speed and Efficiency:* The efficiency of a capability is how fast it performs its mission. More efficient capabilities afford opportunity to be used at a large scale, for example, scanning a large network.[337] Intuitively, very fast capabilities, particularly malicious code that runs on target systems, quickly performing an action and then deleting itself, are less likely to be discovered. Alternatively, depending on the use case, capabilities may be designed to operate very slowly so that the network traffic they create is hidden among routine network traffic over long periods of time. Very fast, but resource intensive, capabilities might slow down the target system noticeably, so a slower approach may be desirable. These examples assume an adversary is trying to avoid detection. If detection doesn't matter, for example in open cyber conflict, more efficient capabilities support agile operations, which can help to gain the initiative.

**Administrative**
Capabilities do not exist in an operational or technical vacuum. Administrative characteristics help the operator understand the cost of using a capability and any policy or legal constraints.

*Cost:* Capabilities are not typically free. Understanding the cost to create the capability will help determine when and where it should be used. Cost is an important point that is misunderstood by new cyber operators. A zero-day vulnerability might cost a million dollars or more to procure or develop. Nevertheless, some might not understand why it probably isn't prudent to use one in a relative low-stakes cyber operation. Making sure operators and their leaders understand the basic economics of building and buying capabilities will help them make wise choices.

*Supplier:* Who developed the capability? Are they available for confidential technical support and capability modification?

*Estimated Lifespan:* The projected shelf-life of the capability before it becomes obsolete. When was the capability developed and when does the actor expect it to become outmoded?

*Usage History:* To perform a better risk analysis, particularly for a valuable or rare capability, actors should track when and how they have used the capability in the past.

*Legal authorities:* Is the capability approved for use, and are there conditions related to its use? May the capability be used for training, even if it isn't legal to use in live operations?[338]

*Prevalence:* Is the capability prevalent in the wild, is it one-of-a-kind, or is it somewhere in between?

*Training and Certification Requirements:* How difficult is the capability to use? How long does it take to gain proficiency? Is there a manual? Where is training available? What are the qualification or certification requirements required by the actor before the tool can be used operationally?

**Capability Taxonomy**
Capabilities come in many different shapes and sizes, from offensive to defensive, software to firmware to hardware, and exist at any cyberspace plane. Table 7-2 provides examples and a look at the range of different types of capabilities. As with all things cyber, capability creation is truly only limited by the creativity of the participants. The future will provide even more

opportunity, and we should think beyond the traditional network security model. At a recent security conference we attended, one of our colleagues suggested that even hearing aids might be targets of compromise. These devices could be placed under control of the attacker and at the attacker's discretion provide normal hearing, the hearing of false things, or nothing at all.[339] As another example, recently security researchers developed a capability that provided long-distance control of more than one million vulnerable automobiles. Potential capabilities are everywhere and researchers have been able to find exploitable vulnerabilities under virtually any rock they look.

*Table 7-2 — Representative Examples of Capabilities by Cyberspace Plane[340]*

| Plane | Examples | Effect |
|---|---|---|
| Command and Control | botnet C2 informant | Software application that serves as a general purpose botnet client, used to gain information on command and control protocols to aid in dismantling a botnet.[341] |
| Persona | password cracker | Performs brute force remote online cracking against HTTP (Basic Authentication, HTTP (HTML Form/CGI) POP3 and Telnet.)[342] |
| | vetted persona | This is a persona of an attractive 25-year old "cyber threat analyst" on social media site X that has been active for three years and has 750+ friends.[343] |
| Virtual | ransomware | Customizable ransomware application, employs AES encryption to lock down files on target system and leaves tailored text file on target desktop with desired demands.[344] |
| | threat emulation[345] | This toolkit provides system profiling, multiple attack packages, spear phishing, covert communications, and beaconing options. |
| | metadata scanner | Scans an organizational website, extracts office suite document and image metadata, and provides supporting analytic tools.[346] |
| | buffer over-read | Allows collection of information, which under normal operation, would be protected under SSL/TLS encryption.[347] |

| | | |
|---|---|---|
| | packet analyzer | General purpose network packet analyzer, capable of parsing most transport layer protocols.[348] |
| | network worm | Customizable network worm that can be configured with desired payload and propagation rate, requires companion exploit capable of compromising desired target system(s).[349] |
| | network tap | Allows passive collection of 10/100 Mbps Ethernet traffic once inserted inline with a network cable.- |
| | malware persistence detection | Utility to analyze common malware persistence mechanisms on different operating systems. Checks startup folder, as well as Run and RunOnce registry keys, among numerous other locations.[351] |
| | firmware rewriter | Rewrites Company X's mobile device firmware to bypass PIN authentication.[352] |
| Physical | ATM skimmer | ATM keypad overlay for X, Y, and Z ATM models that records and stores PIN entries.[353] |
| | cell phone surveillance | Remotely activates the camera and microphone on a Brand X cell phone and smart watch without user permission or knowledge.[354] |
| | full disk encryption | Performs full disk encryption of most commodity hard drives using the AES algorithm.[355] |
| | remote GFCI failure | Causes failure of Ground Fault Circuit Interrupter (GFCI) electric protection devices from a distance of 10 feet.[356] |
| | GPS jammer | Jams reception of most models of GPS receivers from a distance of 100 feet.[357] |
| | directed energy weapon | High Energy Radio Frequency (HERF) device that remotely destroys electronic circuits from a distance of 20 feet.[358] |
| | GPS spoofer[359] | Allows transmission of arbitrary GPS location to target GPS receiver from a distance of 100 |

| | | feet.[360] |
|---|---|---|
| | wireless access point spoofer | Allows man-in-the-middle (MITM) attacks against modern WiFi protocols.[361] |
| Geographic | vehicle tracker | Once installed, tracks location of vehicle and driving history, and can be configured to alert third parties when the vehicle crosses geographic boundaries and speed thresholds.[362] |

## Case Study: A Cyber Capability Rifle

Let's study an example of employing capabilities on the tactical battlefield using a cyber capability rifle (CCR), see Figure 7-3. The concept and prototype of a CCR was created by a group of researchers at the Army Cyber Institute at West Point.[363] The device resembled a rifle, included an antenna, a small onboard computer, and power supply.

The researchers demonstrated the use of the CCR by "shooting down" a small commercial drone by wirelessly transmitting a known exploit which caused the drone to shut off and fall to the ground. In another proof of concept demonstration they used the CCR to compromise a wireless access point and open an electronic lock in a mock military compound from over a mile away. While the form-factor in this case is a rifle, the idea generalizes well and could easily adapted to many shapes, from a ball to a vest to a larger device on a vehicle. Their idea is a powerful one.

*Figure 7-3: Prototype cyber capability rifle, which uses an antenna, power supply, and onboard computer with one or more software capabilities. (Image: Brent Chapman, Matt Hutchison and Erick Waage.)*

As militaries work to integrate cyber capabilities on the battlefield, mobile and easy to use devices are critical. Some platforms will be laptop computers, tablets, and smart phones, but some will take other shapes like the CCR. The key to the CCR is that it contains both a set of capabilities and the technical means to deliver them. These capabilities could be developed on the front lines, but are more likely to be developed farther back from the front and pushed forward electronically. Like all capabilities, the more frequent the use, the more likely adversaries will develop a countermeasure, creating a continual game of one-upmanship that is common across cyber operations and information security. If forward teams require specific hardware-based capabilities, they could fabricate what they need based on their own skill or from plans pushed forward from other experts in the rear. For example, a team might need to fabricate a new type of antenna for the CCR for a different frequency range. Teams must therefore deploy with tactical *making kits*, including a tools and supplies, which they could supplement with local acquisitions, creativity, and if need be, shipments from the rear.[364]

With further development, the CCR could move from a proof of concept to a formally supported family of tactical cyberspace and electronic warfare components. The rifle format could include interchangeable antennas and a laser range finder, and be used for direction finding, eavesdropping via a laser microphone, and even emergency communications. The primary point of highlighting this idea isn't the rifle, the opening of an electronic lock in a mock compound, or the drone takedown. It is the people. Our takeaway is that in an era of uncertain times, ill-defined problems, and adaptive asymmetric adversaries, it is the skilled and empowered individual who will take an operational need and rapidly prototype a solution. Developing people is a clear differentiator. Put more effort into growing people and less emphasis on buying stuff.

*"Vulnerability disclosure is the price of attacking a target."*
*— decius*[365]

**Employment**
Capabilities reside at the tense intersection of offense, defense, and exploitation. For example, an actor may wish to subvert security update mechanisms of software to achieve some objective, but once the technique becomes known a global population of users will disable software updates making the entire ecosystem less secure.[366] One strategy for managing this tension is referred to as NOBUS, or nobody but us, a term used to describe situations in which an actor may decide that they have a sufficient technical

advantage to create a capability with the belief that they will be the only one to discover and weaponize it. Such a situation will make the actor far less likely to make the corresponding vulnerability known to others so that they can develop countermeasures.[367] A given NOBUS decision may or may not be correct. In addition, creators of hardware and software are in a particularly powerful position as they have the ability to design exploitable vulnerabilities into their products, and possess critical knowledge about how to subvert their own security. Actors, such as law enforcement agencies or even criminal groups, might coerce companies into assisting in the creation of capabilities.[368]

As decius indicated in the above quote, using a cyberspace capability often provides a blueprint for others to emulate it.[369] After you use an exploit, expect copycats to emerge, and even expect that their evolved, and perhaps mutated, capability may equal or exceed your own.[370] Some capabilities might be so powerful that they would only be employed in the face of an existential threat and require extensive and time-consuming approvals before use. Others may be dangerous, but clean up after themselves in an attempt to limit proliferation of the technology. Each use brings a greater chance of countermeasures. Other capabilities are low-cost or free, and relatively innocuous.

We must give careful thought to allocations of capabilities inside government and military organizations. Expect bureaucratic infighting and hoarding of capabilities as organizations jockey for supremacy. Possession and subsequent restrictive control of a powerful capability provides not just operational power, but power in the scrabble for budgets and career advancement that occurs in bureaucracies. Organizations will maintain secrecy and may demean other organizations by only sharing trivial capabilities under the guise of being a team player. At the same time, some actors will share dangerous capabilities not fully understanding their societal impact and the chilling effect proliferation will have on the democracies they seek to protect, such as the Stingray device now used by law enforcement and criminal groups to intercept cellular phone calls.

Cyber capabilities will not always be used in isolation, but will often be woven into a combined cyberspace and kinetic operation and buttressed by kinetic capabilities and effects. To better guarantee success, testing, training, certification, and rehearsals are key. Some capabilities can be reduced to a simple playbook of options that can be used by untrained personnel, but others require expert operators who can use, modify, and adapt their tools to increase their probability of success. Placing emphasis on better trained and educated forces is paramount to understanding the capabilities one has, adapting to operational necessities, anticipating the capabilities adversaries have, and finding new capabilities in the highly competitive global arena of cyber operations. We'll cover more on the employment of capabilities in Chapter 9 – Fires and Effects.

## Conclusions

There are no secure computers, and a solution seems far out of reach. Capabilities, and the vulnerabilities and exploits they depend on, are not going away any time soon. The arms race for advanced capabilities will continue as defenders perpetually lag slightly behind, aided by inefficient acquisition processes, misaligned business incentives, and poor prioritization of security by senior leaders. The builders of IT systems require the vulnerability discovery, capability development, and hacker ecosystems to keep them honest, otherwise they will lack appropriate incentives to improve security.

Actors will continue to build arsenals of capabilities, some cutting-edge and rare, others older and well known, depending on the resources and expertise they have available. While finding vulnerabilities and creating capabilities is not easy, we should never underestimate the ingenuity of less resourced actors. Every actor will develop their own capability management strategies to make the most effective use of their capabilities. In particular, we envision established actors maintaining databases of operational, technical, and administrative characteristics of capability arsenals to organize their efforts. There are many known capabilities in the public information security space and more in the classified arsenals of cyberspace actors, but the well is deep and many more capabilities will be discovered as time progresses.

# 8 INTELLIGENCE

*"If I always appear prepared, it is because before entering on an undertaking,*
*I have meditated for long and foreseen what may occur."*
*– Napoleon Bonaparte*

Timely and accurate intelligence is critical to cyberspace operations, particularly when organizations must defend their networks and devices against nation-state adversaries. Intelligence provides an understanding of threats, adversaries, and the environment that inform offensive and defensive operations. Intelligence is enabled by collection systems that facilitate understating of the cyber, physical and human terrain. The intelligence process collects raw data, and through a process of machine and human filtering, synthesis, and analysis seeks to provide actionable information at the right point in time to drive decision making. The intelligence process is iterative and each cycle helps build and refine reconnaissance and surveillance plans that improve subsequent results. Intelligence collection, however, isn't easy. No actor has perfect intelligence, but those adept at performing intelligence planning and collection, processing and exploitation, analysis and production, and finally integration and dissemination have a distinct advantage. Figure 8-1 visually depicts how data is refined into intelligence. The field of intelligence is deep and rich, many books have been written on the subject.[371] In this chapter we focus on key essentials of the discipline and how to best apply them to cyber operations.[i]

---

[i] There are mixed feelings about *threat intelligence* and what it means within the information security community. Some feel that the term is overused, and misunderstandings abound regarding what true intelligence is. Perhaps others have been burned by paying for a threat intelligence feed that consisted of

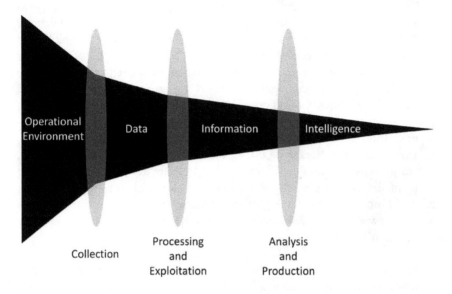

*Figure 8-1: The Intelligence process collects data from the operational environment and through processing and analysis refines the data into intelligence to drive operations.*[372]

## Types of Intelligence

There are many types of intelligence. Designed to be complementary, each intelligence sub-discipline draws upon differing collection methods and sources of information. Human Intelligence (HUMINT) uses spies to collect information from other humans, as well as to gather information requiring access that would be difficult or impossible to acquire through technical means. HUMINT specialists conduct debriefings and interrogations in addition to analyzing patterns and trends of human activity. Signals Intelligence (SIGINT) collects and analyzes information broadcast through the EM spectrum and, since the advent of computer networks, information both at rest on computers systems and in transit via computer communications. Communications Intelligence (COMINT), Electronic Intelligence (ELINT), and Foreign Instrumentation Signals Intelligence (FISINT) are SIGINT sub-disciplines and collect information on

---

unprocessed threat data and was not helpful to their network defense. We would argue that a list of IP address of known threat actors, domain names of botnet C2 servers, and malware signatures are not, in themselves, threat intelligence. These elements fall directly into the data component of Figure 8-1 and cannot be considered intelligence until processed and analyzed in conjunction with other data elements and the context of the network being defended.

communications, radars, and telemetry, respectively. Imagery Intelligence (IMINT) uses sensors to collect and analyze imagery of activities and regions of interest around the world. Measurement and Signature Intelligence (MASINT) collects and studies electronic, acoustic, nuclear, chemical, and biological signatures, such as the sound made by a certain type of vehicle or the specific type of emissions by a radio transmitter. Technical Intelligence (TECHINT) is intelligence gathered from the study of threat equipment, systems, and materiel. Counterintelligence (CI) is the discipline of identifying and countering the intelligence collection efforts of other actors. Open Source Intelligence (OSINT) collects and analyzes publicly available information. Many years ago OSINT was the domain of newspapers, books, and magazines, but has quickly migrated to Internet news sources, blogs, and social media sites. Ironically, where once a country might send a spy to risk life and limb to acquire certain information, say by climbing a fence to peek inside a new adversary tank, there is an overabundance of information freely available, or lightly protected, on the Internet.

There are overlaps between disciplines listed here, but each discipline is mutually supporting and designed to provide a holistic view of adversary, or potential adversary, activities, capabilities, and intents.[373] The intelligence discipline includes an all-source intelligence category for those who specialize not in any one area, but fuse and analyze intelligence from many different sources. While intelligence is used for a broad range of operations, each discipline may be leveraged to support cyber operations at the tactical, operational, and strategic levels. See Table 8-1 for more information about the intelligence disciplines.

*Table 8-1: Major types of intelligence applied to cyber-related activities at the tactical, operational and strategic levels.*

| | Strategic | Operational | Tactical |
|---|---|---|---|
| **SIGINT** | Analyzing the telecommunication networks of an adversary nation. Compromising a server and downloading a database of 22 million background investigation files required for a security clearance. | Collecting telemetry from an adversary drone system. | Collecting WiFi transmissions at a local cyber café or business facility. Performing radio direction finding of a transmitter. |
| **HUMINT** | Using a prostitute to compromise a senior government official. Recruiting spies inside a government facility. Infiltrating a security firm and stealing a secret signing key to support future operations. | Infiltrating a regional insurgent group tied to cyber operations capabilities. | Collecting documents found at a target's home. Installing a keystroke logger on a laptop when target is out of a hotel room. |
| **IMINT** | Satellite imagery collection of a national government facility of interest. | Airborne imagery collection and subsequent analysis of parts shipments from a chip manufacturing factory. | Analyzing photographs taken of employee badges. |
| **CI** | Performing polygraph exams for senior leaders with access to sensitive information. | Investigating adversary collection attempts against an enterprise. Developing enterprise intelligence threat assessments. | Providing counter-threat briefings to personnel travelling to a conference abroad. Scanning a workplace for surveillance devices. |
| **OSINT** | Downloading all webpages and documents from a military organization's website. Performing social media sentiment analysis of a target nation. | Monitoring forums of regional threat actor groups. | Performing open-source recon of a target on websites, blogs, and social media sites prior to initiating a penetration test. |

**Intelligence Tasks**

An essential purpose of intelligence is to inform decision-making for current and future operations. Intelligence supports military operations, business operations, and intelligence collection efforts. To accomplish these objectives we must tightly integrate intelligence into operations and planning. These objectives break down into four major tasks: support situational understanding, conduct intelligence collection, support operational responsiveness, and provide intelligence support for cyber effects.[374] Intelligence and enterprise intelligence feeds into systems that provide a common operating picture (COP) for security analysts, operators, and decision makers. A COP could be as simple as a shared map updated in a headquarters, or as complex as a networked situational awareness tool that draws from shared distributed databases of friendly and threat activity and provides tailored near real time visualizations for the individual all the way up to national leaders. Situational understanding includes feeding intelligence to personnel, helps protect the enterprise, and is supported by the conduct of Intelligence Preparation of the Battlefield (IPB – a topic we will explore later in this chapter), to understand potential adversary courses of action and to inform friendly decisions.

Intelligence collection employs selection and exploitation of available intelligence feeds and prioritizes answering unmet intelligence requirements using any other resources you might have available, or can construct or acquire. Support to operational responsiveness builds pictures of current and potential threat actors, monitors indicators and warnings (I&W) for important adversary actions, and helps conduct planning for future offense and defense. Intelligence support for cyberspace operations provides the detailed intelligence required to provide physical and virtual effects through cyberspace missions.

**Intelligence Process**

The intelligence process cannot occur in a vacuum, but must be closely integrated into day-to-day operations and future planning. The many consumers of intelligence depend on it, and speaking from experience, will not hesitate to complain if they aren't satisfied. Focusing the intelligence process requires guidance from leaders on what information they need, and when. We can visualize intelligence activities as a five step process: Planning and Direction, Collection, Processing and Exploitation, Analysis and Production, and Dissemination and Integration, with continuous evaluation and feedback throughout, see Figure 8-2.

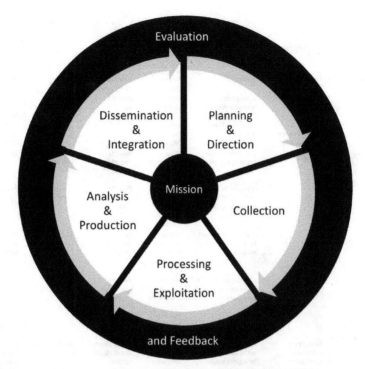

*Figure 8-2: Intelligence Process.*[375] *The Intelligence Process is iterative and breaks the cyber intelligence mission down into manageable steps.*[376]

### Planning and Direction

The intelligence process begins with guidance from senior leaders and a clear understanding of what leaders wish to achieve. Next comes designing collection plans, desired intelligence products, and intelligence architectures to accomplish your objectives. At the high level these objectives may be to keep leaders and the right teams informed, gain a detailed understanding of the threat environment, counter adversary deception and surprise, support friendly deception initiatives, defeat adversary intelligence efforts, and assess the effectiveness of your operations.[377] At this step, it is critical to define and prioritize the specific information requirements, that is, the questions that must be answered. It is here also that you start tasking any organic intelligence collection assets you might have, requesting assistance from others, and acquiring commercial, open source, or governmental intelligence feeds. Table 8-2 represents a collection plan that brings these concepts together.

*Table 8-2: Cybersecurity Focused Collection Plan*[378]

| Priority | Intelligence Requirement | Indicators[379] | Areas of Interest | Agencies to be Employed | Data Sources | Desired Reports |
|---|---|---|---|---|---|---|
| 1 | Where and when has the Enterprise network perimeter been compromised? | a. Suspicious hardware devices being brought into building or found plugged into network. | Office spaces near entrance, wiring closets, data center | Physical Security Group | Security gate guards, all employees | Daily report to Security Operations Center, Weekly report to Chief of Staff |
| | | b. Reports of spear phishing against employees | Senior leader email accounts | Security Operations Center | All employees, IT staff | As needed |
| | | c. Reports of slow or malfunctioning computer systems | Developer, R&D, and senior leader machines | Security Operations Center | All employees, IT staff | As needed |
| | | d. High severity alert for critical system on network IDS | Systems containing critical organization data | Security Operations Center | SEIM | Immediate notification of CISO |
| | | e. Suspicious activity on internal network honeypots | Pivoting through honeynet to R&D, Personnel, and Finance systems. | Security Operations Center | Honeynet administrators | As needed |
| 2 | What threat actors are considering operations against the enterprise? | a. Increased negative social media chatter by activist groups about enterprise. | Twitter, LinkedIn, other sites as appropriate | Public affairs and strategic comms groups. | Twitter, 4chan, other social media sites as appropriate | Daily reports of negative social media to Chief of Staff & CSO |
| | | b. Threats made by activist groups | Credible threats made to personnel | All personnel | Any | Immediately inform senior leadership |
| | | c. Detailed scanning and downloading of enterprise website from overseas location. | Network DMZ | Security Operations Center | Firewall, IDS logs, SIEM system | Daily report by Security Operations Center to CIO |
| | | d. Reports of social engineering attempts against employees | IT help desk, system admins | Security Operations Center | Self-reported | Immediate reporting through supervisor to Security Operations Center. |
| | | e. Attacks against similar enterprises | Peer companies X, Y, and Z | Security Operations Center | STIX/TAXii reporting system, ISAC, personal relationships | Immediate reporting to Security Operations Center |

We've only given representative examples, but you could expand each section as needed and tailor the plan to your specific environment. You may also consider adding other fields such as specific attack vectors/avenues of approach, specific time windows, identifying specific areas of interest (like a given server) and breaking down intelligence requests into finer grain sub-requests. What is important is that you tie together prioritized information requirements with the associated indicators, responsible parties, data sources and reporting mechanisms. The collection plan will also help identify intelligence gaps, such as unwatched avenues of approach, and requirements that necessitate new sources of information. The collection plan is a living document. Each cycle through the intelligence process is an opportunity to improve the plan and keep it current.

### *Collection*

The Collection step is where sensors capture samples of the operational environment. Sources of intelligence may be human or machine-based, organic, or third-party. Most individual sensors can only sample small portions of the operational environment.[380] We want to maximize what we do have available, ensuring to cover the most important information requirements and attack vectors first, and selectively invest in new sensors and data sources to fill gaps. If you've worked through the collection plan process you'll have an organized strategy for assigning and placing your sensors. Collection managers can dynamically reassign their collectors based on information quality and emerging needs.

Collectors, whether machine or human, must be placed at the appropriate location (physical or virtual) in the operational environment. Such placement is driven by the intelligence team's best estimate on which samples of the operational environment will be of the highest value in answering their intelligence requirements. Key places include monitoring avenues of approach (or attack vectors) you might use to reach your target, or that an adversary might use to reach you. Table 8-3 provides a summary of some potential sources of cyber-threat related data.

*Table 8-3: Representative cyber intelligence data sources. There are many sources available, some in-house and others third-party.*[381]

| Source | Example |
|---|---|
| **Network-based** | IDS log, AV log, firewall log, proxy server, NetFlow data, full packet inspection, full packet capture, web server, syslog, database server, SNMP, VPN server, web security gateway, authentication server, fraud analytics systems, honeynet, email server, application server, DNS lookups, network mapping tools, router logs, WiFi logs |
| **Host-based** | IDS log, AV log, Windows event log, operating system logs, application logs, web browsing history, email archives, file system data, system memory |
| **Third-Party** | IP geolocation database, commercial and open source threat intelligence feeds, information sharing collaborations, satellites, social media APIs |
| **Physical** | Facility entrance/exit logs, asset management databases, friendly force tracking systems, reports from human security teams, Internet of Things devices, CCTV security cameras, web cameras, microphones, vibration sensors, employee records, radar, sonar, drone-based sensors, license plate readers, space-based sensors, undersea sensors |

There are limits to the reach of intelligence. Some information will be inaccessible and the team must work to gain the required access. Once you gain access and the desired data begins to flow, the associated sources and methods must be carefully protected to avoid a compromise that will shut down the flow, embarrass the organization, or worse yet, become a source of threat deception efforts.

When analyzing collection systems, whether the system is one you control, or one you pay for access to, it is worth the time and effort to understand the end-to-end flow of the data from sensor to processing and beyond. You should also evaluate the timeliness of the information flow and the sampling rate. People often use the terms "real time" and "continuous monitoring" pretty loosely. In cyber conflict, seconds may matter. The throughput and upstream filtering capabilities of the system also matter. If you collect too much data, your human analysts and machine processors can become overwhelmed. The system should allow you to craft filtering mechanisms to ease the burden, similar to filters you can create for a Security Information Event Management (SIEM) system. You will also want to examine how to best balance the flow of data, such as what is pushed to you and what you need to pull, and how to best define the scope of your efforts. Also consider whether the sensors are active or passive. If they are active, such as a tool that scans portions of the Internet, then there will be traces left behind. If the sensors are passive, for example a network tap, then the activity will be harder to discover.

As intelligence personnel collect information, they will encounter *intelligence gain/loss* decisions, where they must decide whether the potential for gathering worthwhile information is worth the cost of continuing a specific intelligence operation. For example, an organization may discover that an adversary has gained unauthorized access to their network, and might attempt to observe the adversary's activities instead of immediately evicting them from the network. This decision is based not only on the value of the information that could be gained, but also on the level of confidence that one can observe the adversary without the adversary burrowing so deep into the network that they can't remove them later. It is best if organizations develop, in advance, a process for making these determinations routinely rather than responding in an ad hoc fashion in the heat of an attack.

Collection of intelligence has many legal implications. For example, there are strict limits on the information the U.S. Government can collect in its Title 10 (Military), Title 18 (Law Enforcement), and Title 50 (Intelligence) roles.[ii] Private companies and individual citizens face similar limitations. When thinking of performing collection operations, get your lawyers involved early and often.

While the U.S. government draws a clear distinction between military, intelligence, and law enforcement roles, missions, and legal authorities, there is a tension between these fields. For example, engaging in offensive military operations may severely impact intelligence collection while prioritizing intelligence operations over military operations may limit military options. It is important that we do not conflate offensive and defensive military operations with law enforcement efforts and intelligence collection activities. Additionally, legal constraints may vary dramatically across the spectrum of potential actors. For example, terrorist, criminal, or hacktivist groups likely care very little about law, policy, and legal authorities surrounding their intelligence gathering.

---

[ii] These refer to sections of the Code of Laws of the United States of America, usually shortened to U.S. Code. This document codifies the federal statutes of United States Law. Title 10 describes the organization and appropriate application of the armed forces, Title 18 refers to crimes and criminal procedure, and Title 50 covers national security, intelligence and espionage activities.

### Processing and Exploitation

For those with technical experience, the concept of Processing and Exploitation should come easily. Here the raw collected data is converted into formats that can be better digested by automated processing systems, human analysts, and other intelligence consumers. The step includes such tasks as data cleansing, sanitization, correlation, decryption, and normalization, and may include filtering and media translation. As with most forms of cyberspace intelligence, processing and exploitation is often automated to maximize throughput and minimize delay. One thing that is difficult to automate at present, however, is sophisticated language translation. To be effective, intelligence teams must have capable linguists skilled at translating threat actor languages and who possess a deep understanding of the foreign culture. Even more valuable are those that understand the adversary's language and culture *and* who understand technology and the technical jargon of any specific sub-cultures, such as a malicious hacker group.[382] It is difficult to find linguists with these additional skillsets and it can be even more difficult to maintain these skills.

When one designs processing and exploitation systems it is important to consider how much data to collect. The ideal scenario is to collect everything possible, but this often isn't realistic due to cost, storage, compute, or bandwidth limitations. We recommend carefully considering the use-cases you envision and working backward to the most appropriate data sources. It is also useful to consider where processing should take place. In some cases it may make sense to process data in situ, in a remote data center, or using a cloud-based service.

### Analysis and Production

During the Analysis and Production step the analysts and automated systems aggregate, analyze, and fuse the refined data coming from Processing and Exploitation. Here they try to create the larger picture from individual puzzle pieces, answer specific requests for information, and generate intelligence reports on a variety of subjects. In warfare, the U.S. military uses variants of the Intelligence Preparation of the Battlefield step-by-step analysis methodology to do much of their combat-focused analytic work.

There are many different types of cyber intelligence products.[383] Here are examples:

- Warning Intelligence – High priority, time-sensitive reporting to warn enterprises and leaders about imminent threats. As we've learned from terrorist threat reporting, however, care must be taken to strike the right balance between an overabundance of caution and a truly credible threat before raising an alert.

- Current Intelligence – Time-sensitive intelligence reporting in support of an ongoing operation. In enterprise defense scenarios we extend this idea to include routine intelligence reports to those charged with defending the network and information infrastructure.
- General Intelligence – Longer term and less time sensitive intelligence reporting on threat actors and their capabilities. For example, reporting on an APT threat group.
- Target Intelligence – Specific, detailed intelligence on a given target. Target intelligence is a critical component of successful attacks in cyber operations.
- Scientific and Technical Intelligence – Intelligence derived from scientific research and technological advances. This could include known vulnerabilities and results of vulnerability discovery efforts.
- Counterintelligence – Intelligence on adversary intelligence collection efforts. Can be used for workforce hardening and education as well as efforts to disrupt threat collection efforts.
- Estimative Intelligence – Forecasts and predictions about future events and actor capabilities.
- Identity Intelligence – The fusion of identity attributes to de-anonymize individuals and groups, determine key activity patterns, and assimilate biographical, behavioral, and physical details about individuals, to include biometric data.

Intelligence analysis is as much art as science. Analysts must make assumptions based on both available facts and instincts, and be willing to accept risk in their analyses. Intelligence analysts also face the challenge of analytic biases, including the tendency to see what one wants to see in the data.[384] As big data systems become increasingly viable, expect that biased human analysis will start giving way to machine algorithms, which will include biases of their own.

### Dissemination and Integration
Dissemination is the process of distributing intelligence products to the right people at the right time. The "right people" could include those in your own organization, partners, or the general public.[385] Classifying documents at varying degrees of sensitivity (high, medium, and low; or Top Secret, Secret, and Unclassified) helps organizations determine what products personnel can share with whom without compromising sources and methods. With dissemination comes risk, but risk you must accept if you've done your due diligence.[386] There is risk that your analysis is wrong. There is a risk that the information will leak. There is risk that you will get someone killed, certainly

in military operations, but also in business threat intelligence reports that finger threat actors and embarrass their benefactors. There are liability concerns with sharing information. Your operators and intelligence team could also face backlash by the public and personal threats from adversaries. Intelligence is sensitive business and it must be taken seriously.

Standardized reporting formats help aid the consumption of intelligence products by your customers, as well as by intelligence and operational processing systems. We also recommend building appropriately accessible archives of the reports, including databases and protected websites, so that consumers can answer many of their own questions without draining the available time of the intelligence team.[387] The caveat here is that if your system is compromised, your user-friendly approach will make it easier for your adversary too.

Integration is arguably the most critical part of the intelligence process. It is only through integration of your intelligence products, and ideally some of your personnel, into the operational mission, that intelligence becomes relevant. Relevance drives future budgets, too. Intelligence must be trusted or you risk failure of your overall intelligence efforts. Intelligence should be fed into the Common Operating Picture[iii] (COP) systems that customers use to conduct their day-to-day operations, whether business, military, or government. The goal is to generate enough accurate samples from the operational environment through the intelligence process to provide an accurate and timely view of the current situation, help predict future threat actions, and drive friendly decision making.

It may sound like common sense, but you would be surprised how many organizations do not provide intelligence to those tasked with actually defending the network. It helps to create an operations center where threat intelligence, IT staff, and cyber operators work side-by-side. We've seen an example of such integration in the Department of Homeland Security's National Cybersecurity and Communications Integration Center (NCCIC).[388]

---

[iii] A common operating picture is a command and control mechanism provided by interactive systems that is used to visualize friendly and (projected) enemy for information and intelligence for maneuver forces. This concept is described in detail in Chapter 10, Command and Control.

*Evaluation and Feedback* – An enterprise engine that generates intelligence is great, but the intelligence may or may not be of actual value. Throughout the intelligence process those producing intelligence should self-assess their results and gather candid feedback from their consumers. Qualitative and quantitative measurement of results is the goal. You should be asking hard questions of yourself, or if you are a consumer, your intelligence provider.

- Was the intelligence anticipatory and timely, or was it too, little too late?
- Was the intelligence accurate or did it quickly lose your trust?
- Was the intelligence in a usable machine or human format?
- Were there gaps in the intelligence or did it paint as clear a picture as possible?
- Was the intelligence relevant and tailored to your needs?
- Was it skewed by bias or was it objective?
- Did your provider keep the intelligence confidential, as appropriate?
- Did the provider flood you with lots of raw data masquerading as refined intelligence?
- Ultimately, did the intelligence meet enough of these attributes of excellence to be actionable?[389]

By addressing the above questions, you can create desired metrics for success, and evolve and optimize your collection efforts.[390]

The U.S. military uses a straightforward ranking system to evaluate intelligence, and this system can be useful in cyber threat intelligence scenarios. In this system, depicted in Table 8.4, the analyst evaluates the accuracy of a given piece of information and the overall reliability of the source over time. For example, an intelligence tip from a shady intelligence source, but one that is confirmed by other sources, would be rated as C1. This system can be used to weigh the relative reliability of competing information, or determine the likelihood of accuracy of individual data elements.

*Table 8-4: System for evaluating intelligence. Cyber threat analysts can tag individual pieces of information for accuracy and develop overall metrics for a given source's reliability.*[391]

| Reliability of a Source | Accuracy of Information |
|---|---|
| A = Completely reliable | 1 = Confirmed by other sources |
| B = Usually reliable | 2 = Probably true |
| C = Fairly reliable | 3 = Possibly true |
| D = Not usually reliable | 4 = Doubtfully true |
| E = Unreliable | 5 = Improbable |
| F = Reliability cannot be judged | 6 = Truth cannot be judged |

## Counterintelligence

We've just walked through the steps of the intelligence process. Do not forget your adversaries are doing the same for their own intelligence efforts, and you are a likely target. Counterintelligence is your tool to degrade their efforts at each step of their process. Consider Table 8-5.

*Table 8-5: Applying counterintelligence principles to frustrate adversary cyber intelligence collection*

| Step | Countermeasures |
|------|-----------------|
| **Planning and Direction** | Disrupt adversary communication networks, insert spoofed leader guidance, employ jamming |
| **Collection** | Educate and harden your workforce against adversary intelligence efforts, provide organizational reporting mechanisms to identify and aggregate suspicious events, disable sensors, insert spoofed sensors, bypass sensors, reduce information leakage via-TEMPEST and OPSEC, harden physical security perimeter, conduct background checks on personnel, reduce BYOD risks, use trusted couriers, avoid social media, avoid Internet use, avoid mobile device use, use in-house versus "free" online analysis tools and proxies, prohibit public display of workplace badges, provide strong physical access control to sensitive areas, employ point-to-point communication lines or VPNs |
| **Processing and Exploitation** | Flood system with alert triggering activities, create ruses, employ encryption, codes, and obscure languages, use isolated cells to prevent linking activities, create obfuscated code |
| **Analysis and Production** | Compromise adversary intelligence analysts, create deception plans that lead adversary analysts to incorrect conclusions, employ fake personas, create a disinformation campaign, use anti-reverse engineering techniques,[i] use false online banners for network services, use intermediaries and dead drops |
| **Dissemination and Integration** | Insert noise into social media intelligence feeds, create false alarms, create and share fake intelligence products, dispute true reports, employ online trolls, discredit authors, sue authors, threaten authors |

As you examine the table note that defeating adversary intelligence collection efforts requires a mixture of common sense, a trusted, educated and aware workforce, OPSEC, deception and a healthy dose of justifiable paranoia. Like all of intelligence, counter-intelligence applications to cyber operations is a rich area worthy of in-depth study.[392]

## Essential Tools and Techniques

The intelligence and information security communities possess many robust tools and techniques that apply well to cyber threat analysis. In this section we've taken what we believe are some of the best and adapted them as necessary to cyber operations.

*Threat Briefings* – It sounds simple, but to be relevant cyber intelligence teams need to work to develop effective threat briefings, both high-level for senior leaders and more detailed versions for others. Operators and enablers will frequently ask for cyber threat briefings. These briefings are valuable tools to share the results of intelligence analysis, build trust, validate analyses, and gain insight into other scenarios and factors that the intelligence team did not fully consider. Always be sure to take into account the background and experience of your audience when preparing a briefing, as they won't have had the same experiences and may not share your mental models or perceived priorities. You should work to educate your audience, but remember you can learn as much from them as they from you. Another key is to understand your audience's appetite for technical detail, abstracting technical details to the extent required and explaining technical specifics lucidly when necessary. Developing threat briefing skills in your intelligence team is important. We believe every analyst should have the ability to translate technical information for non-technical audiences, but for important engagements like briefing the Board of Directors, send in your best translator. Sometimes this isn't the most technically adept member of your team, but someone who has credibility on both sides of the fence, can speak the language of military operations (or business) and has the credentials respected by the audience, whether this is a Harvard MBA, a Yale Law Degree, or a Ranger Tab. Operators and leaders don't just want to hear about problems that have been revealed by the intelligence process. They want actionable intelligence, key insights, and recommended solutions.

*Intelligence Databases* – Another fundamental tool is the intelligence database. Intelligence is about the collection, processing, analysis and dissemination of large amounts of information. As you read this chapter you will see a number of useful cyber intelligence database strategies, such as creating databases of threat actors and their capabilities, high-payoff target lists[393] you may wish to attack or defend, relationship databases between actors, and numerous others. With these databases in place you have the foundation for automated processing and the development of cyber threat intelligence analytics, automated responses, and increasingly, AI-based command and control. Of course, such databases are critical assets that must be heavily defended.

*"Traffic analysis, not cryptanalysis, is the backbone of communications intelligence."*
*- Susan Landau and Whitfield Diffie*

**Traffic Analysis**[394] – Traffic analysis is the study of communication metadata to provide intelligence. If you consider a typical communication, such as a letter, phone call, or network packet, there are two primary components: the actual content of the communication and the metadata which is the related addressing, processing, and contextual information surrounding the transmission and receipt of the message. Metadata includes data elements like IP addresses, timestamps and message duration, phone numbers, user account names, message size, message priority, radio frequency, operating system version, use of encryption, physical locations, signal strength, protocols used, checksums, message fragmentation, browser version, browser plug-ins, and web pages visited, among others.[395] While it is common practice to encrypt the content of communications and protect the message from prying eyes, it is effectively impossible to hide all metadata.

From analysis of metadata, patterns emerge that provide useful insights, such as the following.

- Transmission of a large message, followed by a number of short responses, may indicate a broadcast from a command and control network node and acknowledgment of receipt from subordinates.
- Late night communication between a married person and someone other than their spouse could indicate an affair.
- Bursty communication could indicate an automated or scripted communication instead of a human typing at a keyboard.
- Timing of encrypted keystrokes could leak information about message content.[396]
- Uncharacteristic enterprise network flow patterns may reveal compromised network nodes and an attacker pivoting between machines.
- Rapid increase in communication might reveal planning for an attack and an absence of communication might reveal deliberate radio silence immediately preceding an attack.

There are some countermeasures to traffic analysis, such as changing communication channels, hiding in crowds of similar traffic, randomizing (or standardizing) communication times, padding communications to all be the same length, inserting random messages, and using "burner"[iv] telephones, but traffic analysis remains a powerful and credible cyber threat analysis tool. Anonymity tools and networks seek to reduce signatures as much as possible, but are never 100% effective.

***Association Matrix***[397] – An association matrix is an analytic tool that shows linkages between entities. Analysts can create an association matrix manually, but the technique is ripe for automation and graph analysis. Figure 8-3 is an example. Note that in this instance the associations are between people, but we can extend the approach to software, websites, hardware, personas, locations, telephone numbers, and any other entities that can be linked in some way. An analyst could further extend this approach with statistics like probability and frequency to show the strengths of the associations as well as run security analytics across multiple dimensions of associations. By analyzing associations, analysts can better understand their threat environment and improve future collection efforts.

There are multiple use cases for association matrices, such as discovering peer-to-peer networks and server-client relationships with no a priori knowledge.[398]

---

[iv] A *burner* is a communication device that is configured as anonymously as possible and used only for the duration of a specific mission to make it difficult to trace back to an individual or organization. A burner phone is usually one that is purchased with pre-paid data, talk, and text time so the user does not have to create an account with a cell provider that might get traced. A burner laptop is one that is minimally configured, used for a brief period, like a visit to a foreign country, and then wiped or even destroyed upon return.

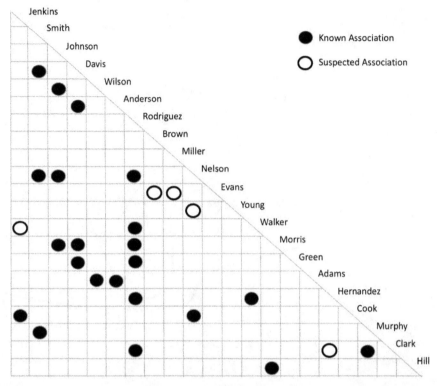

*Figure 8-3: An association matrix is useful for manual or automated analysis of linkages between entities.*

**Contact Chaining**[399] – Where the association matrix analyzes first-order relationships, both the intelligence and social network analysis communities use contact chaining to analyze linkages, such as those found in metadata, between entities to any desired degree of depth. See Figure 8-4.

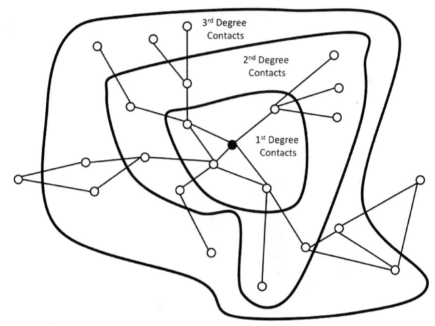

*Figure 8-4: Contact chaining creates a graph of contacts between any desired person, machine, or entity. The figure depicts a network via contacts from a central node out to the 3rd degree.*

Contact chaining has great utility and highlights properties of the network including centrality, influence, clusters, density, and size. There are obvious limitations to this technique. The network grows at an exponential rate and quickly approaches connecting everyone as there are only about six degrees of separation between any two people on the planet.[400] The linkages can also be misleading. For example, a group of individuals may appear to be connected via a given hub, but in reality, they are only ordering pizza from the same restaurant. In general, limiting analysis to 2-3 degrees of separation is most productive. Contact chaining is particularly valuable on internal networks to identify clients interacting with too many disparate servers and clients interacting with too many other clients. Both scenarios are indicative of anomalous and potentially malicious behavior.

***Activities Matrix***[401] – Similar to the association matrix, the activity matrix allows analysts to compare the activities of a large number of people against a large number of activities, locations, tools, TTPs, among many other features. See Figure 8-5 for an example. The activities matrix is similarly a manual technique that is readily adaptable to machine processing and transition from two dimensions to many.

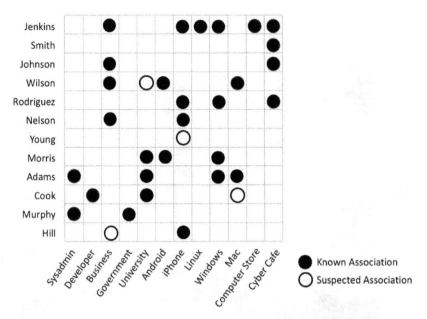

*Figure 8-5: Activity matrices compare entities with user-defined dimensions of interest, such as job role, employer, mobile device usage, operating system usage, and frequented businesses.*

The activities matrix helps highlight similarities among any desired group of individuals or actors. From it, analysts can spot group memberships, organizational structures, cell structures and sizes, communication networks, support structures, linkages with other organizations and entities, group activities and operations, and organizational and national or international ties, as well as identify anomalies and outliers despite apparently fragmentary information.[402] It can further pinpoint optimal targets for further intelligence collection, identify key personalities, and assist the analyst in developing an understanding of the organizational and technical structure of a group.[403]

**Link Diagram[404]** – So far we've discussed tools to depict relationships between entities, the link diagram extends these ideas further by grouping entities into meaningful clusters, and then depicting them using appropriate visualization techniques such as color, size, and shape, as depicted in Figure 8-6.

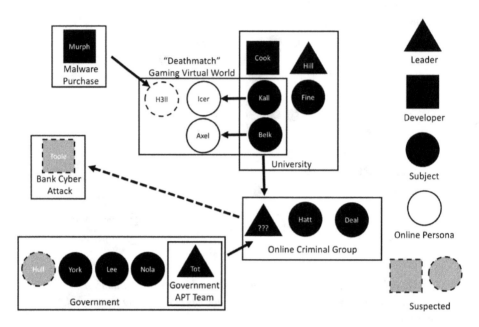

*Figure 8-6: Link diagrams allow you to group activities, locations, and people in intuitive ways. As you examine this notional example, note the use of the virtual gaming world to purchase a malware weapon that is passed to an online criminal group with ties to the government for suspected mission execution.*

Using this flexible technique, analysts can group together entities (people, computers, locations) by a desired attribute. The technique requires a lot of screen real estate, so graph layout algorithms can be helpful. Link diagrams can be paired with activities and association matrices to help show "who knows whom," "who participated in what," "who went where," and "who belongs to what group."[405] The link diagram, combined with these matrices, helps provide a clear and concise picture of a threat environment despite seemingly unrelated data.

***Pattern of Life Analysis*** – Pattern of life analysis studies patterns that emerge from individuals and groups and uses the insights gained to predict the future.[406] Consider your common daily activities: When do you wake up in the morning and when do you sleep? Where do you go and how do you get there? What websites do you frequent? Do you always wait until the last minute and download the same brand of tax preparation software every year? Humans are remarkably predictable animals, but what about machines? Does your computer run maintenance scripts every night at midnight? Does it download patches every Tuesday? Pattern of life analysis intersects with the behavior analysis and user profiling work being done by online companies. Developing key attributes to track and studying the results will aid in a variety of operational activities, from surveillance to arrests to employing targeted advertising.

***Capability Based Analysis***[407] – Capability based analysis is an analytic tool we developed that examines a device, a system, or a threat actor not from the perspective of what they say they do, or even what we see them doing, but what they have the *capability* to do. This type of analysis is admittedly paranoid, but it does provide a worst-case scenario and anticipates unlikely attack vectors and security vulnerabilities. Consider a common mobile device, like you have in your pocket. It isn't just a phone, but a powerful computer with multiple radio transmitters, microphones, and cameras, a GPS, a gyroscope, and perhaps a range of sensors including motion, temperature, ambient light, and moisture. It does appear to be under your control, but in reality it is potentially under the control of those who designed, built, or sold it to you, not to mention the control of whatever software you may have installed.[408] By employing this more rigorous standard you are less likely to be surprised.

### Understanding Adversary Doctrine and TTPs
Thoroughly analyzing adversary doctrine and TTPs is very valuable. Consider kill chain analysis for cyber operations. If you have been working in cybersecurity over the past five years, you've likely heard of the kill chain. Kill chain analysis was developed by the Special Operations community and adapted to the cyber domain by defense contractor Lockheed Martin.[409] It is a model for analyzing network intrusions and represents a generalized, seven-step attack on a network:[410]

1. Reconnaissance – Gathering information on the target either through active means or through open source
2. Weaponization – Developing a weapon for the target
3. Delivery – Transmitting the weapon to the target
4. Exploitation – Executing the attack on the target
5. Installation – Installing additional software to maintain persistence
6. Command and Control – Configuring remote control systems on compromised target
7. Actions on Objective – Attacker performs desired actions

By breaking one link in the cyber kill chain, the defender can stop that specific attack. It can be useful for predicting future threat actions and shutting them down, or for improved intelligence collection. The kill chain is also useful as an example of reversing adversary doctrine and tactics. Note however, that while useful, this particular kill chain applies only to its given context of intrusions. Other actors, such as lone malicious hackers or online criminal groups, may behave very differently. We encourage you to think broadly and as you encounter threat actors, deriving their TTPs and doctrine will help you gain similar anticipatory, real-time, and forensic[411] benefits. At the same time, you should understand that your adversaries are trying to reverse your doctrine and TTPs, so we recommend inserting some degree of randomness and unpredictability into your own operational activities.

*"Never attribute to malice that which is adequately explained by stupidity"*
*— Hanlon's razor*

### Indications and Warnings (I&W)

Indications and Warnings are another useful tool for anticipatory intelligence. Analysts work to create databases of behaviors and signatures that are precursors to important events and feed them into their intelligence collection efforts. We've given you a list of examples in Table 8-6. Indications and Warnings are generally predictive, but can help indicate that an attack is occurring and what stage it is at, as well as provide indicators of compromise after a successful attack. Scales of time are important here as well. Some indications and warnings provide months or weeks of notice, but others are time-sensitive and could only provide seconds or less of warning if they are part of a fully automated operation. We encourage your cyber threat intelligence teams to put effort into developing a full spectrum of indications and warnings, including indicators of compromise, across all timescales. Beyond manual analysis, I&W is particularly helpful if you can automate these signals and tip-off human analysts or sensitize related signature-based, behavioral, or AI-driven security systems to be on the lookout for likely upcoming actions. However, don't be lulled into a sense of complacency, prior indications and warnings for attack may not always reoccur. And don't ignore Hanlon's razor (above).

*Table 8-6: Comparison of cyber and kinetic Indications and Warnings at the strategic, operational, and tactical levels.*[412] *We've provided a few representative examples from the kinetic domain for context.*

| | Strategic | Operational | Tactical |
|---|---|---|---|
| Kinetic Indications and Warnings | - Troops massing on the border of a neighboring country<br>- Executive helicopters practice landings and takeoffs<br>- Government expels foreign press | - Certain military units stop using the radio<br>- Anti-government protests occur around a region | - Host nation employees do not come to work at hotel catering to foreign nationals, a bombing follows<br>- Disparaging propaganda posters appear in town center |
| Cyberspace-related Indications and Warnings | - Foreign diplomats express outrage about a film depicting the assassination of their leader, film production company later attacked<br>- Routing "mistake" misdirects Internet traffic through a given country<br>- Malicious software found in multiple power plant control systems<br>- Certificate signing company compromised<br>- Widely employed secure identification token stolen from security company, attacks using the token later occur against a defense contractor<br>- Academic cryptographers warn of flaw in popular cryptographic or hashing algorithm<br>- Nation-state hacking teams found probing voter registration databases | - Spear phishing emails sent to enterprise senior leaders<br>- Senior enterprise leader makes negative public remarks about a foreign leader, destructive cyber attack follows<br>- Enterprise pre-employment screening detects three separate suspect personnel attempting to gain employment with firm<br>- Senior employee makes inflammatory remarks, Twitter, 4chan, and IRC are buzzing with angry comments about enterprise<br>- Enterprise public affairs issues low-key press release about an attack against their systems<br>- Enterprise smart cards stolen | - Entire corporate website is downloaded by a device with an international IP address<br>- IT Help Desk reports social engineering attempts<br>- IDS detects download of Remote Access Trojan<br>- Several users report their machines are running "slow"<br>- Mobile device and laptop stolen from mid-level manager while travelling<br>- Suspicious vehicle with antennas seen in the parking lot<br>- City residents throw bottles and trash at employee shuttle buses<br>- Organizational website or social media account is compromised<br>- Large increase in outbound traffic |

*"An attack graph is a succinct representation of all paths through a system that end in a state where an intruder has successfully achieved his goal."*
*— Jha, Sheyner, and Wing[413]*

### Attack Graphs

Attack graphs[414] are a technique refined by the academic information security community. Attack graphs model the paths through a system that allow an intruder to achieve their goal. An example is at Figure 8-7. Each path can be weighted to provide probabilities of likely courses of action, as well as the risk and reward each path represents. We believe attack graphs have potential for real world use and are worthy of further exploration, but require further vetting in practice. If initial operational results prove promising, we believe attack graphs can be used for manual or automated analyses, bringing to bear the power of mathematics and graph theory. In addition to modeling real-world threat activities based on threat intelligence, attack graphs might be constructed using red teaming to help train models by contributing attack graph data.[415]

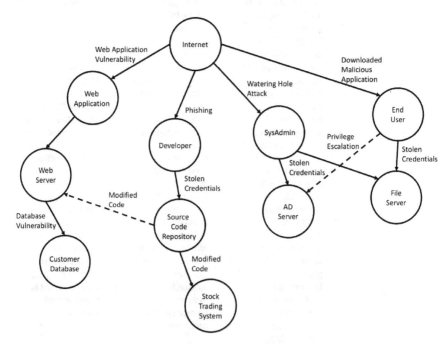

*Figure 8-7: Example of a simple attack graph. Attack graphs model all paths through a system and aid in determining threat courses of action. Very complex attack graph models are possible using an automated approach.[416]*

Beyond attack graphs, there is active research into the application of graph-based models for security that can be applied to cyber operations challenges. These include techniques such as Bayesian Networks, Stochastic Petri Nets, Markov Chains, and associated formal semantics and verification of models. We encourage exploration of these more advanced, automation-driven techniques, but they are beyond the scope of this book.[417]

## Intelligence Preparation of the Cyberspace Battlefield[418]

Intelligence Preparation of the Battlefield (IPB) is the workhorse of military intelligence.[419] The objective of IPB is to understand the battlefield and the options available to friendly and adversary forces.[420] Analysts have adapted IPB to virtually every aspect of military operations, from Joint Service operations to counter-insurgency, and from urban environments to the traditional battlefield. There have been several efforts to adapt IPB to cyberspace operations, and building upon these earlier efforts we provide our framework here.[421] There are four major steps to IPB.

### Step 1 - Define the Operational Environment

As we discussed in Chapter 4, the Operational Environment (OE) describes the conditions, circumstances, and influences that affect military operations. The OE includes political, military, economic, social, information, infrastructure, physical environment and time-based aspects, which we mapped to operations in the cyber domain. It is in Step 1 of IPB that we carefully analyze the environment and how it will impact our operations, whether we are conducting just a single activity, like an offensive action, or the long-term defense of an enterprise. Understanding the OE is critical because the environment either enables or constrains friendly and adversary potential actions. See Figure 8-8 for key components of Step 1.

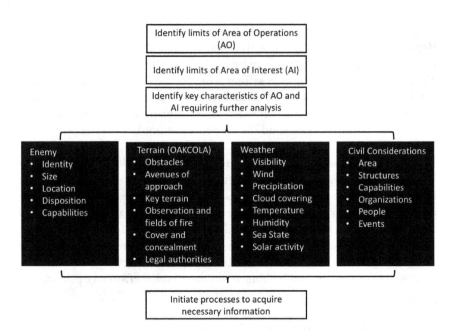

```
┌─────────────────────────────────────┐
│  Identify limits of Area of Operations│
│              (AO)                     │
└─────────────────────────────────────┘
┌─────────────────────────────────────┐
│  Identify limits of Area of Interest (AI)│
└─────────────────────────────────────┘
┌─────────────────────────────────────┐
│  Identify key characteristics of AO and│
│   AI requiring further analysis       │
└─────────────────────────────────────┘
```

| Enemy | Terrain (OAKCOLA) | Weather | Civil Considerations |
|---|---|---|---|
| • Identity | • Obstacles | • Visibility | • Area |
| • Size | • Avenues of | • Wind | • Structures |
| • Location |   approach | • Precipitation | • Capabilities |
| • Disposition | • Key terrain | • Cloud covering | • Organizations |
| • Capabilities | • Observation and | • Temperature | • People |
| |   fields of fire | • Humidity | • Events |
| | • Cover and | • Sea State | |
| |   concealment | • Solar activity | |
| | • Legal authorities | | |

```
┌─────────────────────────────────────┐
│  Initiate processes to acquire        │
│      necessary information            │
└─────────────────────────────────────┘
```

*Figure 8-8: Step 1 of the IPB process – Define the Operational Environment. The key outcomes of step one are to know what areas of cyberspace you are responsible for, what other areas you are interested in, understand the general operational environment, and identify gaps in current intelligence holdings that must be filled.*

To understand the cyber battlefield, we have to understand the boundaries. Kinetic forces have the luxury of drawing lines on a map and assigning responsibilities to commanders in each Area of Operations (AO). This concept applies reasonably well to cyberspace when we consider the geographic location of physical devices, but much of where you will conduct cyberspace operations will be distributed regionally, if not globally. The key here is to clearly define where you are conducting operations and who owns the terrain. When defending an enterprise network, boundaries are reasonably easy to define for facilities you operate, others will be shared with third-parties such as those hosted by a cloud provider and require mutual collaboration. In offensive operations, defining boundaries of immediate objectives is somewhat more difficult, but tractable. However, the broader area of operations can quickly become global and transit, or reside in, regions of cyberspace run by commercial entities, governments, private citizens, neutral third-parties, or adversaries, each with important diplomatic considerations and legal constraints. Such complexity demands more than lines on a map, and a database at a minimum, but more likely advance graph-based automation to track.

After the intelligence team defines the AO, they then identify the limits of the Area of Interest (AI). The AI includes those areas of potential concern outside your AO where actors may impact your operations. This is, again, relatively straightforward in the geographic plane but much harder in cyberspace. Because the cyber AI can be vast, we recommend identifying key areas outside of the AO where you wish to monitor and track activities.

The next step is to closely study the characteristics of the AO and AI and determine where to focus further analysis. Here we search through existing intelligence resources to analyze threat actors and compile an order of battle database containing details about each individual, group, or unit, such as their identity, location, size, disposition and capabilities. Once the AO and AIs have been clearly defined, the next step is to analyze the terrain in detail, using the OAKCOLA model: obstacles, avenues of approach key terrain, observation and fields of fire, cover and concealment, and legal authorities.

For kinetic operations, weather plays an important role and we'd consider things like visibility, wind, precipitation, cloud covering and cloud ceiling, temperature, humidity, and sea state. While weather plays a much less critical role in cyber operations, we should still consider how it might impact operations. Weather may block line-of-sight network communications, the wind may blow satellite dishes out of alignment, high (or low) temperatures can cause malfunctions in electronics or impact battery life, sea air and high humidity can cause corrosion, rain can cause flooding in data centers, and sunspots can enable or disrupt wireless communications. While there is not technically weather in cyberspace, we would also consider general environmental properties like available network bandwidth, times of peak network utilization, and degree of Internet background noise.

Next we consider the population and society at an appropriate degree of granularity depending on whether you are responsible for a small town, an enterprise, or a country. A popular model is: Area, Structures, Capabilities, Organizations, People, and Events (ASCOPE).

- Areas: Key civilian areas or aspects of the terrain, such as radio broadcast areas, political districts, and temporary settlements
- Structures: Key buildings and others structures of significance, such as shopping malls, colleges and schools, telecommunication central offices, radio stations, communication lines and towers, postal services, and government buildings
- Capabilities: Civilian abilities to save, sustain, or enhance life, such as law enforcement, emergency response, education, economic

capacity, and water production

- Organizations: Non-military groups and institutions, such as government, political, industry, unions, economic alliances, as well as media, criminal, insurgent, and non-profit groups
- People: Non-military personnel who can influence operations, such key leaders, media personalities, and online personas
- Events: Major online or physical events of significance, planned or spontaneous, routine and cyclical, such as elections, national holidays, scheduled maintenance, sporting events, and religious celebrations

By conducting these analyses, analysts will understand the environment and the limits of their available information. This step ends with initiating processes, such as intelligence collection planning and purchase of desired information, to fill known gaps required to complete the full IPB analysis.

### Step 2 - Describe Environmental Effects on Operations
In Step One we defined the Operational Environment and systematically gathered available information, identified gaps, and initiated processes to fill them. In Step 2 we seek to take the information we have available and analyze how the OE will affect operations. Key outcomes in this step are a detailed understanding of the terrain, threat actors, the impact of the physical and virtual "weather," and the civil context, see Figure 8-9. Step 2 also provides an additional opportunity to refine intelligence collection efforts as needed. Note that in traditional IPB, the process generates a number of manual products. Here we are assuming the results of this step will be fed into analytic databases and others that support visualizing the environment as part of a common operating picture, although you could create written products, if desired.

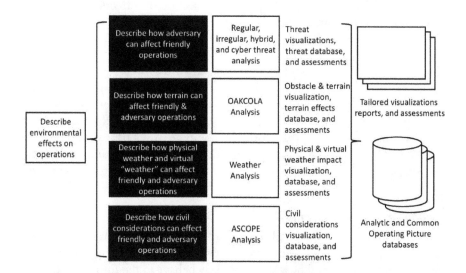

*Figure 8-9: Step 2 of the IPB process – Describe Environmental Effects on Operations.*

At this stage we seek to understand the potential adversaries in the AO. IPB covers the adversary in much greater depth in Steps 3 and 4. Here we want to enumerate the adversaries we are likely to face and understand their general characteristics. Depending on projected missions, the predominate factor in the AO may be adversaries, terrain, weather, or civil considerations. When enumerating adversaries, the objective is to create useful database records, or a manual matrix, listing group name or identity, location (physical and common locations in cyberspace), disposition (distribution of group elements within an area, location of headquarters or leader), and a general description. This information should also be fed into a physical or cyberspace mapping system to create a map overlay or perform data enrichments.

We described the cyber terrain analysis process in Chapter 5 – Terrain. Here is where you apply it. Remember OAKCOLA: obstacles, avenues of approach/attack vectors, key terrain, observation and fields of fire, cover and concealment, obstacles, and legal authorities. Terrain analysis studies each of these aspects in the physical domains, but more importantly from our perspective, across the cyberspace planes. We recommend developing and understanding avenues of approach that will get you to your objective, or the adversary to theirs, as well as identifying key terrain. Contrary to kinetic battles, in cyberspace operations you can be both on the offensive and the defensive at the same time. Once identified you should feed the results of your OAKCOLA analysis, with special emphasis on the effects of the terrain, into your databases and common operating pictures systems, and also create printed versions as necessary.

The next steps are to analyze the physical and virtual "weather" and perform ASCOPE analysis of the civil environment feeding results into your databases and analytic and common operating picture systems, as well as to generate manual reports. We've covered ASCOPE earlier in the chapter, but we wanted to highlight that you can combine ASCOPE with Political, Military, Economic, Social, Information, and Infrastructure (PMESII) aspects, covered in Chapter 4 – Operational Environment, to help enhance your analysis.

### Step 3 - Evaluate the Threat
In Step 3 the analyst digs deeply into current and potential threat actors they may face, gaining insight into what they are capable of, how they have operated in the past, and how they will likely behave in the future. There are several goals at this stage: update the order of battle database of threat actors, analyze the current situation, determine threat capabilities, and identify/refine targets for collection and cyber/kinetic targeting. By evaluating the adversary in depth, friendly forces can best focus and prioritize their offensive, defensive, and intelligence efforts. See Figure 8-10 for an overview.

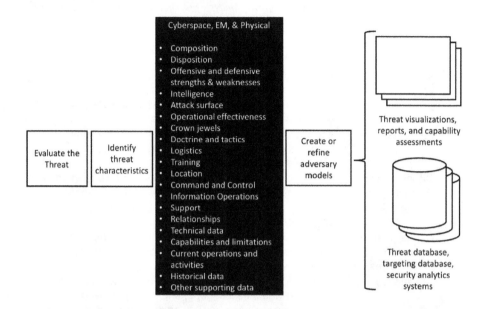

*Figure 8-10: Step 3 of the IPB process – Evaluate the Threat. In this step analysts identify and analyze threat characteristics in cyberspace, the EM spectrum, and the physical domain, then create or refine threat models. Key outputs are a detailed threat actor database / order of battle database, assessments of threat capabilities, and operational targeting lists.*

Traditional IPB focuses on physical threat actor characteristics, but for cyberspace operations we need to also consider the dimensions of cyberspace and the EM spectrum. Adversaries in cyberspace can come from any of the actors described in Chapter 2 – Actors and Adversaries, ranging from lone individuals to organized nation-state cyber forces. It is up to you how deeply you characterize those you are facing or may face, although more information is generally better, especially if you can create automated systems to handle the bulk of the work and reserve human attention for specific in-depth or specialized analysis. See Table 8-7 for an overview of potential characteristics.

*Table 8-7: Characteristics of cyber threat actors. These characteristics can be used for manual analysis or to create an automated Order of Battle database. As you examine these characteristics, note that cyber threat analysts must consider their application in the context of cyberspace and the EM spectrum.*

| Characteristic | Description |
|---|---|
| Composition | High-level identification of adversary and their organizational hierarchy, specific types of sub-units/teams/squads, staff elements |
| Disposition | Location of people, servers, tools in cyber and physical domains under control of the adversary, current offensive and defensive positions |
| Offensive and Defensive Strength | What are the actor's strengths and weaknesses when on the offensive and the defensive? Number of people, servers, amount of bandwidth and processing power, degree of popular support |
| Offensive and Defensive Weaknesses | Weaknesses in how the actor conducts offensive and defensive cyberspace operations, as well as in the physical world |
| Intelligence | How robust is the actor's intelligence collection, including weaknesses, gaps, and strengths, what intelligence methods do they employ and favor? |
| Attack surface | Details on the attack surface of the organization, including systems, workplaces, automobiles, and homes |
| Operational Effectiveness | Overall assessment of the actor's ability to operate effectively both in the cyberspace domain, but also in joint cyber/kinetic operations |
| Crown Jewels | Are there any particular assets of essential value to the actor? |
| Doctrine and Tactics | What patterns emerge from the actor's behavior, are there particular toolsets that they employ, do they publish their doctrine, what are their favored tactics, techniques, and procedures, how do they perform offensive tasks, how do they infiltrate and exfiltrate data, how do they defend both during operations and in day-to-day activities, how do they retreat? |
| Logistics | How the adversary supplies their activities in general, what is their hardware and software supply chain, what are their rapid and routine acquisition timelines, what warehouses, routes, stores, and suppliers do they use, what maintenance/patching/updating do they perform? |
| Training | Level of training of personnel and specific areas of expertise, analysis should include aspects of training, or lack thereof, that could be exploited |
| Location | Beyond current disposition, other areas that they frequent, such as safe houses, base camps, cyber cafes |

| | |
|---|---|
| Command and Control | How the group is given operational directives, who is in charge, how much operational flexibility do subordinate leaders possess, what are the personalities and skillsets of the leaders, any predispositions and tendencies? |
| Information Operations | Social media presence, use of media and other information operations capabilities |
| Support | What are their sources of support, e.g. government officials, media, grassroots |
| Relationships | Relationships and linkages inside the group and between groups |
| Technical data | Specific types and versions of hardware, software, firmware, networking equipment and protocols (wired and wireless), authentication methods, encryption usage, electromagnetic spectrum and frequency usage, types of sensors, transmitters, and receivers |
| Capabilities and Limitations | What technical and kinetic operational capabilities does the actor possess, what is their capacity for operations, do they possess robust deception, jamming, propaganda, hardware fabrication, code-writing, physical security penetration abilities, or other specialized skills? |
| Current Operations and Activities | What operations and activities does the actor currently have ongoing, what are known activities they are planning? |
| Historical Data | What historical activities has the group participated in? Any other key historical information, such as senior leader changes |
| Other Supporting Data | Goals and motivations of actor, biometric data, authentication credentials, network map data, culture, family members, handles/code names, internal reward and punishment mechanisms, internal personality conflicts and organizational fractures, how they replace personnel losses and repair/replace hardware and software |

With a detailed understanding of the adversary's characteristics, we then build an adversary model. Threat modeling, and the related discipline of simulation, are deep areas with significant ongoing research.[422] Here we will keep our discussion at a high level and suggest that you create three primary products at this stage: a list (or database) of high-value targets for offensive or intelligence collection operations, a description of the threat's tactics and options, and analyses of patterns of behavior/doctrine. Reversing the threat's doctrine, tactics, and habitual behavior is very important to anticipating behaviors as a conflict unfolds. With this understanding you can create models, visualizations, templates, and timelines of how an adversary may perform operations to achieve its objectives in a given context. Threat models list options available to the adversary, whether they are successful in any given activity or not, and can help identify when the adversary might transition from operations of one form, or plane, or domain, to another. These models also assist in wargaming what an adversary will do in response to friendly actions or reactions.

> "It's my job to think the way Dark wizards do, Karkaroff —
> as you ought to remember..."
> - Mad-Eye Moody [423]

### Step 4 - Determine Adversary Courses of Action

At this point we have a detailed understanding of the operational environment and the threat actor(s) we are facing. In the final step of IPB we determine what potential courses of action the adversary can take, as depicted in Figure 8-11. By doing so, you can quickly narrow down the nearly infinite realm of the possible to the most likely and most dangerous threat actions you face. It is this at point we apply one of the most valuable skills of the intelligence analyst and operational commander, the ability to get into the mindset of the adversary. What actions would you take as the adversary and when? How would you respond and counter friendly moves in a given conflict scenario? Like a game of chess, the more moves out you can accurately predict threat behaviors the greater the advantage you have. And, like Deep Blue beating chess master Garry Kasparov, automation in the form of predictive analytics and decision-making tools can provide an even greater advantage.

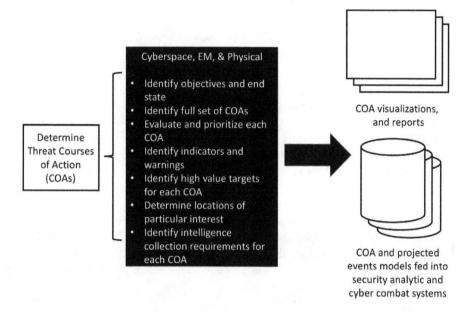

*Figure 8-11: Step 4 of the IPB Process – Determine Adversary Courses of Action*

We recommend brainstorming with the intelligence team to identify enemy objectives and potential attack vectors, understand enemy and friendly weaknesses, and prioritize potential enemy COAs. With the COAs in hand you can develop indications and warnings that focus your intelligence collection efforts, adapt your defenses, and better plan your operations. When determining COAs you should consider:[424]

- Current threat situation
- Threat objectives, incentives, and mission
- How the threat is organized
- Threat capabilities and vulnerabilities
- High value targets the threat may attack
- Threat intent for maneuver, reconnaissance and surveillance, cyber and kinetic fires and effects, logistics, deception, protection and information operations
- How physical, cyber, and human terrain will enable or limit threat activities

- How the threat will employ multi-domain operations, to include air, land, sea, space, cyber and electronic warfare forces
- Key points in time and space where the adversary will have to make decisions
- The likely role and reaction of non-combatants, including those that own or operate cyber infrastructure
- Threat use of obstacles

Coarse of action prediction results can be summarized into Who, What, Where, When, Why, and How, and prioritized into two categories, Most Likely and Most Dangerous. With effort, analysts can estimate timelines of how they expect events to unfold, but they should be very conscious of the marked differences between human, network, and machine time. As part of the process we make a list or database of High Value Targets (HVTs), which are those assets of particular value to the *adversary* in a given operational context. We can then feed the COA predictions, HVTs, and timeline predictions into later operational planning and threat modeling. While kinetic forces frequently conduct this analysis manually, for cyber operations we suggest working to automate the process. The attack graph technique we outlined earlier can play a useful role.

## Conclusions

Cyber operations is an intelligence-led process. Developing high-quality, timely, and relevant cyber threat intelligence isn't easy, but it is possible. Analysts must learn to think like their adversaries and be intellectually honest. Cooperation is critical to bring together diverse information feeds and points of view. Intelligence systems must constantly prioritize and reprioritize their efforts to remain agile. Intelligence must not be collected for its own sake, but to be relevant must be integrated into operations.[425] Operational intelligence consumers will demand actionable intelligence so they can make decisions. Cyber threat analysts must be concerned about the present, but also maintain a long-term perspective, that reaches beyond millions of daily cyber "attacks" and isolated events to campaigns lasting months or years to long-term strategies that may imply death by a thousand cuts rather than a forever looming "Cyber Pearl Harbor."[426] As you read this chapter you probably saw that cyber intelligence is amenable to automation. Expect increasingly powerful threat intelligence analytics in the future, including systems that predict the near-future with a high degree of accuracy.[427]

# 9 FIRES AND EFFECTS

*"The computers take care of all that. They're constantly firing in any direction that won't hurt one of our ships. The computers pick targets, aim; they do all the detail work. You just tell them when and get them in a position to win."*
*- Maezr Rachham[428]*

We've previously discussed types of capabilities, the use of maneuver to place forces in the best offensive or defensive position on cyberspace terrain, and the use of intelligence to deeply understand the adversary, environment, and current situation. In this chapter, we bring these facets together to deliver *fires*, the use of a cyber capability to create specific lethal or nonlethal effects on a target, and *targeting* to select and prioritize those effects to match the appropriate capability to the operational requirement.[429]

The targeting process is rooted in the methods that military artillerymen use to decide where and when to use artillery fires to achieve a commander's intent. During peacekeeping operations in places like Kosovo and Bosnia, and later during counterinsurgencies in Afghanistan and Iraq, the U.S. military began to focus less on firing artillery and more on achieving non-destructive effects, such as improving local living conditions or enhancing capabilities of host nation militaries and law enforcement personnel. Military leaders realized that the flexible and adaptable fires process was well-suited to planning non-lethal effects against targets that are enemy, friendly, or neutral. We usually think of fires as purely a kinetic activity, but we are defining the idea broadly to include effects that are relevant in military cyber operations, the private sector, or even to individuals. Effects are the consequence or result of fires, and include such things as destruction, deception, and degradation of operations. Governments possess a monopoly

179

on the use of force, but individuals can achieve effects on adversaries too, within certain constraints.[430] We'll go into much greater depth on effects in this chapter, as well as the process of selecting targets, executing fire missions, integrating fires into overall operations, and assessing results, see Figure 9-1.

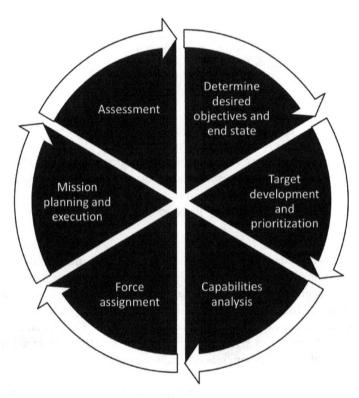

*Figure 9-1: Generating offensive or defensive effects on adversaries is far more efficient and powerful through a systemic process.[431]*

## DETERMINING DESIRED OBJECTIVES AND END STATE

Fires and effects for cyberspace operations sometimes require long-term planning and preparation, but also the ability to respond agilely when circumstances warrant. Planning begins with an analysis of a current mission or projected contingency missions you might have in the future. Short-term fires activities will be driven by the operational mission at hand. Agility in the face of stressful combat situations demands training and rehearsals of the process outlined in Figure 9-1. In the military, a long-term plan might be the defense of an ally in the event of an invasion by a given aggressor, but there is a wide range of possibilities and potential timelines for both planning and execution, from very-long to exceptionally short.

There are two primary categories of targeting: deliberate and dynamic. Deliberate targets are planned in advance; perhaps well in advance. If there is sufficient time to do adequate planning, targets are either scheduled for effects delivery at a given time, or they are categorized as on-call. On-call targets might be low priority and will only be engaged if and when effects delivery becomes worthwhile. On-call targets might also be important targets that have not been located, in which case they are engaged when the location becomes known. Dynamic targeting is much more fluid, occurring[432] in the midst of combat, and prosecuted when an opportunity presents itself, but with insufficient time for deliberate targeting. These targets of opportunity may be known to exist but unplanned, or alternatively, unanticipated targets may appear in the given area of operations. Figure 9-2 breaks out these categories.

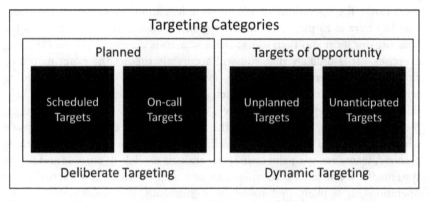

*Figure 9-2: Operational cyber targeting falls into two main categories: deliberate targets which are planned for and targets of opportunity that present themselves in the heat of combat. Each type of target affords significantly different preparation time.*

Targets that fall into any of these four categories may be time-sensitive in that they provide a fleeting window of vulnerability and susceptibility to attack. In kinetic warfare, this might be an adversary senior leader travelling from one secure bunker to another, being vulnerable while en route. In cyber operations, targets may be time-sensitive as well, like attacking a target system before software is patched, or attacking an organization while it is in the midst of configuring a firewall upgrade. Targets may also be classified as *sensitive*. Sensitive targets are those that require additional planning, legal approvals, or present potential for significant collateral damage. Understanding these categories helps an actor organize their targeting rapidly and at scale. Such organization is facilitated by proper planning and training.

*"In preparing for battle I have always found that plans are useless, but planning is indispensable."*
*– Dwight D. Eisenhower*

## Scenario Based Planning

A powerful technique for both short- and long-range planning is to use scenarios that come up as likely during your Intelligence Preparation of the Cyber Battlefield. The scenarios can be strategic, operational, or tactical, depending on the types of forces you have available. A strategic scenario might be the attack on a national stock exchange that manages to corrupt back-ups of trading data. An operational scenario could be a nation-state attack against your business that seeks to steal mission-critical intellectual property. Finally, a tactical scenario could be a cryptomalware attack that shuts down the operations of a hospital unless administrators pay a ransom. The key here is to put time and energy into building realistic scenarios for your organization and then to use these scenarios during you team's training exercises. It is unlikely that you will accurately predict the exact nature or circumstances surrounding future events, but the process of building scenario-based plans and then exercising the most likely to occur will help refine incident response procedures, develop legal responses in advance, prepare your team, and give them the experience and confidence to handle what does come to pass.[433] As modeling and simulation of cyber operations matures, teams can plan and train using realistic models of current and future systems.[434] While legal authorities can be a major constraint on actual cyber operations, it is likely that there are significantly less restrictions in your planning, training, and wargaming activities, contrasted with actual execution, and allow you to explore the unfettered realm of the technologically possible. Through these activities, you will also identify gaps in your processes, capabilities, and authorities that you can work to fill.

## Timelines

Cyber operations are notorious for long preparation times, but there is really a spectrum of time required. Access is often a necessary precursor to effective fires and proper synchronization can have an amplifying effect.

***Access*** – Mission success often comes down to the type of target and whether, and to what extent, access is required. Little preparation is required to conduct simple cyber operations like a DDOS attack, a spam campaign, or triggering IDS false positives. In these cases access to necessary resources, such as an email address of a senior leader, the EM spectrum, or a public facing web server, is assumed. More complex targets require more time depending on their protection level and complexity.[435] For example, nation-state attackers with an apparent goal of gaining access to the internal network of a financial institution used two zero-day exploits to first compromise a popular business news website, which then infected user machines in a multistage effort to gain access to well-protected financial sector systems.[436] In hard targets, like an air gapped network in a secure facility, access may take months or years to acquire. In these cases, access might be achieved through supply chain compromise, penetrating upstream service providers, developing an insider accomplice, or waiting for a window of vulnerability during a system upgrade. We don't think of gaining access as an attack *per se*, but a means of collecting information and an enabler of an attack at some point in the future, or perhaps both. Access can be gained, and sometimes lost, in advance of a cyber conflict, due to accident, compromise, or improved defensive security measures. We see accesses, much like capabilities, as valuable assets that may be stockpiled and brought into play at the right time.[437] See Figure 9-3 for an example of developing accesses in advance and then carefully employing them in a conflict.

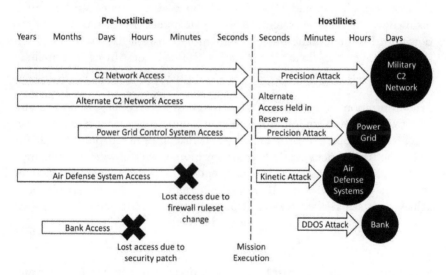

*Figure 9-3: Notional outbreak of hostilities. The attacker has been developing access to key terrain over a course of years awaiting a need. Note that access allows precision cyber attack, but not in the two cases where access is lost. Here the attacker shifts to kinetic attack and a blanket DDOS attack which work without access.*

Note that in the figure, some access has been lost prior to the outbreak of hostilities, so the attackers have chosen to employ kinetic attack and an access-less DDOS attack instead. However, adversaries can seek to develop accesses on the fly, at either network or human speeds, possibly expending capabilities such as valuable zero-day exploits if the circumstances warrant.

*"Battles are won by fire and movement. The purpose of the movement is to get the fire in a more advantageous place to play on the enemy. This is from the rear or flank."*
*— George S. Patton, Jr.[438]*

**Synchronization** – While some threats are asynchronous and do not require specific timing to achieve a desired effect. Synchronization of cyber operations alone or in conjunction with kinetic operations is a force multiplier, helping to produce the right effects at the right time to accomplish objectives. If you refer to Figure 9-3, you will see that the attacker prepared accesses in advance of the outbreak of hostilities and then launched a series of precision, kinetic, and DDOS attacks in an orchestrated effort. First, taking down air defense systems to enable air superiority, then taking out the power grid to undermine the government and disrupt day-to-day life, then shutting down the financial system, and finally destroying the military command and control network, with a presumed ground invasion to follow.

Synchronization is best achieved through prior planning, practice, and effective command and control during execution. We will discuss more on synchronizing operations of humans and machines in Chapter 10, but for now note that maneuver and fires are far more powerful when coordinated. Maneuver along an attack vector or avenue of approach allows attackers to reach the attack surface. If access is required and hasn't already been achieved, attackers then seek to gain access to penetrate defenses, and then to employ capabilities to achieve desired effects.

**Speed**
Speed matters. Attacks must be swift and decisive to gain the initiative and to prevent the defender from negating the attack through patching, reconfiguration, counterattack, or simply pulling the plug on a network cable.

## TARGET DEVELOPMENT AND PRIORITIZATION

Central to fires and effects is targeting. Targeting is the selection and prioritization of potential targets and the selection of specific effects that you want to achieve against those targets. When performing targeting, the goal is to achieve overarching objectives and create the desired effects on the target, and to limit collateral effects on unintended targets. To be performed effectively targeting requires close integration between kinetic, intelligence, information, and electronic warfare operations, as well as a variety of other supporting disciplines. In cyberspace operations, these disciplines include fires specialists, operators, developers, domain experts, and technologists. The ultimate goal being to achieve effects in a systematic, synchronized, and adaptive manner in support of the mission.[439] In cyberspace operations, targeting functions across many scales of time, from years to milliseconds, and requires both human and machine decision making. In target development and prioritization we identify targets and nominate them for prosecution, analyze potential target systems, develop packages that map capabilities to specific targets, develop prioritized target lists, and understand when, where, and what effects may be legitimately employed.

### Dynamic Targets

In situations where there is not sufficient time to perform deliberate planning, units will request immediate fire support. In the kinetic realm this is straightforward. A unit will make a request, typically by radio, to a supporting artillery unit to fire at a given map location. In this case, the process turns very quickly. The requesting unit reports on the nature and the location of system they wish to target. One rapid reaction scenario is counter-battery fires, which occur when a unit is receiving incoming indirect fire and seeks to destroy or disable the source of the attack. In cyber operations, expedited requests are possible but trickier. The notion of counter-battery fire in cyber operations is relevant, as the debate over "hacking back" against attackers illustrates. The distinction between hacking back, returning fire from cyber operations units, or some notion of "cyber artillery" isn't yet well defined, but the concept is important. There will be instances where one unit will want to return fire before the attacking unit causes severe damage or shifts location. Finally, while intelligence is important for all forms of fires and effects, intelligence is doubly important for dynamic targets. You cannot fire on a target that you cannot detect and locate. Recall the collection planning discussion from the Intelligence chapter and our recommendation to carefully place sensors to detect attack. These sensors will be crucial to detecting adversaries and firing upon dynamic targets.

*"The Center of Gravity is the hub of all power and movement,*
*on which everything depends."*
*– Clausewitz*

## Center of Gravity Analysis
The U.S. Military defines a center of gravity (CoG) as "the source of power that provides moral or physical strength, freedom of action, or will to act." By performing CoG analysis, actors can undermine adversary centers of gravity while shielding their own. CoG analysis is very powerful, and rather than striking in an ad hoc fashion, allows military forces to strike the key pressure points on their adversary to achieve the desired outcome.

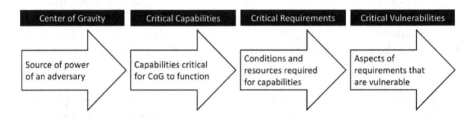

*Figure 9-4: Center of Gravity analysis, which studies key sources of power for actors, helps friendly forces prioritize their defenses and to better undermine their adversary. Centers of Gravity depend on critical capabilities to function which can be further analyzed for vulnerabilities.[440]*

As you examine Figure 9-4, note that each center of gravity is built upon a foundation of critical capabilities[441] that are essential for the targeted entity to function. Each critical capability in turn has certain requirements and those requirements have vulnerabilities, creating a nested framework to decompose each center of gravity and identify underlying vulnerabilities that may be targeted. CoG analysis also helps identify key terrain. Center of gravity analysis may be used at the strategic, operational, or tactical level. In Table 9-1, we've taken a global resource, cyberspace, and broken it down into its constituent critical capabilities, and then provided representative critical requirements and critical vulnerabilities. If you've read the news, you will have seen that many of these vulnerabilities have already been exploited or attacked.

## Table 9-1: Partial Center of Gravity Analysis of Cyberspace[442]

| Critical Capability | Critical Requirements | Critical Vulnerabilities |
| --- | --- | --- |
| Hardware Supply Chain | Chip foundries, chip design firms, trusted routers, transportation, warehousing | Computer engineers, chip design software, vehicle drivers, warehouse personnel |
| Software Supply Chain | Operating system companies, open source repositories, software update mechanisms, App stores | Popular operating systems (closed and open source), popular applications in App stores, volunteer developers |
| Internet | DNS, Time synchronization, PKI, routing | DNS root name servers, Internet core routers, Internet backbone, core routing protocols |
| Search | Search engine companies | Web crawlers, search logs, search query histories |
| Internet Governance | Internet governance bodies, national and international telecommunication policy and standards groups | Cryptographic standards, networking standards, choice of when to deprecate technologies, committee members |
| WWW | Browser companies, web server companies and open source projects | Browser source code, web publishing framework, web servers, popular websites, web browsers |
| Email | Email service providers, email servers and clients, email protocols | Email servers, email clients |
| Telecommunication Infrastructure | Undersea cables, communication satellites, electromagnetic spectrum | Physical access, system fingerprinting, cloned network routers |

You can use CoG analysis on a nation, city, company, group, individual, or even a system. If you consider how dependent nations are on cyberspace, and that keeping IT and network resources efficiently up and running is difficult, you'll understand that cyberspace is fragile and possesses many vulnerabilities. As you read the news about nation-state level cyberspace activities, you'll likely see that much of the malicious activity occurs in areas like those listed in Table 9-1 as actors seek to infiltrate or undermine aspects of cyberspace both during times of conflict, and in peacetime espionage. On the other hand, defenders at the strategic, operational, and tactical level can perform CoG analysis on their own assets and institutions to better prioritize defenses.

*"This isn't painful.*
*Getting shot is painful.*
*Getting stabbed in the ribs is painful.*
*This ... isn't painful."*
*– Tony Soprano*[443]

## Effects

Effects-based operations represent a powerful evlolution in the conduct of war. By focusing on a desired end-state and then considering a range of potential approaches to achieving that end-state, commanders leveraged more options and achieved goals with a better chance of success, fewer casualties, and fewer resources. A simple example is a commander's approach to counterinsurgency operations. One way to disrupt an insurgency is to kill or capture most or all of the insurgents. This method requires a huge resource investment, potentially high casualties, and does not have a high likelihood of success. Insurgents are hard to identify among the general population, and killing one insurgent often results in their family members and close associates joining the insurgency. Another approach is to improve governance and public services for local populations. Doing so brings the will of the people to the side of the counterinsurgents rather than the insurgency. Since an insurgency needs material assistance and secrecy from the local population to survive, effectively turning the population to the side of the counterinsurgents is likely to cause the insurgency to wither and die with relatively fewer casualties and potentially lesser resource investment.

Effects can be narrowly targeted and tailored, or broadly applied. Cyberspace operations can create many effects; some occur in cyberspace only, some in the physical world, and some affect human decision making and cognition.[444] The opposite is also true, effects in the physical world and in human decision making can also impact cyberspace. Table 9-2 illustrates how actions in one domain can achieve effect in another.

188

*Table 9-2: Examples of actions taken in one domain creating effects in another.*

| Effect | Strategic | Operational | Tactical |
|---|---|---|---|
| **Cyberspace → Cyberspace** | Electronic trading disrupted via data corruption | Enterprise web server knocked offline by DDOS | Corrupting a key application on an end user workstation |
| **Cyberspace → Physical Domain** | Power grid disabled, globally popular insulin pump implant line gives lethal dose to hosts | Stolen CEO emails used to destroy company[445] | Hacked geolocation data used for arresting individual, [446] attackers remotely open electronic lock[447] |
| **Cyberspace → Cognitive Domain** | Disenfranchised populations organize by social media resulting in mass protests and overthrow of governments throughout the Middle East | Threatening emails sent to general officers undermining their will to fight, destabilized currency causes population to lose trust in financial system | Individual radicalized by online extremist forum, dissident blogger shouted down by online trolls |
| **Physical Domain → Cyberspace** | Bombs destroy data network hubs shaping the Physical layer and forcing leadership onto desired communication networks[448] | Backhoe destroys facility fiber optic lines which provide network connectivity | User connects rogue access point into secure network, local attackers penetrate WiFi network, electromagnetic jamming disconnects wireless network users |

Effects are rarely used in isolation. They are more often massed and directed at a given target to create even more impact. Combatants may also combine physical and kinetic effects as they plan for or conduct a given engagement. As you examine Table 9-3 consider how these effects may be combined in various operations and how they might be generated by cyberspace or kinetic means.

*Table 9-3: Example Effects Possible Through Cyber Fires* [449]

| Effect | Definition | Cyberspace → Cyberspace | Cyberspace → Physical |
|---|---|---|---|
| **Convert** | Change the loyalty of a human or the effective control of a device or system | Gain root access on a weapon system control computer | Placement of material on a web forum that (de)radicalizes readers[450] |
| **Deceive** | Mislead through manipulating understanding of reality | Tricking malware to run in a sandbox | Deceptive command and control email sent to insurgent leader [451] |
| **Degrade** | Reduce effectiveness or efficiency | Insert disconnect requests on wireless network | Jam GPS receiver |
| **Delay** | Slow operations or activities | Malware that slows down a system, man-in-the-middle attack that slows network traffic | Exploiting a file sharing fairness algorithm to delay a user access to information |
| **Deny** | Prevent use of some resource such as space, personnel, terrain, or EM spectrum | Filling up the storage on an email server | Cutting fiber optic cables to data center, gaining administrator access and locking out authorized users |
| **Destroy** | Physical or virtual damage that cannot be repaired without replacement | Erasing a critical application or data from disk | Industrial control system sends instructions that destroy generator, erasing firmware to make a mobile device unusable |
| **Deter** | Discouraging a given behavior | Misadvertising router availability | Deter a potential insurgent group recruit due to worry over communications security,[452] using location data in a photo to arrest an individual |
| **Disrupt** | Disturb or upset an activity, process, or event | Sending out spurious router advertisements | Shutting down power production system, using data |

| | | | manipulation to prevent an extremist group from paying its members.[453] |
|---|---|---|---|
| **Divert** | Turn aside from a course of action | IP hijacking to divert network traffic to your country[454] | Known compromise of email servers diverts users to cell phones, fax machines, and couriers |
| **Interdict** | Intercept and prevent a course of action | Performing a man in the middle attack and altering packets | Detection of an adversary on your network and performing defensive actions |
| **Neutralize** | Render incapable of interference | Crashing an anti-virus application | Plant child pornography on a political leader's computer that leads to their removal from office |
| **No Effect**[455] | Create no effect or one below a detection threshold | Defensive security software does not notice an attack and data exfiltration | Defender never recognizes a data center break-in took place |
| **Suppress** | Temporarily degrade performance | Forcing a reboot of a security system | Suppression of enemy air defense systems, create spurious intrusion detection system alerts |

## Destructive Effects

Make no mistake, cyberspace effects can be destructive and lethal.[456] Effects may be felt directly (1st Order), indirectly (2nd Order), or through an extended and sometimes uncontrollable chain of actions and reactions (Nth Order), as depicted in Figure 9-5. First order effects for cyberspace operations occur in cyberspace-only where they might destroy virtual constructs like personas, data, and software, or provide instructions to computing devices that set the conditions for destructive physical effects as a second order consequence.

Despite occasional depictions in popular movies, we aren't able to cause computers to explode using a virus,[457] but cyber operations can render systems inoperable by deleting data in firmware or on a system hard drive. In some cases, permanent damage can be caused by simply setting the system date to a particular invalid value.[458] Cyber operations can also relay spoofed instructions to humans, or to physical control systems, to cause destruction. Examples include sending incorrect targeting information to a weapon system, sending malicious instructions to a medical device,[459] shutting down power to a hospital's intensive care unit, or triggering a nuclear power plant meltdown.[460] Even without malicious instructions, the lack of a computer to guide a process can cause physical destruction. For example, widespread disruption of automated air traffic control systems during busy periods could lead to disaster.

Destructive effects may also be brought to bear in training environments. If you consider risky training courses, like the U.S. Army's Airborne and Ranger Schools and dangerous training environments like the National Training Center (NTC) in the Mojave Desert, training accidents sometimes lead to serious injury or death. We aren't suggesting using cyber effects to kill people, but we believe simulated destruction should certainly be used, and it is worth considering careful use of actual destructive effects on machines. Participants and Generals will then better understand the destructive power of cyber, and repair technicians will gain experience recovering from a destructive cyber attack.

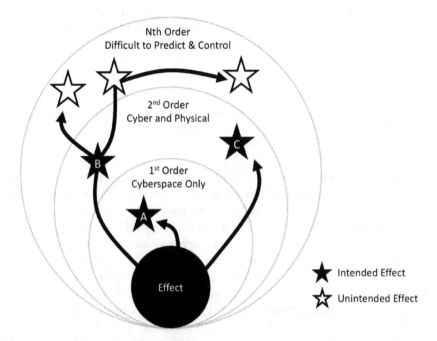

*Figure 9-5: Cyber operations cause effects that impact cyberspace directly (first-order effects) or create a chain of one or more additional effects. Second-order or greater effects may cause physical damage. However, effects from cyberspace operations are notoriously difficult to predict and control, and may create numerous unintended consequences.*

## Self-Inflicted Effects

Effects aren't always directed against an adversary. There are circumstances where an actor may unintentionally generate adversarial effects on friendly forces (fratricide) or even deliberately target friendly forces.

***Unintentional*** – Sadly fratricide occurs all too frequently in kinetic operations and cyber operations are not immune. Whether it is a first order effect create by a typographical error in a target list or a misunderstanding, leakage of a capability, or uncontrolled propagation of malware, there is an all too real possibility of accidently striking oneself, friendly forces, or an ally.[461] The high risk of fratricide underscores why leaders and operators need to know how their tools work at a meaningful level.

***Deliberate*** – There is also a rarely used kinetic technique, calling in artillery fire dangerously close to friendly positions when an enemy force threatens to overrun a position. This is referred to as a "danger close" artillery mission. We can envision scenarios where cyber effects may be directed against friendly systems, such as corrupting data being infiltrated by an attacker, blocking lower priority network traffic to free up bandwidth, or destroying a friendly server that is under the administrative control of an attacker. At the extreme, a friendly element may initiate human or machine controlled self-destruction to prevent system compromise. This might include erasing ("zeroing out") the crypto key in a secure telephone, wiping data, or destroying large systems, among many possibilities.[462] An example of this is remotely wiping a lost or stolen mobile phone and resetting it to factory settings.

***Reversible Effects*** – When we first heard of reversible effects as a tool in cyber operations we thought it was a solution looking for a problem.[463] We admit we were wrong. Reversible effects, are just that, effects that can be reversed when necessary. For example, an attacker could lock adversary users out of their computer systems by changing passwords, but return control of the machines after the end of hostilities. The advent of Bitcoin as a quasi-anonymous currency has opened up the potential for reversible effects as a tool for extortion.[464] *Ransomware* is a class of malware that encrypts a user's system, then demands a ransom, usually in Bitcoin because of the anonymity it offers. If the ransom is paid, a decryption key is (usually) provided so that the effects can be reversed. If not, the information is effectively destroyed. Criminals usually do provide the necessary decryption key and (ironically) some level of customer service, otherwise future victims will be unlikely to pay the ransom. Of course, some effects, like death, physical destruction, and secure wiping of data, cannot be reversed, but much in cyberspace is just the state of a given set of zeroes and ones. By saving and later restoring this state, the attacker can reverse the effect. When you create capabilities, consider including the ability to reverse the effect to add another option to your range of cyber capabilities.

Simulated and reversible effects are also useful for training. For those who have served in the military, you probably have used the Multiple Integrated Laser Engagement System (MILES) for force-on-force combat. Others may be familiar with the *Ender's Game* battle room in which student team members' suits would freeze when shot, preventing the "casualty" from moving their limbs until the battle was over. The same is possible for cyber operations. We can envision a future in which combat simulators, and possibly even combat systems, will allow for simulated and reversible effects.

A topic related to reversible effects is the duration of effects. Reversible effects are a special case where the duration is variable and determined by the attacker. Attackers can chose the time to lift the effect at their discretion. Some effects are irreversible such as permanent destruction and others only last for a given period of time dependent upon the target's response actions. The target may have multiple remediation options at their disposal, depending on their resiliency, preparation, and training. For example, a defender might reflash firmware or restart a virtual machine to eradicate a malware infection, or shift to a backup data center. In many cases, the attacker will attempt to maintain persistence in a target system in order to extend the effect or retain access even when the defender employs countermeasures.

> *"Behind every E-mail, Tweet, #hashtag, and avatar, – or better yet, behind every phishing scam, denial of service attack, Honey Pot, or Remote Action Tool in cyberspace – there is a person."*
> *- Command Sergeant Major Rodney Harris and Master Sergeant Jeff Morris[465]*

## Identification and Nomination

Intelligence Preparation of the Battlefield, Center of Gravity analysis, and Terrain Analysis, especially key terrain, provide the starting point for identifying candidate targets. We use the concept of nomination because there will not be enough resources to address every potential target, and every potential target may not be operationally, legally, and morally valid to strike. By wargaming[i] upcoming combat and developing a prioritized list of targets operational forces can then begin to deeply analyze target systems and create mission packages designed to achieve the desired effects. Over time, a playbook will emerge of common target types, ranges of potential effects, common delivery mechanisms, and resultant TTPs that operational forces can rehearse in training and execute decisively when called upon. Ideally this playbook will contain pre-approved options that can be executed agilely, without lengthy legal reviews, by the lowest level of command. New scenarios, types of targets, and mission scenarios will certainly be encountered, but planners can develop options and add them to the playbook over time.

---

[i] *Wargaming* is a military staff process that involves walking through a planned operation with someone playing the part of an adversary in order to refine the plan. The operations officer usually plays the part of the friendly force and the intelligence officer plays the part of the adversary. Unlike no-holds-barred combat simulation, military wargaming is disciplined and carefully choreographed in an action (taken by friendly force), reaction (predicted to be taken by the adversary), and counteraction (friendly action to counteract the adversary's reaction) process. When done by a well-practiced staff, it can be done very efficiently and serves to quickly identify gaps in planning.

Wargaming the battle with cyber and operational planners is essential to developing targets. Targets will likely emerge from the Critical Capability, Critical Requirement, and Critical Vulnerability outputs of CoG analysis, and may be strategic, operational or tactical. Other targets will emerge dynamically, and the more often wargaming can identify these targets in advance the better planners will be able to create anticipatory mission packages which speed dynamic mission execution despite not knowing all the details in advance. Planners won't be able to identify all targets in advance. Some targets will unanticipated, which due to limited available time, necessarily constrains the range of potential options and may call for more generic, versus precision, mission options such as jamming, DDOS attack, or physical attack.

Cyberspace operations bring additional challenges. You might know where a target exists logically in cyberspace, and can even reach it, but not know its location in the physical domain, or vice versa. Because it is very difficult to draw crisp boundaries in cyberspace around operational areas of responsibility for subordinate units, planners will need to work extensively to deconflict[ii] targets with other stakeholders across the government, allies, and other third parties, and take part in intelligence gain/loss discussions. The bureaucratic results will likely be messy at first, but will improve over time and can be assisted by creating effects that are logically or geographically constrained. Long-term planning timelines are essential, particularly while a pre-approved playbook of options is immature.

Potential targets exist at the tactical, operational and strategic level. Cyber operations afford a very wide range of potential targets from individuals, to businesses, cities, and critical infrastructure, to strategic assets, even entire populations. There aren't crisp lines defining the cyber battlespace, so expect actors to target not just the local battlefield, but deep into the rear area where it would be difficult to strike using conventional means. Depending on the constraints actors face, self-imposed or otherwise, targets may well include garrison facilities of military units, national governments, financial markets, business entities, elections, even the homes of service members. There is no sanctuary and returning safely home from "the war." We should not naively think otherwise. Cyber conflict can affect entire populations, innocent or not.[466]

---

[ii] *Target Deconfliction*: In physical conflict, each potential target is the responsibility of a specific organization, and that responsibility is usually defined by *unit boundaries* – the borders that specify how an area of operations is divided among units. In some cases, unit borders overlap and targets are divided among units operating in the same area of operations by their higher headquarters.

Some general categories of potential targets include data,[467] code, devices, servers, networks, services, systems, facilities, places. People can also be targets of cyberspace operations. It often makes sense to target the human actors behind a given type of activity.[468] Interdependencies also play a critical role, as you think through desired effects remember you aren't constrained to only first-order effects. An army that doesn't get food, ammunition, water, power, pay, or fuel won't be an army for long. See Table 9-4 for examples.

*Table 9-4: Example cyberspace targets at the strategic, operational, and tactical levels of war.*

| | Strategic | Operational | Tactical |
|---|---|---|---|
| **Military** | National military command and control systems,[469] logistics systems,[470] nuclear weapons[471] | Reachback support for deployed forces, drone fleet command and control,[472] Air Defense Artillery (ADA) systems[473] | Communication devices and combat systems used on the battlefield |
| **Communications** | Presidential email,[474] senior military staff email[475] | Web portals used for collaboration among subordinate organizations | Tactical networks used by deployed units |
| **Commerce and Finance** | Online banking,[476] trading exchanges,[477] strategic backups of financial transactions for global corporations[478] | Enterprise data centers,[479] CISOs | Business hotels, point of sale terminals, system administrators |
| **Defense Industrial Base** | Plans of next generation weapon systems | Developer teams | Contractor home computers |
| **Emergency Services** | Emergency alert systems | Regional 911 systems | Dispatching systems |
| **Energy** | National energy grid[480] | Nuclear power plants[481] | Installation power supply |
| **Education** | Research funding agencies | University research and prototypes[482] | Graduate students, faculty members |
| **Food and Agriculture** | Next generation agricultural system research at a federal agency | Automated food production systems | Food shipment logistic systems |
| **Government** | Senior government officials, tax collection services, security | City-level critical infrastructure and governance | Voting machines |

| | | | |
|---|---|---|---|
| | clearance processing | systems,[483] voter registration databases | |
| **Homes and Personal** | Nationally deployed networking and entertainment equipment, mobile device networks[484] | Consumer grade IoT devices brought into the enterprise workplace[485] | Baby monitors,[486] electronic picture frames, smart-grid power meters, fitness bracelets, laptops, tablets, mobile devices, home routers |
| **Information Technology** | App stores,[487] code signing keys,[488] open source software repositories | Enterprise clouds[489] | End-user consumer technology |
| **Manufacturing** | Chip manufacturing[490] | Just-in-time logistics systems | Warehouse shipping system |
| **Medical** | Medical laboratories | Corporate plans for next generation medical devices | Automated pharmacy systems |
| **Social** | Global social media sites | Dating sites[491] | Personas of influential social media personalities |
| **Transportation** | Smart vehicles, networked vehicles, GPS systems, seaports, airports, air traffic control systems[492] | City-level traffic systems, fuel processing plants, passenger jets[493] | Aircraft, gas stations |
| **Water** | SCADA systems that control water supply of arid country | Water purification plants, dams[494] | Town/village water purification systems, sewage treatment systems |

As you examine the table, note that we've heavily cited sources from the news to demonstrate how many of these targets have already been engaged in some way. These engagements have played out over an extended period, but it is not hard imagine what might happen if many or most of these targets were engaged simultaneously in an intense conflict scenario. Intelligence and access play a key role in targeting. Analysts believe many of these initial cyber-related incidents are for reconnaissance purposes and to develop access in case of future conflict. We are even seeing incidents of criminal groups gaining access to information systems to gain lists of other high-payoff targets.[495]

The hardness of the target matters a lot when choosing which targets to prosecute and how. Some will be soft targets and easier to exploit, others are much harder and perhaps cyber operations aren't the right tool. We've seen what appears to be a bell curve of target hardness, from old, supported, and highly vulnerable to modern and reasonably well protected to bleeding edge and again vulnerable.

> *"Perhaps the most challenging aspect of attributing actions in cyberspace is connecting a cyberspace actor (cyber-persona) or action to an actual individual, group, or state actor, with sufficient confidence and verifiability to hold them accountable."*
> – *U.S. Department of Defense Cyber Operations Doctrine*[496]

## Attribution

You cannot target well if you can't detect an actor or activity. Even when you can detect these things, it would be reckless to shoot at humans, machines, systems, or facilities without knowing if they are friendly, neutral, or enemy. While not necessarily easy in kinetic warfare, the laws of warfare require service members and their equipment to be readily identifiable. Medical teams and equipment are similarly identified with a Red Cross or Red Crescent to show their non-combatant status. Accidents sometimes occur, but deliberately violating these principles, a common tactic of extremist groups, is considered a war crime. In an attempt to prevent fratricide, traditional militaries have created Identify Friend or Foe (IFF) systems. For example, a surface to air missile system might interrogate a transponder on an aircraft to determine if it is a threat before firing.

In cyberspace there is little in the way of IFF systems to help combatants differentiate between friendly, neutral, and enemy. Perhaps the closest we have are digital signatures and Public Key Infrastructure.[497] There are certainly no equivalent of uniforms or the Red Crescent. Short of an evil bit,[iii,498] combatants need to put deliberate effort into determining both responsibility and lawful targets. This challenge is key to the attribution problem.[499]

Attribution is rarely clear cut, even when an actor "claims" responsibility. In actuality, attribution is a spectrum from no confidence to very high confidence. When the President of the United States appeared on national television and pointed the finger at North Korea after the Sony Hack, most observers were fairly confident that he had incontrovertible evidence.[500] Between the two extremes of no confidence and high confidence is a context-dependent threshold of uncertainty and plausible deniability that makes counterattacks or sanctions difficult or impossible on the global stage.[501] Speed of attribution is important and while it would be great to employ high speed automated attribution systems, such systems aren't feasible in many circumstances. It wouldn't take long before attackers realized that you were naively targeting, say, source IP addresses of purported "attackers" and endeavor to trick your automated systems into attacking a neutral target like a hospital, or even yourself.

Depending on the scenario, attribution may require confirmation through multiple sources of intelligence, reverse engineering of hardware and software, and extensive forensic analyses.[502] The work required to accurately attribute a cyber attack can be even greater if the analyst must punch through the noise of deception and disinformation campaigns. Attribution is another area that is prime for additional research.[503] Table 9-5 includes examples of information that can be used for attribution.

---

[iii] *The Evil Bit:* Internet Request for Comments (RFC) 3514. Released on April Fool's Day in 2003, RFC 3514 is a tongue-in-cheek recommendation for network packets to include a header field set to 1 if the packet is sent with malicious intent, or 0 otherwise. Of course, no malicious cyber actor would ever follow such a recommendation.

*Table 9-5: Types of information useful for attributing a cyber attack to a particular actor in cyberspace. Note that many can be spoofed as part of a deception strategy.*

| Carrier Objects Employed | Target Systems | Construction |
|---|---|---|
| • Executable files<br>• Memory<br>• Exploits<br>• Processes<br>• Macros<br>• Network packets<br>• Scripts<br>• Data files<br>• Update mechanisms | • Operating System<br>• Applications<br>• Processes<br>• Hardware<br>• Purpose<br>• Provenance<br>• Organization | • Compiler(s) / Interpreter(s)<br>• Source programming language<br>• Custom or open source tools<br>• Tool suite used<br>• Payloads<br>• 0-day<br>• Code signing certificates |
| **Behavior** | **Transport Mechanism** | **Defensive Mechanisms** |
| • Targeting<br>• Propagation<br>• Collateral damage safeguards<br>• Time of attacks<br>• Frequency and volume of attacks<br>• C2 requirements<br>• Targeted information<br>• Clean-up behaviors<br>• Tactics simularity<br>• Code complexity and size<br>• Time zone<br>• Patient zero<br>• Effects caused<br>• Coding errors | • EM Spectrum<br>• WWW<br>• Email<br>• LAN<br>• Hardware<br>• Removable Media<br>• Peripheral<br>• TCP/IP<br>• App Store<br>• Humans | • Anti-Virtual Machines<br>• Anti-Forensics<br>• Anti-Reverse Engineering<br>• Code obfuscation<br>• Deception<br>• Packing<br>• Encryption<br>• Proxies |

While attribution is the objective of those attacked, it is useful to consider the perspective of the attacker whose objective is non-attribution. Non-attribution TTPs are those measures an actor takes to frustrate attribution attempts. There will be instances where attribution is obvious or unnecessary, but oftentimes actors, especially those with weaker traditional military capability, will actively seek to avoid attribution. Expect actors to take measures to reduce their online signatures[504] and operate through anonymizing proxies including personas, anonymity networks, public WiFi access points, hotels, and compromised machines of innocent bystanders. However, even if an attacker is operating through an anonymizing screen and cannot be readily attributed, those attacked may very well return fire and start attacking the proxies themselves, even if the systems were once innocent bystanders. Expect deception as well, ranging from spoofed IP addresses to complex false flag operations implicating innocent parties.

## CAPABILITIES ANALYSIS

With a prioritized target list in hand, the next step is to match appropriate capabilities with targets, a process called weaponeering, and to estimate potential collateral damage.[505] In Chapter 7 we discussed technical capabilities in depth, but targets need not be engaged by technical means alone, any of the traditional levers of power or other forms of leverage can be brought to bear against a given target, even if it is beyond the reach of technical means. Planners should be open minded and think beyond kinetic and cyber operations, if needed. The U.S. Military calls this larger team effort *Unified Action*, and is illustrated in Figure 9-6.

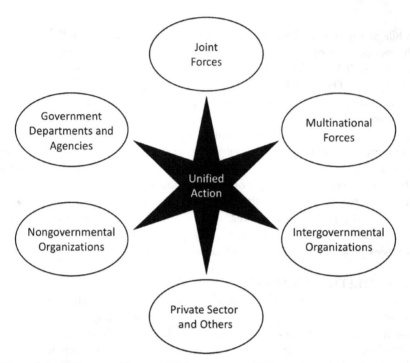

*Figure 9-6: When matching capabilities to targets think not just of organic cyber and operations capabilities, but the capabilities possessed by other arms of government, international allies, law enforcement, and across the public and private sector.*[506]

Each of these actors possesses differing kinetic and cyber weapons, but also various degrees of access to information, legal authorities for action, and elements of power such as law enforcement, diplomacy, intelligence assets, economic power, and information sharing policies that may be leveraged to gain a desired effect. For example, a law enforcement agency in conjunction with a national government may issue an indictment against foreign military hackers or extradite an alleged malicious hacker.[507] The entire spectrum of hard and soft tools can be employed to achieve the effects you desire, both when initiating an offensive operation and as a defensive counter.[508] Counterattacks need not be only hacking back, sometimes tracking down the actual humans behind an activity or undermining centers of gravity through soft power can be equally effective.

As we discussed in the Chapter 7, capabilities are a precious commodity. We propose a Law of Conservation of Capabilities, to use the least valuable capability first to achieve a desired effect.

**Weaponeering**

Weaponeering is a military term for determining or developing the means to create a desired effect on a target.[509] In Chapter 7 we discussed the importance of creating a database of available capabilities and metrics for evaluating the cost and other implications of their use, here is where we bring that database to bear by evaluating the desired effects and mapping them to available capabilities. See Table 9-6. There are myriad potential weapon platforms that actors may employ, at the most basic level any node or device capable of transmitting traffic is a potential weapon system. We envision many potential platforms, from hardware only devices, such as a DDOS in a box that simply needs a target IP and a network connection then fires off packets to hardened war computers to battle-oriented data centers optimized for combat. We have already seen the Mirai botnet which consisted of IoT devices organized into bot armies. Regardless of the specific platform, actors will employ management consoles to manage their assets and evaluate their health and performance, like Metasploit or Armitage but designed to operate at a grand scale.[510] There is a lot of potential for innovation in this area.

*Table 9-6: Examples of weaponeering, the matching of appropriate capabilities to targets*

| Priority | Target | Capability | Effect |
|---|---|---|---|
| 1 | Offensive nation-state cyber operations teams | Law enforcement indictment | Deter recruiting efforts and chill appetite for future exploitative operations |
| 2 | Offensive nation-state affiliated cyber operations teams | Extradition | Disrupt government enabled criminal group operations |
| 3 | Insurgent group C2 | Trojan Horse | Send spoofed messages from insurgent group leader to deceive subordinates[511] |
| 4 | Government C2 | Router exploitation[512] | Deny government key command and control communication links |
| 5 | Media Outlet Websites | DDOS | Degrade ability to share news of combat events |
| 6 | Financial System | Logic Bombs | Create loss of confidence in national currency |

## Constraining Effects

Firing a rifle is straightforward and the effects are well understood; aim at a target, pull the trigger and a bullet flies the direction the rifle is pointed. The maximum effective ranges of standard caliber rifles are well known, and short of a ricochet nothing really surprising happens. Bombs are more complex, but behave in predictable ways. Drop a bomb on a target and there will be predictable damage within a certain blast radius. As we've discussed, cyber effects spread rapidly and are much more difficult to constrain geographically and virtually. Beyond just the effects, even the weapon system itself and knowledge of the vulnerability, in the form of code, may spread rapidly. It's as if firing a rifle gives everyone else the knowledge of how to build the rifle at near zero cost. There are many reasons to constrain effects, including to:

- Limit collateral damage
- Prevent cascading effects[513]
- Comply with law or policy
- Avoid angering home country government or law enforcement[514]
- Respect moral or ethical limits[515]
- Avoid no-strike areas
- Allow autonomy of command by respecting assigned areas of responsibility
- Avoid being detected or identified
- Limit disclosure of vulnerabilities or tools used[516]
- Avoid or limit the effects an adversary may have on you

Cyber effects are notoriously difficult to control, a lesson we started learning early on with the Morris Worm. However, constraining effects is often possible across each of the planes of cyberspace. Examples of this are provided in Table 9-7. [517] Research is ongoing to estimate and measure cyberspace effects.[518] There is also the risk that containing effects to avoid certain activities, actors, or regions will provide clues that allow attribution.

*Table 9-7: There are many strategies for containing cyberspace effects. This table provides examples across each of the cyberspace planes.*

| Cyber Plane | Examples |
|---|---|
| **Command and Control** | Employ administrative control measures such as no-strike lists, restricted target lists, and off limits areas, provide active command and control of deployed capabilities, use highly trained personnel, require mandatory verification and re-verification of key parameters like target IP addresses, require a human in the loop for decision making, provide update mechanism for capability |
| **Persona** | Target only specific identities (e.g.: specific administrator accounts, email addresses or social media accounts), conduct identity verification before executing operations |
| **Logical** | Assign logical areas of responsibility to unit commanders, use commodity vs. custom capabilities first, use capabilities without built-in propagation mechanisms, employ capabilities that self-destruct/delete themselves after a period of time, encrypt capability until used against very precise system,[519] perform very robust testing before use of a capability, confirm hardware, software, and network technical specifications match those of target, employ propagation counters |
| **Physical** | Limit transmission power of wireless hacking systems, use directional and/or low gain antennas, limit more virulent attacks to air gapped networks, restrict propagation to certain physical devices, confirm presence of known hardware on target before execution |
| **Geographic** | Assign geographic areas of responsibility to unit commanders, employ fire support control measures such as coordinated fire lines and kill boxes,[520] conduct attacks only through physical access, use geographically constrained propagation strategies such as dropping a thumb drive in a target parking lot |

## FORCE ASSIGNMENT

With the prioritized target list in hand, it is time to assign targets to given forces. Some targets can be assigned to traditional military forces, some to special operations units, and some to cyber operations forces, providing that each possesses the right access, operational reach, experience, and cyber weaponry, see Figure 9-7. As you assign missions, make sure that forces understand the *Rules of Engagement* (ROE)–when, where, and under what circumstances they may perform their activities. Keep in mind that cyber conflict is asymmetric and cyber operational missions can be assigned to a wide variety of actors with different levels of ability to prevent attribution.

We've seen collaborations between governments, online criminal groups, activist organizations, and hacker collectives in cyber conflict. Expect some combatants to assign cyber missions to non-traditional forces. Virtually anyone with a computer and a network connection could play a part.[521]

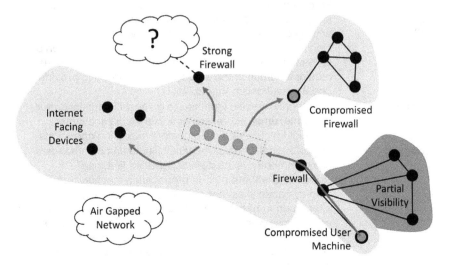

*Figure 9-7: "Range Fan" a given team has to engage various targets. In this example the team can directly engage Internet facing devices, as well as a target network via a compromised firewall. The team has partial ability to strike a user machine compromised through a drive-by download[iv] on a website which may enable strikes deeper into the network despite a firewall. The team can also strike another firewall, but has no current ability to strike deeper into the network. An air gapped network remains out of reach.*

## MISSION PLANNING AND EXECUTION

After planners identify and prioritize targets, mission planning and rehearsals begin in earnest by the team assigned to the operation. For complex operations, particularly those involving new capabilities or new types of targets, proper rehearsals will include development of mockups of the target and the network environment to increase the likelihood of mission success.[522] Acquiring the requisite hardware and software of the target may disclose intent to third-parties and teams must exercise care in acquiring such components. Sources range from open source repositories, commercial

---

[iv] *Drive-by Download*: This term refers to malware embedded in web pages, usually as scripts associated with the page. Most major websites have one or many small programs embedded in them written in JavaScript or other scripting languages. An attacker will often use a phishing email to entice a user at a targeted organization to click on a link that hosts a webpage with a malicious script that causes the victim's system to download and install a piece of malware.

suppliers, second-hand sources like eBay and Craigslist, and black markets. Replicating the exact target environment is the goal, but operators must always assume their rehearsal environment is imperfect and plan for contingencies. The requirement for such flexibility underscores the importance of highly skilled operators who can go off-script when necessary while understanding the risks and advantages of their actions. Given the wide range of expertise required for teams to execute missions, teams may have to bring in subject matter experts in given technologies and target domains as advisors.

Extensive planning and rehearsals are luxuries that circumstances might not permit, particularly for dynamic targeting. Teams should be given flexibility and authority to achieve the intent of the mission to the greatest extent possible. A playbook of techniques and pre-established fires options will help here, as will rules of engagement that define the broader boundaries of when and where teams can create effects. For example, military ROE typically provide for self-defense regardless of the actor. Additionally, fires in the heat of battle require decision making and approval authority at the lowest level of command possible. Clearly you wouldn't want nuclear weapons in the hands of junior soldiers, but placing authority to use cyber capabilities in the hands of field commanders is important. The playbook can create tiers of capability and effects options that push authority downward for agility, but require higher levels of approval as the risk and cost increases.[523] Ideal playbooks should be written as flexibly as possible, otherwise you may have a very hard time coming up with options that are effective, remain relevant over time, and aren't too tailored to any specific scenario.[524] From the operational perspective, the goal is to reduce approval time to zero, but this isn't always possible or prudent for operations that could generate dangerous or widespread effects.

Mission planning gives way to execution, as depicted in Figure 9-8. When possible, fires should be automated to create rapid and decisive attacks that function at machine or network speed, leaving adversaries to respond slowly at human speed. Automated target deconfliction and weapons assignment is used in kinetic weapons, such as the Phalanx weapon system found aboard combat ships, and may be used with great effect in cyberspace operations.[525] Specific nodes may be assigned targets based on assets they possess, such as bandwidth, storage, processing power, protective screens of anonymizing proxies, or physical or logical proximity to the target. Rotating firing nodes limits potential for counterattack and deconflicting targets allows maximum efficient use of the forces of available, see Figure 9-9.

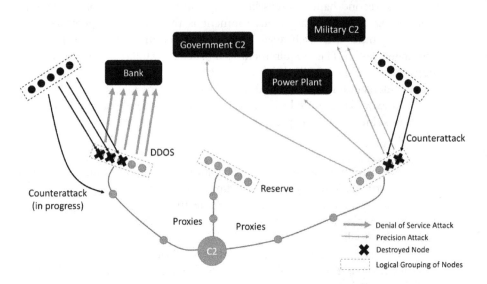

*Figure 9-8: Notional cyber combat scenario.*[526]  *In this example, one actor maintains control of three teams protected by a series of proxies that help provide protection from counterattack and attribution.  One team (right) executes precision attacks against Government C2, a Power Plant, and Military C2.  The next team (left) performs a noisy DDOS attack against a bank.  The third team is held in reserve.*[527]  *The other actor counterattacks knocking some attacking nodes offline.*

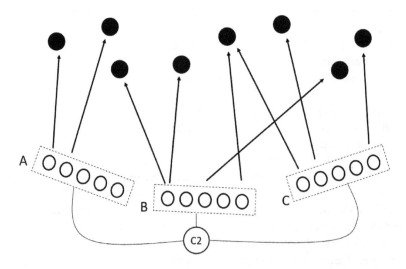

*Figure 9-9:  Sharing targeting information between attacking nodes via a secure command and control communication channel allows target deconfliction and optimal allocation of systems against various classes of targets.*

Teams should consider the duration of their fires. Unlike kinetic attack, some cyberspace attacks will not be noticed, particularly precision attacks, in this case seeking shorter timespans to initiate and conduct operations is desirable to decrease the likelihood of detection and response.

With extensive efforts to train and rehearse, events *should* unfold smoothly, but there are no guarantees. Success is always probabilistic. Of course, kinetic fires and effects are still prone to issues, but the odds of success are often higher with kinetic options. Teams can improve their chances of success with thorough planning and rehearsal. After the team executes the mission, the next step is to confirm proper execution and reattack if necessary until they've accomplished their objectives. From here we move to Assessment where you determine your impact and what, if any, unanticipated or undesirable effects you may have caused.

## ASSESSMENT

Firing without checking to assess whether you hit your target is foolhardy. The Fires and Effects process we've been discussing includes an important last step – Assessment, which provides critical feedback into the overall process and will help inform future targeting and determine whether reattack is necessary.[528] During Assessment we seek to measure the effectiveness of a cyber operation by monitoring the attack as it unfolds, evaluating what happened, and making necessary adjustments to future plans.[529] Assessment in cyberspace can be particularly challenging. It is often difficult to observe your targets and many effects are difficult to assess reliably. Intelligence planning is critical to making sure there is proper overwatch of the target to either observe the operation as it takes place, or to examine the state of the target after the fact. When possible, use passive observation, rather than active observation, to limit the possibility that your observation will be traced back to you.

We want to measure three primary things during the assessment phase: battle damage, collateral damage, and capability effectiveness. Battle Damage Assessment (BDA) considers the effects on the target, collateral damage assessment considers other effects beyond the target, and capabilities (or munitions) assessment examines how well the capability performed. The key then is to feed back these insights into future planning and operations.

## Conclusions

Fires and Effects are at the core of cyber operations. Cyber operations can have devastating effects, both as first-order consequences in cyberspace and second-order and beyond in cyberspace and the physical world. Effects in cyberspace must be carefully considered and operational forces must carefully employ safeguards to prevent collateral damage.

Speed of operations matters. A vetted playbook and delegated release authority gives operational commanders a suite of potential options to employ on the battlefield and gain trust in. Success is never guaranteed, but proper planning, training, and rehearsal of cyber operators alongside kinetic warfighters are keys to success. Fires and Effects requires a team that brings together kinetic and cyberspace planners and enlists domain experts on specific target systems.[530] Cyber operations organizations must develop both long-term, deliberate planning processes as well as very rapid processes to handle fleeting opportunities on the battlefield. Pre-planned targets and the development of access in advance, perhaps years in advance, will aid in rapid cyber fires prosecution when the need arises. Expect the role of automation to increase in order to create fires and effects that are rapid, decisive, deconflicted, and far outpace human response. We must seek to improve attribution. Sometimes attribution will be easy, fast and accurate, but at other times attribution will be tedious, time consuming, and error prone. Commanders will be faced with hard risk and benefit decisions in terms of intelligence gain/loss as well as when and whom to attack or counterattack. Sometimes their decisions will be wrong.

Cyber fires and effects will remain a challenging, but surmountable problem. We are preparing for cyber operations and technologies that haven't even been invented yet. The high rate of technological change ensures that those that stand still will be left behind, those that move quickly will gain operational advantage.

# 10 COMMAND AND CONTROL

*No single activity in war is more important than command and control. Command and control by itself will not drive home a single attack against an enemy force. It will not destroy a single enemy target. It will not effect a single emergency resupply. Yet none of these essential warfighting activities, or any others, would be possible without effective command and control. Without command and control, campaigns, battles, and organized engagements are impossible, military units degenerate into mobs, and the subordination of military force to policy is replaced by random violence. In short, command and control is essential to all military operations and activities.*

*- United States Marine Corps Doctrine*[531]

Command and Control (C2) is what organizes individuals into effective units, or mobs into armies. Command provides instructions efficiently to these units and Control regulates their activities and provides feedback to the leader. In this chapter we study command and control as it applies to cyberspace operations.

Understanding command and control principles and how to apply them is valuable to both military cyberspace operators and information security professionals. Command and control will help you scale your operations, make better decisions, employ software intelligence, maximize the power of your human capital, and gain a shared understanding of your operational environment.

## Uncertainty and Speed

Combat is replete with uncertainty.[532]   Command and control reduces uncertainty in any combat situation by working to provide personnel, especially the commander, the right information at the right time.   The information flows two ways.  Command includes the guidance and directives from the leader to subordinates designed to achieve the leader's intent and objectives.  Control includes the feedback the leader receives from her forces to confirm her directions are being followed, to understand the current situation, and provides opportunity to make adjustments as necessary.[533] Included in Command and Control are information gathering and analysis, decision making, operational planning and coordination, communicating directives, and supervising execution, with the ultimate objective being the effective conduct of operational action.[534]  Contrary to traditional military thinking we assume that humans aren't just leading other humans, but also code-based systems of varying degrees of intelligence and autonomy.  There are three primary parts of a command and control system:  decision makers, information, and the C2 infrastructure.  Here we include in decision makers both humans and machines.   Machines will give commands to other machines, and while admittedly rare at present, machines will provide directives to humans.  We believe machine oversight of humans is something that will grow over time.   In this fashion C2 weaves together the primary functions of cyber operations: movement and maneuver, protection, intelligence, logistics, fires and effects, and capabilities, see Figure 10-1.  We'll explore different organizational models and C2 topologies later in the chapter.

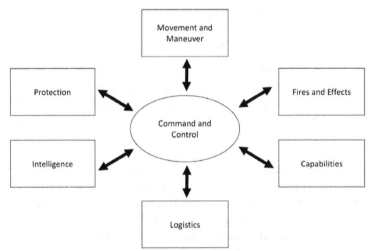

*Figure 10-1: Command and Control is integral to all primary functions of cyber operations.*[535]

Speed is essential to Command and Control. The objective is to reduce uncertainty to the degree possible within available time, make informed decisions, and act to faster than your adversary. Historical command and control was slow and limited to the sound of the leader's voice, but was soon extended using drums, gongs, flags, and written directives. More modern automated command and control systems greatly expanded the leader's reach and reduced the time required to communicate, but are still bound to human speed decision making. Automated offensive and defensive systems are now emerging with increasing degrees of autonomy. We expect these trends to continue. With cyber operations in particular, machine and network speed decision making will quickly become a necessity.

*"Whatever the age or technology, the ultimate measure of C2 effectiveness will always be the same: can it help us act faster and more effectively than the enemy?"*
*- United States Marine Corps Doctrine*[536]

**Approaches to Command and Control**
Command and control is inherently cooperative. Units of one side work together to achieve a common end. The adversary doesn't cooperate with your stratagems, but does cooperate amongst themselves. There are two basic models of command and control: mission command and detailed command. Each makes different assumptions about war, autonomy, organization, and leadership methods. Figure 10-2 compares the two models.

Mission Command is the predominant approach employed by the U.S. military. It assumes that war is probabilistic and difficult to predict and embraces the ever-present disorder and uncertainty in combat. The philosophy behind mission command empowers subordinates and decentralizes authority affording spontaneity and individual initiative. Mission Command works best with trained and self-disciplined subordinates who understand the leader's intent. The leader's intent, or in the parlance of the military "Commander's Intent," is an essential tenet of Mission Command. If subordinates understand the commander's intent, or what he expects to achieve in the overall mission, they can be resilient and adaptive in the myriad ill-defined situations they will face in combat. Mission Command's empowering nature helps forces remain agile, exploit opportunities on the battlefield, and function effectively if communications with headquarters break down.[537]

| Detailed | Command & Control | Mission |

Assumes war is:
**Deterministic**
**Predictable**

Assumes war is:
**Probabilistic**
**Unpredictable**

Accepts:
**Order**
**Certainty**

Accepts:
**Disorder**
**Uncertainty**

Tends to lead to:
**Centralization**
**Coercion**
**Formality**
**Tight Rein**
**Imposed Discipline**
**Obedience**
**Compliance**
**Ability Mostly at Top**

Tends to lead to:
**Decentralization**
**Spontaneity**
**Informality**
**Loose Rein**
**Self-Discipline**
**Initiative**
**Cooperation**
**Ability Throughout**

Communication:
**Explicit**
**Vertical**
**Linear**

Communication:
**Implicit**
**Vertical & Horizontal**
**Interactive**

Organization:
**Mechanistic**
**Bureaucratic**

Organization:
**Organic**
**Ad Hoc**

Leadership:
**Authoritarian**
**Telling**

Leadership:
**Persuasive**
**Delegating**

Appropriate to:
**Science of War**
**Technical/Procedural Tasks**

Appropriate to:
**Art of War**
**Conduct of Operations**

*Figure 10-2: Comparison of Detailed Command and Mission Command-based C2 models. While Mission Command is better suited to traditional kinetic operations and human cyber operators, Detailed Command is better suited for automated cyber operations and cyber capabilities.*[538]

As Figure 10-2 illustrates, Detailed Command is the mirror opposite of Mission Command and makes fundamentally different assumptions about war. Detailed Command assumes that war is deterministic and predictable which leads to centralization of authority, ability mostly at the top, tight discipline, and detailed, sometimes stifling, instructions to subordinates. Because of these factors, Detailed Command is usually slower, far less adaptive, and fails to exploit opportunity.

Which model is better? Well, both are right, or wrong, depending on the individual circumstances. In general, the U.S. Military greatly prefers mission command and its benefits. Detailed Command is an anathema. However, U.S. doctrine admits there is a time and place for each model. We believe C2 of cyberspace systems and capabilities frequently requires Detailed Command despite its tight rein and consolidation of authority. Code, even "autonomous code," requires close human supervision. We want to draw an important distinction however; we mean Detailed Command is more important when humans are giving instructions to machines. Machine intelligence is simply not mature enough to merit the trust Mission Command implies. Today it may be harder legally to "kill" a computer than a human, sometimes for good reason. However, and this is important, Detailed Command breaks down when the flow of information to or from the higher echelon is broken or disrupted. This combination of the need for close control of capabilities, and the fact that most machines aren't intelligent enough to handle disruption of their C2, will remain an Achilles heel of emerging cyber capabilities. Another challenge is that Mission Command provides subordinate leaders autonomy over a specific physical region. Providing similar autonomy over regions of the highly interconnected networks of cyberspace remains an unsolved technical problem.

### Coup d'oeil

Much responsibility rests on the shoulders of the leader, whether employing Mission Command or Detailed Command.[539] Commanders must develop a "feel" for the situation gained through experience and personal observation. They need an overview of the situation to watch how patterns of events unfold and to envision the situation from the perspective of the enemy to anticipate adversary actions and intentions.[540]

Much of what is expected from the leader is captured in the French term, *coup d'oeil*. Literally, *coup d'oeil* means "stroke of the eye," but has grown to mean the inherent ability of a leader, typically a senior commander, to survey the terrain and discern the tactical advantages and disadvantages.[541] *Coup d'oeil* is master-level leadership at its best. We've seen it in senior general officers, but also in financial sector veterans who can look at the New York Stock Exchange trading board and immediately grasp the implications, security engineers who can look at a network configuration and know if the design is flawed, and doctors who can quickly diagnose patients. We need to grow *coup d'oeil* in cyber leaders. You won't find *coup d'oeil* in the amateur.[542] The technical skill requirements are very different than that required of kinetic warfare leaders, but the value to cyber operations is immeasurable. Cyber leaders who develop *coup d'oeil* will be highly sought after by professional cyber forces around the world and the commercial sector.

**Command and Control by Whom of What?**
Personnel, networks, information systems, processes and procedures, and facilities and equipment all make up a C2 system, shown in Figure 10-3, but what exactly is being commanded and controlled, and by whom? We've suggested that humans and machines are both potential decision makers and subordinates in cyber operations. Let's take a look at some different scenarios. Humans have historically directed humans in military operations (H2H). Humans have also directed machines (H2M). For example, a human botnet operator may have a million or more zombie computers under their control. Machines also direct other machines (M2M). We see M2M command and control in a group of swarming drones or the autopilot of a jet.[543] Finally, machines sometimes direct humans (M2H). For example, a GPS directing a driver, who complies with the instructions. Figure 10-4 illustrates these four relationships. An interesting side aspect of M2H command and control is that the human may or may not know that they are being directed by a machine, such as in a work order system.[544] Interestingly, humans will sometimes follow machine instructions even if the guidance is bad, such as the driver who could have died when her GPS took her deep into the desolation of Death Valley.[545]

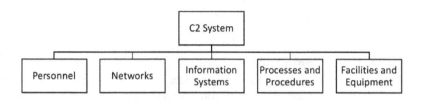

*Figure 10-3: Components of a Command and Control System.*[546]

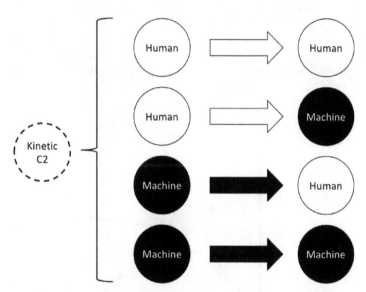

*Figure 10-4: There are four basic models of C2 relationships: Human to Human (H2H), Human to Machine (H2M), Machine to Human (M2H), and Machine to Machine (M2M). In some cases these relationships may be nested under traditional kinetic command and control.*

*1. Serve the Public Trust*
*2. Protect the Innocent*
*3. Uphold the Law*
*4. Classified*
        *— RoboCop's Prime Directives*[547]

## Command and Control of Machines

We've stated that machines can give or receive instructions, being either the leader or the led, but what exactly does this mean? Machines are simply information processing systems with varying degrees of intelligence, ranging from simple algorithms to advanced artificial intelligence.[548] Even the most "intelligent" systems were created by humans, at least until machines are truly capable of creating other machines, and the human designers imbued their intelligent creation with a certain degree of autonomy and bias. As organizations place these machines into service, the organization may increase or decrease the autonomy of their machines beyond that of the creator's original intent. Intuitively, we might think that an increase in intelligence results in a proportional increase in autonomy, but the human masters of these machines may very well decide to keep some features disabled and keep their inventions in a tightly controlled box, see Figure 10-5.

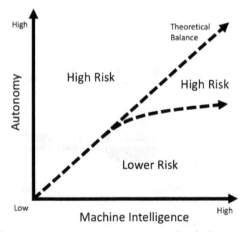

*Figure 10-5: It is dangerous to give autonomy to systems that lack appropriate intelligence, but it is also very dangerous to provide a high degree of autonomy to highly intelligence machines.*

Autonomy is what gives Mission Command its power. By understanding their commander's intent and the bigger picture of the conflict, leaders can exploit opportunity and function effectively despite a breakdown in communication. In short, leaders are empowered. What then is the role of autonomy in cyberspace systems? We frequently hear the phrase mentioned: autonomous drones, autonomous cars, and autonomous weapon systems.

Autonomy is the ability to make decisions and take actions without interference. Autonomy provides speed, flexibility, and agility. As the tempo of combat, especially cyber combat, increases, autonomy is a necessity. Code that can fight and move without human interaction will best human speed in almost every situation. Machines are increasingly beating human performance in the physical realm, and automated systems that reside exclusively in cyberspace can maneuver many orders of magnitude faster than humans.[549] Autonomy combined with intelligence provides machines the flexibility to exploit opportunity, the ability to execute highly complex actions, to behave without obvious patterns that humans can grasp, and to act with prescience.[550] As machine intelligence grows, we will see autonomous anti-malware and isolated machine detachments that function effectively even when isolated from their human command and control.[551] Such autonomy isn't trivial to achieve. The automated system requires appropriate knowledge of the leader's objectives and the big picture, much as we see in the kinetic warfighter's employment of Mission Command for traditional military operations.

The powerful lure of machine autonomy is obvious, but is it wise to give a robot a shotgun or trust that our intelligent code will act in ways that we intend? Probably not, at least not without putting in place high standards for quality control, carefully fielded deployment, and strict constraints on behavior.[552] There are many ethical concerns we must work through before even considering putting such dangerous systems to use.[553] Intelligent systems must be able to cope with damage and loss of contact with their leaders in resilient and safe ways. Providing machine autonomy without secure failsafe mechanisms and human overrides is foolhardy. The more intelligent systems become, the more difficult they will be to control. [554]

There is a trade-off between machine autonomy and human control. As machine autonomy increases, human control decreases, as shown in Figure 10-6. However, about where the two lines intersect, there is an important region where humans and machines collaborate. Interestingly, overall performance by human/machine teams seems to be better than either the best humans or best machines. In their book, *The Second Machine Age,* authors Erik Brynjolfsson and Andrew McAfee state this concept clearly; a "weak human + machine process was superior to a strong computer alone, and more remarkably, superior to a strong human + machine + inferior process" and that the key insight was that "human strategic guidance combined with the tactical acuity of a computer was overwhelming."[555]   These insights suggest machines don't need full autonomy, but should collaborate with humans for best performance.

*Figure 10-6: Human control declines as machine autonomy increases, however there is an important middle ground where overall system performance may be higher when machines and humans collaborate.*

*"Line tanks carry only a driver and the blower chief who directs the tank and its guns when they are not under the direct charge of the Regiment's computer."*
*-David Drake, in "Hangman"* [556]

Human control of machines can take many different forms, on both the physical and virtual planes.  Physical control means a device can be turned off, disconnected from the network, or destroyed.  Full virtual control means you can issue the machine any instructions you desire.  We may or may not have full virtual control even over the machines we own.  System creators may design in third-party control we can't remove,[557] create nagware we can't delete, update systems against user wishes, or limit users' administrator or root access.  Conversely, system creators may deliberately choose *not* to give themselves full control, for among many reasons, legal liability and to prevent governments from gaining access to corporate and customer data.  The logic being that you can't turn over data to the government if you can't access it yourself, even as the creator of the system.[558] A major part of cyber conflict is compromising adversary machines and placing them under friendly control.

Positive control prevents undesirable effects and prevents systems from behaving in ways the designers did not intend. For dangerous cyberspace capabilities, we must be able to guarantee control to the greatest extent possible.

There are varying degrees of control one can have over machines. Table 10-1 illustrates this concept. At one end of the spectrum, humans have full control over the machine and at the other end, machines operate fully autonomously. As we shift from one extreme to the other, the human increasingly delegates their authority and resources, but not necessarily their responsibility, to the machine for various actions.[559] While a human may be able to only control three to seven immediate subordinates, by increasing machine autonomy they can control far more virtual subordinates, albeit at a more abstract level. For example, a human may initiate an automatic firing sequence on a Phalanx weapon system, bring to bear multiple firing batteries across multiple ships all prioritizing their firing and deconflicting their targets. The ultimate decision as to what degree of control one should have is based on the level of acceptable risk.

*Table 10-1: Degrees of Human-in-the-Loop Decision Making [560]*

| Degree | Human | Machine |
|---|---|---|
| 1 | Makes decision | Offers no assistance |
| 2 | Makes decision | Offers full list of alternative courses of action |
| 3 | Makes decision | Offers filtered list of alternative courses of action |
| 4 | Makes decision | Suggests single recommended course of action |
| 5 | May override decision in limited time period | Executes single course of action |
| 6 | Kept informed of decision | Makes decision and executes automatically |
| 7 | Kept informed of decision if human asks machine | Makes decision and executes automatically |
| 8 | Machine may inform human at machine discretion | Makes decision and executes automatically |
| 9 | Ignored by machine | Makes decision and executes automatically |

The degree of human-in-the-loop control need not be fixed. You may design systems that operate at one level for routine use and other levels in combat. Such a model allows for tighter, but slower, human control when necessary and gains the advantage of high speed decision making and firing when toggled to a more automated mode. However, this design implies that the human retains an ultimate authority, outside of the system, to change the degree of human control. This was the problem with the fictional Skynet in the Terminator movie series.

### Control Measures

We mentioned earlier that commanders are assigned by their superiors a given sphere of responsibility (usually a geographic region), called an area of operations, where they have autonomy, An example area of operations is shown in Figure 10-7.[561] This autonomy is an implicit assumption in Mission Command. However, a geographically-based approach doesn't necessarily map well to cyber operations. As we discussed in the Fires and Effects chapter, while cyberspace is built upon physical devices it is difficult to constrain effects to geographic areas, particularly areas as small as a battalion, brigade or division might cover, typically about a mile or less, several miles, and tens of miles, respectively. Controlling effects in both the physical and virtual domains, however, is not impossible.[562] The military uses control measures to limit kinetic fires and effects, and to synchronize operations. The simplicity of these control measures is an advantage in traditional operations, but they lack sufficient fidelity for complex cyberspace operations. However some of these concepts and techniques are useful to inform appropriate cyberspace operations controls.

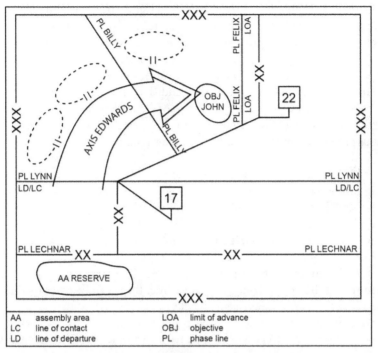

| AA | assembly area | LOA | limit of advance |
| LC | line of contact | OBJ | objective |
| LD | line of departure | PL | phase line |

*Figure 10-7: Geographic control measures used in traditional military operations are insufficient to properly control cyberspace operations, but are nonetheless useful to inform appropriate virtual controls.*[563]

As a starting point, we can assign nodes, links, or specific networks geographically if a specific context allows us to do so, such as an air gapped network, physical data center, or a cyber café. We can then assign additional areas of responsibility based on logical, not physical, attributes.

If we anticipate that activities, effects, or even presence on these systems will escape areas of responsibility, we must coordinate with appropriate stakeholders in advance (or after-the-fact if something unexpected occurs). Similar coordination is necessary if multiple units share responsibility for a given area. It will be up to the policymakers and lawyers to decide when and if forces should alert neutral third parties and how to cope with congested or ambiguous areas. Cyberspace is vast and not all areas need to be assigned immediately. Leaders can assign areas of responsibility based on emerging operational requirements as needed.

Control measures in cyberspace are often not as straightforward as in the physical domain. For example, some wireless attacks could be controlled using directional antennas, antenna gain, and signal strength. Control is aided by the natural attenuation of radio transmissions. But some physical control measure concepts are helpful. Here are some examples. Assembly Areas are locations units occupy to prepare for future operations.[564] In the cyberspace context, assembly areas might be virtual locations were operators meet online prior to operations and place software and data, ideally on a system where they have full control, or at least have not been detected. Compromised servers and end-user workstations are frequently employed by online criminals as assembly areas, and to stockpiles data and weapons.

After a leader is assigned an area of operations, planners divide up the region adding additional control measures, such as a Phase Lines (PL) which indicate when a unit has crossed a given geographic, physical or virtual threshold. These phase lines should be readily referenced by members of the unit.[565] Planners create a virtual Line of Departure (LD), that indicates the starting point of the operation and the Line of Contact (LC) where the unit may expect to be in contact with the enemy.[566] In cases where the line of departure and the line of contact are the same, these can be combined into a single LD/LC. The planners also assign Objectives (OBJs) that, again in the cyber operations context, indicate the target system, node, or network, and a Limit of Advance (LOA) that cautions forces to move no further. An Axis of Advance, provides the desired route for forces to move and maneuver, while a Direction of Attack provides a more general direction. These features can be combined with other control measures that designate certain areas off limits, such as a humanitarian aid organization headquarters, and possible positions from which to initiate fires and effects. As you think about these control measures realize that each concept is quite appropriate for synchronizing online automated or interactive operations, as well as amenable to graphical presentation and automated processing.

Control measures may also be embedded in the (semi) autonomous code. Examples include setting triggers for self-destruction, deleting forensic artifacts, encrypting payloads to prevent leakage and frustrate reverse engineering, limiting or not allowing automated propagation, and providing a strict set of requirements that must be met before creating effects.

Ultimately, these measures are only a starting point. In the future we anticipate that humans will not just be given autonomy in an area of operation, but also machines will be given virtual and physical areas of operations where they possess autonomy.

*Dave: Open the pod bay doors, HAL.*
*HAL: I'm Sorry Dave, I'm afraid I can't do that.*
*- 2001 A Space Odyssey* [567]

*"Please put down your weapon. You have twenty seconds to comply."*
*- ED-209* [568]

## Command and Control of Human Cyber Forces

We've discussed command and control of machines, but what about human cyber forces? Cyber forces may be employed at all three levels of war: tactical, operational and strategic. At the strategic level, operations can be global and most likely will happen outside of battlefield command and control. At the tactical and operational level, forces will be integrated into the kinetic warfighter's planning and C2. See Figure 10-8.

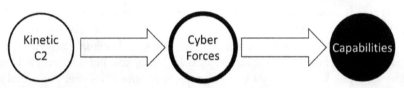

*Figure 10-8: At the operational and tactical levels of war, embed at least a small staff element in the kinetic force that can translate between operational requirements in the field and technical realities of cyber capabilities.*

These forces supporting kinetic C2 can follow several different models: permanently assigning cyber forces directly to maneuver units, integrating cyber forces temporarily for the duration of specific missions or operations, or providing support remotely. These models aren't an all or nothing affair, but may be used in combination. It is beneficial to have a staff officer or element integrated with tactical forces who understands the tactical requirements and planning processes, as well as how to properly request cyber support and the strengths and limitations of cyberspace capabilities. At the lowest tactical level where cyber might be employed, say a brigade, the element may consist of a single individual, with cyber elements growing more robust in size, experience, and rank at higher levels of headquarters.

For cyber operations to be taken seriously by the kinetic warfighting community, they must be responsive to kinetic warfighters' requests for support, and they must provide a liaison that is either permanently or temporary assigned for quick access. To best institutionalize and professionalize cyber operations into the kinetic force we suggest creation of a formal staff position at the brigade level and higher. More specifically, consider a traditional military staff, which includes a Personnel Officer (S1/G1/J1), Intelligence Officer (S2/G2/J2), Operations Officer (S3/G3/J3) and Logistician (S4/G4/J4).[i] Since Cyberspace Operations is operational, the position should be nested under the Operations Officer as the S3X at the brigade level, G3X at the division and higher, and J3X for Joint staffs. A formal staff position will build credibility and better integrate and institutionalize cyber operations into the larger effort rather than being an afterthought. However, military units are known to misuse personnel, for example putting an outlier staff officer in charge of mundane tasks such as creating briefing slides, so cyber leaders must be careful to guard against improper use of their people.

**Cooperation and Trust**

Until cyber operations become routine, there will be friction between government officials, partners, kinetic warfighters, and cyber operators. This friction can be reduced by close coordination and clear relationships that dictate lanes of responsibility and specify exactly who is in charge. These relationship define which organization is *supporting* another and who is being *supported*. The U.S. military's basic command relationships that are useful to understand:

---

[i] Continental Staff Numbering System. With its origins in the mid-19th century Napoleonic Army, the continental staff number system is used by Western militaries to identify staff roles. These numbers are below.
1. Manpower or personnel
2. Intelligence
3. Operations
4. Logistics
5. Plans
6. Signal (communications or IT)

Higher numbers are often used but are less standardized among Western countries. In a U.S. Army command that is not led by a flag (General) officer, staffs sections begin with the 'S' designation; the S1 is the personnel officer, the S2 is the intelligence officer, etc. In organizations that have a General officer commander (normally Division or larger), staff elements begin with a 'G' designation (G1, G2, G3, etc.). Joint staffs, those staffs that support commanders of units from multiple branches of the military (Army, Navy, Air Force, etc.) begin with a 'J' designation.

- Combatant Command (COCOM), which provides an organization full authority to accomplish its assigned missions
- Operational Control (OPCON), which places one organization fully under the control of another, typically for a limited duration
- Tactical Control (TACON), which places one organization under another for the limited purpose of directing movements and maneuvers in a given area of operations
- Direct Support, where one organization aids, protects, or complements another organization for the duration of an operation or mission.[569]
- General Support, where an organization provides support to a large number of organizations long-term on an as-needed basis.

Clearly applying these relationships up-front will prevent misunderstandings and misuse of human or machine assets, in a crisis or the heat of combat.

Efficient cooperation is what enables C2 to scale. More importantly, cooperation allows execution of complex operations all in support of an overarching goal.[570] Cooperation makes Command and Control powerful, and cooperation depends on trust. Trust is a challenge between both humans and machines. In formal military organizations, cyberspace operations C2 will not occur in isolation. The human or machine leader will be nested into the larger kinetic warfighting system. Kinetic warfighters' lives depend on a team that delivers results as promised. Their trust must be earned. Cyberspace operations are probabilistic and cyber operations planners must communicate the candid truth to their kinetic brethren. If requested cyberspace effects fail to achieve the desired outcome, warfighters will quickly lose trust or deem cyberspace operations as irrelevant. Humans come to trust machines after they perform in a reliable fashion. At best, machines will perform as specified. At worst humans and machines can deceive each other in any combination of H2H, H2M, M2H, and M2M, or fail in unanticipated ways. Technologies such as digital signatures and reputation systems help build trust, but sometimes falter by failing to account for the full threat model. Many security issues spring from misplaced trust.

We've discussed trust between the kinetic warfighting force and cyber operations forces. There always has been, and probably always will be, tension between various arms of government: military, intelligence, judicial, law enforcement, diplomatic, and executive, as well as with the private sector, and cyber operations is no exception. This balance of powers is important, lest one overly-aggressive entity jeopardize the larger system of government in overzealous, but myopic efforts to accomplish its individual mission.

Cyber operations absolutely have the potential to impact interagency, state, local, and international activities and requires coordination.[571] Cyberspace operations are, by necessity, a team sport. Building relationships and trust is essential.

**Organization**

It is possible, actually desirable, to organize forces both physically and logically based on command and control attributes. For example, traditional leadership theory states that a single leader can have approximately three to a maximum of seven direct subordinates, but C2 of automated forces affords the opportunity to control far more, depending on the automated system's degree of intelligence and desired autonomy. A single human could control a convoy of many semi-intelligent wheeled vehicles, much like a train conductor controls a train more than a mile long. Or a single fighter pilot could control more than their aircraft, such as a number of semi-autonomous wingmen or even swarms of drones. These are cyber-physical examples, but far greater scale is possible when dealing solely with code which can be replicated in any number of copies. Humans have a finite budget of time and attention, so the greater the desired span of control, the simpler, more intelligent, or more autonomous the automated systems must be. Remember that some capabilities may be entirely autonomous, pre-loaded with their mission and then fired, similar to fire-and-forget missiles.

We see extreme examples of scale in botnets, where a single botnet operator can control a million or more zombie computers. The human may use enabling tools to issue commands, leveraging the inherent intelligence in each end device, or there may be intervening tiers of control, such as a human Wing Commander who issues commands to automated Squadron Commanders who then issue commands to individual aircraft. More and more warfighting is being automated. Ours may be the last generation of human fighter pilots and vehicle drivers.[572]

There are multiple topologies for organizing command and control of automated forces including: hierarchical, random, peer-to-peer, and mesh, among others. Each has strengths and weaknesses. In a hierarchical organization, narrowing span of control introduces additional layers of hierarchy, which increases complexity and communication delay. However, this provides the opportunity to employ proxies that mask the humans who are ultimately directing the C2. A random topology can have surprising efficiencies and may prove difficult to reverse engineer.[573] Mesh and peer-to-peer topologies provide redundancy and eliminate the single point of failure of a central node. Importantly, with the aid of automated C2, virtual organizational structures need not be static, but can be reorganized dynamically around missions or a given operational situation, a key advantage over relatively static human organizations.[574]

The organization of humans in cyber operations units is also important. Militaries are historically wed to hierarchical organizations, but team-based approaches, such as those found in the U.S. Special Forces, provide additional agility. In some traditional military systems, supporting units, such as intelligence, have deliberately labeled their units using the same terminology as mainstream operational branches like infantry, even when those labels don't necessarily fit well. For example, traditional command titles such as brigade, battalion, and company are applied to organizations that look nothing like their combat arms counterparts. This labeling is helpful in militaries that employ centralized promotion and command selection boards to prevent confusion. If cyber operations leaders were to make promotion and command selections of cyber leaders, this labeling is much less relevant.[575]

Contrary to U.S. kinetic forces, which enjoy long breaks from combat in today's environment, cyber operations forces are engaging adversaries every day. There is no return from the front to the safety of the homeland. This is a reality that leaders must communicate well to kinetic warfighters. Cyber operations organizations must be built with additional redundancy by at least 20-30% to allow for personnel to take time away for both short-term training and long-term education to remain current in the latest techniques. It is up to the commander how to best manage the training, but they should not be so blinded by near-term requirements that they forget about long-term individual and force development. Cyberspace C2 system training requirements can be reduced by providing common tools with a straightforward user interface. DARPA's Plan X cyberspace command and control project makes the key assumption that more than 6,000 new personnel in U.S. Cyber Command won't be experts and will need easy-to-use tools.[576]

There are other models employed by cyberspace actors beyond the military. For example, insurgent groups are often cell-based with a high degree of autonomy. At the greatest extreme, there is the radicalization of lone-wolf actors that receive abstract guidance through online content, and choose their own targets without direct instructions. This relationship provides plausible deniability to the instigator. Command and control can also flow across diverse organizational boundaries, such as a government providing guidance to a criminal organization or patriotic hacker group. However, the same decisions regarding autonomy based on capability and trust still apply.

*"We need computers to understand our computers.*
*Help in managing the complexity [of defense] is going to be fundamental."*
*- Richard Hale, Deputy CIO of the U.S. Department of Defense*[577]


*"Ender waited, waited for the flash of insight that would tell him what to do,*
*how to destroy the enemy."*
*— Orson Scott Card*[578]


## Common Operating Picture

To direct operations, decision makers need to have a shared understanding of the situation. As discussed in the Intelligence chapter, a C2 system generates understanding by collecting and processing data, which turns the data into actionable information. Leaders must analyze the information over time, creating knowledge and applying their judgment to develop a true understanding of the situation. All of this leads to informed decision making.[579] A core technique for generating understanding is the Common Operating Picture (COP), which is provided by interactive systems that visualize friendly force information and intelligence for operators.[580] The best cyber COP systems exploit the strengths of humans and the strengths of machines, seeking to complement both, and create a hybrid system whose sum is greater than its parts.[581]

The cooperation and unity of effort that makes command and control so powerful requires a shared understanding of the current situation. A cyber COP system cannot stand alone, it must be integrated into other kinetic C2 systems and decision making processes. An ideal cyber COP system provides shared understanding across all domains and cyberspace planes. A COP system isn't a "dashboard" that you might encounter in the business context. It is far more detailed and integral to operations.

A COP system isn't just for a few key leaders. Staffs need an understating of the situation, often acting as analysts and filters, using their professional judgment to provide the commander with the right information at the right time. In mission command systems, individual operators need to be well informed of their unit's operations and the larger context, and will likely have tailored COP systems for their use. Care must be taken to push the right information to each, but also provide self-service repositories where personnel can pull what they need on demand.[582] Even automated systems and code-based capabilities may require digital COP information, particularly as these systems gain intelligence and autonomy.

Leaders have many tasks and information requirements in high stress situations. Most importantly, they must know the status of friendly, threat, and neutral forces, both physical and virtual. Leaders must assess risk for each of their decisions, prioritize efforts, conserve resources, and anticipate future events. Leaders will need to pay particular attention to their cyber operations, especially software agents, to ensure these capabilities are performing as intended.[583] A cyber COP system can address each of these challenges, particularly when supported by analytics, modeling, simulations, and AI systems. We shouldn't, however, feed the illusion that precision in war is attainable.[584] A COP will never be perfect.

### *Visualization* [585]

Kinetic operators are accustomed to employing COP systems in command posts at various levels, so they are familiar with the general concept. Cyber operators are used to visualization tools from penetration testing, such as Cobalt Strike.[586] However, there is no cure-all scalable cyber COP system at present, although DARPA's Plan X effort pointed toward a solution.[587] An even farther reach is an integrated system that merges kinetic and cyber operations into a single unified cyber-physical picture with the appropriate degrees of abstraction, for the kinetic warfighter, the cyber enabler, and the cyber operator.[588]

As we saw in Figure 10-7, in the heat of combat visualizations need to be simple. Properly designed automated solutions can provide this simplicity, but also provide the ability to drill down to specifics as required. A mantra from the information visualization community certainly applies here: "overview first, zoom and filter, then details on demand."[589] Applying these and other usability best practices will help prevent information overload.

There are robust graphics, iconography, and symbol standards for kinetic warfighting visualization, but we lack the same for cyber operations.[590] Future work needs to be done to incorporate existing symbology from the military lexicon in cyberspace COPs. This will reduce the training burden for kinetic warfighters and ease the communications between cyber operators and kinetic warfighters. Where there are gaps, this work should then incorporate common standards from the information security community. New graphics, icons, and symbols should only be created as a last resort.

The military possesses another useful concept, the overlay. Historically, overlays were clear acetate sheets placed over physical maps. Examples include a threat overlay that highlights suspected or known threat locations, an obstacle overlay that depicts the location of obstacles, and an operational overlay that shows the location of friendly forces and the planned scheme of maneuver. These overlays, and many others, have migrated to automated systems, where they can be toggled on and off by operators as needed.[591] These traditional overlays should be augmented with cyber overlays which show relevant cyber operations information where geographic location is relevant, and in tailored network visualization systems appropriate for virtual information.

Even with reliable intelligence and friendly force status information, uncertainty increases with the passage of time. Video games often model this uncertainty by providing current information in areas under direct observation, depicting formerly observed physical terrain as grayed out, fading out previously observed enemy unit locations as they age, and blacking out unknown territory. These techniques may work well in conveying information to human operators in cyber C2 systems, with the understanding that while physical terrain may be unlikely to change when not being observed, cyberspace may change far more rapidly.[592]

Cyber common operating picture systems should be extensible and customizable. Rather than a top-down driven approach where a contractor dictates the capabilities of the system, the best systems can be augmented with user-created widgets or apps from an app store.[593] Facilitating innovation starting with the end users will help lift the maturity and utility of cyber common operating picture systems across the force. Existing visualizations are shown on screens ranging from very small mobile devices to wall size displays. In the future we will see virtual reality and augmented reality technologies in wider use.[594]

*Figure 10-9: Soldiers of the U.S. 10th Mountain Division and the 101st Airborne Division gather around a network visualization tool during a network evaluation exercise. (Photo: U.S. Army).* [595]

### Technology

Technology provides the infrastructure for the COP system and the C2 system in general. The goal is to provide confidentiality, integrity, and availability on a foundation of resilient infrastructure that can function in austere environments, including 24/7 use, as well as extremes of heat, moisture, and contaminants. The communication systems should facilitate communication to superiors, subordinates, and peer organizations to enable unity of effort for offensive and defensive operations. These systems should also allow rapid emergency communications to any node in exigent circumstances. Importantly, the system must cope with a breakdown in electronic communications with higher headquarters, and the human team should be well trained in employing manual C2 methods, something that is very rare today.

Humans may be able to function, albeit inefficiently, using manual C2 systems, but automated systems and capabilities requires automated C2. Existing COP systems are designed specifically for human consumption, but while the presentation format may be different (graphical for humans and binary for machines) automated cyber capabilities will need a common operating picture as well. These requirements can both be met with a common operating database that accumulates information and presents it to all consumers in a format that is useful to each. Old information can be dangerous, but refreshing situational data too frequently will cause networks to bog down and the extra communications will make the C2 system more visible to attackers. Systems need to strike the right balance between information required and conservation of bandwidth, storage, machine processing power, and human time and attention.

Having a secure communication channel that provides confidentiality and integrity is the backbone of a Common Operating Picture system. Information should flow smoothly, getting to the human or machine decision maker at the right time, place, and pace. In human-only networks, distortion will occur as information transits the C2 network, but in automated C2 networks with adequate error correction algorithms, distortion should not occur (or should be readily identifiable). In either case, delay will accumulate at human, network, or machine speed depending on the topology of the network and the degree of humans in the loop. No C2 network will be completely real-time.

Interoperability is a central aspect of a common operating picture. This makes sense because if your systems can't share information, you can't generate a common view of the operational environment. However, interoperability isn't something to be taken for granted. Large organizations will likely have systems from numerous vendors, each of which have little incentive to design systems that interoperate with their competitors unless contractually required.[596] The design of the systems should be based on operator requirements, not trumped-up features with little true value, hawked by the purveyors of these systems. When nation-state allies team up, such as in NATO, interoperability will certainly be a major C2 issue.[597] The solution is to train and exercise together to find the shortfalls before a real-world crisis.

*"Now, fractions of a millisecond later, the Lady May was directly in line.*
*Here was where the skill and speed of the Partners came in.*
*She could react faster than he…*
*She could fire the light-bombs with a discrimination which he might miss.*
*He was connected with her mind, but he could not follow it."*
*- Underhill, in "The Game of Rat and Dragon"* [598]

**Attacking and Defending C2**
Command and Control is a point of vulnerability for cyber operations. The powerful organizing and amplification benefits of command and control can

be nullified or subverted by successful attack. An adversary inside a C2 system is dangerous indeed, and may lead to exposure of operations, attribution, loss of control of forces, disruption of operations, capture of systems, and fires and effects against the wrong targets. Expect adversaries to target command and control networks, while attempting to protect their own.

Some of the most interesting evolutions in cyber C2 attack and defense comes from botnet operators and the law enforcement agencies that try to stop them. We'll draw insights from this game of one-upmanship, apply traditional military strategies, and extend and generalize these ideas to the scale of cyber combat.

## Attacking

Adversary overconfidence and overreliance on C2 systems is a common rationale for attack. If the C2 system and the entities it helps orchestrate lack resiliency, then just disrupting their C2 can have devastating effects on operations. Importantly, the attacker may wait for routine upgrades or random failures as opportunities to launch an exploit against an otherwise secure system. Attackers may also compromise C2 and not exploit the system immediately, biding their time until it is most useful.

The first step is identifying command and control systems and networks. C2 networks are commonly identified by the content of intercepted communications, such as identifying bot-like behavior or keywords on a social media account. If only metadata is available, then communication patterns, such as a centralized server routinely sending commands to a number of compromised machines as part of a botnet, is another common technique.

With knowledge of the system and how it communicates, the attacker may then be able to deny, destroy, or disrupt the communications infrastructure, such as directing traffic to a sinkhole, jamming network links, or destroying a key router or central node, to cut off C2. Less obvious attacks are also possible such as exploiting dependencies. For example, a botnet might rely on a weakly protected time server, or traffic could be delayed, slowing the operational response time of the adversary.[599] As another example, a weapon system may rely on a GPS feed that forces a system into a failsafe mode that could be exploited. This is what purportedly happened to a U.S. RQ-170 drone when it was captured by Iran in 2011.[600] Other non-military forms of attack are also possible, such as law enforcement agents seizing key servers or forcing domain registrars to disable threat actor Internet domains.

If the attacker is able to break into the C2 network directly and compromise the information flows or the systems themselves then a full range of effects is possible, ranging from depleting the resources of the enemy to physical destruction. The attacker could insert deceptive spoofed commands, selectively filter commands, flood the network with spurious reports, or insert a malicious node into the C2 network to collect intelligence.[601] The attacker could prevent legitimate commands from getting through or stop software updates from taking place. The most dangerous course of action may be to take full control of the defender's systems without their knowledge.

## Defending

The first steps in defending C2 are enumerating friendly C2 systems in use and then mapping out the their attack surface, potential vulnerabilities, and interdependencies. It is important to think broadly and candidly assess your dependence upon, and confidence in, these systems and how your C2 might be attacked. Proper training is necessary to defend C2. Personnel should be on guard for anomalous behavior and should report discrepancies. Units should conduct kinetic and cyber operations with varying degrees of disruption to C2 from mild to simulated catastrophic. Better to figure out what to do in these circumstances in an exercise than attempt to cope in a high stakes combat situation. These exercises should stress-test not just your people, but also machine decision making. In both circumstances, an opposing force that simulates threat tactics is beneficial. Those on the opposing force will be able to better think like an adversary and they might even find vulnerabilities in your C2 before an adversary does. You don't want one of your ships sailing into a hostile area because of a GPS spoofing attack.[602] With this foundation in place you can then move to more advanced strategies including: stealth, maneuver, deception, and resiliency.

### *Stealth*

Identifying a C2 network is a prerequisite for its compromise. Defenders employ stealth to mask their C2 when possible. The best case is that an adversary never discovers the existence of a C2 system. C2 requires communication, and in the event of conflict, communication networks will be among the first disrupted. Don't expect any communication system to be immune to attack. The Internet, cellular networks, wired telephones, and radio are each vulnerable in their own way and enemies *will* target them. Recall as well that many military networks rely on commercial communications infrastructure creating an expansive attack surface and myriad avenues of approach leading to your C2.

There are multiple ways to lower the profile of cyberspace C2 networks. Creating smaller isolated "armies" helps reduce the amount and frequency of communications, a tactic that was recently employed by botnet operators. Creating more intelligent software that requires less supervision also reduces communications overhead. Encryption helps prevent an observer from viewing the actual content of communications. While it doesn't completely mitigate the threat, encryption may prevent or delay the identification of a C2 network. Even if the channel is detected, encryption limits an adversary to simple traffic analysis attacks, rather than analysis and reverse engineering of the full protocol and content.[603] Anonymity networks provide an even higher degree of protection, eliminating some of the metadata that aid in traffic analysis.[604] From the perspective of avoiding detection, less communication is better. Avoiding verbose communication protocols, communicating only when needed, and employing data compression will reduce the C2 network's online footprint, as will limiting the unit size to reduce communication requirements. Easy metrics for self-assessment of this footprint are available: including the number of bytes of C2 traffic and the frequency and number of messages sent in each direction.[605] Reducing these attributes will help increase stealth. More advanced strategies include comparing C2 traffic to legitimate benign traffic and attempting to normalize C2 properties to blend in.

When attempting to defend a C2 network you control, try to make the terrain as defensible as possible. When communicating across a network controlled by an adversary, be doubly careful. Physical network access is a powerful enabler that provides one's adversary significant advantages, such as the ability to tap network communications covertly or to use Man-In-The-Middle attacks to compromise some forms of encrypted communication. It is dangerous, but sometimes necessary, to perform command and control over the same network that you are using to conduct operations. If possible, seek out another covert communication C2 channel isolated from operational activities, and beware of bridging the two networks together by accident.[606]

### Maneuver
The concepts of maneuver are also applicable to defending C2 networks. We see excellent examples from the designers of botnets, including rapidly changing C2 domains,[607] using encrypted tunnels to provide cover and concealment, using domain generation algorithms to constantly change C2 to predictable (to the botnet operator) Internet domains. Botnet operators also switch their command and control channels frequently, using HTML, Internet Relay Chat (IRC), social networking sites, and peer-to-peer networks to stay one step ahead of defenders.

## Resilience

The idea of a strong network perimeter has long been a mainstay of cybersecurity, as is the related concept of defense in depth. A newer concept, resiliency, is particularly useful. In this model, we assume the attacker has penetrated perimeter defenses. The goal of resiliency is to develop response mechanisms for when there is a successful attack or compromise. These well-rehearsed procedures help reduce downtime and lower costs. In addition to routine system and network hardening, resiliency measures include standard operating procedures and repair and restoration procedures, well established order of leadership succession in the event a leader or automated system is damaged or out of contact, training exercises, and multiple redundant communication options, to prepare for events that will likely occur. An essential component is frequently backed-up data, where some copies are stored offsite and offline, and regularly checked.

Resilient defenses are engineered so that there are no single points of failure. They include plans for the loss of command and control. For example, what should an automated system do if it were to lose its command and control link, even if it is just for the code to shut down or delete itself? Humans may improvise well, but we don't necessarily want a dangerous cyber weapon or armed drone improvising. Loss of C2 should be planned for early in system design. In addition to these failsafe modes, your systems should include manual overrides when appropriate. For example, we don't want a jumbo jet or nuclear power plant to be run entirely by computers without any way for the pilot or plant operator to regain control, or at least carefully land the aircraft or shut down the reactor.

*"Ideally, [military organizations] must combine the precision and reliability of computers with the creativity and flexibility of humans"*
*– Colonel Patrick Duggan* [608]

## Conclusions

Effective Command and Control is essential to cyber operations. It reduces, but can never eliminate, the uncertainty found in combat. C2 helps forces agilely cooperate, synchronize efforts, and gain a relative speed advantage over adversaries. It can also provides a decisive edge in bringing the right forces to bear at the right place and time.

To be effective, command and control must be tailored to the leader and the led, whether human or machine. Machine intelligence is the future of cyberspace C2, but at present, humans must be in the decision-making loop (except, perhaps, in rare circumstances). These humans perform best when under flexible Mission Command and we should cultivate *coup d'oeil* in cyberspace leaders. Machines best operate under Detailed C2 and we should always carefully assess what autonomy and authority we delegate to machines. That being said, machine autonomy is on the rise. Common Operating Picture systems will help alleviate some of the complexity and training burden found with cyberspace operations, and common operating picture databases will provide a similar shared understanding to automated systems.

In the near-term, there will be friction between traditional kinetic warfighting forces and cyber operators over the proper command and control of cyber operations, as each side struggles to communicate with the other. Trust is essential to bridging this gap and to ensuring the efficacy of cyber C2 and cyber operations in general. Forces, both human and code-based, can organize their units to help facilitate efficiency and effectiveness.

At its best, command and control helps forces organize and gain insight into the problems they face. Each of the facets of C2: intelligence, identifying threat capabilities and vulnerabilities, as well as one's own, help the entire force understand the friendly and enemy situation allowing for unified action at a faster pace than one's adversary with potentially devastating effects.[609]

At its worst, command and control is a critical vulnerability which attackers are sure to exploit. C2 must be defended. Otherwise, the amplifying effects C2 provides will be negated, or worse yet, turned against oneself. It is possible to create defensible C2 that is difficult to detect and even harder to compromise by employing physical and logical C2 topologies that are stealthy and resilient.

# 11 DECEPTION

*Though fraud [deception] in other activities be detestable, in the management of war it is laudable and glorious, and he who overcomes an enemy by fraud is as much to be praised as he who does so by force."*
*– Niccolo Machiavelli*

Deception has always been part of warfare, and likely always will be.[610,611] Deception is also a great tool for offensive and defensive cyber operations. In cyberspace, humans and machines view the world through interfaces and data consisting of sets of zeroes and ones in specific states. Attackers and defenders can shape this data, and the tools and hardware used to view it, to their liking. In general, the attacker has the advantage in cyberspace and the (non-governmental) defender's hands are tied because they cannot retaliate, or "hack back," at least not without the potential for severe legal consequences. Deception is a tool that a defender can use to turn the tables on the attacker, and offers a full range of potential effects on adversaries. Deception is also useful for identification of malicious activity, including insider threats. Helping the workforce to understand social engineering and deception will make your people harder targets. Leaders ignore deception at their personal and organizational peril.

Denial and deception are often used together, as they are two sides of the same coin. Deception paints a false picture of reality. Denial restricts an adversary's access to true information. It is hard to conduct an effective deception campaign without also denying the enemy access to the true reality. Together, denial and deception control the flows of information into and out of your organization and are used in peacetime and in war at the tactical, operational, and strategic levels of war. At the strategic level (National Policy / Theater Strategy) deception "disguises basic objectives, intentions, strategies, and capabilities."[612] At the operational level (Campaigns / Major Operations) deception helps "confuse an adversary regarding a specific operation you are preparing to conduct," and at the tactical level (Battles / Engagements / Small Unit Actions) deception "misleads others while they are actively involved in competition with you, your interests, or your forces."[613]

The U.S. Military considers deception part of its Information Operations (IO) discipline, which includes five main areas: Electronic Warfare (EW), Computer Network Operations (CNO), Psychological Operations (PSYOPS), Operations Security (OPSEC) and Military Deception (MILDEC).[614] Collectively EW, CNO, PSYOPS, and OPSEC are key enablers for denial and deception operations.[615] While deception is commonplace in traditional warfare, we are seeing cyberspace deception techniques increasingly employed by civilian organizations. Early deception efforts were pioneered by the Honeynet project and today there is growth in deception-focused information security companies.[616]

Attribution is at the heart of cyber operations and we should assume every actor will employ deception to avoid attribution. When you read news or industry reports of attributing attacks and malware to a threat actor, be suspicious. For example, if malware used against major retailer's credit card readers contained Kransnovian[i,617] language strings, compiled using a Kransnovian-language build environment, during working hours in the time zone of the Kransnovian capital, it doesn't mean the Kransnovians were responsible. Everything is malleable. With advanced actors all attempts at naïve attribution analysis will be flawed.

We've seen deception used throughout the history of war. Common techniques include demonstrations, fictional units and equipment, spoofed communications, masked capabilities, feigned attacks and retreats, and False Flag operations.[618] Militaries have formed special units designed to conceive, design, and execute deception operations. Perhaps the most famous is the 23rd Headquarters Special Troops or "Ghost Army" from World War Two. This 1,100 person special unit recruited creative talent including actors, artists, and designers and unleashed their creativity in developing battlefield deceptions. Their tactics included visual deception, such as dummy airfields, sonic deception, such as the sound of tanks moving in the night, spoofed

---

[i] Krasnovia is a notional country once used as a foil in U.S. military exercise scenarios.

radio broadcasts, and simulating actual units deployed elsewhere.[619] The unit was innovative and powerful. It is interesting to consider which country's military might be the first to create a similar unit for cyberspace deception?

We also see deception as a common practice in information security and cyber operations. When you ask someone about cyber deception, honeypots probably are the first thing that come to mind. Honeypots, or honeynets, are computers designed to attract attackers, but have no legitimate purpose. Activity on a honeypot is always suspect. People have created many variants of the honeypot, including SCADA honeypots that appear to be vulnerable internet facing systems controlling equipment like power plants and factories.[620] Such systems have attracted swarms of attackers. Honeypots are a valid deception technique, but are only one of many. Cyberspace deception includes social engineering,[621] phishing, modified log files, misattribution attempts, and false DNS records, among many others. We'll discuss the full spectrum of techniques later in the chapter.

### Human and Machine Deception

Classical deception sought to deceive the human through physical subterfuge, but cyberspace operations afford the opportunity to deceive the human through their machines, or even the machines themselves, as illustrated in Table 11-1. Machines are dependent on their algorithms to make decisions, if you understand how the algorithms work you can feed them false input to shape their decisions. The same is true for humans. At present, most deception comes through human agency, but as machines become more intelligent, they will be capable of deception directly. Intelligent machines are on the cusp of passing the Turing test, where a machine attempts to trick a human into believing the machine is a human. The Turing test is inherently about deception, expect viable deceptive machines in the near future.

*Table 11-1: Targets for Cyber Deception*

|  | Attacker | Defender |
| --- | --- | --- |
| **Human** | Honeynets, "hackable" appearing websites, decoy database, file, and backup servers, decoy sysadmin machines with SSH and RDP services[622] | Fake social media personas, phishing emails, convincing IT Help Desk to reset password |
| **Code/Machine** | Spoofed network service banners, virtual machine environment convinces malware it is "real" hardware, emulated botnet C2 | Spoofing source IP address, other spoofed packet header data, false browser user agent strings, triggering false IDS alerts |

*"The ideal deception makes the victim certain but wrong."*
*— Barton Whaley* [623]

## Deception Effects

Throughout this book we've analyzed a wide range of effects possible through cyber operations, here we will take a closer look at effects caused by deception. As a first order or second order outcome, the entire spectrum of effects is possible, including degrade, delay, deny, destroy, disrupt, divert, exploit, neutralize, herd[624] or suppress, among many others. To accomplish these effects, there are many degrees of freedom, such as altering the perceived who, what, where, when, why, and how engendered by the deception.

When considering deception effects it is useful to look at effects from the perspective of the attacker and the defender, such as those listed in Table 11-2. As you examine the table, note that many of the techniques listed in the attacker column are things that happen commonly in real life, such as the relatively recent use of DDOS attacks to tie up incident response teams while other targeted attacks are taking place. We discussed such a coordinated attack in Chapter 6 - Maneuver.

*Table 11-2: Example Cyber Deception Effects for the Attacker and Defender* [625]

|  | Attacker | Defender |
|---|---|---|
| **Fail to observe** | Prevent the defender from detecting the attack. | Prevent the attacker from discovering their target. |
| **Sow Distrust** | Cause the defender to lose trust in trustworthy systems, data, or people. | Cause the attacker to lose trust in trustworthy systems, data, or people |
| **Reveal** | Trick the defender into providing access. | Trick the attacker into revealing their presence. |
| **Waste Time** | Focus the defender's attention on the wrong aspects of an incident. | Focus the attacker's efforts on the wrong target. |
| **Underestimate** | Induce the defender to think the attack is unsophisticated, not carefully tailored. | Induce the attacker into thinking the defender is not sophisticated. |
| **Disengage** | Induce the defender into thinking that the attack is contained or completed. | Induce the attacker into thinking that they have already achieved their goal. |
| **Misdirect** | Focus the defender on a different attacker. | Encourage the attacker to target a different victim. |
| **Misattribute** | Induce the defender into thinking that the attacker is someone else. | Induce the attacker into thinking that they've compromised the wrong network. |

On the defender side, we'd like to emphasize two things. First, "Security Through Obscurity," a term applied to cyber defenders who try to hide critical assets and information without rigorous safeguards, can be an effective, albeit temporary, tactic. Security through obscurity is the reason that Soldiers wear camouflage clothing and employ OPSEC. It is a time-tested technique that works. Second, when dealing with persistent adversaries, you aren't necessarily going to win on a technical level over the long term. Some of the outcomes listed here for defenders speak to the need to target the person on the other side of the screen and get them to decide to stop attacking you, because they've concluded that there is no point in continuing to do so. That's how you win. Third, deceptions are like obstacles in that they will usually delay, but not stop an adversary. They are only effective as long as they are actively maintained and believed by defenders.

**Deception Operations**

When planning a deception campaign there are many considerations. Consider your ultimate aim, what effects you wish to cause, and the resources available to you and your adversary. The skill level of each will inform your range of potential options. If you possess strong technical skills you'll be better able to mask subtle clues in the technical detail. An adversary with strong technical skills may find inconsistencies that reveal the deception. Strong target cultural and language skills are essential. Understanding the target deeply, human or machine, yields insights into their susceptibility to deception, and what type will work the best. The target will have intelligence team to help penetrate deception, and your friendly intelligence personnel will better shape your efforts for maximum effect. Financial resources allow more extravagant operations. Deception operations always incur risk, make sure leaders fully understand the risk they are accepting and that you consult with your legal advisors. Cyber deception operations are almost always conducted in the context of some larger cyberspace or cyber/kinetic operation. For three recent examples, see Figure 11-1. Note in each case, Russia/Ukraine, Iran, and Syria, cyberspace deception was closely integrated with kinetic operations to great effect.

| Russia / Ukraine "Mass Hallucination" | Iran "Mass Intimidation" | Syria "Foreign Intervention" |
|---|---|---|
| • Special forces teams seize armories and government buildings<br>• Disrupt communications (digital and analog)<br>• Employ patriotic hackers<br>• Wage massive disinformation campaign, including troll army<br>• Cyber enabled violence<br>• Gray area between peace and war | • Threatening emails<br>• Doxing activists<br>• Offering rewards for activist capture<br>• Infiltrate social media<br>• Staging false events to arrest activists<br>• Sowing mistrust in activist leadership<br>• Misattributable / Nonattributable cyber actions | • Employed Iranian advisors, but masked by disinformation campaign<br>• Cause physical harm without causing international backlash<br>• DDOS<br>• Overloaded networks<br>• Jammed social media<br>• Disseminated propaganda<br>• Professionalized hacker field training |

*Figure 11-1: Cyberspace deception is often used in conjunction with other kinetic and cyberspace operations. We've seen cyberspace deception used in the Russian incursion into Ukraine, and Iran and Syria's crackdowns on social unrest.* [ii,626]

---

[ii] Note that Figure 11-1 introduces the concept of *doxing*. This term was coined in recent years to describe a situation in which sensitive documents related to a specific person or organization are stolen through a cyber attack and shared widely on the Internet with intent to harm the target's reputation or safety. This is usually

## Principles of Deception[627]

To help design and refine your operations, the military's time-tested principles of deception help provide guidance. These principles are described here.

**Focus** – Clearly identify your target for deception, typically the adversary decision maker, and focus your efforts accordingly.

**Objective** – Understand your desired objective. Deceiving an adversary is of little value if they do not act upon the deception in a desirable way. The key is for the adversary to detect the deceptive events, incorporate the deceptive information into their decision making, and then act upon it in a way favorable to you. Alternatively, you could paralyze their decision making, cause them to reveal strengths, intentions, weaknesses and preparations, or condition the adversary to a particular pattern of behavior.[628]

**Centralized Planning and Control** – Centralizing planning and control of deception efforts avoids confusion, and prevents multiple unsynchronized, and possibly counterproductive or dangerous, deception campaigns. The deception planning process typically involves the following steps: 1. Analyzing the mission, 2. Receiving leadership guidance, 3. Developing a tentative plan, 4. Leadership and legal review, 5. Revise plan 6. Final review and approval.[629] The first step, analyze the mission is particularly important. You should ask yourself:

- Why deception?
- What capabilities and assets do I have to support the deception operation?
- What are my constraints and limitations?
- What assumptions am I making and are they truly valid?
- Does my deception plan induce a risk to operations that would not be present without it?
- How will I mitigate risks?[630]

---

done in retaliation for some real or perceived injustice perpetrated by the target of the doxing.

U.S. military deception planning uses a "see, think, do" methodology.[631] This is intended to highlight the importance of the adversary acting in response to the deception. Simply believing the mistruth is not enough.

- **See**: What will the adversary observe as a result of the deception?
- **Think**: Based on their observations, what do we expect the adversary will believe?
- **Do**: What action de we expect the adversary to take based on their (mistaken) belief?

**Security** – Deception operations are very sensitive and knowledge of the deception should be tightly controlled, even from your own people. In addition to people, in cyberspace operations it is particularly important to secure any technical systems you employ from attack. Compromising a system, particularly at the root or administrator level, is likely to provide clues that a deception is taking place. Honeynet operators have long been aware of the risk of system compromise, but a recent event at the DEF CON hacker conference provides a timely example. In this case an individual was using a WiFi Pineapple device, which spoofs legitimate wireless access points. Under normal circumstances this is a potent and hard to detect deception technique, but not so at a hacker conference. A skilled hacker turned the tables on this deception and compromised the WiFi Pineapple device, destroying its firmware.[632]

**Timeliness** – Deceptions must be carefully orchestrated and synchronized. The right deception at the wrong time will be ineffective or worse. Timing matters. As an example, recall the Cyber Kill Chain: Reconnaissance, Weaponization, Delivery, Exploitation, Installation, Command & Control, and Actions on Objectives. To best frustrate the kill chain, deceptions must be tailored for the correct step and occur at the right time. Attempting to deceive an attacker after they have successfully conducted a given step would likely be a waste of time and energy.

**Integration** – Deception alone will rarely win the day. It must be carefully integrated into overall kinetic and cyberspace operations. When designing deceptions, avoid the overly complex, as complexity can increase the odds of failure. The best deception strategies are often simple, practical in the context of the larger effort, and support the overall goals and objectives of the operation. However integration doesn't imply a lack of secrecy, nor does it suggest that one should fail to share information only on a need-to-know basis. In fact in the days before the Egyptian invasion that began the Yom

Kippur War, an estimated 85% of the Egyptian forces involved did not know it was a deception operation, even up until the time they started crossing the Suez Canal.

These principles are simply guidelines to be considered during the preparation and execution of deception operations. However, you should consider carefully before deviating from them.

## Deception Techniques

Deception in cyberspace operations may occur across all layers: Command and Control, Persona, Logical, Physical, and Geographic, and potential techniques are limited only by the imagination. To develop techniques, gather some of your most devious and cunning people and put them together to brainstorm. It is almost certain that something interesting will emerge. To help add structure to the discussion we recommend breaking down potential deception strategies by cyberspace plane, from both the attacker and defender perspective. Doing so will help elicit ideas and gain insight into not just offensive strategies, but also how an attacker might deceive you and your organization. Table 11-3 lists potential cyberspace deception techniques by cyberspace plane for both offensive and defensive operations. Armed with this information you can work to develop the right offensive techniques and protect your enterprise from enemy deception.

*Table 11-3: Example deception techniques from the offensive and defensive perspectives. In addition to planning for the offense, understanding how you might be attacked helps you better defend your organization.*[633]

| | Attacker | Defender |
|---|---|---|
| **Command and Control Plane** | Social Engineering, Phishing, damage target leadership reputations, DDOS as a diversion,[634] trigger false alerts, fake attacks, spoofed text messages[635] | Spoof botnet C2 server, fake C2 traffic |
| **Cyber Persona Plane** | Spoofed social media personas,[636] privilege escalation, stolen credentials, stolen certificates, Troll armies,[637] spoofed caller ID | Decoy employee social media personas, decoy user accounts and email addresses |
| **Logical Plane (OSI 2-7)[638]** | Modify log files, forged certificates, create a watering hole, leave false trail of clues in malware, Trojan horse software, code obfuscation, build environment spoofing, trojan adversary build environment,[639] spoofed websites,[640] compromised machines as proxies | Decoy file and database servers, poisoned documents, beaconing documents, fake documents, false HTML comments, false robots.txt directories, false DNS records, fake cheating tools,[641] disguise system characteristics,[642] network camouflage |
| **Physical Plane (OSI 1)** | Spoof GPS data,[643] IMSI catcher (Sting Ray), WiFi Pineapple, blue box (phreaking), use of indigenous hardware and software | WiFi honeypot, spoofed transmissions, transmission antennas remoted from transmitters |
| **Geographic Plane** | Insert fake components into supply chain,[644] thumb drive in the parking lot, mailing fake DVD to target, disguised PwnPlug, ATM skimmer | Printer microdots, false signage on facilities, disguised surveillance cameras and other sensors |

## Deception Maxims[645]

The military deception community has long-standing deception maxims which we have listed below. Applying these maxims to your deception planning, execution, and counter-deception efforts will help ensure you stay on track.[646]

***Magruder's Principle*** – Magruder's Principle warns against confirmation bias. If your target already suspects an activity may take place, you can feed this predilection and your deception is more believable. It is far more difficult to make a target change their beliefs altogether. In World War Two, the Allies sought to deceive German High Command as to the primarily landing point for the Allied D-Day invasion. They used a "rubber army" of inflatable vehicles and equipment and fake radio transmissions to create a fake army, notionally led by top field commander General George Patton. This deception only served to reinforce the German belief that the main invasion force would arrive at Calais, even long after the Allies landed and secured a beachhead at Normandy. The fact that one can fabricate a fake *army* against an already suspicious and well informed adversary shows the power of confirmation bias.[647] As an example in the cyberspace operations context, an attacker might apply Magruder's Principle by purporting to be a threat actor that the target already expects, rather than appearing to be something out of the ordinary or unexpected. As a defender, if you're creating honeypots, you want them to look like systems that are popular and normally found on your network. The key is that the deceptive thing should be what the target expects to find.

***Limitations to Human and Machine Information Processing***[648] – In Chapter 3 - Laws of Physics, we discussed human and machine cognition and sensing. Deception deliberately exploits these limitations. Humans fall prey to the Law of Small numbers, where people draw conclusions based on an insufficient number of data points, are susceptible to conditioning (recall the story of the Boy who Cried Wolf), and assume that unlikely (Black Swan) events are impossible. As an attacker I might benignly trigger the same IDS alarms on a regular basis, so the Security Operations Center (SOC) gets used to seeing them and won't carefully investigate when they see them again.

From the perspective of the defender, assume you've got an application server with lots of valuable data on it and you fear that attackers on your network might get into the application easily because authentication is tied to domain credentials. So you stand up a second system alongside the first one, running the same application, but with no data. You then configure several sub-interfaces on that second machine, each with a different IP address, filling your entire available network space. From an attacker's perspective, there aren't two machines - there is a forest of them, and they are all serving the same application. This achieves 3 effects.

1. Reveal - if anyone is probing the honeypots, you know they are up to no good.
2. Delay - the attacker has to check a large number of systems, which will slow them down, and give you time to react.
3. Condition - Once the attacker investigates 20 of these IP addresses and sees that the system contents are all the same and don't have any valuable data, the attacker may abandon the lot and never find the real one hidden in the crowd.

Each of these also applies in the machine context, based on the machine's algorithms. For example, it is possible to condition an intrusion detection system to believe malicious traffic is normal, an algorithm could base decisions on too few samples, and a system designer may fail to provide safeguards in code to handle unlikely failure modes. All of the limitations we mention in the Laws of Physics chapter apply. A related concept we'd add is something we call *sensor aperture*; deceptions need only be as effective as demanded by the bandwidth of the tool that is used to observe them.

***Multiple Forms of Surprise*** – Surprise catches the target at a disadvantage. There are many dimensions of surprise that one can attempt to achieve including the number of personnel you have, their activities and locations, the equipment you use, the intent of your actions, and your overall style of operations, among many others.

***Jones' Dilemma*** – Jones' dilemma deals with the balance of true versus deceptive information sources. The more sources of real information, the more likely the adversary will discover the deception. The attacker can choose deceptions where the target has few resources to determine the ground truth, and the attacker could work to eliminate or disrupt those sources they do have. You want to undermine your adversary's trust in the truth.[649] Defenders would best do the opposite, seek to add trustworthy information sources if they sense a vulnerability or if something may be amiss.

***The Monkey's Paw***[650] – The Monkey's Paw is a short story published in England in 1902, later turned into a film. In it, a magical monkey's paw would grant three wishes. As you might expect in tales where magic items grant wishes, things quickly go awry. While the wishes were fulfilled, each came with unanticipated side effects. The deception community uses the Monkey's Paw maxim to remind itself to watch for unanticipated reactions to their deception activities, especially effects on friendly forces. In the cyber context, we should extend this watchfulness to our own computing systems, especially systems that inform the actions of security personnel. You sometimes see unanticipated reactions with penetration tests. People believe the penetration test is real and take actions accordingly. If you don't ever tell employees it was a drill, years later they may be telling war stories about the sophisticated attack their organization experienced when it was really just a pen test. This is just a benign example, far worse is possible. Ask an experienced penetration tester to tell some horror stories about their experiences with guards with guns, for example.

***Don't Make it Too Easy*** – This is one of our favorite maxims, and it applies well to cyberspace operations. Consider carefully where you place and how you protect your deceptive material. Make the target "work" for it. Don't boldly announce what you are doing. As an attacker you might make the analyst unpack your malware or fiddle with some poorly designed "encryption" or encoding before they can get to the phony list of IP addresses you've embedded in an executable program. If they have to work to discover the deceptive information you have placed, they are more likely to think that the product of their efforts is something valuable you didn't want them to find. Make them feel clever. In Operation MINCEMEAT during World War Two, Allied Forces successfully convinced Axis power that their main effort would be in the Balkans rather than Sicily. In 1943, they took the body of a man who died of pneumonia, dressed him as a British staff officer, placed false documents on his person indicating the Balkans, and dropped him off the coast of Spain. He was picked up by a fisherman and the documents made their way to German officials who believed the ruse. To add to the realism, they gave the dead man a fictitious "girlfriend," actually an MI5 staff member, see Figure 11-2.

*Figure 11-2: "Pam," the notional girlfriend used as part of a World War Two ruse that misled German officials into thinking the Allies would invade the Balkans rather than Sicily.* [651]

**Husband Deception Assets** – This maxim is straightforward. Deception assets are scarce resources, employ them carefully, and protect them from misuse.

***Choice of Types of Deception*** – In military parlance, you'll hear these referred to as "A-Type" (Ambiguity Deception) and "M-type" (Misdirection Deception). Ambiguity deception increases uncertainty in the eyes of the target. Misdirection deception is ambiguity reducing, decreasing doubt in the mind of the target regarding a specific falsehood. From the perspective of the attacker, let's say you create a piece of malware that has a group of IP addresses in it that look like command and control points, but are really just there to throw off the analyst and cause misattribution. Including the IP addresses of a bunch of random servers associated with different threat actors is going to be much less effective, as a deception, than listing addresses of servers that are only associated with one nation state. In the latter case you are focusing the target on one falsehood rather than presenting many.

***Carefully Sequence Deception Activities*** - The best deceptions tell a convincing story. As you develop a deception plan, think through how the actual events would have played out in real life, much like one would storyboard a television program. Lead with the most believable and leave the riskiest or incredible parts to the end. The believable parts at the beginning will help prepare the target to accept the riskier later parts. Even if the target eventually discovers the ruse there will be less time to react.[652]

The Egyptian deception operation prior to their attack across Suez Canal to start the Yom Kippur war in October 1973 is a great example. The story began with a series of Egyptian tactical exercises over several months, starting in May, to condition Israelis regarding the Egyptians movement of forces and buildup along the canal. At first, the Israelis responded to early exercises by mobilizing their armed forces to defend against a possible Egyptian attack across the Canal, at considerable expense. As the exercises continued off and on over several months, the Israelis eventually stopped responding. The Egyptians moved ammunition and other supplies at night under cover of darkness, so Israeli intelligence would not detect the buildup. They also announced the exercises in local media to convey 'saber rattling' for internal consumption. When the Egyptian army eventually invaded in October, about 85% of Egyptian troops didn't know about the deception until immediately before crossing the Suez.

**Get Feedback** – As with Battle Damage Assessment, it is important to learn of the effect of deception efforts. For example, did the target actually witness the deceptive event or encounter the deceptive material? Did the target believe them? During the Persian Gulf War coalition forces planned a "Hail Mary" left hook maneuver into the heart of Iraq. For the success of the mission, it was important that the Iraqis not be prepared for this strategy. U.S. and Allied forces created a deception involving a supposed amphibious landing along the Kuwaiti coastline on the Persian Gulf, supported by lengthy rehearsals and demonstrations.[653] Feedback from the deception came in the form of satellite and aerial imagery that showed Iraqi units positioning to repel a landing force and mounting an 'economy of force' mission along the border with Saudi Arabia.[654] In cyberspace deception efforts you won't have the luxury of satellite imagery, but it is possible to collect intelligence regarding the success of deception strategies. For example, experienced incident response teams will try to work in the same physical room. If you're all on a conference call together, that conference call could be compromised by the attackers. This has been known to happen. As a defender, you'd be amazed at the things that people who run IRC botnets will simply say in the channel that the bots are attached to.

*You and I in a little toy shop*
*Buy a bag of balloons with the money we've got*
*Set them free at the break of dawn*
*'til one by one they were gone*
*Back at base bugs in the software*
*Flash the message: "something's out there!"*
*Floating in the summer sky*
*Ninety-nine red balloons go by*
                                    *— Nena* [655]

## Conclusions

Deception is commonplace in offensive cyberspace operations, including operations by criminal groups, hacktivists, and nation-states, as well as legitimate penetration testing teams. Deception is a powerful strategy when technical barriers are strong. By targeting the human, deception allows attackers to sidestep even the strongest technical defenses. Leaders should ensure their workforce is aware of common deception techniques, so team members will be better prepared to defend against them. No one is immune to deception.

Deception isn't only for the offense. It allows the defender to employ their superior knowledge of their own networks, systems, and data to great effect, consuming attacker resources and misdirecting efforts, in some cases even convincing a persistent adversary, incorrectly, that they have accomplished their mission.

We believe that deception is underutilized by defenders, but defensive deception bears great promise. While there are certainly legal implications of employing deception, these techniques give defenders a viable toolset to impact an attacker without crossing legal limits.

We commonly think of deceiving humans, but deception works well against machines too. Machine algorithms, whether naïve pattern matching or advanced artificial intelligence, are susceptible to deception. Sometimes trivially so.

Deception is only limited by the creativity of the actor.[656] Thinking in terms of the five domains: Air, Land, Sea, Space, and Cyberspace will help elicit new ideas. Furthermore, by considering each of the cyberspace planes: Command and Control, Persona, Logical, Physical, and Geographic we can identify very specific areas ripe for the deployment of deception. Perhaps the greatest tool of all is to look for overextended or misplaced trust, with a little nudge such trust may easily be exploited.

Deception must be employed with care. It is entirely possible to deceive members of your own organization, your government regulators, your customers, or other innocent parties by accident.

# 12 A LOOK TO THE FUTURE

*"I see the future, but only the bad things."*[657]
— *Roger Kelim*


Attempting to predict the future is notoriously difficult, and while we can't predict specific events we can identify trends that indicate where things are heading. Understanding the trajectory of cyber security and cyber operations is important to those with a stake in the outcome, which is all of us. If we see where things are going we can make better decisions and investments today that will help protect ourselves, our businesses, and our way of life in the future.

Security will not be "solved" in the foreseeable future. We are making incremental progress toward strengthening systems, but most solutions come at the cost of decreased functionality.[658] A security panacea remains out of reach. The engines of business and the creativity of technologists will continue to create software and devices designed to transform our lives for the better.

When looking to the future of cybersecurity we are unfortunately pessimistic. If history is any guide, each technological advance will create new societal dependence and new vulnerabilities. We wish we could assume the best in people, but being realists and security professionals, we assume the worst. We believe each technological advance, no matter how enticing on the surface, will be exploited by those with the power to do so. Technologies and organizational structures will converge, creating cost efficient gains, but also creating homogenous ecosystems with single points of failure and broad attack surfaces. Some new technologies will fail in spectacular ways, others will go through a survival of the fittest process and painstakingly become more secure. Many new commercial devices and systems will be veiled honeypots designed to collect personal information, making people the product. Like the lobster who doesn't notice the water getting slowly warmer until becoming cooked, companies will push data collection limits and field rapidly produced insecure products as far and as fast as they can to increase profit.

Militaries and law enforcement agencies will chafe at the limits of legal authorities in order to better pursue their missions. While these feelings are honest and well intentioned, some of the restrictions aren't mistakes. Governments will constrain their law enforcement and military arms until they are mature enough to use the authority correctly and understand the larger diplomatic picture. Even if an organization does have a legal ability to perform some action it doesn't mean it should. Leaders must make balanced decisions to protect us, while also protecting our values.

Becoming a Luddite recluse isn't a solution. To be citizens of the 21st century we must learn to cope with these new realities. With each passing day we lose elders who lived before the advent of the connected world. These are the people who can help us understand what life was like before massive interconnectedness, give us points of reference, and help us understand what we are giving up to technology.

Cyber organizations, in the military, in the private sector, and in rogue formations are ascendant and will continue to thrive, but the early days will be painful for the technology community. Governments will create law and policy that will incrementally fix problems, but will sometimes overreact and threaten the values they intend to protect. Conducting independent information security research will become increasingly difficult. People may be forced to join nation-state sponsored teams to avoid their work being considered illegal, creating a chilling effect and self-censorship dynamic that will undermine independent points of view and public discourse. Companies will create security products that marketing teams will portray as a cure all, but many will provide only incremental gains and a false sense of security at best, and create new vulnerabilities at worst. Some organizations will create bureaucratic solutions that shift responsibility and liability to those unable to protect themselves.[659] Ultimately however, despite bureaucratic pressure, human nature will not change, and organizations should not expect unrealistic behavior from their workforces. Humans will remain insecure points of entry into even the most technologically protected systems.

The threat is real and critical. Combat will take place on the Internet, in data centers, in military systems, and the myriad electronic devices in our homes, workplaces, and communities. As technologies advance, the battlefield will include devices embedded in our bodies and eventually our brains. Cyber attacks will grow in frequency, severity, and destructiveness. A catastrophic cyber attack against a highly advanced and technologically dependent nation is possible, and will likely occur. In the meantime, nations will quietly spar in the shadows seeking to gain access, positional advantage, and to acquire sensitive information that furthers their aims. The death of a thousand cuts currently draining the intellectual capital of the United States over the course of decades will continue, as will the information operations occurring against democracies, and the United States risks waking up one morning to realize it isn't a super power anymore.[660] Many would like to see this happen. One of the biggest risks to the United States as a nation is that these attacks continue at a level that fails to catalyze deliberate long-term action from senior leaders in government and the private sector.

We are in the early days of the era of cyber conflict. There will be mistakes and lessons learned by governments, militaries, and all other parties along the way. Militaries are working hard to integrate cyber operations, electronic warfare, information operations, and traditional kinetic warfare into unified methods of waging war. Much work remains to be done, but over the course of the next decade and beyond, they will figure it out. Increasingly intelligent automation will play a growing role for both security and cyber operations. We expect cyber operations to become a routine part of the spectrum of conflict.

> *Kyle Reese: The 600 series had rubber skin. We spotted them easy, but these are new. They look human... sweat, bad breath, everything. Very hard to spot. I had to wait till he moved on you before I could zero him.*
>
> *Sarah Connor: [frustrated] Look, I am not stupid, you know. They cannot make things like that yet.*
>
> *Kyle Reese: Not yet, not for about 40 years.*
>
> *Sarah Connor: [disbelieving] Are you saying it's from the future?*
>
> *Kyle Reese: One possible future.*
>
> — *The Terminator (1984)* [661]

## TECHNOLOGIES

Technology will drive future cyber combat. In this section we've identified emerging technologies that will play an increasingly central role. Note that each technology may or may not begin as a tool for warfare, but we should assume that each will be designed, adapted, or subverted to the extent possible and that like all technologies will spread beyond their creators, typically nation states and large corporations, to other actors. As you look at our analysis, consider the trends that emerge: greater embedded computational devices and instrumentation of the physical world via the Internet of Things, the immersive and increasingly intimate relationship between humans and machines through augmented reality, virtual reality, nanotechnology, biotechnology, implants, and neural interfaces, and the steady growth of data driven analytics and AI. Each advance requires serious thinking about the security implications, not just the purported business, societal, or recreational advantages. Each of these advances will raise questions of the correct balance between human control and machine autonomy, ultimately bringing future cyber operations face-to-face with the specter of artificial intelligence that outstrips human capacity. For the next fifty years it's going to be an interesting ride, and after that, all bets are off.

### Internet of Things

The Internet of Things is the overarching term for the myriad interconnected physical objects that are increasingly being embedded in the physical world. These devices contain sensors that sample the environment, possess small but powerful processors, and most communicate without human interaction. Like many other technologies, the IoT promises much, like giving us the ability to control our homes from a distance, save money by smarter load balancing of the electric grid, or order consumer products with the touch of a button, but will eventually become essential for life in the 21st century. Each component of the IoT is a potential part of the cyber battlespace and will be used for surveillance by governments and corporations, and as infrastructure and weapons for cyber combat.[662] The density of such devices will be higher around humans, and will be especially dense in Smart Cities and Mega Cities.[663]

### Exploitable Man-Machine Intimacy

Humans will enjoy a closer coupling with machines. Augmented reality will overlay data onto the human's perception of the physical world, initially through glasses, but eventually contact lenses and implants. Virtual reality will take things a step further and create immersive virtual games, worlds, and experiences that draw in participants for extended periods of time. Lesser known is teledildonics, which brings sexual intimacy via machines. Direct neural interfaces will emerge, first with simple "hello world" applications like

"What time is it?" and your neural co-processor will provide the answer, but quickly moving to a deeply interconnected symbiosis of man and machine. See Table 12-1 for a summary of some potential risks.

*Table 12-1: Man and machine will grow more intimate, but the promise of benefit is counterbalanced with significant risks.*

| Technology | Promise | Risk |
| --- | --- | --- |
| **Augmented Reality** | Intelligent overlays onto the human's view of the world to make life easier, more fun, and more productive | Surveillance, invasive advertising, misleading information displays, malicious applications like theft assistance, law enforcement detection, covert lie detection, and stalking aids[664] |
| **Biotechnology** | Life extension and eradication of disease[665] | Malicious implants, mutations, rogue gene editing[666] |
| **Nanotechnology** | Science, technology, and engineering at microscopic scales capable of creating new materials, commercial products, and medical treatments | Severe health and environmental issues, grey goo existential threat[667] |
| **Neural Interfaces** | All the power of computers and networking seamlessly integrated with the mind[668] | Direct observation of thought and manipulation of human actions and memories,[669] invasive advertising, targeted assassination |
| **Teledildonics** | Increased sexual gratification locally and at a distance, between humans or humans and machines | Surveillance of the most intimate of human activities, blackmail, manipulation |
| **Virtual Reality** | Immersive virtual experiences for recreation, commerce, communication, and governance | Illicit funds transfer using in-game currencies, insurgent training, surveillance and manipulation of online populations |

Machines will grow more intelligent and humans will provide them with more responsibility and authority. Today, there is a human-in-the-loop for many critical decisions, but machines will gain greater and greater autonomy alongside a subsequent decline in human autonomy and oversight. While this transfer of power is often beneficial, subversion of the machine logic prior to fielding or in the field through incorrect sensory inputs, algorithmic bias or other vulnerabilities will put the trust humans place in machines at risk.[670]

## Robotics

Robotics are transforming warfare and will continue to do so in increasingly powerful ways. Robots, whether they be land, sea, air, or space-based will provide reach for human controlled systems and mobility for automated systems to sense and interact with the physical world. This interaction will include robots with weapons and increasing autonomy. We anticipate as there are field manuals for tanks on the battlefield today, we will see similar doctrine emerge for robots, like swarming and employing arsenal planes loaded with drones, tomorrow.[671] Robots will eventually be capable of self-repair, and mechanical, albeit not biological, replication.[672] Counter-robot tactics will grow into a military focus area of significant importance.

*"I for one welcome our new computer overlords."*
*- Ken Jennings* [673]


*"In cybersecurity, offense has permanent structural advantage. AI applied to offense will result in Mexican standoff, which will be called 'peace.'"*
*- Dan Geer* [674]


## Artificial Intelligence

In the not too distant future, we will be fighting AIs, not just humans, in cyberspace.[675] Every few years disruptive technologies upset the balance of power and the competitive business environment. In recent times, the Internet has been the textbook example of disruption. Mobile devices and drones are more recent examples. Artificial Intelligence is poised to impact the human population in unprecedented ways. We see glimpses of the potential now with the cloud-based intelligent agents embedded in our phones, video recommendations on YouTube that are almost impossible to resist, and cyber forces moving to big data analytics.[676] Throughout the Industrial Revolution machines made entire classes of jobs redundant, forcing humans to adapt and move to other professions. AI is doing the same, but more rapidly and with an ability to take on work that was once thought impossible to automate. Consider self-driving cars. A few years ago, the task of piloting vehicles across roads and highways seemed clearly restricted to humans, now informed predictions state that self-driving cars will move from prototypes to mass production in as few as five years.[677] This may be the last generation of human drivers. Not only is AI matching human capability, but AI is quickly exceeding it. Complex games like Jeopardy, chess, and Go, where humans once ruled supreme, have fallen to machine competitors. Cyber operations will become the purview of AI-based systems, for the offense and the defense.

Such a transition begins with where we are now, big data initiatives, early commercial AI agents, hybrid man-machine teams, and automated capture the flag hacking contests.[678] At present, hybrid man-machine teams seem to provide better results than the best humans or the best machines in many domains, but we believe over time the human will become less and less important. We anticipate nations and powerful corporations will develop strong AI systems. As the power of AI grows, it will serve as a unifying force for some of the most advanced security technologies, including big data analytics, behavioral models, machine learning, datamining, and self-modifying code, and exceed isolated capabilities, ultimately transcending human intelligence, sensing, and biological response times.[679] First movers will have a significant advantage. At first, these AIs will be domain specific and optimized for finance, commerce, medicine, and war, but will then move to general purpose strong AI. A strong AI may very well be the last technology that mankind creates, as super intelligences will soon follow.

## REQUIREMENTS FOR CYBER DOMINANCE
Given the context of ubiquitous and powerful emerging technologies, how do cyber forces cope today and set the conditions for success tomorrow? Here are some recommendations.

### Find Senior Leader Champions and Create an Agile Culture
Cyber forces will flourish in a culture that is agile, adaptive, and values what cyber operators bring to the fight, but will flounder in a hegemony run by myopic kinetic operators. For more than a decade, knowing that cyber security was important and cyber operations essential to military operations, we ran a grassroots campaign to prepare future cyber leaders and help prepare the Army for upcoming conflicts in cyberspace. We grew more than a hundred at West Point and sent them into the Army. These were unique individuals, but largely unappreciated by the Army at the time. Nonetheless, each went out and made a difference, but only isolation. A grassroots effort in a large bureaucratic and hierarchical organization can only take you so far.

We can point to the day when things changed; it was the birth of U.S. Cyber Command and service cyber commands. Now we had senior leader champions that actively sought out cyber talent. A senior leader, especially a general or admiral in charge of a branch of service, can enable change far faster than a grassroots community. One challenge of senior leader champions, however, is that they are only in positions of power for a limited period. You'll want to plan ahead and build a diverse base of support in the up and coming ranks, until the day when senior leader champions aren't necessary and the entire force understands the value of cyber alongside kinetic forces. Our takeaway is that if you want to create cyber forces, you need both senior leader champions at the highest level possible, to include political leaders, *and* grassroots support.[680]

Resistance to change is normal in large organizations. When forming cyber forces, be on the lookout for entrenched power and those with something to lose due to the rise of cyber. Hotspots might include the signal and communications communities, who provide telecommunications utility-like service to military customers. Over time, signal organizations will be on the wane as technology miniaturizes and converges, so we anticipate smaller communicator forces in the future. Partnership with signal leaders is key. Another potential hotspot is the acquisition community. The military invests billions into large military systems that take years, sometimes decades, to produce. Cyber demands far more agility than such large scale acquisition processes can handle. Look to agile models found in the Rapid Equipping Force (REF), Asymmetric Warfare Group (AWG), and the Joint Improvised-threat Defeat Agency (JIDA) for inspiration.[681] AWG, REF, and JIDA have all made a positive difference, but the best example in the cyber community is probably DARPA's Cyber Fast Track program which provided small-scale research funding for innovative independent security researchers, yet produced phenomenal output.[682] We are optimistic that the U.S. Department of Defense's Defense Innovation Unit experimental (DIUx) can achieve similar innovation, agility, and high impact as it gets traction, but only if it can win over the Silicon Valley entrepreneur community and remains a priority across changes in senior DoD leadership.[683] Alumni of the Israeli Defense Forces' cyber-focused Unit 8200 have created a post-government service entrepreneurial model to emulate as well.[684]

Depending how you staff your cyber forces, expect a battle for the heart and soul of cyber culture inside and outside the cyber workforce. Cyber brings together diverse tribes, including technologists, intelligence specialists, and kinetic warfighters, and the intersection can be messy. We've experienced what we call the "cyber warrior in the mirror syndrome," where each group looks in the mirror and sees the ideal cyber warrior. In reality there is no "ideal" today. The desired goal is probably a balance between all the tribes. Letting one group achieve dominance early in the process could be dangerous to achieving the best possible end result. The kinetic warfighting community is particularly powerful as they run each of the services. Their natural inclination may be to create tactical formations at the expense of strategic preparedness. The best solutions will create powerful forces and capabilities across the entire spectrum from tactical to strategic. Beware as well an inherent anti-intellectual and anti-technologist bias found in some kinetic warfighting communities. They tend to have a fixed view of the world and you don't want your technical experts sidelined in favor of "good leaders" who don't know the cyber domain. Exceptions to the rule exist. Find them, and enlist their support. For others, you may just have to wait until they retire.

Champions aren't constrained to just military leaders. Public support is a powerful thing, as is media attention. Both will help draw attention to problem areas, as well as reinforce successes. Those seeking solutions to cyber problems are aided by the drumbeat of cyber compromises that we see in the media each day. From our experience, the most influential cyber incidents are those that make cyber security personal. An example is the U.S. Office of Personnel Management (OPM) breach that disclosed detailed personnel information on virtually every person working for the government with a clearance, and the data spills surrounding the 2016 U.S. presidential election. Such surges of support will last only a limited period of time. Plan for black swan events and use these surges of support wisely.

In the United States, some of the most powerful champions are those found in Congress. Through the power of law and the power of the purse they can break through roadblocks inside the military. Be careful however, the military likes to tightly control its communications with political leaders, operating outside formal channels can be dangerous. This is unfortunate, as we've found political leaders and their staffers to be bright, well intentioned, and eager for partnership. We would have engaged policymakers on the subject of cybersecurity more often if allowed to do so.

**Create Diverse, Multi-Disciplinary Teams**
Cyber conflict is inherently multi-disciplinary. At the birth of cyber, we'd admit we were biased toward thinking that cyber was the domain of only technical experts. Every member of the cyber workforce needs a technical foundation of appropriate depth, but virtually every other discipline has important intersections. Cultivate an enabler community with skillsets in law and policy and keep them in the community once they overcome the initial learning curve. Other disciplines such as systems engineering, psychology,

operations research, mathematics, history, foreign languages, among numerous others are important for a well-rounded team. Personnel with domain knowledge of areas of cyber operation targets are also essential to bring in as needed. For example, you may want to bring in a Wall Street MBA to help secure financial markets or a pilot to help secure an aircraft. Partnerships, cultivated well before a crisis, are essential to building the requisite trust and understanding.

> *"The Capacity of the United States military to fund and field*
> *an institutional force is an asymmetric advantage over enemies*
> *and adversaries around the globe."*[685]
> *- Daniel Sukman*

## Adapt or Create Cyber Institutions

The U.S. military has refined training pipelines for military leaders over decades, and senior military leaders are the product of institutional programs that got them where they are. These programs include the entire spectrum of military education from basic training to general officer finishing school, as well as civilian education prior to entry and during service.

The challenge is to provide the right amount of cyber education at the right point in service members and civilians' careers to prepare them for future assignments and responsibilities. We can break down the potential audiences into three groups: all, some, and few, with each group having different requirements:[686]

- All – The entire workforce. The baseline knowledge required of the entire workforce, both in general and at a specific rank or grade, such as basic anti-phishing and anti-social engineering training.
- Some – The cyber enabler community. The in-depth knowledge required for cyber enablers such as kinetic planners, lawyers, and policy makers to perform their roles in an informed fashion, such as key cyber-related laws and legal precedents, as well as a sufficiently developed technical foundation for context.
- Few – The cyber operations community. The expert level knowledge required by those who make a career out of cyber operations.

While an in-depth study of cyber training and education requirements is beyond the scope of this book, our key takeaway is that each service needs to develop training programs for each group that are efficient and effective. The "All" group should encounter appropriate content embedded in their routine instruction in common educational events like basic training, staff colleges and the war colleges, as well as in annual workplace training. The "Many" group should be able to pursue additional knowledge via electives in required service schools and receive job specific training upon arrival at cyber-related assignments. The military schooling for the "Few" group should be focused on cyber topics and when taking required mandatory training like a staff school, should seek to exhaust all available cyber-related electives.

If done correctly, military cyber training can be a powerful recruiting and retention draw, but until organizations are fully functional there may not be enough talent to fully staff the instructor population. Ideally, instructors will be cyber operations veterans from inside the force, but as a bridging strategy, training centers may need to contract out course development and instruction from high-end civilian sources. Formal academic educational programs are likewise important. Training and education are distinct entities. Training programs provide shorter term hands-on experience and education programs provide longer lasting underlying principles. Selection for cyber operations personnel should include assessment of pre-service college degrees to link prior cyber-related education to positions in the cyber workforce. As individuals in the "Many" and "Few" groups progress, graduate degrees in areas like computer science, data science, networking, and computer engineering will be useful. Also useful are degrees in business, policy, economics, psychology, human factors, law, and many other disciplines, as long as the degree program includes substantial study of the intersection of the given discipline and cyber operations. These complementary degrees will help prepare people for assignments at higher levels of responsibility where non-technical cyber expertise is essential. Note that civilian degree programs will take people out of the operational force for one or more years, so it is important to encourage a culture that values civilian education.

We'd also like to discuss institutions beyond just those for traditional military school house training and civilian education. We believe there is a need for a service academy for cyber. Right now, cyber is bolted onto traditional Army, Navy, Air Force, and Marine officer development programs. Wedded in tradition, each academy is unlikely to change its core mission. The academies do what they do for their specific branch of service and they do it well, but cyber competes for fragments of student and faculty time and resources. It would be powerful indeed to create a dedicated service academy for cyber, where the entire program would be designed to recruit and develop the highest possible quality cyber talent. Imagine that instead of extensive high school recruiting for football players, this cyber academy recruited in high schools for the best potential cyber operators. A cyber academy could feed graduates into the Joint force just like any other service academy. We believe an investment in a new service academy would make a dramatic difference in both quality and quantity of cyber talent that would be unmatched in the world.

Another consideration is to create a war college for cyber. At present each of the services has highly-selective year-long war college programs for senior officers, but these programs are focused on largely service-specific concerns and include only cursory cyber content.[687] It would be powerful to create a war college for cyber that was built from the ground up to cover cyber conflict issues. Senior cyber leaders would attend from all the services along with appropriate individuals from cyber-enabler communities. Kinetic warfighters might also desire to attend as a broadening experience. A war college for cyber is a non-trivial investment, but another key step in making a professionalized cyber operations force.

A service academy and war college for cyber are great steps forward, but the ultimate answer is to create a new military service for cyber, alongside the Army, Navy, Air Force, and Marines. The United States did this in 1947 for the air domain with the creation of the U.S. Air Force to serve as the aerial warfare branch. We first heard the idea of a military service for cyber in 2002 from a colleague at West Point and it has since received occasional discussion in the press.[688] Left to their own devices, we should assume that each of the traditional services will focus on their specific areas of responsibility, often focusing on their comfort zone of the tactical level. A separate service could tackle greater concerns to the nation at the strategic level and fill the critical void of who protects the nation in cyberspace. Having seen the tumultuous birth of homeland security, joint force, and service cyber components, we shouldn't naively assume the transition to a service for cyber will occur quickly and easily, it will take a decade or more from inception until the service would start reaching maturity.[689]

If you want to be best in the world in cyberspace operations, these are the steps required. Anything less will fall short of the mark. The resources required aren't trivial, but they aren't impossible either, the key challenges to overcome are cultural and political, not resource limitations.

## Create Credible Doctrine

Doctrine provides the framework in which organizations operate. Good doctrine springs from best practices developed in the field that are then codified into formal written documents. Whether you call it doctrine, best practices, or something else, the frameworks need to be flexible so they can be applied in a variety of circumstances. Doctrine isn't holy writ, however, and leaders must understand that previous military doctrine, while good, is focused on kinetic warfare and may or may not apply well to cyber operations.

Military organizations should be willing to invest some of their precious cyber talent to develop cyber operations doctrine and make sure we begin with a solid foundation. Without this investment, doctrine will be written by those without experience in the domain and you'll later have to spend more energy to retroactively get it right.[690] To the extent possible, it is important to get it right up front.

The rate of change of technology and the cyberspace domain create additional challenges. Cyber doctrine will need to be flexibly written, and you'll want to work hard to capture and codify best practices rapidly.

Doctrine written in a vacuum is dangerous, as is outdated doctrine. Beware the hubris of the kinetic warfighter who dismisses cyber as well as your colleagues that color only inside the lines. Challenge your doctrine before your adversaries do. Study the doctrine and the tactics, techniques, and procedures of your adversaries. By analyzing adversary doctrine you can get inside their heads, prepare defenses, and execute offensive operations. Your adversaries will be working hard to do the same to you. Avoid the "not invented here" syndrome. Learn from your adversaries, other cyberspace actors, industry, academia, and independent security researchers.

## Acquire and Grow Cyber Talent

We end this list with the subject of people. Technology is important, but at the end of the day, it is the people who make cyber operations possible. The better the people you have the more successful you will be. When the doctrine of cyber operations was introduced in the U.S. Army, it seemed to us that senior leaders were surprised by the people. They anticipated recruiting talent for whom cyber operations was just another job, but instead they found believers who wouldn't accept lowered standards for motivation and expertise, believers for whom cyber security was wired into their DNA. You can, of course, just recruit talent, but with believers you get individuals for whom cybersecurity is more than just a job. You don't need to supervise them closely, you just need to give them broad left and right boundaries and a general direction to head, and they will do the rest. Beware the careerist, however. You don't want isolated careerists undermining the morale and performance of cyber organizations because they view cyber as trendy and career enhancing. Militaries haven't been historically kind to dedicated cyber talent, so moves like the U.S. Army creating cyber career paths and a Cyber branch provide a rallying point.[691] As part of creating a branch, it is important to work hard to acquire the authority to make promotion decisions within the community, rather than via larger service-wide generalized systems who may employ the wrong metrics to judge success and promotion potential.

You can't take your existing cyber talent for granted. These are people who are highly marketable and, frankly, can find a better paying job elsewhere. You retain cyber talent by treating them with respect, valuing their contributions, feeding their insatiable appetite for knowledge, and creating a culture and environment where they want to work. Contrary to traditional career development, we found an inversion of expertise, the more junior the individual, the more cyber expertise they possessed, so focus on recruiting, developing, and retaining this high-end talent.

Like any service member, cyber operators want to look up at their leaders and see people they aspire to be. As you fill the more senior ranks, it is important to select leaders who are equally passionate about cyber operations and are dedicated to growing people who are better than themselves. Perhaps the most important role of leaders is to shield their talent from the relentless press of military and government bureaucracy, so the workforce can accomplish their missions.

The challenge of cyber leaders will be to forge individuals into cohesive teams. Such bonding comes through collective training, exercises, and operational experiences. For those in the kinetic warfare ranks, be advised that what you see developing in the cyber operations community will appear uncomfortably unorthodox, like the Special Operations community appears to the traditional military. Please don't kill these nascent cyber communities because they look different than you. These communities are innovative, entrepreneurial, and essential, even if different.

For an organization to be truly world class there must be an increasingly high bar for expertise. High levels of expertise cannot be achieved piecemeal. A dedicated cyber career path is essential. If you look at kinetic warfighting generals officers, you will see experts in infantry, armor, field artillery, and aviation whose expertise in their field was honed over 20-30+ year careers of progressively challenging assignments, work roles, and educational opportunities. The end result is senior leaders that are among the best in the world. Cyber service members can be the same, if they are allowed to succeed. After much thought and experience at developing and employing cyber talent, we firmly believe that cyber officers need a solid technical foundation to understand the domain in which they operate, the capabilities that they employ, and the risk they accept. After initial assignments in cyber operations, service members should have the choice between following a technical track to hone their technical skills to the highest level, and a leadership track that creates cyber-savvy leaders up to the General Officer ranks. In the cyber operations arena, possession of technical skills cannot be the job of junior enlisted soldiers alone, or you will quickly hit a ceiling that limits the potential of the entire organization.

A cyber career path should allow onboarding of talent at the higher ranks from the civilian workforce and acknowledge that some service members will leave along the way. Even after departure from the service, alumni should be encourage to remain part of the larger cyber operations ecosystem and to create their own companies, perform research in academia, or serve as contractors, government civilians, and mentors.

The most powerful cyber workforce is a team that brings together active duty, civilian, contractor, and reserve personnel, of all ranks, around a common mission. No nation has fully broken the code on the proper use of reservists in the cyber operations community, but the reserves can play a decisive role. Reservists possess skillsets absent in the active force, understand the business community, and the role of protecting individual states, business sectors, and communities. They can serve as translators, ambassadors, and key extra-governmental entry points in times of crisis, not just a pool of talent to quasi-draft when needed.

*"Just because there's not a war doesn't mean there's peace."*
*- Raven Darkhölme* [692]

## Parting Thoughts

Cyber brings new capabilities to bear and will fundamentally alter warfare. However, at its heart, war will remain war. War is ugly, despicable, and something that will remain with us. Actors from nation-states to individuals will seek to employ cyberspace operations to achieve their aims and gain advantage, both in intense conflict and in campaigns that exist over years or more. Just as airpower alone cannot solve all problems, nor can cyber. Cyberspace operations however, will play an increasingly important role in all future conflict. By understanding the future landscape, you can make better informed decisions today to set the conditions for tomorrow. Now is the time for cyber operators to be audacious and bold.

*Si vis pacem, para bellum*[693]

# REFERENCES

[1] Steve Bellovin, "The Security Flag in the IPv4 Header," Request for Comments: 3514, 1 April 2003. Cyber combat would certainly be much more straightforward if combatants honored the evil bit.

[2] Ironically, the same nuclear weapons prevented warfare due to the threat of mutually assured destruction.

[3] Lawrence Lessig, "Code Is Law: On Liberty in Cyberspace," *Harvard Magazine*, 1 January 2000.

[4] Mark Wilson, "The clock is ticking for the US to relinquish control of ICANN," BetaNews, 25 January 2016. See also Patrick O'Neill, "French government considers law that would outlaw strong encryption," The Daily Dot, 12 January 2016 and Sam Thielman, "US and European officials reignite 'back door' encryption debate after Paris," The Guardian, 18 November 2015.

[5] U.S. Cyber Command Fact Sheet, U.S. Strategic Command Organizational Website, March 2015. Available online at https://www.stratcom.mil/factsheets/2/Cyber_Command/. See also Aliya Sternstein, "US Cyber Command Has Just Half the Staff It Needs," DefenseOne, 8 February 2015.

[6] Note that the U.S. Air Force, created an earlier, provisional, Air Force Cyber Command in 2008 led by Major General William Lord.

[7] David Alexander, "Pentagon to treat cyberspace as 'operational domain'," Reuters, 14 July 2011.

[8] "Army Cyber branch offers Soldiers new challenges, opportunities," Fort Gordon Public Affairs Office, U.S. Army, 24 November 2014.

[9] As one of our favorite information security voices, Josh Corman, likes to state: cynicism is InfoSec's core competency. If you believe these examples are exaggerated, ask yourself what you could pull off if you had the resources of a nation-state and a 10,000-30,000+ member trained cyber army under your command. If anything, we've understated what might happen.

[10] Cyber Operations is a term applying to any activities or actions in the cyber domain, similar to the U.S. military's concept of "Land Operations," but not limited exclusively to campaigns at the operational level of war.

[11] Roy Ragsdale, "Cyber from First Principles," Cyber Talks, National Defense University, 2015. Available online at https://www.youtube.com/watch?v=qbwroHUuMzk

[12] Some argue against, see Thomas Rid, *Cyber War Will Not Take Place*, Oxford University Press, 2013. *Cyber War Will Not Take Place* is an important work and

recommended reading.

[13] Joint Publication 3-12(R) Cyberspace Operations, U.S. Department of Defense, 5 February 2013.

[14] Everett Rosenfeld, "US-China agree to not conduct cybertheft of intellectual property," CNBC, 25 September 2015. Michael Schmidt and David Sanger, "Russian Hackers Read Obama's Unclassified Emails, Officials Say," New York Times, 25 April 2015. Adam Kredo, "U.S. Power Grid Being Hit With 'Increasing' Hacking Attacks, Government Warns," Free Beacon, 24 June 2015. Peter Elkind, "Sony Pictures: Inside the Hack of the Century," Fortune, 1 July 2015. Ben Elgin and Michael Riley, "Now at the Sands Casino: An Iranian Hacker in Every Server," Bloomberg Business, 11 December 2014. Jose Pagliery, "The inside story of the biggest hack in history," CNN Money, 5 August 2015.

[15] Each of these has been proven feasible though. See Jordan Robertson and Michael Riley, "How Hackers Took Down a Power Grid," Bloomberg Businessweek, 14 January 2016, Jose Pagliery, "Russian hackers placed 'digital bomb' in Nasdaq," CNN Money, 17 July 2014, and Steve Ragan, "Ransomware takes Hollywood hospital offline, $3.6M demanded by attackers," CSO Online, 14 February 2016.

[16] Marc Lindemann, "When the Screens Go Dark: Rethinking Our Dependence on Digital Systems," Small Wars Journal, 2 March 2015.

[17] Patrick Duggan, "Man, Computer, and Special Warfare," Small Wars Journal, 4 June 2016. For a discussion on hybrid war, see Damien Van Puyvelde, "Hybrid war - does it even exist?," NATO Review Magazine, 2015.

[18] Current U.S. doctrine calls this concept the "range of military operations." We used the previous "spectrum of conflict" model from the U.S. Field Manual FM 3-0 Operations, 2011 because we felt it to be a closer match in the context of cyberspace.

[19] RussR and Jericho, DEF CON Recognize Awards, DEF CON, 2013.

[20] The U.S. military prefers the terms lethal and non-lethal to kinetic and non-kinetic. We prefer to use kinetic framing because non-kinetic activities can be lethal.

[21] The correct use of terminology is important, but challenging, as the cyberspace operations field is so dynamic. We tend to think of language as organic and new terms will eventually come into common use and some will make their way naturally into a dictionary. This has not stopped the U.S. Department of Defense from trying to drive adoption of approved terminology. We've met the individual responsible for the "Cyber Lexicon," who tries to standardize top-down driven terminology into the ranks. He is a great guy, but has a thankless job.

[22] The U.S. Department of Defense currently utilizes Offensive Cyber Operations (OCO) and Defensive Cyber Operations (DCO). We prefer the DoD's

deprecated terminology, *Computer Network Attack (CNA)*, *Computer Network Defense (CND)*, and *Computer Network Exploitation (CNE)*, which is more precise and draws a distinction between attack (CNA) and intelligence collection (CNE).

[23] The U.S. Department of Defense defines *cyberspace* using the unwieldy, "A global domain within the information environment consisting of the interdependent network of information technology infrastructures and resident data, including the Internet, telecommunications networks, computer systems, and embedded processors and controllers" in Joint Publication 1-02 Department of Defense Dictionary of Military and Associated Terms, 8 November 2010 (As amended through 15 January 2016).

[24] The definition is derived from FM 3-38 Cyber Electromagnetic Activities, U.S. Army, February 2014.

[25] The U.S. Department of Defense calls this DODIN Ops, for the operation of the DoD Information Network. A slightly older DoD term you might encounter is GIG Ops, for the operation of the Global Information Grid. The concepts are largely the same, just the name and acronym were updated.

[26] James Holmes, "Unorthodox and Chaotic: How America Should Fight Wars," The Diplomat, 27 September 2013.

[27] FM 3-38 Cyber Electromagnetic Activities, U.S. Army, February 2014.

[28] Joint Publication 3-12(R), Cyberspace Operations, U.S. Department of Defense, 5 February 2013.

[29] In 2012 we made an attempt at convincing some of the naysayers, see Jonalan Brickey, Jacob Cox, John Nelson, and Gregory Conti, "The Case for Cyber," Small Wars Journal, 13 September 2012. Read the comments section, too.

[30] The U.S. military calls these six categories "warfighting functions." See ADRP 3-0 Unified Land Operations, U.S. Army, May 2012.

[31] Ibid.

[32] The concept of freedom of action is embedded in the mission statement of U.S. Army Cyber Command: "Army Cyber Command and Second Army directs and conducts cyberspace and information operations as authorized or directed, to ensure freedom of action in and through cyberspace, and to deny the same to our adversaries." See http://www.arcyber.army.mil/

[33] These definitions are derived from Martin Dunn, "Levels of War: Just a Set of Labels," Research and Analysis: Newsletter of the Directorate of Army Research and Analysis, Australian Army, No. 10, October 1996, available online at http://www.clausewitz.com/readings/Dunn.htm The levels of war aren't necessarily firm and fixed. Edward Luttwak in his book *Strategy: The Logic of*

*War and Peace,* Belknap Press, 2002, includes a "technical" level below tactics, which we might call hardware and software tools. The technical level is usually ignored in traditional military discussions, which we think is a mistake, because it's very relevant to cyber. Note also that the business community uses the same three terms, but differently. Strategy is associated with policy, procedures are considered Tactical, and execution is Operational.

[34] We first heard this idea from Richard Bejtlich, and his thinking was spot on. See Richard Bejtlich, "Strategy, Not Speed: What Today's Digital Defenders Must Learn From Cybersecurity's Early Thinkers," Brookings Institution, May 2014.

[35] This graphic, excluding the cyber operations examples, is derived from FM 3-0 Operations, U.S. Army, February 2008.

[36] This section is based on the initial message sent out by the 39th Chief of Staff of the U.S. Army, General Mark Milley, 2015, available online at http://ec.militarytimes.com/static/pdfs/Initial_Message_39th_CSA.pdf In this letter he outlines three priorities: Readiness, Future Fight, and Taking Care of the Troops. See also, Michelle Tan, "Milley: Readiness for ground combat is No. 1 priority," Army Times, 28 August 2015.

[37] The current shortage of cyber security talent is well documented. See Monty Munford, "Skills Shortage Means Salaries Soar As US Cities Vie For Cybersecurity Talent," Forbes, 30 August 2016 and Steve Morgan, "Market expansion adds to cybersecurity talent shortage, CSO Online, 13 July 2016 as examples.

[38] ADP 5-0 The Operations Process, U.S. Army, May 2012.

[39] Read Michael Lewis' *Flash Boys*, W. W. Norton & Company, 2015 for an in-depth look at this arena.

[40] Riley Walters, "Russian Hackers Shut Down Ukraine's Power Grid," Newsweek, 14 January 2016.

[41] See Army Cyber Institute, http://cyber.army.mil/.

[42] Baron De Jomini, *The Art of War*, Wilder Publications, 2008, p. 11.

[43] John Greenough, "How the 'Internet of Things' will impact consumers, businesses, and governments in 2016 and beyond," Business Insider, 14 April 2015.

[44] In U.S. military doctrinal symbology friendly forces are color coded as blue, enemy forces as red, and neutrals as white.

[45] For a detailed study of insider threats see Dawn Cappelli, Andrew Moore, and Randall Trzeciak, *The CERT Guide to Insider Threats: How to Prevent, Detect,*

and *Respond to Information Technology Crimes*, Addison-Wesley Professional, 2012.

[46] Gunter Ollmann, "Letter Of (Cyber) Marque and Reprisal," Dark Reading, 13 June 2013.

[47] As an example, the well-known Russian Business Network (RBN), became a world hub for child pornography, spamming, and identity theft. One group allegedly used RBN's infrastructure to steal about $150 million from bank accounts in a single year. See Brian Krebs, "Shadowy Russian Firm Seen as Conduit for Cybercrime," Washington Post, 13 October 2007. In 2013, Kreb's was subject to a simultaneous denial of service attack on his website and a misdirected police raid on his home. Kreb's believed the attacks were connected to a story he had published exposing a black market website offering Social Security numbers for sale. See Carl Franzen, "Security blogger Brian Krebs suffers simultaneous cyber attack, police raid," The Verge, 15 March 2013.

[48] We've used the term "corporations" here, but non-incorporated companies are equally valid.

[49] Larisa Epatko, "Is It Fair to Describe Corporations as Sociopaths?," PBS NewsHour, 12 April 2010.

[50] Andy Greenberg, "Founder of Stealthy Security Firm Endgame To Lawmakers: Let U.S. Companies 'Hack Back,'" Forbes, 20 September 2013.

[51] For examples of the impact of public disclosures, see Andy Greenberg, "HBGary Federal's Aaron Barr Resigns After Anonymous Hack Scandal," Forbes, 28 February 2011, Clare O'Connor, "Target CEO Gregg Steinhafel Resigns In Data Breach Fallout," Forbes, 5 May 2014, and Lisa Richwine, "Cyber attack could cost Sony studio as much as $100 million," Reuters, 9 December 2014.

[52] As an example, the United States' Intelligence Community (IC) has 17 diverse organizations, organized around various missions and intelligence specialties including: Signals Intelligence (SIGINT), Human Intelligence (HUMINT), Imagery Intelligence (IMINT), Counter Intelligence (CI), and Tactical Intelligence. See "Member Agencies," The United States Intelligence Community, https://www.intelligencecareers.gov/icmembers.html.

[53] Michael Kolton, "The Inevitable Militarization of Artificial Intelligence," Cyber Defense Review, 8 February 2016.

[54] Andrew Clevenger, "'The Terminator Conundrum': Pentagon Weighs Ethics of Pairing Deadly Force, AI," Army Times, 23 January 2016.

[55] Rogue AI's have been explored extensively in science fiction, with the T-800 cyborg from the 1984 Terminator movie and the HAL 9000 from Arthur C. Clarke's 2001: A Space Odyssey being classic examples. See also Daniel

Wilson's *Robopocalypse*, Doubleday, 2011 for another interesting study.

[56] International standards organizations possess great power and help define the function and openness, or lack thereof, of cyberspace. For example, a standards body could mandate the use of strong encryption in a given type of protocol, or use their bully pulpit to speak out on an issue. The latter was seen when the Internet Engineering Task Force (IETF) created the 451 HTTP status code. The number 451 pays homage to Ray Bradbury's anti-censorship book *Fahrenheit 451* and the 451 HTTP code was enacted to indicate potential censorship on the Web.

[57] The term *survival of the fittest* was first used by Herbert Spencer in his 1864 book *Principles of Biology* in his explanation and analysis of Darwin's theory of natural selection.

[58] "What if DOTMLPF?," United States Army Capabilities Integration Center, http://www.arcic.army.mil/AboutARCIC/dotmlpf.aspx. See also Wikipedia, "DOTMLPF," https://en.wikipedia.org/wiki/DOTMLPF.

[59] For high quality research on economic incentives, see the Workshop on the Economics of Information Security, http://econinfosec.org/

[60] HP Security Research, "Profiling an enigma: The mystery of North Korea's cyber threat landscape," Hewlett Packard, August 2014.

[61] Scott Henderson, *The Dark Visitor*, Lulu, January 2007.

[62] The phrase *turning a blind eye* is attributed to an incident involving Admiral Horatio Nelson. Nelson, during the Battle of Copenhagen in 1801, ignored orders from his superiors, by placing a telescope to his blind eye and stating "I really do not see the signal [flags]" directing him to discontinue engaging the enemy. A short summary of this incident may be found at https://en.wikipedia.org/wiki/Turning_a_blind_eye

[63] See Jose Pagliery "NSA is world's best hacker thief, says former director," CNN Money, 12 January 2016 and Brian Bennett, "NSA chief says Chinese government encourages cybertheft," Los Angeles Times, 24 September 2015. Typically U.S. attempts at drawing a distinction between theft of intellectual property for national security versus financial gain do not play well on the global stage.

[64] A *zero-day*, or *0-day*, is an undisclosed computer software vulnerability. For more information, see https://en.wikipedia.org/wiki/Zero-day_(computing)

[65] Paul Rexton Kan, "Anonymous vs. Los Zetas: The Revenge of the Hacktivists," Small Wars Journal, 27 June 2013.

[66] Fred Brooks, *The Mythical Man-Month*, Addison-Wesley, 1975.

[67] The fall of the Soviet Union, which was partially precipitated by attempting to match defense spending with the United States is one clear example. See "Fall of the Soviet Union," The Cold War Museum, http://www.coldwar.org/articles/90s/fall_of_the_soviet_union.asp. For an excellent analysis of the cost efficiencies of large actors versus small agile actors see Peiter "Mudge" Zatko, "Keynote: Analytic Framework for Cyber Security," ShmooCon, 2011.

[68] For a good overview of order of battle see https://en.wikipedia.org/wiki/Order_of_battle.

[69] For an excellent discussion see Thomas Wadlow, "Who Must You Trust?," Communications of the ACM, July 2014, Vol. 57, No. 7, pp. 42-49.

[70] Ken Thompson, "Reflections on Trusting Trust," Communications of the ACM, August 1984, Vol. 27, No. 8, pp. 761-763.

[71] We will discuss capabilities in far greater detail in Chapter 7 - Capabilities.

[72] Shane Harris, *@War: The Rise of the Military-Internet Complex*, Eamon Dolan / Houghton Mifflin Harcourt, 2014, p. xxiii.

[73] In addition to the mutually beneficial or ideological reasons for partnerships, a stronger party may coerce a weaker party into a partnership.

[74] Leslie Groves, *Now It Can Be Told*, Da Capo Press, 1962.

[75] See Leo Taddeo, "Hacker-For-Hire Markets Can Turn Ordinary Insider Threats into Top Tier Adversaries. Time to Rethink Tools and Strategies," LinkedIn, 6 February 2016. Available online at https://www.linkedin.com/pulse/hacker-for-hire-markets-can-turn-ordinary-insider-threats-leo-taddeo?trk=hb_ntf_MEGAPHONE_ARTICLE_POST

[76] North Atlantic Treaty Organization, "Collective defence - Article 5," North Atlantic Treaty Organization, http://www.nato.int/cps/en/natohq/topics_110496.htm. See also, Paul McLeary "NATO Chief: Cyber Can Trigger Article 5," Defense News, 25 March 2015.

[77] Cheryl Pellerin, "DoD's Silicon Valley Innovation Experiment Begins," U.S. Department of Defense, 29 October 2015.

[78] Idan Tendler, "From The Israeli Army Unit 8200 To Silicon Valley," TechCrunch, 20 March 2015.

[79] Margaret Warner, "An exclusive club: The five countries that don't spy on each other," PBS NewsHour, 25 October 2013.

[80] As examples, see Jim Sciutto, Nicole Gaouette and Ryan Browne, "US finds growing evidence of Russia feeding emails to WikiLeaks," CNN, 14 October 2016

and Gadi Evron, "Authoritatively, Who Was Behind The Estonian Attacks?," Dark Reading, 17 March 2009.

[81] Clifford Stoll, *The Cuckoo's Egg*, Doubleday, 1989.

[82] See Gunter Ollmann, "Botnet Communication Topologies: Understanding the intricacies of botnet command-and-control," White Paper, Damballa, 2009.

[83] Aliya Sternstein, "Pentagon Grants Contractors An Extension On Hack Detection Rules," NextGov, 4 January 2016.

[84] Claire Miller, "Revelations of N.S.A. Spying Cost U.S. Tech Companies," New York Times, 21 March 2014.

[85] Alistair Charlton, "Did the FBI pay Carnegie Mellon University $1M to hack Tor and reveal Silk Road 2 staff?," International Business Times, 12 November 2015.

[86] Amir Efrati and Siobhan Gorman, "Google Mail Hack Blamed on China," The Wall Street Journal, 2 June 2011.

[87] Kim Zetter, *Countdown to Zero Day: Stuxnet and the Launch of the World's First Digital Weapon*, Crown, 2014. Other good example are the many security industry generated threat reports which implicate nation-state actors. See Nick Selby, "One Year Later: The APT1 Report," DarkReading, 8 April 2014.

[88] Dennis Fisher, "Final Report on Diginotar Hack Shows Total Compromise of CA Servers," Threatpost, 31 October 2012.

[89] "Stingray Tracking Devices: Who's Got Them," American Civil Liberties Union, https://www.aclu.org/map/stingray-tracking-devices-whos-got-them. See also Gordon Corera, "How the British and Americans started listening in," BBC News, 8 February 2016.

[90] Brent Chapman and Frederick "Erick" Waage, "Going Native: A Career Pipeline for U.S. Military Success Out in Silicon Valley," Foreign Policy, 14 January 2016 provides a thoughtful analysis.

[91] As an example, the United States employs the NOFORN caveat to label classified information that cannot be shared with non-U.S. citizens. Such restrictions hamper international collaboration.

[92] Sean Lyngaas, "Sorry, DOD. Silicon Valley's just not that into you," Federal Computer Weekly, 20 October 2015.

[93] *The Matrix*, Warner Brothers, 1999. Quote retrieved from http://www.imdb.com/title/tt0133093/quotes

[94] Newton's Laws, paraphrased: 1) Every object in a state of uniform motion tends to remain in that state of motion unless an external force is applied to it; 2)

The relationship between an object's mass *m*, its acceleration *a*, and the applied force *F* is $F = ma$; 3) For every action there is an equal and opposite reaction.

[95] Famed military theorist, Colonel John Boyd, brought together diverse theories from science and applied them to military operations, such as Godel's incompleteness theorems, the Second Law of Thermodynamics, and Heisenberg's uncertainty principle, see John Boyd, "Destruction and Creation," White Paper, 3 September 1976. We are taking a similar approach here, partially inspired by his work.

[96] Another way to view these laws of physics is as the physics of information flows within systems and networks.

[97] For a discussion of the powerful capabilities of Silicon Valley firms, see Fred Kaplan, "What Role Should Silicon Valley Play in Fighting Terrorism?," Technology Review, 23 February 2016. See also Jim Acosta, "First on CNN: Government enlists tech giants to fight ISIS messaging," CNN, 25 February 2016.

[98] In Douglas Adams' *Hitchhiker's Guide to the Galaxy* it took 7.5 million years to calculate the answer to the "Ultimate question of Life, The Universe, and Everything." Certainly not the lifespan of the universe, but still a significant investment of computational power. [Spoiler Alert] The answer was 42.

[99] David Goodstein, "Mechanics," Encyclopedia Britannica, 2016.

[100] The study of information is a rich and relevant field. See James Gleick, *The Information*, Vintage, 2012 and John Pierce, *An Introduction to Information Theory*, Dover, 1980.

[101] This applies in general, of course there are also non-deterministic (stochastic) sources employed in computing systems, such as using random number generators based on quantum properties or atmospheric noise. There is also the possibility of errors, such as "soft errors" that could cause a bit flip based on stray cosmic radiation. These errors have practical implications, such as domain name hijacking. See Artem Dinaburg, "Bitsquating," Black Hat, 2011.

[102] Robbie Gonzalez, "10 Limits to Human Perception … and How They Shape Your World," Gizmodo, 17 July 2012.

[103] This graphic was inspired by "The Electromagnetic Spectrum," National Aeronautics and Space Administration (NASA), March 2013. http://imagine.gsfc.nasa.gov/science/toolbox/emspectrum1.html.

[104] One example is the limit on the precise measurement of the position and

momentum of a particle.

[105] To be more precise, the hardware components of each node reside in the physical world as well, but our intent with this graphic is to demonstrate how sensors allow the virtual machine to perceive the physical world.

[106] These are the sensors included in the current version of the Apple iPhone.

[107] Olivia Solon, " iPhone Accelerometer Could Spy on Computer Keystrokes," Wired, 19 October 2011.

[108] William Herkewitz, "With 'MyShake' App, Your Phone Feels Earthquakes and Automatically Warns Scientists," Popular Mechanics, 12 February 2016.

[109] Kyle Hill, "Your Brain Has a Frame Rate and It's Pretty Slow," Nerdist, 26 June 2014. See also https://en.wikipedia.org/wiki/Phi_phenomenon.

[110] If you are interested in learning more, see Gregory Conti and Edward Sobiesk, "Malicious Interfaces and Personalization's Uninviting Future," IEEE Security and Privacy, May/June 2009.

[111] Chris Matyszczyk, "Police to experiment with blinding 'Dazer Laser'?," CNET, 23 July 2010.

[112] Zoz, "Hacking Driverless Vehicles," DEF CON, 2013. For a discussion of laser dazzling of electo-optical sensors see Gunnar Ritt and Bernd Eberle, "Sensor Protection Against Laser Dazzling," SPIE – The International Society for Optical Engineering, 27 October 2010.

[113] For a useful discussion on the memory capacity of the human brain, Paul Reber, "What Is the Memory Capacity of the Human Brain?," Scientific American, 1 May 2010.

[114] The software engineering discipline seeks to overcome weaknesses in the human development of code allowing greater scale and complexity, while reducing errors. Machines can also write code, albeit in a very structured way ultimately designed by humans, and machines may even adjust their own programming via self-modifying code and machine learning.

[115] We are using the more general definition here, work factor is also used in the context of cryptography as a metric of effort an attacker would need to invest to defeat a given cryptosystem. For an example of creating computational complexity and using it as a weapon see the *I, Mudd* episode of the original Star Trek where the characters overwhelm an android by posing to it the Liar's Paradox. See https://en.wikipedia.org/wiki/Liar_paradox and

https://en.wikipedia.org/wiki/I,_Mudd for details of the episode.

[116] For an early attempt at overwhelming the human operator through deception, see Samuel Patton, William Yurcik, and David Doss, "An Achilles' Heel in Signature-Based IDS: Squealing False Positives in SNORT," Recent Advances in Intrusion Detection (RAID), 2001.

[117] For a science fiction depiction of precognition, see the movie, *The Minority Report*, 20th Century Fox, 2002.

[118] Law enforcement agencies are actively employing predictive analytics, see Walter Perry, Brian McInnis, Carter Price, Susan Smith and John Hollywood, "The Role of Crime Forecasting in Law Enforcement Operations," RAND, 2013.

[119] Christopher Malmo, "Bitcoin Is Unsustainable," Vice, 29 June 2015.

[120] Mark Barnett, "Small Business Brief," Office of Small Business Programs, National Security Agency, 26 April 2011 via The Greater Baltimore Committee, retrieved 11 June 2013.

[121] John Markoff, "Microsoft Plumbs Ocean's Depths to Test Underwater Data Center," 31 January 2016.

[122] Dan Farber, "Facebook turns on data center at edge of the Arctic Circle," CNET, 12 June 2013.

[123] John Herman, "Why Everything Wireless Is 2.4 GHz," Wired, 7 September 2010. As a benchmark, a recent world WiFi distance record was 237 miles using specialized gear. See Nilay Patel, "Venezuelans set new WiFi distance record: 237 miles," 19 June 2007.

[124] FM 3-0 Operations, U.S. Army, February 2008

[125] Somini Sengupta, "A Homemade Drone Snoops on Wireless Networks," New York Times, 5 August 2011.

[126] Sean Gallagher, "Pwned again: An exclusive look at Pwnie Express' newest hack-in-a-box," ArsTechnica, 30 July 2013.

[127] There are different types of race conditions, but the one we've just described is called a time-of-check-to-time-of-use (TOCTTOU) bug.

[128] For one example regarding humans see @JRRaphael on Twitter's apparent testing of a non-chronologically-ordered timeline. Available online at https://twitter.com/JRRaphael/status/674276087145365504.

[129] For a discussion on propagation timing and geolocating sources of network traffic see Ari Juels, *Tetraktys*, Emerald Bay Books, 2009.

[130] Shane Harris, *@War: The Rise of the Military-Internet Complex*, Houghton Mifflin Harcourt, 2014.

[131] Mixed human, machine, and network speed attacks are also certainly possible. We'll discuss these issues in more depth in Chapter 10: Command and Control.

[132] See Jan Kallberg, "In Cyber, Time is of the Essence," Cyber Defense Review, 28 January 2016.

[133] Baron De Jomini. *The Art of War*, Wilder Publications, 2008.

[134] In the language of computer science, this end-to-end flow is a session. Sessions may be stateless or stateful. A stateful session means that at least some of the communicating devices must store some information about the session. A stateless session is one that each interaction is acted upon independently as individual requests and responses.

[135] For a classic example of using intermediate proxies see Cliff Stoll, *The Cuckoo's Egg: Tracking a Spy Through the Maze of Computer Espionage*, Pocket Books, 2005. For pivoting see "VPN Pivoting," InfoSec Institute, 11 February 2013.

[136] M-Labs, "Malware Persistence without the Windows Registry," FireEye, 15 July 2010.

[137] Ken Than, "A computer's microphone and speakers can covertly send and receive data," Inside Science, 11 December 2013. See also Dan Goodin, "Beware of ads that use inaudible sound to link your phone, TV, tablet, and PC, Ars Technica, 13 November 2015.

[138] For our earlier thinking on counterintuitive aspects of cyber conflict, see Matthew Miller, Jon Brickey, and Gregory Conti, "Why Your Intuition About Cyber Warfare is Probably Wrong," Small Wars Journal, 29 November 2012. We build upon this effort here.

[139] See Yu-Tzu Chiu, "Flash Memory Survives 100 Million Cycles," IEEE Spectrum 30 November 2012 to learn about limitations of flash memory. For the textbook example of physical destruction, see the Aurora Generator Test run by Idaho National Laboratory in 2007 in which a cyber attack violently destroyed a generator. An account is found in Bruce Schneier, "Staged Attack Causes Generator to Self-Destruct," Schneier on Security, 2 October 2007.

[140] Sharon Gaudin, "NASA conducts Martian tech support to repair Curiosity," Computerworld, 5 March 2013.

[141] Nola Taylor Redd, "How Long Does It Take to Get to Mars," Space.com, 13 February 2014.

[142] See https://en.wikipedia.org/wiki/Die_(integrated_circuit) for an overview of processor dies.

[143] Laszlo Kish and Claes Granqvist, "Does Information Have Mass?," Proceedings of the IEEE, Vol. 101, No. 9, September 2013, pp. 1895-1899.

[144] An excellent overview of research on directed energy weapons and electromagnetic bombs may be found at Air Power Australia's website, http://www.ausairpower.net/dew-ebomb.html.

[145] This section heading is derived from one of our favorite cyber conflict quotes, made by Brigadier General Mark Kimmitt, who quipped "I'm an artillery officer, and I can't fire cannons at the internet." See James Westhead, "Planning the US 'Long War' on terror," BBC News, 10 April 2006.

[146] An interesting example is that of BIFF, Backhoe Induced Fiber Failure. See Fred Lawler, "The 10 Most Bizarre and Annoying Causes of Fiber Cuts," Blog Posting, Level 3 Communications, 4 August 2011.

[147] Greg Miller, "Undersea Internet Cables are Surprisingly Vulnerable," Wired, 29 October 2015.

[148] For seminal work on clock synchronization in distributed systems, see Leslie Lamport, "Time, clocks, and the ordering of events in a distributed system," Communications of the ACM, Vol. 21, No. 7, July 1978.

[149] We see hibernation in laptops and in virtual machines.

[150] Hope Hodge Seck, "Navy Wants to Unplug From Some Networks to Stay Ahead of Cyberattacks," Military.com, 19 February 2016. This sounds a lot like the science fiction series, Battlestar Galactica, where Commander Adama orders that no computers may be networked. His foresight allowed his ship to survive the Cylon attack. See http://en.battlestarwiki.org/wiki/Colonial_Computer_History.

[151] See Darren Pauli, "Patient monitors altered, drug dispensary popped in colossal hospital hack," The Register, 25 February 2016.

[152] Sean Gallagher, "Pwned again, An exclusive look at Pwnie Express' newest

hack-in-a-box," ArsTechnica, 30 July 2013.

[153] John Mearsheimer, "Assess the Conventional Balance: The 3:1 Rule and Its Critics," International Security, Vol. 13, No. 4, Spring 1989, pp. 54-89.

[154] Richard Bejtlich calls this the "intruder's dilemma," see Richard Bejtlich, "Defender's Dilemma vs Intruder's Dilemma," TaoSecurity, 23 May 2009.

[155] Tom Cross, David Raymond, and Gregory Conti, "Deception for the Cyber Defender: To Err is Human; to Deceive, Divine," ShmooCon, 2015. See also Martin Libicki, Lillian Ablon, and Tim Webb, "The Defender's Dilemma: Charting a Course Toward Cybersecurity," RAND, 2015.

[156] Rob Joyce, "Disrupting Nation State Hackers," USENIX Enigma, 2016. This is a groundbreaking talk and highly recommended.

[157] We first heard the clear distinction between cyber tool users and cyber tool makers from Roy Ragsdale. See Roy Ragsdale, "Cyber from First Principles," Cyber Talks, National Defense University, March 2015.

[158] We are talking line-of-sight frequency ranges here. Certain frequencies, like HF, will bounce around the world on only a few watts of power.

[159] Stuxnet did just this. See Gregg Keizer, "Why did Stuxnet worm spread?," Computerworld, 1 October 2010.

[160] This analogy was suggested by Giorgio Bertoli during his talk on cyber effects at Cyber Talks, National Defense University, September 2015.

[161] MC Frontalot, "Secrets From the Future," Musical Lyrics. Available online at http://frontalot.com/index.php/?page=lyrics&lyricid=41. Note that last line of the quotation comes immediately before the preceding text, but we have moved it after to provide better context short of listing the entire song.

[162] A recent example can be seen in Stingray cell phone surveillance technology, which was once a classified program, then a more widespread law enforcement program, and now commercially available. See Stephanie Pell and Christopher Soghoian, "Your Secret Stingray's No Secret Anymore: The Vanishing Government Monopoly over Cell Phone Surveillance and Its Impact on National Security and Consumer Privacy," Harvard Journal of Law and Technology, Vol. 28, No. 1, Fall 2014.

[163] Take for example the, likely true, claims made by Britain's Government Communications Headquarters (GCHQ) that they had discovered public key cryptography several years before the open research community. See Bruce

Schneier, "The Secret Story of Nonsecret Encryption," Dr. Dobb's Journal, April 1998. We believe public knowledge of secrets will approach, but never reach 100%, some things will likely remain a permanent debate such as the Kennedy assassination and alien contact in Roswell, but we argue the overall principle holds true. Much information will become public with time.

[164] See https://en.wikipedia.org/wiki/Moore%27s_law.

[165] "Frequently Asked Questions (FAQ) About the Electronic Frontier Foundation's 'DES Cracker' Machine," Electronic Frontier Foundation, 16 July 2016.

[166] In the early 2000s we overheard a security researcher at the Black Hat security conference quip that "56 bits is plaintext." He was right. (56 bits is the length of DES's key) For fun we got t-shirts made up with "56 bits is plaintext" on the front.

[167] Perfect forward secrecy properties of some cryptographic algorithms can frustrate retroactive decryption. A system that employs perfect forward secrecy, which uses separate session keys for communications, is resistant to cryptanalytic attack even if long-term keys are compromised. This increases the attacker's work factor, but doesn't necessarily prevent future decryption. Advances in quantum cryptography, if successful, could lay bare secrets hidden with many of today's cryptosystems. However, the provably secure, one-time-pad algorithm, if properly employed, will remain secure into the future, but it is infrequently used because of the difficulties of sharing identical, truly random keys with all communicating parties.

[168] See https://en.wikipedia.org/wiki/Information_wants_to_be_free.

[169] For a compelling science fiction story about near-future armies that hide in the population, organize and fight cyber-enabled kinetic battles, and dissolve back into the population see Adam Roberts, *New Model Army*, Gollancz, 2011.

[170] Rachel Nuwer, "Will machines eventually take on every job?," BBC, 5 August 2015.

[171] For information on IBM's Deep Blue and its defeat of chess champion Gary Kasparov, see "Deep Blue," IBM, http://www-03.ibm.com/ibm/history/ibm100/us/en/icons/deepblue/, for Go see Alan Boyle, "AI software masters the game of Go, takes aim at the world's top player," Geek Wire, 27 January 2016, and for Jeopardy see Sharon Gaudin, "Watson triumphs in Jeopardy's man vs. machine challenge," Computerworld, 16 February 2011.

[172] Ray Kurzweil, *The Singularity is Near*, Penguin Books, 2006. See also, Nick

Bostrom, "What happens when our computers get smarter than we are?," TED, 2015.

[173] Edward Cardon, "Cyber Capabilities Key to Future Dominance," Army, February 2016, Vol. 66, No. 2.

[174] See Patrick Tucker, "How the Army Plans to Fight a War Across the Electromagnetic Spectrum," DefenseOne, 26 February 2014 and Sydney Freedberg, "DoD CIO Says Spectrum May Become Warfighting Domain," Breaking Defense, 9 December 2015.

[175] Various versions of military doctrine use the term "Battlespace" for essentially the same concept.

[176] Joint Publication 3-0 Joint Operations, U.S. Department of Defense, 11 August 2011.

[177] Joint Publication 5-0 Joint Operational Planning, U.S. Department of Defense, 11 August 2011.

[178] ADRP 5-0: The Operations Process, U.S. Army, May 2012.

[179] This table format and the traditional application content it contains is derived from the "Regional Analysis Worksheet" made available by West Point's Department of Geography and Environmental Engineering. See http://www.usma.edu/gene/siteassets/sitepages/publications/regional%20analysis%20worksheet.pdf.

[180] See Nick Fielding and Ian Cobain, "Revealed: US spy operation that manipulates social media," The Guardian, 17 March 2011, Anonymous, "How to Spot a State-Funded Chinese Internet Troll," Foreign Policy, 17 June 2015, and Max Seddon, "Documents Show How Russia's Troll Army Hit America," BuzzFeed, 2 June 2014.

[181] For an overview of the extensive instrumentation in our world, see Greg Conti, "Our Instrumented Lives: Sensors, Sensors, Everywhere," DEF CON, 2010.

[182] There was a ground breaking article entitled "My Second Implant" written by Estragon in 2600 magazine, Vol: 27, No. 2, 2010. It is difficult to know if the article represents truth or fiction, but it provides a compelling story regarding life with implants.

[183] See Lisa Shay, Gregory Conti, Dominic Larkin, and John Nelson, "A Framework for Analysis of Quotidian Exposure in an Instrumented World," IEEE Carnahan Conference on Security Technology, October 2012.

[184] See the important work of Katina Michael and M.G. Michael on Uberveillance,

including "A Note on 'Uberveillance,'" IEEE Technology and Society Magazine, Summer 2010 and Roger Clarke's "What is Uberveillance? (And What Should Be Done About It?)," IEEE Technology and Society Magazine, Summer 2010.

[185] Andrea Peterson, "Yes, terrorists could have hacked Dick Cheney's heart," Washington Post, 21 October 2013, Katie Shilton, "Four Billion Little Brothers?: Privacy, Mobile Phones, and Ubiquitous Data Collection," Communications of the ACM, Vol. 52, No. 11, November 2009, Sean Gallagher, "Patients diverted to other hospitals after ransomware locks down key software," Ars Technica, 17 February 2016, and Kim Zetter, "Inside the Cunning Unprecedented Hack of Ukraine's Power Grid," Wired, 3 March 2016.

[186] David E. Sanger, "Obama strikes back at Russia for election hacking," The New York Times, 29 December 2016

[187] Ryan Browne, "U.S. military spending millions to make cyborgs a reality," CNN, 7 March 2016.

[188] A personal favorite dystopian technology is Amazon's Dash Button, see Ian Crouch, "The Horror of Amazon's New Dash Button," The New Yorker, 2 April 2015.

[189] Meghan DeMaria, "Samsung warns customers not to discuss personal information in front of smart TVs," The Week, 9 February 2015.

[190] James Clapper, "US intelligence chief: we might use the internet of things to spy on you," The Guardian, 9 February 2016. For an excellent example of user tracking via commercial technology, consider printer microdots. Printer microdots are a little known, but widely deployed technique for tracking the origin of printed documents back to their original source. See Jason Tuchey, "Government Uses Color Laser Printer Technology to Track Documents," PC World, 22 November 2004.

[191] Cory Doctorow, "Lockdown: The coming war on general-purpose computing," BoingBoing, 10 January 2012.

[192] John Leyden, "Polish teen derails tram after hacking train network," The Register, 11 January 2008.

[193] Robert Neurbecker, "Lower your car insurance bill, at the price of some privacy," The New York Times, 15 August 2015.

[194] Julia Davis, "OnStar- watching over you or watching you?," Examiner, 13 January 2010.

[195] Jamey Heary, "Defcon: Hacking Tire Pressure Monitors Remotely," Network World, 31 July 2010.

[196] Kashmir Hill, "E-ZPasses Get Read All Over New York (Not Just At Toll Booths)," 12 September 2013.

[197] Annie Karni, "Cabbies May Strike To Protest Mandatory GPS Systems," The Sun, 24 August 2007.

[198] Andy Greenberg, "Hackers Remotely Kill a Jeep on the Highway – With Me in It," Wired, 21 July 2015.

[199] For a study on automation trends in law enforcement, see Greg Conti, Lisa Shay and Woody Hartzog, "Life Inside a Skinner Box: Confronting our Future of Automated Law Enforcement," DEF CON 2012 and Lisa Shay, Woodrow Hartzog, John Nelson, Dominic Larking, and Gregory Conti, "Confronting Automated Law Enforcement," We Robot, 2012.

[200] "BCN Smart City," Barcelona, Spain, http://smartcity.bcn.cat/en.

[201] Greg Conti, Tom Cross, and David Raymond, "Pen Testing a City," Black Hat, August 2015.

[202] See Heather Somerville, "Sochi airport uses Silicon Valley facial recognition software," The Mercury News, 10 February 2014 and Vickie Chachere, "Biometrics used to detect criminals at Super Bowl," ABC News, 13 February 2016.

[203] Brent Rose, "Police used facial recognition software to ID suspects in UK riots," Gizmodo, 15 August 2011.

[204] Robert Dixon, "Bringing Big Data to War in Mega-Cities," War on the Rocks, 19 January 2016.

[205] Darryl Ward, "Operational Environment Implications of the Megacity to the US Army," Small Wars Journal, 9 February 2016.

[206] John Vidal, "UN report: World's biggest cities merging into 'mega-regions,'" The Guardian, 22 March 2010.

[207] Nate Anderson, "How China swallowed 15% of 'Net traffic for 18 minutes," Ars Technica, 17 November 2010.

[208] For one example of many possible ways to hack satellites and their services, see J. M. Porup, "It's Surprisingly Simple to Hack a Satellite," Motherboard, 21 August 2015.

[209] Baron De Jomini, *The Art of War*, Wilder Publications, 2008.

[210] The U.S. military has put a great deal of emphasis on *human terrain*, "the human population... as defined and characterized by sociocultural, anthropologic and ethnographic data and other non-geographic information," see Jacob Kipp, "The Human Terrain System: A CORDS for the 21st Century," Military Review, October 2006.

[211] See David Raymond, Gregory Conti, Tom Cross, and Michael Nowatkowski, "Key Terrain in Cyberspace: Seeking the High Ground," NATO Conference on Cyber Conflict, 2014.

[212] A simplified concept of layers can be found in JP 3-12: Cyberspace Operations, U.S. Department of Defense, 5 February 2013, which includes a Physical Network Layer, Logical Network Layer, and Cyber-Persona Layer.

[213] Brett Stone-Gross et al, "Your Botnet is My Botnet: Analysis of a Botnet Takeover," ACM Conference on Computer and Communications Security, 2009.

[214] See David Meyer, "Top NATO officer impersonated on Facebook," ZDNet, 12 March 2012. Seminal research in fake profiles can be seen in the Robin Sage experiment, where an attractive women who developed a popular, but fake online identity was friended by many governmental and non-governmental security professionals. See Joan Goodchild, "The Robin Sage experiment: Fake profile fools security pros," Network World, 8 July 2010.

[215] We are using the generalized idea of a packet here, a more specific term in this example is an *Ethernet frame*.

[216] At this point we want to acknowledge the fine work of Shawn Riley, "'Cyber Terrain': A Model for Increased Understanding of Cyber Activity," LinkedIn 7 October 2014. As we were writing this chapter, we found that he had done important work on cyber terrain and the fine grain aspects of the logical layer, in particular.

[217] Ryan Naraine, "Blue Pill Prototype Creates 100% Undetectable Malware," eWeek, 28 June 2006.

[218] Roger Grimes, "Should you worry about memory-only malware," InfoWorld, 4 February 2014.

[219] Dan Goodin, "Meet 'badBIOS,' the mysterious Mac and PC malware that jumps airgaps," Ars Technica, 31 October 2013. See also the Unified Extensible Firmware Interface Forum, http://www.uefi.org/.

[220] Dan Kaminsky, "Secure Random by Default," DEF CON, 2014. Another way to think about computers residing in other computers is to consider them "systems of systems."

[221] Dan Kaminsky, "Secure Random by Default," DEF CON, 2014.

[222] Thomas Friedman is a New York Times columnist and author of several books including *The Lexus and the Olive Tree: Understanding Globalization*, and *The World is Flat: A Brief History of the Twenty-first Century*.

[223] In cyber security, physical access is frequently considered a game-over scenario, such as when U.S. Department of Defense medical contractor TriWest was subject to a theft of 14 hard drives which contained the medical records and personal information of millions of beneficiaries.

[224] For the student of military acronyms OAKOC was formerly OCOKA, but the concept largely remains the same. See also Dwight Hobbs, "Application of OCOKA to Cyberterrain," White Paper, White Wolf Security, June 2007 for the earliest work we've seen that applies OCOKA to cyber terrain.

[225] In military parlance, the term *engage* means to apply lethal force to an adversary or to some tactical target with firearms or artillery. In the context of cyber operations, we use it to refer to applying a cyber weapon or tool to an asset in cyberspace.

[226] David Gioe, "Can the Warfare Concept of Maneuver be Usefully Applied in Cyber Operations?" Cyber Defense Review, 14 January 2016.

[227] CALEA is the Communications Assistance for Law Enforcement Act which requires telecommunication carriers to build law enforcement friendly surveillance capabilities into their services.

[228] An insider is an individual with malicious intent that is inside an organization and often has access to network resources and information that an external threat would not have.

[229] Whaling is a variant of phishing where attackers target senior leaders.

[230] FM 101-5-1 Operational Terms and Graphics, U.S. Army, 30 September 1997.

[231] On Unix systems, the /etc/passwd or /etc/shadow files contain hashes of system passwords. If compromised, attacker would attempt brute force attacks to determine the actual passwords.

[232] Thirteen root name servers sit atop the DNS hierarchy and perform a critical role in Internet function.

[233] An RS-232 port is found on some network devices and allows direct connection of a computer and issuance of commands without security checks. Typically used for legitimate administration, RS-232 ports are a valuable target for attackers.

[234] Option ROMs are read only memory that contain firmware for a given device.

[235] FM 3-21.8 The Infantry Rifle Platoon and Squad, U.S. Army, 28 March 2007.

[236] A tarpit is a service that deliberately slows network connections, such as delaying the transmission of bulk email.

[237] Our favorite story on web filtering is that we were once searching for "proxies" on Wikipedia and the mere act of visiting Wikipedia was blocked by an overzealous security policy.

[238] William Jackson, "U.S. understanding of cyber war still immature, says former NSA director," Government Computer News, 29 July 2010. See also Peter Dombrowski and Chris Demchak, "Cyber War, Cybered Conflict, and the Maritime Domain," Naval War College Review, Vol. 67, No. 2, Spring 2014.

[239] Prior to the use of Unrestricted, Restricted, and Severely Restricted classifications, the U.S. Army used Go, Slow-Go, and No-Go categories. We suspect doctrine writers made the change because No-Go terrain implied that the terrain was impassable, which was not always the case, particularly when facing a determined adversary.

[240] This innovation was invented by SGT Curtis Culin, who was serving with the 102nd Cavalry Reconnaissance Squadron, 2nd Armored Division. When tanks drove over the hedgerows, their bellies were exposed, thus making them easy targets for German tanks. The retrofitted "Rhino tanks" were able to cleanly cut through the bocage. SGT Culin was awarded the Legion of Merit for his innovation.

[241] Nate Anderson, "How China swallowed 15% of Net traffic for 18 minutes," Ars Technica, 17 November 2010.

[242] One popular passive network fingerprinting tool is p0f by Michal Zalewski see the project page at http://lcamtuf.coredump.cx/p0f3/.

[243] A honeypot is a system deployed by a network defender that appears to be a legitimate, and often lucrative, target designed to draw attackers' attention away

from real assets.

[244] *War driving* is the use of wireless sniffing technology to locate wireless access points.

[245] *War dialing* is the repeated calling of a range of telephone numbers looking for connected electronic devices.

[246] Noah Shachtman, "Military Networks 'Not Defensible,' Says General Who Defends Them," Wired, 12 January 2012.

[247] William Jackson, "U.S. understanding of cyber war still immature, says former NSA director," Government Computer News, 29 July 2010.

[248] David Gioe, "Can the Warfare Concept of Maneuver be Usefully Applied in Cyber Operations?," Cyber Defense Review, 14 January 2016.

[249] The U.S. military's Joint doctrine defines *maneuver* as "[a] movement to place ships, aircraft, or land forces in a position of advantage over the enemy." See JP 1-02 Dictionary of Military and Associated Terms, U.S. Department of Defense, 2010.

[250] This mixing and matching of one's available units and capabilities to accomplish a given mission is called *task organization*.

[251] This exact example of a cyber/kinetic attack occurred in the 2008 Russian invasion of Georgia. See John Markoff, "Before the Gunfire, Cyberattacks," New York Times, 12 August 2008.

[252] Frank Tiboni, "DOD cyberwarriors in a war of attrition," Federal Computer Weekly, 11 July 2005.

[253] For a useful overview of attrition warfare see https://en.wikipedia.org/wiki/Attrition_warfare.

[254] Details and analysis of the Battle of Verdun can be found at http://www.wereldoorlog1418.nl/battleverdun/.

[255] For a thorough discussion of Blitzkrieg, see https://en.wikipedia.org/wiki/Blitzkrieg.

[256] Our discussion of maneuver warfare is drawn from ADP 3-0 Unified Land Operations, U.S. Army, October 2011.

[257] ADP 3-0 Unified Land Operations, U.S. Army, October 2011.

[258] Qiao Liang and Wang Xiangsui, *Unrestricted Warfare*, PLA Literature and Arts Publishing House, 1999. For an overview see https://en.wikipedia.org/wiki/Unrestricted_Warfare.

[259] "Hybrid war – does it even exist?" NATO Review, 2015.

[260] "Flanking Maneuver," Wikipedia, https://en.wikipedia.org/wiki/Flanking_maneuver.

[261] Ibid.

[262] Map Courtesy of the Department of History, United States Military Academy. See https://commons.wikimedia.org/wiki/File:Battle_of_Marathon_Greek_Double_Env elopment.png.

[263] Carl Von Clausewitz, *On War*, Princeton University Press, 1989, p. 149.

[264] Brian Krebs, "Hospital Declares 'Internal State of Emergency' After Ransomware Infection," Krebs on Security, 22 March 2016.

[265] We've used FM 100-5 Operations, U.S. Army, 1986 as a starting point for these classical techniques.

[266] For example, some e-commerce companies may go out of business if their online systems go down for more than a few hours.

[267] In kinetic operations, an encirclement cuts off means of resupply, reinforcement, and escape.

[268] JP 3-12(R) Cyberspace Operations, U.S. Department of Defense, 2013.

[269] HTTPS does not provide complete concealment. There are enterprise tools that allow network defenders to monitor user HTTPS content if the organization controls access to the trusted certificates in the users' browsers.

[270] Sam Bowne and Matthew Prince, "Evil DoS Attacks and Strong Defenses," DEF CON, 2013.

[271] These attacks are called algorithmic complexity attacks. See Douglas McIlroy, "A Killer Adversary for Quicksort," Software: Practice and Experience, Vol. 29, No. 4, April 1999 and Scott Crosby and Dan Wallach, "Denial of Service via Algorithmic Complexity Attacks," USENIX Security, 2003.

[272] This is called MAC flooding, where an attacker fills up the table on a networking switch which maps Media Access Control (MAC) addresses used at

the link layer to physical ports on the switch. If this table is filled up, the switch will broadcast all traffic to all links, behaving like a networking hub. There are countermeasures to MAC flooding, but it makes for a good example of unintended behaviors when under an attack.

[273] Baron De Jomini, *The Art of War*, Wilder Publications, 2008, p. 134.

[274] In his paper "The Principle of Maneuver in Cyber Operations," Scott Applegate describes six characteristics: speed, operational reach, access and control, dynamic evolution, stealth and limited attribution, and rapid concentration." We incorporate and build upon his work here.

[275] This model folds OSI's Presentation and Session layers into the Application layer and was popularized by Kurose and Ross in *Computer Networking: A Top-Down Approach*, Pearson, 2012.

[276] Todd Frankel, "Mini flash crash? Trading anomalies on manic Monday hit small investors," The Washington Post, 26 August 2015.

[277] See Michael Lewis, *Flash Boys*, Norton, 2015.

[278] Whether such trust is justified depends on the proxy.

[279] As an example, if you would like to see just how unique you are on the web, visit the Electronic Frontier Foundation's Panopticlick website, https://panopticlick.eff.org/.

[280] For an in-depth propagation analysis of one such worm see Cliff Zou, Weibo Gong, and Don Towsley, "Code Red Worm Propagation Modeling and Analysis," ACM Conference on Computer and Communications Security, 2002.

[281] See Kevin McCaney, "DoD puts emphasis on Navigation Warfare, accurate GPS signals," Defense Systems, 9 February 2015 and Jeff Schogol, "Commandant to Marines: 'Get out your map and your compass,'" Marine Corps Times, 11 February 2016.

[282] These estimates are back of the envelope calculations. Of course mapping isn't easy, and some of those being mapped won't like it, but we are thinking of the determined and well resourced threat actor here. Even individuals have mapped the entire Internet address space.

[283] David Gioe, "Can the Warfare Concept of Maneuver be Usefully Applied in Cyber Operations?," Cyber Defense Review, 14 January 2016.

[284] The U.S. Army has a maneuver damage claims program designed to

compensate third-parties for damage due to physical maneuver. See Jerrett Dunlap, "The Economic Efficiency of the Army's Maneuver Damage Claims Program," U.S. Army Judge Advocate Officer Graduate Course, April 2006. In the future we may see calls for a similar program for cyberspace maneuver damage.

[285] In other forms of conflict, such as in legal battles, adversaries will similarly maneuver and attempt to shape terrain, such as seeking court precedents, to gain future advantage.

[286] Note that while we consider code having the ability to move, if properly constructed, we do not consider data as having this ability without being acted upon.

[287] The concept of shaping terrain combined with cyber maneuver was a key thesis put forth by Carl Hunt, Jeffrey Bowes, and Doug Gardner in their seminal "Net Force Maneuver: A JTF-GNO Construct," paper published in the proceedings of the 2005 IEEE Information Assurance Workshop.

[288] The six phases of the continuum of military operations are: Phase 0: Shape the Environment, Phase 1: Deter the Enemy, Phase 2: Seize the Initiative, Phase 3: Dominate the Enemy, Phase 4: Stabilize the Environment, Phase 5: Enable Civil Authority.

[289] See Aaron Brantley, Strategic Cyber Maneuver, Small Wars Journal, 17 October 2015 for additional discussion of maneuver at the strategic level.

[290] As an example, see Yong Guan et al, "NetCamo: Camouflaging Network Traffic for QoS-guaranteed Mission Critical Applications," IEEE Transactions on Systems, Man, and Cybernetics, Vol. 31, No. 4, July 2001.

[291] For an example, the country of Georgia moved key web hosting to the United States while under cyber attack. See Jeremy Kirk, "Estonia, Poland Help Georgia Fight Cyber Attacks, PC World, 12 August 2008.

[292] Baron De Jomini, The Art of War, Wilder Publications, 2008, p. 69.

[293] FM 3-0 Operations, U.S. Army, February 2008.

[294] Somini Sengupta, "A Homemade Drone Snoops on Wireless Networks," New York Times, 5 August 2011. See also Sydney Freedberg, "Wireless Hacking In Flight: Air Force Demos Cyber EC-130," Breaking Defense, 15 September 2015.

[295] Sean Gallagher, "Pwned again: An exclusive look at Pwnie Express' newest hack-in-a-box," ArsTechnica, 30 July 2013.

[296] Jeff Becker and Todd Zwolensky, "Making Sense of Military Doctrine: Joint and Service Views on Maneuver," War on the Rocks, 9 July 2014.

[297] Scott Applegate conducted the initial analysis of exploitive maneuver in Scott Applegate, The Principle of Maneuver in Cyber Operations, International Conference on Cyber Conflict, 2012.

[298] Moving target defense is an active research area, see the ACM Workshop on Moving Target Defense, http://mtd.mobicloud.asu.edu/.

[299] John Keller, "Raytheon cyber maneuver technology to help safeguard Army networks from information attacks," Military & Aerospace, 18 July 2012.

[300] the grugq, Twitter, 6 February 2015. https://twitter.com/thegrugq/status/563964286783877121

[301] Joint Publication 3-12(R) Cyberspace Operations, U.S. Department of Defense, 5 February 2013.

[302] Hasherezade, "Le Chiffre, Ransomware Ran Manually," Malwarebytes, 22 January 2016.

[303] "Ten epic Windows 7 pranks you absolutely must try," ZDNet, 21 November 2011.

[304] Kim Zetter, "Hacking Team Leak Shows How Secretive Zero-Day Exploit Sales Work," Wired, 24 July 2015.

[305] Amber Corrin, "Air Force launches first cyberspace weapons system," C4ISR & Networks, 20 January 2016.

[306] Metasploit, http://www.metasploit.com/

[307] Dual Core, "The Game," Music Lyrics, Next Level, 2009. Lyrics from Wikia, http://lyrics.wikia.com/wiki/Dual_Core:The_Game

[308] A great example is the Pwn2Own hacking contest where contestants save their capabilities for a chance to win prizes. See Steven Vaughan-Nichols, "Pwn2Own 2015: The year every web browser went down," 23 March 2015. Other examples, which mirror cyber combat, are capture the flag competitions. See Sabrina Korber, "Cyberteams duke it out in the World Series of hacking," CNBC, 8 November 2013.

[309] Jake Kouns and Carsten Eiram, "Screw Becoming a Pentester - When I Grow Up I Want to Be A Bug Bounty Hunter," DEF CON, 2014. See also Andy Greenberg, "New Dark-Web Market Is Selling Zero-Day Exploits to Hackers," Wired, 17 April 2015.

[310] See Richard Bejtlich's post on Twitter as well as associated commenter

discussion, https://twitter.com/taosecurity/status/666989716374466560, last accessed 25 January 2016.

[311] An example is that of medical devices that run older operating systems and are frequently left unpatched. See Scott Erven and Shawn Merdinger, "Just What The Doctor Ordered?," DEF CON, 2014.

[312] Parts of this definition are derived from R. Shirey, "Internet Security Glossary," RFC-2828, Internet Society, May 2000.

[313] These flaws are so prevalent that security researchers have coined the phrase "weird machines" for the exploitation of systems by finding and programming systems with carefully crafted malicious input data. See Sergey Bratus, Michael Locasto, Meredith Patterson, Len Sassaman, and Anna Shubina, "Exploit Programming - From Buffer Overflows to 'Weird Machines' and Theory of Computation," ;login:, December 2011. See also Sergey Bratus and Anna Shubina, "Computerization, Discretion, Freedom," White Paper, Dartmouth University, 31 December 2015. Available online at http://www.cs.dartmouth.edu/~sergey/drafts/computerization-discretion-freedom.pdf

[314] A classic vulnerability that keeps reappearing was described in 2008 in Microsoft Security Bulletin MS08-067. See "MS08-067 Still Alive and Kicking," SecureState, 3 October, 2012. Available online at https://www.securestate.com/blog/2012/10/03/ms08-067-still-alive-and-kicking

[315] See Marc Gaffan, "The 5 Essentials of DDOS Mitigation," Wired, December 2012 and Sam Bowne and Matthew Prince, "Evil DoS Attacks and Strong Defenses," DEF CON 21, 2013.

[316] See MITRE's excellent Common Vulnerabilities and Exposures catalog for a listing of publicly known information security vulnerabilities, https://cve.mitre.org/

[317] David Kushner, "The Real Story of Stuxnet," IEEE Spectrum, 26 February 2013.

[318] Stephen Northcutt, "The Attack Surface Problem," SANS Technology Institute, http://www.sans.edu/research/security-laboratory/article/did-attack-surface

[319] "Cyber Fraud at SWIFT - $81 Million Stolen from Central Bank," ZeroHedge, April 26 2016.

[320] Joel Johnson, "What is LOIC?," Gizmodo, 8 December 2010.

[321] "Resilient Military Systems and the Advanced Cyber Threat," Defense Science Board, January 2013.

[322] David LeBlanc and Michael Howard, *Writing Secure Code*, Microsoft Press, 2002.

[323] Michael Sutton, Adam Greene, and Pedram Amini, *Fuzzing: Brute Force Vulnerability Discovery*, Addison Wesley, 2007.

[324] Eldad Eilam, *Reversing: Secrets of Reverse Engineering*, Wiley 2005.

[325] Jenna McLaughlin, "TSA Doesn't Care That Its Luggage Locks Have Been Hacked," The Intercept, 17 September 2015.

[326] Joe Grand, Jake Appelbaum, and Chris Tarnovsky, "'Smart' Parking Meter Implementations, Globalism, and You," DEF CON 17, 2009.

[327] See Sai Sathyanarayan, Pankaj Kohli, and Bezawada Bruhadeshwar, "Signature Generation and Detection of Malware Families," Australasian Conference on Information Security and Privacy, 2008 for one example.

[328] Eric Limer, "This Tactical Cyber Rifle Is a Glimpse Into the Future of High-Tech Warfare," Popular Mechanics, 15 October 2015.

[329] Michael Riley and Ashlee Vance, "Cyber Weapons: The New Arms Race," Bloomberg Business, 20 July 2011.

[330] For an important related discussion see the Common Vulnerability Scoring System (CVSS) operated by the Forum of Incident Response and Security Teams (FIRST). CVSS is designed for the related problem of rating vulnerabilities, but includes useful insights from the defense perspective. We'll incorporate these insights in this section as appropriate.

[331] As a point of comparison, it is useful to examine CVSS. CVSS includes three categories similar to effects, called impact metrics, that cover confidentiality impact, integrity impact and availability impact. While valid, we extend these concepts to consider the full range of effects possible by the capability. See "Common Vulnerability Scoring System Version 2 Calculator," National Vulnerability Database, NIST.

[332] When constructed in software, one example of this class of capability is called a logic bomb by the information security community. See https://en.wikipedia.org/wiki/Logic_bomb for an overview.

[333] Dan Goodin, "Puzzle box: The quest to crack the world's most mysterious malware warhead," ArsTechnica, 14 March 2013.

[334] See the October 2013 issue of eForensics Magazine for an overview of metadata analysis and Stephen Northcutt, "Traffic Analysis," SANS, 16 May 2007 for a related discussion.

[335] Brian Krebs, "Microsoft, Symantec Hijack 'Bamital' Botnet," Krebs on Security, 7 February 2013.

[336] See Peiter "Mudge" Zatko, "Keynote: Analytic Framework for Cyber Security," ShmooCon, 2011 for a thoughtful analysis of defender's lines of code versus that of attackers.

[337] "Masscan: the entire Internet in 3 minutes," Errata Security, 14 September 2013.

[338] Rodney Harris, "Army Braces for a Culture Clash," Signal Magazine, 1 January 2016.

[339] New York Institute of Technology Cybersecurity Conference, New York 2015.

[340] We've generalized in this table due to space limitations, but have cited real world examples of each of our notional capabilities. We anticipate capabilities will be stored in a database with far greater detail. This table contains just representative examples, the full spectrum of potential capabilities could be a book of its own. The cyber kill chain is also an effective way to classify capabilities. See Eric Hutchins, Michael Cloppert, and Rohan Amin, "Intelligence-Driven Computer Network Defense Informed by Analysis of Adversary Campaigns and Intrusion Kill Chains," Lockheed Martin Corporation, 2011 and note they map kill chain steps to the effects that capabilities create: deny, disrupt, degrade, etc.

[341] See the work of the Botnet Research Group at the University of Michigan, http://vhosts.eecs.umich.edu/fjgroup/botnets/

[342] Pavitra Shankdhar, "10 Most Popular Password Cracking Tools," InfoSec Institute, 2016.

[343] Thomas Ryan, "Getting in Bed With Robin Sage," Black Hat, 2010. See also Joan Goodchild, "DefCon contest to spotlight social engineering," CSO Online, 6 July 2010.

[344] Darren Pauli, "Ransomware blueprints published on GitHub in the name of education," The Register, 18 August 2015. See also Sara Peters, "Big Week for Ransomware," Dark Reading, 28 January 2016.

[345] "Cobalt Strike - Advanced Threat Tactics for Penetration Testers," Cobalt Strike, https://www.cobaltstrike.com/

[346] Fingerprinting Organizations with Collected Archives (FOCA), Eleven Paths, 2016. See https://www.elevenpaths.com/labstools/foca/index.html

[347] "The Heartbleed Bug," Heartbleed.com, last accessed 8 April 2016.

[348] For an example see, Wireshark, https://www.wireshark.org/

[349] There are many real-world examples of network worms, from the Morris Worm to Code Red to the present.

[350] Joe, "Make a Passive Network Tap," Instructables.com

[351] Mark Russinovich, "Autoruns for Windows v13.51," Windows Sysinternals, Microsoft, 4 January 2016.

[352] Russell Brandom, "How dangerous is the tool the FBI is asking Apple to build?," The Verge, 19 February 2016.

[353] For an example, see "KeyGrabber - Hardware Keylogger," KeeLog, https://www.keelog.com/

[354] Declan McCullagh, "FBI taps cell phone mic as eavesdropping tool," CNET, 4 December 2006.

[355] "TrueCrypt," Project Page, SourceForge, http://truecrypt.sourceforge.net/

[356] Andy Greenberg, "Watch a Hacker Fry a Hair Dryer with her Radio," Wired, 8 August 2014.

[357] John Brandon, "GPS Jammers Illegal, Dangerous, and Very Easy to Buy," Fox News, 17 March 2010.

[358] Kevin Poulsen, "Zap! … and your PC's dead," ZDNet, 10 September 1999. See also Mike Nathan, "HERF Gun Zaps More Than Your Dinner," HACKADAY, 21 March 2011.

[359] James Armstrong, "Keep Talking, We're Listening: Multinational EW Operations at JMRC," Small Wars Journal, 28 September 2015.

[360] Lisa Vaas, "$80 million yacht hijacked by students spoofing GPS signals," Naked Security, Sophos, 31 July 2013.

[361] WiFi Pineapple, https://www.wifipineapple.com/

[362] Chris Morran, "Verizon's 'Hum' Device For Your Car Will Rat Out Speeding Teens," Consumerist, 17 February 2016.

[363] Brent Chapman, Matt Hutchison, and Erick Waage, "It is time for the U.S. Military to Innovate Like Insurgents," War on the Rocks, 28 October 2015. Note that prior to the development of the CCR, the hacker community made several gunstock-based WiFi-devices, but not with the intent of military employment

[364] See Erick Waage, "Phreaker, Maker, Hacker, Ranger: One Vision for Cyber

Support to Corps and Below in 2025," Small Wars Journal, 11 August 2015 and Brent Chapman, Erick Waage, and James Finocchiaro, "Makers in the Military," World Maker Faire, 2015.

[365] Tom "Decius" Cross, "The Risks of Vulnerability Disclosure in International Conflict," Cyber Talks, Atlanta, March 2016.

[366] Dan Kaminsky, Twitter, 28 February 2016. See https://twitter.com/dakami/status/704138989649813504.

[367] Herb Lin, "Further Reflections on NOBUS, Lawfare, 21 March 2015. See also Herb Lin, "Making Progress on the Encryption Debate," Lawfare, 24 March 2015.

[368] CBS/AP, "FBI debates sharing iPhone hacking details with Apple," CBS News, 7 April 2016.

[369] One example of a cyberspace capability that has so far resisted full analysis is Gauss. Analysts believe Gauss' encrypted malware payload is tied to very specific parameters of the target system creating an exceptionally difficult cryptographic key that has remained unbroken. See Dan Goodin, "Puzzle box: The quest to crack the world's most mysterious malware warhead," Ars Technica, 14 March 2014.

[370] Matthew Schwartz, "Shamoon Malware Might Be Flame Copycat," Dark Reading, 22 August 2012.

[371] To get a small sample of the vast body of intelligence literature, see the U.S. Army's doctrine and training publications library. The library contains more than 45 book-length current documents, http://armypubs.army.mil/doctrine/30_Series_Collection_1.html. In this chapter we will draw heavily from multiple sources, but recommend FM 2-0 Intelligence, U.S. Army, May 2004 and JP 2-0 Joint Intelligence, U.S. Department of Defense, October 2013, in particular.

[372] Image is derived from JP 2-0 Intelligence, U.S. Department of Defense, 22 October 2013. Note that "exploitation" in this context refers to exploitation of information

[373] We've left out RUMINT which is intelligence community slang for Rumor Intelligence.

[374] These tasks are modified forms of U.S. Military doctrine. See "Intelligence Tasks (METL)," FM 2-0 Intelligence, U.S. Army, May 2004.

[375] Image is from JP 2-0 Intelligence, U.S. Department of Defense, 22 October

2013.

[376] Again please note that "exploitation" in this context is that of exploiting information, not exploiting a vulnerability in a network or system.

[377] JP 2-0 Intelligence, U.S. Department of Defense, 22 October 2013.

[378] "The Collection Plan," Appendix A, FM 34-2 Collection Management and Synchronization Planning, 8 March 1994.

[379] For more on indicators, see the Indications and Warnings section later in the chapter.

[380] However, nation-state intelligence can be very robust. The U.S. Intelligence Community has a budget of more than $65 billion, see "U.S. Intelligence Community Budget," Office of the Director of National Intelligence, and a formal 16 member Intelligence Community: Air Force Intelligence, Army Intelligence, Central Intelligence Agency, Coast Guard Intelligence, Defense Intelligence Agency, Department of Energy, Department of Homeland Security, Department of State, Department of the Treasury, Drug Enforcement Administration, Federal Bureau of Investigation, Marine Corps Intelligence, National Geospatial Intelligence Agency, National Reconnaissance Office, National Security Agency, and Naval Intelligence. See "Members of the IC," Office of the Director of National Intelligence.

[381] There are many possible expansions of this table. Intra-network, network ingress, and network egress is one such way to consider network traffic. Hosts may be further broken down to include clients and servers as each provides a different vantage point. Third-party data sources may be useful for detecting planning and access attempts, as well as provide a sense of the broader external threat environment, whereas internal network and host-based data will be useful for detecting mapping and reconnaissance, data collection, and data exfiltration. As a result, one can map data sources to one or more stages of the steps required for an attack to be successful.

[382] A great example is the Chinese "rou ji" which translates to "meat chicken," but is slang for a compromised computer in certain hacker communities. See Peijin Chen, "The not-so-secret life of Chinese hackers," Shanghaiist, 8 June 2009.

[383] "Categories of Intelligence Products," JP 2-0 Intelligence, U.S. Department of Defense, 22 October 2013.

[384] See the "Report of the Select Committee on Intelligence on the U.S. Intelligence Community's Prewar Intelligence Assessments on Iraq," U.S. Government Printing Office, 9 July 2004, for intelligence analyst biases leading

up to the U.S. invasion of Iraq.

[385] Some organizations share threat intelligence reports publicly to aid the larger community, sometimes for altruistic reasons, and other times for marketing purposes.

[386] This acceptable risk does not include naïve document redaction. It seems every few months another government agency accidently spills sensitive information because they put black boxes over text in a document, not realizing the text was still there in the underlying binary data. Sometimes even a simple Select All followed by Copy and Paste revealed the "secret" data. Refer to one of the many guides available for handling redaction properly.

[387] As an example, the The Washington Times reported that China was compiling an easy to use Facebook-like interface of U.S. Government employees with data from the Office of Personnel Management (OPM) hack. See Todd Wood, "Chinese compiling 'Facebook' of U.S. government employees," The Washington Times, 16 September 2015.

[388] See "National Cybersecurity and Communications Integration Center," Department of Homeland Security, https://www.dhs.gov/national-cybersecurity-and-communications-integration-center.

[389] See JP 2-0 Intelligence, U.S. Department of Defense, 22 October 2013 for attributes of intelligence excellence.

[390] There are several high-quality books on security metrics, see Andrew Jacquith, *Security Metrics: Replacing Fear, Uncertainty, and Doubt*, Addison-Wesley, 2007 as a good starting point.

[391] This table is from FM 2-22.3 (FM34-52) Human Intelligence Collector Operations, U.S. Army, September 2006.

[392] See FM 34-60 Counterintelligence, U.S. Department of the Army, 3 October 1995 for one in-depth study of traditional counterintelligence.

[393] A *High-Payoff Target* (HPT) is "a target whose loss to the enemy will significantly contribute to the success of the friendly course of action." See JP 3-60, Joint Targeting, U.S. Department of Defense, 13 April 2007.

[394] Raven Alder, Riccardo Bettati, Jon Callas, and Nick Matthewson, "Traffic Analysis: The Most Powerful and Least Understood Attack Methods," Black Hat, 2007.

[395] For an amazing array of information that can be derived from just network flow

data see the archives of FloCon, http://www.cert.org/flocon/.

396 Dawn Song, David Wagner, and Xuqing Tian, "Timing analysis of keystrokes and timing attacks on SSH," USENIX Security Symposium," 2001.

397 "Association Matrix," FM 34-60 Counterintelligence, U.S. Department of the Army, 3 October 1995.

398 Including when a client starts acting like a server when it shouldn't, sometimes called "client/server schizophrenia." Association matrix analysis may be extended with metadata, like volume of traffic into a system, which might indicate downloading of tools, the receipt of instructions, or some sort of collection and processing function, as well as volume of traffic going out, which might reveal data exfiltration.

399 "Contact Chaining," The Network Thinkers, 28 June 2013.

400 For a more detailed overview of six degrees of separation see, https://en.wikipedia.org/wiki/Six_degrees_of_separation. There is also ongoing research implying that as the world becomes more connected, there are, on average, fewer than six degrees of separation, see Sergey Edunov, Carlos Diuk, Ismail Filiz, Smriti Bhagat, and Moira Burke, "Three and a half degrees of separation," Research at Facebook, Facebook, 4 February 2016.

401 "Activities Matrix," FM 34-60 Counterintelligence, U.S. Department of the Army, 3 October 1995.

402 Ibid.

403 Ibid.

404 "Link Diagram," FM 34-60 Counterintelligence, U.S. Department of the Army, 3 October 1995.

405 Ibid.

406 See Michael Flynn, Rich Juergens, and Thomas Cantrell, "Employing ISR SOF Best Practices," Joint Forces Quarterly, Issue: 50, 3rd Quarter 2008.

407 Our Capability Based Analysis strategy is not to be confused with Capability-based security from the secure computing systems community. Ours is an analytic tool that examines the true capabilities of a device, system, or actor, and capability based security is a security model which provides unforgeable tokens that reference objects and associated access rights.

408 If you really want security from a given device, don't just turn some feature off

in the operating system, but physically remove the hardware from the device, such as a WiFi board from a laptop.

[409] Eric Hutchins, Michael Cloppert, and Rohan Amin, "Intelligence-Driven Computer Network Defense Informed by Analysis of Adversary Campaigns and Intrusion Kill Chains," Information Warfare and Security (ICIW) Conference, 2010.

[410] Other kill chain models exist, such as 1. Planning, 2. Access, 3. Mapping/Recon, 4. Collection, 5. Exfiltration. Note that 3, 4, and 5 happen in your environment, but many focus on steps 1 and 2 which usually do not. In some cases, steps 1 and 2 are fleeting, while steps 3, 4, and 5 may repeat more often.

[411] "A 'Kill Chain Analysis' of the 2013 Target Data Breach," Committee on Commerce, Science, and Transportation, United States Senate, 26 March 2014.

[412] Many of these examples are ours or appeared in the headlines, others came from the following: "Indicators in OOTW," U.S. Army Intelligence Center and School, February 1995, Ericka Chickowski, "Top 15 Indicators of Compromise," Dark Reading, 9 October 2013, and Scott Swanson, Craig Astrich, and Michael Robinson, "Cyber Threat Indications and Warning: Predict, Identify, and Counter," Small Wars Journal, 26 July 2012.

[413] Somesh Jha, Oleg Sheyner, and Jeannette Wing, "Two Formal Analyses of Attack Graphs," IEEE Computer Security Foundations Workshop (CSFW), 2002.

[414] Attack Graphs have a close cousin called Attack Trees, both approaches are relevant to the discussion here.

[415] "Red Teaming for Program Managers," Project Web Page, Sandia National Laboratories, 2009.

[416] This graph was inspired by the work of Daniele Sgandurra, Imperial College London.

[417] As a starting point see the output of GraMSec, the International Workshop on Graphical Models for Security, http://gramsec.uni.lu/.

[418] In this section we've drawn heavily from two source documents that served as our starting point for adapting intelligence preparation of the battlefield: ATP 2-01.3, Intelligence Preparation of the Battlefield/Battlespace, U.S. Army 26 March 2015 and FM 34-130 Intelligence Preparation of the Battlefield, U.S. Army, 8 July 1994.

[419] There are several variations of Intelligence Preparation of the Battlefield, including Intelligence Preparation of the Battlespace and Joint Intelligence Preparation of the Operational Environment, among others. For clarity and ease of use we will simply use the term IPB.

[420] FM 34-130 Intelligence Preparation of the Battlefield, U.S. Army, 8 July 1994.

[421] Steven Winterfeld, "Cyber IPB," White Paper, SANS Reading Room, December 2001.

[422] For deeper study of threat modeling, see Adam Shostack, *Threat Modeling: Designing for Security,* Wiley, 2014, and Frank Swiderski and Window Snyder, *Threat Modeling*, Microsoft Press, 2004.

[423] J.K. Rowling, *Harry Potter and the Goblet of Fire*, Scholastic, 2002, p.280.

[424] "Identify the Full Set of COAs Available to the Threat," ATP 2-01.3 Intelligence Preparation of the Battlefield, U.S. Army, November 2014.

[425] "Principles of Joint Intelligence," JP 2-0 Intelligence, U.S. Department of Defense, 22 June 2007.

[426] Security strategist Richard Bejtlich has studied this subject in detail, see his "Strategic Defence in Cyberspace: Beyond Tools and Tactics," NATO CCD COE, 2015.

[427] For a look at a modern advanced intelligence analysis system see "Distributed Common Ground System – Army (DCGS-A)," Project Site, U.S. Army, https://dcgsa.army.mil/. For a look to the future of prediction see Kevin Maney, "Prediction Machines will see the Future for Hedge Funds, CIA," Newsweek, 12 January 2016.

[428] Orson Scott Card, "Ender's Game," *The Best Military Science Fiction of the 20th Century,* (Harry Turtledove and Martin Greenberg Ed.), Ballantine Books, 2001, p.166.

[429] JP 1-02 Dictionary of Military and Associated Terms, U.S. Department of Defense, 2010 (definition of fires) and ATP 3-60 Targeting, U.S. Army, May 2015 (definition of targeting). In this chapter we draw heavily from ATP 3-60 and JP 3-09 Joint Fire Support, U.S. Department of Defense, 20 June 2010.

[430] Please consult your legal advisor before doing so however.

[431] "Joint Fire Support Planning Process," JP 3-09 Joint Fire Support Process, 30 June 2010. The utility of using Joint Fires processes for cyber operations is reinforced by Maj. Gen. Brett Williams, then Chief of Operations (J3) of U.S.

Cyber Command, who wrote "... the joint targeting cycle, which begins with an endstate and commander's objectives and continues with target development, weaponeering, execution, and assessment, readily accommodates cyberspace targeting" in Brett Williams, "The Joint Force Commander's Guide to Cyberspace Operations," Joint Forces Quarterly, No. 73, 1 April 2014.

[432] These targeting categories and Figure 9-2 were derived from ATP 3-60 Targeting, U.S. Army, May 2015.

[433] We recommend that your planners read Nassim Nicholas Taleb, *The Black Swan: The Impact of the Highly Improbable*, Random House, 2010.

[434] Mike Jackson, "Designing a Digital Crystal Ball," Modern Warfare Institute at West Point, 2 February 2016.

[435] Access may also be rented from a third-party. See Catalin Cimpanu, "You Can Now Rent a Mirai Botnet of 400,000 Bots," Bleeping Computer, 24 November 2016. The Mirai botnet consists of embedded systems and Internet of Things (IoT) devices with weak default credentials allowing easy takeover by an attacker and formation into a botnet.

[436] Fahmida Rashid, "Chinese Attackers Hacked Forbes Website in Watering Hole Attack: Security Firms," Security Week, 11 February 2015.

[437] "Ongoing Sophisticated Malware Campaign Compromising ICS (Update E)," U.S. Industrial Control Systems Emergency Response Team, 2 March 2016. See also Sean Gallagher, "Researchers try to hack the economics of zero-day bugs," Ars Technica, 14 April 2015.

[438] As quoted in JP 3-09 Joint Fire Support, U.S. Department of Defense, 30 June 2010.

[439] "Targeting Principles," ATP 3-60 Targeting, U.S. Army, May, 2015.

[440] This graphic was inspired by Chris Cleary, "Operational Use of Offensive Cyber," DEF CON, 2011. This is an excellent talk and highly recommended. See https://www.youtube.com/watch?v=lEDCiUyJa2U

[441] Not that we use the phrase "capability" here in the conventional, not cyber operations, sense.

[442] You can also visualize center of gravity analysis as a tree data structure.

[443] Alice Vincent, "James Gandolfini: Tony Soprano's 20 best lines," The Telegraph, 20 June 2013.

[444] JP 3-12(R) Cyberspace Operations, U.S. Department of Defense, 5 February 2013 states that "Cyber operations may support Information Operations objectives."

[445] Peter Bright, "With arrests, HBGary hack saga finally ends," Ars Technica, 10 March 2012.

[446] Bryan Lee, "The Impact of Cyber Capabilities in the Syrian Civil War," Small Wars Journal, 26 April 2016.

[447] Darren Orf, "Samsung's Smart Home Platform is Full of Security Holes," Gizmodo, 2 May 2016.

[448] Michael Hayden, *Playing to the Edge: American Intelligence in the Age of Terror*, Penguin Press, 2016. See also associated discussion at https://twitter.com/thegrugq/status/722848532680454144.

[449] Some of these effects and definitions came from ATP 3-60 The Targeting Process, U.S. Army, November 2010. We've added several others.

[450] Jeremy White, "Virtual Indoctrination and the Digihad: The Evolution of Al-Qaeda's Media Strategy," Small Wars Journal, 19 November 2016.

[451] David Sanger, "U.S. Cyberattacks Target ISIS in a New Line of Combat," New York Times, 24 April 2016 and Fred Kaplan, "What Cyberwar Against ISIS Should Look Like," Slate, 2016.

[452] David Sanger, "U.S. Cyberattacks Target ISIS in a New Line of Combat," New York Times, 24 April 2016.

[453] Ibid.

[454] Nate Anderson, "How China swallowed 15% of 'Net traffic for 18 minutes," Ars Technica, 17 November 2010.

[455] We've included "No Effect" here because some operations, particularly espionage, desire to have no discernable effect.

[456] See Aliya Sternstein, "Pentagon Contractors Developing Lethal Cyber Weapons," Nextgov, 4 November 2015.

[457] Not that people haven't tried. There are conflicting reports, for example, that networked printers can be hacked and made to catch fire. Paul Wagenseil, "Printers Can Be Hacked to Catch Fire," Scientific American, 29 November 2011 and "HP Refutes Reports That Printers Can Be Remotely Set on Fire," Fox News, 29 November 2011. With respect to making laser printers catch fire and in

talking with some hardware security colleagues recently, the answer is probably not, but that a cheap sensor is the only thing preventing a fire. Science Fiction likes to explore the idea of security Intrusion Countermeasures Electronics (ICE) killing off cyberpunks via the hacker's neural interface. Once we have direct neural interfaces, such damage may well be possible.

[458] Samuel Gibbs, "Setting the date to 1 January 1970 will brick your iPhone, iPad or iPod touch," The Guardian, 12 February 2016.

[459] Andrea Peterson, "Yes, terrorists could have hacked Dick Cheney's heart," Washington Post, 21 October 2013.

[460] Canonical examples of physical destruction include Jose Pagliery, "The inside story of the biggest hack in history," CNN Money, 5 August 2015 (Saudi Aramco), Jose Pagliery, "Iran hacked an American casino, U.S. Says," CNN Money, 27 February 2015 (Sands Casino), Jeanne Meserve, "Sources: Staged cyber attack reveals vulnerability in power grid," CNN, 26 September 2007 (Aurora Generator Test), and Mark Seal, "An Exclusive Look at Sony's Hacking Saga," Vanity Fair, 4 February 2015 (Sony Entertainment). Medical devices are particularly troubling and vulnerable, as they are responsible for direct care of people. See Kelly Jackson Higgins, "Medical Device Security Gets Intensive Care," Dark Reading, 20 January 2016. See also Aliya Sternstein, "Pentagon Contractors Developing Lethal Cyber Weapons," Nextgov, 4 November 2015 (Nuclear Power Plant Meltdown).

[461] The Morris worm is a textbook example of uncontrolled propagation, see https://en.wikipedia.org/wiki/Morris_worm for an overview. See also, Catalin Cimpanu, "KeyBase Keylogger Usage Explodes After Getting Leaked Online," Softpedia, 25 March 2016.

[462] Instructing the computer on Star Trek to destroy the Enterprise comes to mind here.

[463] Here "we"=Greg.

[464] Catalin Cimpanu, "Hackers Demand $3.6 Million from Hollywood Hospital Following Cyber-Attack," Softpedia, 14 February 2016.

[465] Rodney Harris and Jeffrey Morris, "Cyber Talent for Unified Land Operations," Small Wars Journal, 18 January 2016.

[466] Steven Winterfeld pointed out that "with the advent of asymmetrical and asynchronous warfare the battlefield no longer has a forward edge and a rear echelon." See Steven Winterfeld, "Cyber IPB," SANS, December 2001.

[467] See Maggie Overfelt, "The next big threat in hacking – data sabotage," CNBC, 9 March 2016.

[468] Shane Harris, *@War: The Rise of the Military-Internet Complex*, Houghton Mifflin Harcourt, 2014.

[469] JP 3-12(R) Cyberspace Operations, U.S. Department of Defense, 5 February 2013.

[470] Ibid.

[471] Russ Wellen, "Yes, Hacking Into Our Nuclear Command and Control Could Actually Happen," Foreign Policy in Focus, 19 June 2015. See also Rachel Oswald, "Congress Wants Pentagon to Upgrade Nuclear Command and Control," Defense One, 18 December 2013.

[472] Remy Stern, "Computer Virus Hits U.S. Drone Fleet," Gawker, 7 October 2011.

[473] Richard Clarke and Robert Knake, *Cyber War*, Ecco, 2011.

[474] Michael Schmidt and David Sanger, "Russian Hackers Read Obama's Unclassified Emails, Officials Say," New York Times, 25 April 2015.

[475] Tom Vanden Brook and Michael Winter, "Hackers penetrated Pentagon email," USA Today, 7 August 2015.

[476] Tracy Kitten, "New Malware Attacks Prey on Banks," InfoRiskToday, 6 April 2015.

[477] Michael Riley, "How Russian Hackers Stole the Nasdaq," Bloomberg, 21 July 2014.

[478] This was a plot arc in the Mr. Robot television program, see Matthew Giles, "Every Single Question You Have About Mr. Robot, Answered," Vulture, 19 August 2015.

[479] Karen Frenkel, "What's Worse Than Stolen Data? Altered Data," CIO Insight, 3 February 2016.

[480] Jose Pagliery, "ISIS is attacking the U.S. energy grid (and failing)," CNN Money, 16 October 2015. See also Paul Roberts, "How cyber attacks can be overlooked in America's most critical sectors," Christian Science Monitor, 23 March 2015.

[481] "German nuclear plant hit by computer viruses," BBC News, 28 April 2016.

See also Paul Roberts, "How cyber attacks can be overlooked in America's most critical sectors," Christian Science Monitor, 23 March 2015.

[482] Shane Harris, "Chinese Hackers Target U.S. University With Government Ties," The Daily Beast, 21 August 2015.

[483] Gregory Conti, Tom Cross, and David Raymond, "Pen Testing a City," Black Hat, 2015.

[484] Katie Shilton, "Four Billion Little Brothers?: Privacy, Mobile Phones, and Ubiquitous Data Collection," Communications of the ACM, Vol. 52, No. 11, November 2009, pp. 48-53.

[485] Our favorite, albeit dated, example is the Furby. See Lauren Davis, "The NSA once banned Furbies as a threat to national security," Gizmodo, 20 February 2014. For more modern examples, see Lisa Phifer, "BYOD security strategies: Balancing BYOD risks and rewards," Search Security, Tech Target, January 2013.

[486] Lucian Constantin, "Despite reports of hacking, baby monitors remain woefully insecure," IT World, 2 September 2015.

[487] Jim Finkle, "Apple's iOS App Store suffers first major attack," Reuters, 20 September 2015.

[488] Olaf Miltenburg, "D-Link blundered by releasing private keys of certificates," Tweakers, 17 September 2015.

[489] Paul Roberts, "Big Data Means Big Risks," Digital Guardian, 28 September 2015.

[490] Brian Benchoff, "The Trouble with Intel's Management Engine," Hackaday, 22 January 2016.

[491] Geoff White, "Adult dating site hack exposes millions of users," Channel 4 News, 21 May 2015.

[492] David Szondy, "World-first remote air traffic control system lands in Sweden," GizMag, 28 April 2015.

[493] Jim Finkle, "Hacker says to show passenger jets at risk of cyber attack," Reuters, 4 August 2014. See also Kim Zetter, "Is It Possible for Passengers to Hack Commercial Aircraft?," Wired, 26 May 2015.

[494] Shimon Prokupecz, "Former official: Iranians hacked into New York dam," CNN, 22 December 2015.

[495] Sean Gallagher, "Pirates hack into shipping company's servers to identify booty," Ars Technica, 3 March 2016.

[496] JP 3-12(R) Cyberspace Operations, U.S. Department of Defense, 5 February 2013.

[497] Robert Zager and John Zager, "Combat Identification in Cyberspace," Small Wars Journal, 25 August 2013.

[498] Steve Bellovin, "The Security Flag in the IPv4 Header," Request for Comments: 3514, 1 April 2003. Cyber combat would certainly be much more straightforward if combatants honored the evil bit.

[499] For a related discussion on attribution in cyber conflict, see Michael Poznansky and Evan Perkoski, "Attribution and Secrecy in Cyberspace," War on the Rocks, 8 March 2016.

[500] Some were less certain about North Korea's involvement. Regardless, even at this level mistakes take place, see the famous "weapons of mass destruction" argument senior U.S leaders made to justify the invasion of Iraq in 2003. In addition, attribution may or may not deter attackers, see Andrea Peterson and Ellen Nakashima, "The hackers that took down Sony Pictures are still on the attack, researchers say," The Washington Post, 24 February 2016.

[501] Analysts have speculated that Russia was behind the 2007 cyber attacks on Estonia, but Russia was able to maintain plausible deniability.

[502] See Harrison Kieffer, "Can Intelligence Preparation of the Battlefield/Battlespace Be Used to Attribute a Cyber-Attack to an Actor?," Cyber Defense Review, 22 March 2016. Table 9-5 is built upon the framework provided by Kieffer and includes some of his examples.

[503] As this book was going to press the U.S. Department of Defense awarded a $17.3 million research grant to the Georgia Institute of Technology to develop a "science of cyber attribution." The project's goals include "Efficient algorithmic attribution methods able to convert the research team's experience with manual attack attribution to novel, tensor-based learning methods. The algorithms will allow expansion of existing efforts to create a science of attribution and traceback; Actionable attribution, in which the application of the algorithms will produce attribution reports to be shared with the attribution community; and Historic public attack datasets brought together into a single distributed environment."

[504] Reducing signatures is possible to a point, but tricky to implement. Much of cyberspace, particularly the WWW, is heavily instrumented. See Panopticlick,

Electronic Frontier Foundation, https://panopticlick.eff.org/ and Lance Cottrell, "Browser fingerprints, and why they are so hard to erase," Network World, 17 February 2015.

[505] "Capabilities Analysis," JP 3-09 Joint Fire Support, U.S. Department of Defense, 12 December 2014.

[506] This figure is an adaptation of "Unified Action," JP 3-0 Joint Operations, U.S. Department of Defense, 11 August 2011.

[507] "U.S. Charges Five Chinese Military Hackers for Cyber Espionage Against U.S. Corporations and a Labor Organization for Commercial Advantage," Press Release, U.S. Department of Justice, 19 May 2014 (Indictment) and "Hacker 'Guccifer,' who uncovered Clinton's private emails, to be extradited to US," RT, 7 March 2016 (Extradition).

[508] Joseph Nye, "Cyber Power," Belfer Center for Science and International Affairs, Harvard University, May 2010.

[509] JP 3-60 Joint Targeting, U.S. Department of Defense, 31 January 2013.

[510] The criminal botnet community has been very active developing command and control consoles for their bot armies.

[511] Fred Kaplan, "What Cyberwar Against ISIS Should Look Like," Slate, 25 April 2016.

[512] Darren Pauli, "Pair publishes python framework for rapid router wrecking," The Register, 26 April 2016.

[513] Jill Treanor, "The 2010 'flash crash': how it unfolded," The Guardian, 22 April 2015.

[514] Peter Kruse, "MazarBOT: Top class Android datastealer," CSIS Security Group, 14 February 2016.

[515] The "Powersniff" macro virus actively avoided healthcare and education machines, and targeted financial systems, see Richard Chirgwin, "Attackers packing malware into PowerShell," The Register, 15 March 2016.

[516] Tom Cross, "The Risks of Vulnerability Disclosure in International Conflict," Cyber Talks – Atlanta, 29 March 2016.

[517] For a detailed study of constraining cyberspace effects, see David Raymond, Gregory Conti, Tom Cross, and Robert Fanelli, "A Control Measure Framework to Limit Collateral Damage and Propagation of Cyber Weapons," NATO

Conference on Cyber Conflict (CyCon), 2013. Table 9-7 is derived from the framework proposed by Raymond et al in the paper.

[518] Giorgio Bertoli and Lisa Marvel, "A proposed 'Exploit Collateral Effect Potential (ECEP)' metric," Cyber Talks, 2015.

[519] Dan Goodin, "Puzzle box: The quest to crack the world's most mysterious malware warhead," Ars Technica, 14 March 2013.

[520] For a detailed discussion of fire support control measures, see Appendix A, JP 3-09 Joint Fire Support, U.S. Department of Defense, 12 December 2014.

[521] We saw this in attacks against Estonia and in various Anonymous operations where organizers would disseminate target lists via online forums to willing participants.

[522] Stoney Trent, Robert Hoffman, and Scott Lathrop, "Applied Research in Support of Cyberspace Operations: Difficult, but Critical," Cyber Defense Review, 2 May 2016.

[523] For a discussion of cyber weapon release authority, see Shane Harris, *@War: The Rise of the Military-Internet Complex*, Houghton Mifflin Harcourt, 2014, p. 9.

[524] On a related topic, some have attempted creating manuals of common tasks to train security analysts. This is possible, but time intensive and the documents are difficult to maintain. The trick is balancing between underlying concepts and detailed tasks required for specific tools and OS versions. We've found erring on the side of concepts provides longer term utility.

[525] A similar system was used on the Battlestar Galactica. Beware though that automated targeting systems may be subject to deception, maintaining white and black lists of targets is prudent here.

[526] This scenario is just one of many and a full treatment of this subject could fill a book of its own. For an example of the complexities of maneuver in cyberspace operations, consider the use of domain generation algorithms to rapidly move command and control servers. See Jason Geffner, "End-To-End Analysis of a Domain Generating Algorithm Malware Family," White Paper, CrowdStrike, 2013.

[527] As an example of reserves, botnet herders are employing back-up botnets in case a primary botnet is compromised. See Mathew Schwartz, "Police Reveal Botnet Herders' Disaster Recovery Secrets," Data Breach Today, 13 May 2016.

[528] JP 3-09 Joint Fire Support, U.S. Department of Defense, 12 December 2014. See also Appendix D, JP 5-0 Joint Operation Planning, U.S. Department of

Defense, 11 August 2011.

[529] Ibid.

[530] For studies on the cyber operations planning, see Jason Bender, "The Cyberspace Operations Planner," Small Wars Journal, 5 November 2013 and Don Barber, Alan Bobo, and Kevin Strum, "Cyberspace Operations Planning: Operating a Technical Military Force beyond the Kinetic Domains," Military Cyber Affairs, Vol. 1, No. 1, 2015. For an overview of military planning in general see FM 3-0 Operations, U.S. Army, February 2008, pp. 95-99.

[531] MCDP-6 Command and Control, United States Marine Corps, 4 October 1996. We use MCDP-6 as our primary reference for military command and control doctrine throughout this chapter. See also the newer, ADRP-6 Mission Command, U.S. Army, May 2012, but if you compare the two, you'll see that MCDP-6 is superbly written, shorter, and clearer.

[532] Clausewitz calls this uncertainty the "Fog of War."

[533] Note that our use of the word Control is different than the Center for Internet Security's Top 20 Controls (and other similar usage), which are safeguards put in place to minimize security risks.

[534] MCDP-6: Command and Control, United States Marine Corps, 4 October 1996.

[535] For those keeping score, this figure is not doctrinal. We've based the figure on Fig 3-1 of ADRP 6-0 Mission Command, U.S. Army 2014. However, the U.S. Army views Mission Command as their model of command and control, but for cyber operations we view both Mission Command and Detailed Command as necessary, complementary models. We've also added Capabilities to the set of warfighting functions because we feel capability development and capability management play a much larger role in cyber operations in contrast with traditional kinetic operations. As you examine the figure, note that we haven't left off offensive aspects as a counterbalance to protection. Offensive aspects are included in Movement and Maneuver, Fires and Effects, and Capabilities. Finally, we carefully considered adding Personnel and Plans to the diagram, but opted not to. You are free to include Personnel and Plans if you feel it useful.

[536] MCDP-6 Command and Control, United States Marine Corps, 4 October 1996.

[537] For additional background on Mission Command, see Victor Delacruz, "Mission Command In and Through Cyberspace for Army Commanders," Cyber Defense Review, 10 December 2015.

[538] This figure is slightly modified version from one found in MCDP-6: Command and Control, United States Marine Corps, 4 October 1996.

[539] In cyberspace, much likewise rests on the shoulders of the software developer. See Ari Shapiro, "What Do Self-Driving Cars Mean For Auto Liability Insurance?," All Things Considered, National Public Radio, 1 March 2016.

[540] MCDP-6 Command and Control, United States Marine Corps, 4 October 1996. It is an interesting problem to consider how many of these attributes will be technically feasible in automated cyberspace C2 tools and AI systems.

[541] For a useful discussion of coup d'oeil see https://en.wikipedia.org/wiki/Coup_d'%C5%93il.

[542] Although the amateur may think they have it.

[543] David Ignatius, "The exotic new weapons the Pentagon wants to deter Russia and China," Washington Post, 23 February 2016.

[544] Albeit science fiction, for plausible M2H scenarios see Daniel Suarez, Daemon, Signet Books, 2009. For a vision a little farther in the future, but not out of the realm of the possible, see Marshall Brain's excellent Manna, BYG Publishing, 2012.

[545] Marc Dorian and Megan Reilly, "My GPS Almost Killed Me: 5 GPS Mishaps," ABC News, 14 March 2013.

[546] This figure is a modified version of one found in MCDP-6 Command and Control, United States Marine Corps, 4 October 1996.

[547] RoboCop, film, Orion, 1987. We could have instead chosen Isaac Asimov's famous laws of robotics here: 1. A robot may not injure a human being or, through inaction, allow a human being to come to harm, 2. A robot must obey orders given it by human beings except where such orders would conflict with the First Law, and 3. A robot must protect its own existence as long as such protection does not conflict with the First or Second Law. However, we liked RoboCop's aspect of a classified directive.

[548] For an interesting discussion on military use of artificial intelligence, see Michael Kolton, "The Inevitable Militarization of Artificial Intelligence," Cyber Defense Review, 8 February 2016.

[549] For example, the world record for a robot solving the Rubik's cube puzzle mechanically is 0.887 seconds, the human world record is about 5 seconds. See Sarah Griffiths, "Blink and you'll miss it! Video shows robot solving Rubik's cube

in 0.887 seconds, beating the world record time by a whisker," Daily Mail, 11 February 2016 (robot solution) and Jamieson Cox, "A teenager just pushed the Rubik's Cube world record under 5 seconds," The Verge, 24 November 2015 (human solution). Consider the Code Red (2001) and Slammer (2003) worms which caused rapid and significant global effects. The Slammer worm infected 90% of vulnerable hosts across the planet in about 10 minutes, see David Moore, Vern Paxson, Stefan Savage, Colleen Shannon, Stuart Staniford, and Nicholas Weaver, "Inside the Slammer Worm," IEEE Security and Privacy, July/August 2003.

[550] For example, a rock-paper-scissors robot can observe, orient, decide, and act so quickly against a human opponent that it always wins. See Matthew Wall, "Superfast rock-paper-scissors robot 'wins' every time," BBC News, 4 November 2013.

[551] Enn Tyugu, "Command and Control of Cyber Weapons," NATO Conference on Cyber Conflict (CyCon), 2012. For a real-world example of autonomous anti-malware, see Jeremy Kaplan, "Japan Reportedly Building Vigilante Virus Assassin Squad," Fox News, 3 January 2012.

[552] Enn Tyugu, "Command and Control of Cyber Weapons," NATO Conference on Cyber Conflict (CyCon), 2012.

[553] Andrew Clevenger, "'The Terminator Conundrum': Pentagon Weighs Ethics of Pairing Deadly Force, AI," Army Times, 23 January 2016. See also, Stephen Goose, "The Case for Banning Killer Robots," Communications of the ACM, December 2015, Vol. 58, No. 12, pp. 43-45.

[554] Enn Tyugu, "Command and Control of Cyber Weapons," NATO Conference on Cyber Conflict (CyCon), 2012.

[555] Erik Brynjolfsson and Andrew McAffee, The Second Machine Age: Work, Progress, and Prosperity in a Time of Brilliant Technologies, W. W. Norton & Company, 2014.

[556] David Drake, "Hangman," The Best of Military Science Fiction of the 20th Century, Ballantine Books, p. 180.

[557] As seen in the rise of Digital Rights Management (DRM).

[558] See Cory Doctorow, "Lockdown: The coming war on general-purpose computing," BoingBoing, 10 January 2012 (loss of full control) and Mark Skilton and Irene Ng, "What the Apple vs. FBI Debacle Taught Us," Scientific American, 20 May 2016 (denying government access).

[559] For an interesting discussion on responsibility, see Nicholas Diakopoulos, "Accountability in Algorithmic Decision-making, ACM Queue, 25 January 2016.

[560] This table is derived from Raja Parasuraman, Thomas Sheridan, and Christopher Wickens, "A Model for Types and Levels of Human Interaction with Automation," IEEE Transactions on Systems, Man and Cybernetics, Vol. 30, No. 3, May 2000.

[561] For a discussion on Areas of Operation see, ADP 3-0 Unified Land Operations, U.S. Army, October 2011, p. 20.

[562] David Raymond, Gregory Conti, Tom Cross, and Robert Fanelli, "A Control Measure Framework to Limit Collateral Damage and Propagation of Cyber Weapons." International Conference on Cyber Conflict (CyCon), June 2013.

[563] Figure 1-3, "Example envelopment control measures," FM 3-90-1 Offense and Defense, U.S. Army, Vol. 1, March 2013, p. 23.

[564] See Rick Baillergeon and John Sutherland, "Tactics 101 081 – The Assembly Area," Arm Chair General, 13 February 2013.

[565] For a useful discussion on Areas of Operations in the context of cybersecurity, see Matthew Stern, "Applying Military Doctrine to Cyberspace: Areas of Operation, Influence and Interest," Security Week, 17 September 2012.

[566] These kinetic control measures came from FM 3-90 Tactics, U.S. Army, 4 July 2001.

[567] 2001: A Space Odyssey, MGM, 1968.

[568] RoboCop, Orion, 1987.

[569] JP-1 Doctrine for the Armed Forces of the United States, U.S. Department of Defense, 25 March 2013. From JP-1, there are also four sub-categories of Support: General Support where an organization provides support to an entire force, not one specific entity; Mutual Support where organizations work together; Direct Support, where one organization provides support to a specific other organization; and Close Support where members of one organization are effectively integrated into another.

[570] Enn Tyugu, "Command and Control of Cyber Weapons," NATO Conference on Cyber Conflict (CyCon), 2012.

[571] JP 3-12(R) Cyberspace Operations, U.S. Department of Defense, 5 February 2013.

[572] Kevin Gray, "The Last Fighter Pilot," Popular Science, 22 December 2015 (fighter pilots) and Joson Torchinsky, "This Last Generation of Human-Driven Cars Will Be Better Than Any Before," Jalopnik, 3 October 2014. Despite the obvious advantage of being able to exceed human capability, there will be much cultural and bureaucratic resistance to these changes. We are concerned as well, that delegating too much to machines is very risky as the machines will likely be compromised at some point, but at the same time current aircraft and vehicles are so complex that the human driver is just issuing commands to a computer anyway.

[573] Michihiro Koibuchi, Hiroki Matsutani, Hideharu Amano, D. Frank Hsu, and Henri Casanova, "A case for random shortcut topologies for HPC interconnects," International Symposium on Computer Architecture, 2012.

[574] This isn't to say human organizations are entirely static, just that they are slower to change. In the military, units are frequently task organized, by building desired forces from modular organizational building blocks. Similarly, resources are cross leveled (think load balancing) between individuals and between larger units.

[575] For examples of potential cyber operations command posts, consider the U.S. CERT, Carnegie Mellon University's CERT, the Joint Information Operations Warfare Center, and the National Security Operations Center (NSOC), as well as examples from industry, such as the temporary cyber-operations headquarters for the Super Bowl. See Harriet Taylor, "Inside the Super Bowl cyber-ops headquarters," CNBC, 29 January 2016.

[576] See Cheryl Pellerin, "DARPA's Plan X Gives Military Operators a Place to Wage Cyber Warfare," DoD News, 12 May 2016.

[577] Sydney Freedberg, "Moving Mountains In Cyber War: Automated Virtual 'Maneuver,'" Breaking Defense, 8 December 2014.

[578] Orson Scott Card, "Ender's Game," *The Best Military Science Fiction of the 20th Century*, Del Rey, 2001. (Eds. Harry Turtledove and Martin Greenberg)

[579] See ADRP 6-0 Mission Command, U.S. Army, 7 May 2012. For an excellent framework on human decision making in a cyber security context, see Lorrie Faith Cranor, "A Framework for Reasoning About the Human in the Loop," Conference on Usability, Psychology, and Security, 2008.

[580] For additional analysis on cyber common operating picture systems, see Gregory Conti, John Nelson and David Raymond, "Towards a Cyber Common Operating Picture," NATO Conference on Cyber Conflict (CyCon), 2013.

[581] MCDP-6: Command and Control, United States Marine Corps, 4 October 1996. As an example, MSDP-6 notes that machine aren't yet "capable of devising tactics, operations, and strategies," areas where humans excel. See also Thomas Limoncelli, "Automation Should Be Like Iron Man, Not Ultron," ACM Queue, 31 October 2015, Vol. 13, No 8. Also see Justin Edgar, "A Scout's Perspective on Network Defense," BSides Augusta, 2015, Monzy Merza, "Active Response: Automated Risk Reduction or Manual Action," RSA, 2015, and Richard Bejtlich, "Not So Fast! Boyd OODA Looping Is More Than Speed," TaoSecurity, 5 December 2015.

[582] MCDP-6 Command and Control, United States Marine Corps, 4 October 1996. MCDP-6 also cautions against higher headquarters making too many requests for information from subordinates and creating a stifling "demand cascade."

[583] Enn Tyugu, "Command and Control of Cyber Weapons," NATO Conference on Cyber Conflict (CyCon), 2012.

[584] MCDP-6 Command and Control, United States Marine Corps, 4 October 1996.

[585] For an in-depth study of cyber common operating pictures, see Gregory Conti, John Nelson, and David Raymond, "Towards a Cyber Common Operating Picture," NATO Conference on Cyber Conflict (CyCon), June 2013 and for two well-regarded books on security data visualization, see Raffael Marty, *Applied Security Visualization*, Addison-Wesley, 2008 and Gregory Conti, *Security Data Visualization*, No Starch Press, 2007.

[586] See Cobalt Strike, https://www.cobaltstrike.com/.

[587] Graham Templeton, "DARPA's Plan X to bring 'military mindset' to cyber-war," Extreme Tech, 31 July 2015. See also, Amy Walker, "Army enhances NetOps, the eyes and ears of the network," Army.mil, 12 May 2016.

[588] One risk, shared with kinetic operators, is that a common cyber operating picture system will invite micromanagement from far-removed superiors.

[589] Ben Shneiderman, "The Eyes Have It: A Task by Data Type Taxonomy for Information Visualizations," IEEE Symposium on Visual Languages, 1996.

[590] The U.S. has very refined symbology for traditional and asymmetric warfare; you can find the canonical reference in ADRP 1-02, Terms and Military Symbols, U.S. Army, December 2015.

[591] For a useful overlay reference, see Battle Staff Graphics Workbook, U.S.

Army Sergeants Major Academy, 16 November 2015.

[592] For numerous examples of video games that employ these techniques, see https://en.wikipedia.org/wiki/Fog_of_war.

[593] See Cheryl Pellerin, "DARPA's Plan X Gives Military Operators a Place to Wage Cyber Warfare," U.S. Department of Defense, 12 May 2016 (app store) and Ozone, http://ozone-development.github.io/ozone-website/ (widget framework).

[594] See Andy Greenberg, "DARPA Turns Oculus Into A Weapon for Cyberwar," Wired, 23 May 2014.

[595] U.S. Army Photo, work of the U.S. Government, Public Domain, https://www.army.mil/media/434758.

[596] To prevent vendor lock-in make sure you embed interoperability into any contracts you generate, else you'll likely be disappointed.

[597] Devon Bistarkey, "Network interoperability key to common operating picture," Army.mil, 22 January 2016.

[598] Cordwainer Smith, "The Game of Rat and Dragon," *The Best Military Science Fiction of the 20th Century*, Del Rey, 2001. (Eds. Harry Turtledove and Martin Greenberg)

[599] See cHaOsOfWar, "Why are hackers often associated with Game Lag," CNET, 22 May 2012.

[600] Scott Peterson, "Downed US drone: How Iran caught the 'beast,'" Christian Science Monitor, 9 December 2011.

[601] See Gregory Conti, Mustaque Ahamad, and John Stasko, "Attacking Information Visualization System Usability: Overloading and Deceiving the Human," Symposium on Usable Privacy and Security (SOUPS), July 2005 (inserting malicious information) and "Detecting and Dismantling Botnet Command and Control Infrastructure using Behavioral Profilers, and Bot Informants," University of Michigan / US Department of Homeland Security, http://vhosts.eecs.umich.edu/fjgroup/botnets/ (malicious nodes).

[602] Dana Goward, "Opinion: Were US sailors 'spoofed' into Iranian waters," Christian Science Monitor, 15 January 2016.

[603] Leyla Bilge, Davide Balzarotti, William Robertson, Engin Kirda, and Christopher Kruegel, "DISCLOSURE: Detecting Botnet Command and Control

Servers Through Large-Scale NetFlow Analysis," Annual Computer Security Applications Conference, 2012.

[604] Guofei Gu, Junjie Zhang, and Wenke Lee, "BotSniffer: Detecting Botnet Command and Control Channels in Network Traffic," Network and Distributed System Security Symposium, 2008.

[605] For example, are messages sent continuously, at regularly scheduled times, based on events, randomly, or never?

[606] For example, consider the networked multi-function printer/scanner/fax machine you probably have in your home. The device is a fax machine connected to your phone line and a networked printer attached inside your firewall to your home network. This situation, could be fine, but is an accident waiting to happen.

[607] A popular technique is using fast flux DNS, which allows attackers to use a single domain to screen a number of malicious hosts at various IP addresses.

[608] Patrick Duggan, "Man, Computer, and Special Warfare," Small Wars Journal, 4 January 2016.

[609] MCDP-6 Command and Control, United States Marine Corps, 4 October 1996.

[610] For two excellent resources on military deception see, JP 3-13.4 Military Deception, U.S. Department of Defense, 13 July 2006 and FM 90-2 Battlefield Deception, Department of the Army, 3 October 1988. See also Jon Latimer's superb *Deception in War*, Thistle Publishing, 2016.

[611] It is with some irony that we note that while military academies enforce strict honor codes, "A cadet will not lie, cheat, steal, or tolerate those who do," much of warfare, cyber or otherwise, involves lying, cheating and stealing. The United States Corps of Cadets PAM 15-1, The Cadet Honor Code, System, and Committee Procedures, 11 November 2009 states "Cadets violate the Cadet Honor Code by lying if they deliberately deceive another person by stating an untruth, or by any direct form of communication, to include the telling of a partial truth or the vague or ambiguous use of information or language, with the intent to deceive or mislead." Luckily deception in war occurs after graduation. For an example of teaching students to cheat see Gregory Conti and James Caroland, "Embracing the Kobayashi Maru - Why You Should Teach Your Students to Cheat," IEEE Security and Privacy, July/August 2011.

[612] Joseph Caddell, "Deception 101 – Primer on Deception," Strategic Studies Institute, U.S. Army War College, December 2004.

[613] Ibid.

[614] The U.S. military has since relabeled PSYOPS as Military Information Support Operations (MISO), but here we use PSYOPS as this term is more illustrative. Note that historically CNO was a sub-component of information operations, but the declaration of cyberspace as an operational domain and the creation of major cyber force structure puts this doctrinal distinction in serious doubt.

[615] As an example of apparent CNO enabled IO see Duncan Gardham, "MI6 attacks al-Quada in 'Operation Cupcake,'" The Telegraph, 2 June 2011.

[616] See information security firm Cymmetria, https://www.cymmetria.com/, and the Honeynet Project, https://www.honeynet.org/.

[617] For real world instances of our Krasnovian examples see Danny Yadron, "Target Hackers Wrote Partly in Russian, Displayed High Skill, Report Finds," Wall Street Journal, 16 January 2014 and Jeremy Kirk, "Clues point to Russia in long-running spying campaign," PC World, 28 October 2014.

[618] False flag operations cause misattribution, by making the evidence look like an innocent third party was responsible.

[619] Megan Garber, "Ghost Army: The Inflatable Tanks That Fooled Hitler," The Atlantic, 22 May 2013.

[620] John Leyden, "SCADA honeypots attract swarm of international hackers," The Register, 1 June 2016.

[621] For a great introduction to social engineering, see Kevin Mitnick, *The Art of Deception: Controlling the Human Element of Security*, Wiley, 2003. See also, Sean Bodmer, Max Kilger, Gregory Carpenter, and Jade Jones, *Reverse Deception: Organized Cyber Threat Counter-Exploitation*, McGraw Hill, 2012.

[622] See Nitsan Saddan, "Opinion: Hacking Team and Defense through Deception," Security Ledger, 6 May 2016.

[623] Bill Gertz, "Counterdeception unit to close," Washington Times, 11 May 2016.

[624] Cyber herding is to drive "individuals, groups, and organizations to a desired location in the digital realm" see Patrick Duggan, "Strategic Development of Special Warfare in Cyberspace," National Defense University Press, 1 October 2015.

[625] This table is based on our previous work, Tom Cross, David Raymond, and Gregory Conti, "Deception for the Cyber Defender: To Err is Human; to Deceive,

Divine," ShmooCon, January 2015.

[626] Patrick Duggan, "Strategic Development of Special Warfare in Cyberspace," National Defense University Press, 1 October 2015.

[627] JP 3-13.4 Military Deception, U.S. Department of Defense, 13 July 2006.

[628] Ibid.

[629] We've derived these steps from the U.S. military's deception planning process. See JP 3-13.4 Military Deception, U.S. Department of Defense, 13 July 2006.

[630] Tom Cross, David Raymond, and Gregory Conti, "Deception for the Cyber Defender: To Err is Human; to Deceive, Divine," ShmooCon, January 2015.

[631] JP 3-13.4 Military Deception, U.S. Department of Defense, 13 July 2006.

[632] Ms. Smith, "Hacker hunts and pwns WiFi Pineapples with zero-day at Def Con," Network World, 11 August 2014.

[633] This table is based on our previous work, Tom Cross, David Raymond, and Gregory Conti, "Deception for the Cyber Defender: To Err is Human; to Deceive, Divine," ShmooCon, January 2015.

[634] The purpose of the diversion is to deceive the target as to the true point of the attack.

[635] Shane Harris, @War, Houghton Mifflin Harcourt, 2014, p. 8.

[636] These personas will often portray themselves as insiders, see Patrick Duggan, "Strategic Development of Special Warfare in Cyberspace," National Defense University Press, 1 October 2015.

[637] See Shai Oster, "China Fakes 488 Million Social Media Posts a Year: Study," Bloomberg Technology, 19 May 2016, Daisy Sindelar, "The Kremlin's Troll Army," The Atlantic, 12 August 2014, and Dmitry Volchek and Daisy Sindelar, "One Professional Russian Troll Tells All," Radio Free Europe, 25 March 2015.

[638] Due to space we haven't expanded the Logical Plane to specifically enumerate OSI Layers 2-7 and system components listed in Chapter 5 - Terrain, but doing so for brainstorming would help elicit additional ideas.

[639] Ken Thompson, "Reflections on Trusting Trust," Communications of the ACM, Vol. 27, No. 8, August 1984.

640 Spoofed websites are often combined with deceptive domain names that closely resemble a legitimate site, like a bank, or combined with DNS manipulation to make the domain appear authentic. In a recent case, foreign hackers set up legitimate appearing news websites to support APT intrusions. See Shane Harris, *@War*, Houghton Mifflin Harcourt, 2014, p. 205.

641 See AdroidL, "How I got 3,000+ hackers VAC banned!," Global Offensive, Redit, 2016.

642 Michael Cooney, "DARPA extreme DDOS project transforming network attack mitigation," Network World, 20 May 2016.

643 Dana Goward, "Opinion: Were US sailors 'spoofed' into Iranian waters?," Christian Science Monitor, 15 January 2016.

644 Andrew Clevenger, "GAO: DoD Needs Better Intel on Fake Parts," Army Times, 16 February 2016.

645 JP 3-13.4 Military Deception, U.S. Department of Defense, 13 July 2006.

646 For an interesting take on counter deception in the context of expert systems see, Gregory Courand, "Counter Deception," Office of Naval Research, 1 December 1989.

647 Two other related concepts are *cognitive dissonance* where one ignores vital information because it interferes with preexisting beliefs and *inertia at rest*, the tendency to hold certain beliefs even after they have been undermined by events.

648 Traditional military doctrine considers this maxim "Limitations to Human Information Processing," which we believe is too limited in the cyber context.

649 An example of unknown provenance is the alleged manipulation of the Anarchist Cookbook, a 1970s countercultural book that provided instruction on the manufacture of explosives and drugs, amongst a wide assortment of other illicit activities. There is an urban legend that the CIA may have sabotaged versions of the book and modified some of the contents to cause the death of the would-be anarchist or to make the recipes fail. Whether true or not, this meme undermines trust in the document's content. See the Anarchist Cookbook FAQ, http://files.righto.com/anarchy/.

650 An important related concept is *Information Fratricide*: "Information fratricide is the result of employing information operations elements in a way that causes effects in the information environment that impede the conduct of friendly operations or adversely affect friendly forces." A classic example is a friendly

force's attempts at jamming enemy communications also degrading friendly communications. See FM 3-07.22 Counterinsurgency Operations, U.S. Army, October 2004.

[651] The photo is in the public domain, see https://commons.wikimedia.org/wiki/File:UK_National_Archives_-_WO_1065921.jpg

[652] Tom Cross, David Raymond, and Gregory Conti, "Deception for the Cyber Defender: To Err is Human; to Deceive, Divine," ShmooCon, January 2015.

[653] In military terms, this is a "demonstration" because forces are deployed to distract the enemy, but the deployment did not include actual contact or combat.

[654] *Economy of force* means employing the majority of resources on a primary effort and only minimum essential resources against secondary efforts.

[655] Nena, "99 Red Balloons," http://www.azlyrics.com/lyrics/nena/99redballoons.html.

[656] For additional creative insights see Mark Mateski and Matt Devost, "The Devil Does Not Exist – The Role of Deception in Cyber," Black Hat, 2014.

[657] This quote from Roger Kelim's Twitter profile, @RogerKelim, https://twitter.com/RogerKelim, last accessed 13 April 2016, is one of our favorites. It captures the mission and the curse of foresight the information security community deals with.

[658] Security solutions don't always inhibit functionality, some like secure coding, provable security, and language-theoretic security build security into the code itself, eliminating important classes of vulnerabilities without impacting function. As an example, see "LANGSEC: Language-theoretic Security," http://langsec.org/, 2016.

[659] Holding line employees accountable for cybersecurity decisions can have positive benefits, but also risks creating a zero-defect workplace where no one will want to work, if not properly implemented. See James Winnefeld, Christopher Kirchhoff, and David Upton, "Cybersecurity's Human Factor: Lessons from the Pentagon," Harvard Business Review, September 2015.

[660] As an example, see "U.S. Steel Files ITC Complaint," Press Release, United States Steel Corporation, 26 April 2016.

[661] The Terminator, Orion, 1984. Quote from the Internet Movie Database, see http://www.imdb.com/title/tt0088247/quotes.

662 David Kravets, "Internet of Things to be used as spy tool by governments: US intel chief," Ars Technica, 10 February 2016.

663 Frank Prautzsch, "U.S. Army Mega City Operations: Enduring Principles and Innovative Technologies," Small Wars Journal, 22 February 2016 (Megacities), Michael Bailey, Robert Dixon, Marc Harris, Daniel Hendrex, Nicholas Melin and Richard Russo, "A Proposed Framework for Appreciating Megacities: A US Army Perspective," Small Wars Journal, 21 April 2014 (Megacities), and "Securing Smart Cities," Securing Smart Cities initiative, http://securingsmartcities.org/, 2015 (Smart Cities).

664 Gregory Conti, Edward Sobiesk, Paul Anderson, Steven Billington, Alex Farmer, Cory Kirk, Patrick Shaffer, and Kyle Stammer, "Unintended, malicious and evil applications of augmented reality," InSecure, Issue 35, September 2012, pp. 20-27.

665 For one possible future see Kim Stanley Robinson's Mars Trilogy Series published by Bantam Books.

666 See Alan Yuhas and Kamala Kelkar, "'Rogue scientists' could exploit gene editing technology, experts warn," The Guardian, 12 February 2016.

667 Grey goo is a hypothetical scenario when out-of-control self-replicating nanotechnology kills off life on Earth.

668 Neural interfaces technology is an early stage research area, see "Bridging the Bio-Electronic Divide," DARPA, 19 January 2016.

669 See Matthew Tobin Anderson's science fiction novel Feed, Candlewick Press, 2002 for an exploration of the risks of neural interfaces.

670 See Mark Harris, "FBI warns driverless cars could be used as 'lethal weapons,'" The Guardian, 16 July 2014.

671 Kris Osborn, "Pentagon 'Arsenal Plane' Likely to be Modified B-52," Scout, 10 March 2016 (arsenal plane) and David Ignatius, "The exotic new weapons the Pentagon wants to deter Russia and China," Washington Post, 23 February 2016 (swarming). See also Gary Anderson, "To Beat ISIS, We Ought to Try Robotskrieg," Small Wars Journal, 3 February 2016 (urban combat tactics).

672 Chris Edwards, "Self-Repair Techniques Point to Robots That Design Themselves," Communications of the ACM, Vol. 59, No. 2, February 2016, pp. 15-17. See also Bill Steele, "Researchers build a robot that can reproduce," Cornell Chronicle, 25 May 2005.

[673] Ken Jennings wrote this remark on his screen as he was defeated by IBM's Watson in Jeopardy in 2011. See the video online at https://www.youtube.com/watch?v=Skfw282fJak.

[674] Sara Sorcher, "Influencers: Trump won't improve cybersecurity," Passcode, Christian Science Monitor, 21 November 2016.

[675] This will include AI-enabled robocallers.

[676] Robert Ackerman, "Convergence Dominates Army Cyber Activities," Signal, 1 October 2015.

[677] Neal Boudette and Mike Isaac, "Head of Fiat Chrysler Sees Self-Driving Cars in Five Years, Not 20," New York Times, 6 May 2016. See also Bill Vlasic, "U.S. Proposes Spending $4 Billion on Self-Driving Cars," New York Times, 14 January 2016.

[678] Russell Brandom, "DARPA's million-dollar search for software that can defend itself," The Verge, 3 June 2015.

[679] Nick Bostrom, "What happens when our computers get smarter than we are?," TED, March 2015.

[680] For one of the best articles we've seen that describes the cyber culture clash in the military see "Army Braces for a Culture Clash," Signal, 1 January 2016 written by the outgoing Command Sergeant Major of U.S. Army Cyber Command, Rodney "Dale" Harris.

[681] See Ian Duncan, "Elite Army unit at Fort Meade searching for ways to fight ISIS," Baltimore Sun, 20 July 2015 (AWG), Dan Lafontaine, "Army continues to provide rapid engineering, prototyping in Afghanistan," Army.mil, 13 April 2015 (REF), and Jen Judson, "As JIEDDO Becomes JIDA, IED Threat Builds in Theater," Defense News, 19 November 2015 (JIDA).

[682] Dennis Fisher, "Groundbreaking Cyber Fast Track Research Program Ending," Threatpost, 6 March 2013.

[683] Cheryl Pellerin, "DoD's Silicon Valley Innovation Experiment Begins," DoD News, 29 October 2015.

[684] Idan Tendler, "From The Israeli Army Unit 8200 To Silicon Valley," Tech Crunch, 20 March 2015.

[685] Daniel Sukman, "The Institutional Level of War," The Strategy Bridge, 5 May 2016.

[686] The "All, Many, Few" model came out of an inter-service academy working group founded circa 2011.

[687] See Francesca Spidalieri, "Joint Professional Military Education Institutions in an Age of Cyber Threat," Pell Center, 7 August 2013 and Francesca Spidalieri, "One Leader at a Time: The Failure to Educate Future Leaders for an Age of Persistent Cyber Threat," Pell Center, 26 March 2013.

[688] John "Buck" Surdu and Gregory Conti, "Join the Cyber Corps," IEEE Information Assurance Workshop, June 2002. (Author's note: Colonel (ret) Surdu conceived the idea of a cyber service, he just kindly afforded me the opportunity to collaborate.) See also Gregory Conti and John "Buck" Surdu, "Army, Navy Air Force, Cyber: Is it Time for a Cyber Warfare Branch of the Military," Information Assurance Newsletter, Vol. 12, No. 1, Spring 2009, pp. 14-18 and James Stavridis and David Weinstein, "Time for a U.S. Cyber Force," Proceedings, January 2014.

[689] Currently U.S. Cyber Command is planned for elevation to a Unified Combatant Command which will provide it more autonomy. See Richard Sisk, "Cyber Command to Become Unified Combatant Command," Military.com, 18 August 2017. Some have suggested an additional step to provide even more flexibility, the creation of a Cyber Joint Special Operations Command. See Frank Cilluffo and Sharon Cardash, "A Cyber JSOC Could Help the US Strike Harder and Faster," Defense One, 25 April 2016. At present, Admiral Rogers, the commander of U.S. Cyber Command has gone on the record stating there isn't a need for a separate military service for cyber. See Mark Pomerleau, "Rogers: Cyber doesn't need its own military branch," Defense Systems, 21 January 2016.

[690] FM 3-38 Cyber Electromagnetic Activities, U.S. Army, February 2014.

[691] "Army Cyber branch offers Soldiers new challenges, opportunities," Fort Gordon Public Affairs Office, Army.mil, 24 November 2014.

[692] X-Men: Apocalypse, 20th Century FOX, 2016.

[693] Latin adage – "If you want peace, prepare for war." This sentiment has been echoed by many, including Clausewitz and Metallica.

www.ingramcontent.com/pod-product-compliance
Lightning Source LLC
Chambersburg PA
CBHW070932050326
40689CB00014B/3175